The Origin of Goods

Centre for Economic Policy Research (CEPR)

The Centre for Economic Policy Research (CEPR) was founded in 1983 to enhance the quality of economic policy-making within Europe and beyond, by creating excellent, policy-relevant economic research, and disseminating it widely to policy influencers in the public and private sectors and civil society. A second goal was to unify and integrate the European economics research community.

CEPR is based on a new model of organization called a 'thinknet': a distributed network of economists who are affiliated with, but not employed by, the Centre, collaborating through CEPR on a wide range of policy-relevant research projects and dissemination activities. CEPR's network of Research Fellows and Affiliates comprises around 600 economists, based primarily in Europe in universitites, research institutes, central bank research departments, and international organizations. No research is performed at CEPR's London headquarters, which serve a purely administrative function, defining research initiatives with the network, seeking funding, organizing research-related activities, such as meetings and publications, and working to disseminate the findings of project teams.

This distinguishes CEPR from traditional thinks-tanks, which employ researchers directly, and typically take an institutional position. In contrast, CEPR has a pluralist and non-partisan stance: the Centre takes no institutional policy positions, and its publications carry a wide range of policy conclusions and recommendations. The opinions expressed in this book are those of the authors and not necessarily those of CEPR or its supporting funders.

Chairman   Guilermo de la Dehesa
President   Richard Portes
Chief Executive Officer   Stephen Yeo
Research Director   Mathias Dewatripont

Centre for Economic Policy Research
90–98 Goswell Road
London EC1V 7RR
UK

Tel: + 44 (0)20 7878 2900   Fax: + 44 (0)20 7878 2999
Email: cepr@cepr.org   Web site: www.cepr.org

The Origin of Goods

Rules of Origin in Regional Trade Agreements

Edited by

Olivier Cadot
Antoni Estevadeordal
Akiko Suwa-Eisenmann
and
Thierry Verdier

UNIVERSITY PRESS

HF
1713
.075
2006

OXFORD
UNIVERSITY PRESS

Great Clarendon Street, Oxford OX2 6DP

Oxford University Press is a department of the University of Oxford.
It furthers the University's objective of excellence in research, scholarship,
and education by publishing worldwide in

Oxford New York

Auckland Cape Town Dar es Salaam Hong Kong Karachi
Kuala Lumpur Madrid Melbourne Mexico City Nairobi
New Delhi Shanghai Taipei Toronto

With offices in

Argentina Austria Brazil Chile Czech Republic France Greece
Guatemala Hungary Italy Japan Poland Portugal Singapore
South Korea Switzerland Thailand Turkey Ukraine Vietnam

Oxford is a registered trade mark of Oxford University Press
in the UK and in certain other countries

Published in the United States
by Oxford University Press Inc., New York

© CEPR, 2006

British Library Cataloguing in Publication Data
Data available

Library of Congress Cataloging in Publication Data
Data available

Typeset by Newgen Imaging Systems (P) Ltd., Chennai, India
Printed in Great Britain
on acid-free paper by
Biddles Ltd., King's Lynn, Norfolk

ISBN 0–19–929048–2   978–0–19–929048–2

10 9 8 7 6 5 4 3 2 1

Acknowledgments

The initial idea of a conference and edited volume on Rules of Origin goes back several years when Robert Devlin, then Deputy Manager at the Integration and Regional Programs Department of the Inter-American Development Bank (IDB), encouraged and enthusiastically supported research on what seemed at the time an arcane topic, of interest only to a handful of specialists. It is a testimony to the initiative's achievement that the topic is not arcane anymore.

Final plans for the two conferences in which the essays collected in this volume were discussed were drawn up between the Integration and Regional Programs Department of the IDB in Washington, D.C. and two leading research centers and networks in Europe, the Department and Laboratory of Applied and Theoretical Economics (DELTA) and the London-based Center for Economic Policy Research (CEPR). The first conference, held at Paris-Jourdan Campus in Paris in May–June 2003, was organized by INRA and sponsored by the IDB, DELTA, CEPR, INRA, Fédération Paris-Jourdan and ADRES. The second and final one, held in Washington, D.C. in February 2004, was organized and sponsored by the IDB.

Our debts, as editors, are multiple. First and foremost, the enthusiastic support shown, from the outset, by all sponsors greatly helped us to carry this project forward to successful completion. In particular, the Inter-American Development Bank's financial contribution through its integration and Regional Programs department was outstandingly generous. Several individuals stand out for their support and encouragement: in particular Nohra Rey de Marulanda, Robert Devlin, and Carlo Binetti at the IDB, and Stephen Yeo at the CEPR.

Second, our thanks go to all authors, whose combined efforts and commitment made this book possible. Special thanks are also due to Martha Skinner and Ziga Vodusek at the IDB as well as Madeleine Roux and Beatrice Havet at INRA for their effort and commitment in the organization of the two conferences. For their critical contribution to the

v

final conference and its invaluable impact on the quality of the papers in this volume, we would also like to thank the distinguished team of discussants: Rafael Cornejo (IDB); Michael Ferrantino (USITC); Jeremy Harris (IDB); Bernard Hoekman (World Bank); Stefano Inama (UNCTAD); William James; Maria Mayda (Georgetown University); Marcelo Olarreaga (World Bank); Antonio Spilimbergo (IMF); Brian Staples (Trade Facilitation Services, Ottawa) and Robert Teh (WTO). Last but not least, the process of producing a book goes beyond the technical competence of the authors. We are deeply grateful for the skilled work of all involved, in particular, Jennifer Wilkinson, Assistant Commissioning Editor and Carol Bestley, Production Editor at Oxford University Press.

The views expressed in these papers are solely those of the authors, and they do not represent the views of the institutions they are affiliated with.

O.C.
A.E.
A.S.-E.
T.V.

Contents

List of Figures   ix
List of Tables   x
List of Contributors   xii

Introduction   1
  Olivier Cadot, Antoni Estevadeordal, Akiko Suwa-Eisenmann, and
  Thierry Verdier

Part I. Rules of Origin: Theoretical perspectives   17

1 Understanding Rules of Origin   19
  Kala Krishna

2 The impact of Rules of Origin on strategic outsourcing:
  an IO perspective   35
  Mathias Thoenig and Thierry Verdier

**Part II. Rules of Origin in Regional Trade Agreements
          around the world**   67

3 Mapping and measuring Rules of Origin around
  the world   69
  Antoni Estevadeordal and Kati Suominen

4 Rules of Origin for services: economic and legal
  considerations   114
  Americo Beviglia Zampetti and Pierre Sauvé

Part III. The political economy of Rules of Origin   147

5 Rules of Origin as export subsidies   149
  Olivier Cadot, Antoni Estevadeordal, and Akiko Suwa-Eisenmann

Contents

6 Rules of Origin and US trade policy   173
I.M. (Mac) Destler

Part IV. Measuring the impact of Rules of Origin   189

7 Are different Rules of Origin equally costly? Estimates
from NAFTA   191
Céline Carrère and Jaime de Melo

8 Implementing PTAs in the Southern Cone region
of Latin America: Rules of Origin   213
Pablo Sanguinetti and Eduardo Bianchi

9 Preferential trade arrangements production, and trade with
differentiated intermediates   237
Joseph Francois

Part V. Rules of Origin and development   257

10 Rules of Origin as tools of development? Some lessons
from SADC   259
Hennie Erasmus, Frank Flatters, and Robert Kirk

11 Trade preferences for Africa and the impact of Rules
of Origin
Paul Brenton and Takako Ikezuki   295

Index   315

List of Figures

1	Vertical trade in a two-stage framework	4
2	The effect of tariff preferences	5
3	Tariff preferences and RoO combined	6
4	PSRO restrictiveness and regime-wide facilitation, selected PTAs	10
1.1	Physical content RoO and costs	25
1.2	Demand, price and cost in an FTA	27
2.1	Reaction curve of outsourcing	40
2.2	Nash equilibrium in outsourcing	41
2.3	Profit functions	44
2.4	Reaction curve under the RoO	45
2.5	(a) Some useful notations; (b) Equilibrium with a binding RoO; (c) Multiple equilibria in outsourcing with RoO	46
2.6	Effects of RoO on profits	48
2.7	Equilibrium in the no-RoO regime	56
2.8	Effect of a RoO on local supplier's investment	59
2.9	Effect of a RoO on monopoly's output and profit	60
2.10	Positive effect of a RoO on equilibrium	61
2.11	Perverse effect of a RoO on equilibrium	62
3.1	Distribution of CTC criteria by agreement	82
3.2	Restrictiveness of RoO in selected PTAs	94
3.3	Facilitation index for selected PTAs	97
9.1	Turkey's motor vehicle exports to Germany	251
9.2	Mexico's auto exports to the US	251

List of Tables

1	Textile & Apparel exports under AGOA	3
3.1	VC criteria by agreement	84
3.2	Distribution of RoO combinations, selected PTAs (1st RoO only)	86
3.3	Regime-wide RoO in selected PTAs	88
3.4	Certification methods in selected PTAs	91
3.5	Sectoral restrictiveness of sectoral RoO in selected PTAs	96
3.6	Operation of outward processing in Singapore's FTAs	101
5.1	Descriptive statistics	162
5.2	(a) Regression results, RoO equation	165
5.2	(b) Regression results, RoO equation	166
5.3	(a) Regression results, market-access equation	167
5.3	(b) Regression results, market-access equation	168
7.1	RoO map, preferences and utilization rates	194
7.2	Determinants of utilization rates and total costs of RoO	201
7.3	Costs and preference rates	203
7.4	Comparison of Estevadeordal's index and costs estimates	205
7.5	RVC and compensating preference margins	208
8.1	Mercosur average tariffs	220
8.2	Tariff concessions in Mercosur-Chile FTA	221
8.3	Main characteristics of RoOs in the Southern Cone	226
8.4	RoO restrictiveness index	227
8.5	Structure of Rules of Origin in Mercosur by manufacturing sector (ISIC R.2) (percentage of tariff subheadings in each category)	228
8.6	Structure of Rules of Origin in Mercosur-Chile FTA by manufacturing sector (ISIC R.2) (percentage of tariff subheadings in each category)	229
8.7	Structure of Rules of Origin in Mercosur-Bolivia FTA by manufacturing sector (ISIC R.2) (percentage of tariff subheadings in each category)	230

8.8   RoOs index by manufacturing sector   230

8.9   Normative determinants. RoO, MNF tariffs differences and CET
       tariff exceptions. Ordered logit estimation. Dependent variable:
       RoO restrictiveness index   232

8.10   Political-economy determinants. RoO and tariff preferences   233

9.1   OLS estimates with robust standard errors: ς1 partner share of
       total imports of parts   254

11.1   US preferences under the GSP and AGOA—the number of tariff
       lines liberalized   298

11.2   EU preferences under the GSP and Cotonou Agreement—the
       number of tariff lines liberalized   300

11.3   Japanese preferences under the GSP—the number of tariff
       lines liberalized   301

11.4   The value of preferences and preference utilization for African
       countries exports to EU, US and Japan   302

11.5   The average costs of complying with requirements to obtain
       preferential access (2002)   312

List of Contributors

Belviglia Zampetti, Americo, United Nations Conference on Trade and Development (UNCTAD)

Bianchi, Eduardo, Instituto de Políticas y Estrategias de Comercio International (IPECI), Argentina

Brenton, Paul, International Trade Department, The World Bank

Cadot, Olivier, HEC Lausanne, Switzerland, CERDI and CEPR

Carrère, Céline, CERDI and CNRS, University of Auvergne, France

De Melo, Jaime, University of Geneva and CEPR

Destler, I.M. (Mac), School of Public Policy, University of Maryland and Institute for International Economics, USA

Erasmus, Hennie, SADC Secretariat

Estevadeordal, Antoni, Integration and Regional Programs Department, Inter-American Development Bank

Flatters, Frank, Queens's University, Canada

Francois, Joseph, Tinbergen Institute and CEPR

Ikezuki, Takako, International Trade Department, The World Bank

Kirk, Robert, The Services Group, USA

Krishna, Kala, Pennsylvania State University and NBER

Sanguinetti, Pablo, Universidad Torcuato Di Tella, Argentina

Sauvé, Pierre, Institut d' Etudes Politiques, France

Suominen, Kati, Integration and Regional Programs Department, Inter-American Development Bank

Suwa-Eisenmann, Akiko, DELTA and INRA

Thoenig, Mathias, CERAS and CNRS

Verdier, Thierry, DELTA and CEPR

Introduction

*Olivier Cadot, Antoni Estevadeordal, Akiko Suwa-Eisenmann,
and Thierry Verdier*

The spread of Preferential Trading Arrangements (PTAs) is rapidly altering the multilateral system created at Bretton Woods. The WTO reckons that if the sixty PTAs currently under negotiation are eventually formed, there will be in total twice as many of them as there are WTO members.[1] Just by themselves, the EU's future Economic Partnership Agreements[2] with ACP countries will cover over half of the WTO's membership. Seen from a different angle, the World Bank estimates that roughly one third of world trade takes place, at least nominally, on a preferential basis (World Bank 2005).[3] As encroachments to the MFN principle have multiplied—whether covered by GATT Article XXIV[4] or by particular waivers such as the one secured by the EU to cover the Cotonou Convention—new rules have gained prominence, among which those used to confer originating status to preferential exports, so-called Rules of Origin (RoOs).

The rise of regionalism has far-reaching implications not just for the multilateral trading system's philosophy but also for the day-to-day conduct of business. For good or for bad, preferential trading rules are of

---

[1] Two hundred and fifty-four PTAs have been notified so far, 124 to the GATT prior to 1994 and 130 to the WTO since 1995. In 2005, an estimated 300 will be in force. It should be kept in mind, however, that many of these agreements are essentially empty shells.

[2] The Economic Partnership Agreements (EPAs) currently under negotiation between the EU and the 77 African, Caribbean and Pacific (ACP) countries will replace the current Cotonou Convention (itself the successor of the Lomé Conventions) by end 2007. They will involve, *inter alia*, replacing the EU's unilateral preferences by a GATT-consistent free-trade zone.

[3] The proportion, however, drops to about 20% if one takes out lines for which MFN tariffs are zero.

[4] GATT Article XXIV allows WTO members to eliminate tariffs on a preferential basis provided that they do not simultaneously raise them against non-members and that 'substantially all trade' between preferential trading partners is liberalized, i.e. that they form a genuine free-trade area.

increasing relevance to traders on the ground.[5] To take but one example, a Mauritian garment today enjoys an average tariff preference of 11.9% on the European market provided that its originating status can be established. On the one hand, in a commodity sector this can mean a substantial cost advantage over MFN competitors. Moreover, tariff-free status combined with export-processing zone treatment in the source country speeds up customs clearance, adding to the cost advantage a time element that can prove critical in the garment industry's intense time-based competition. On the other hand, however, if RoOs impose the use of expensive local materials and burdensome administrative procedures to confer originating status, they can also render the preference margin worthless.

Thus, notwithstanding the classic debate about whether PTAs are good or bad for world welfare (i.e. whether they generate 'trade diversion' or 'trade creation'), how they are designed matters a lot if one is to understand how much market access they really confer. This is particularly important in view of the developmental justification often put forward in favor of North-South PTAs such as the United States' Africa Growth & Opportunity Act (AGOA) or the EU's Everything But Arms (EBA) initiative.

In parallel to the rise of preferential agreements, world trade has also been transformed by the rise of so-called 'vertical trade'. Anecdotal evidence supported by case studies[6] suggests that multinational companies have, over the last three decades, set up in many sectors and regions what Gordon Hanson called 'regional production networks', involving extensive outsourcing and the use of cross-border supply chains. Lesotho's garment industry, whose exports to the US have boomed at an annual rate of about 30% per year since the mid-1990s, is a case in point. Over 90% of Lesotho's exporting factories are owned and managed by East Asian nationals. They get large orders from US brands placed through company headquarters in Asia and use inputs provided by the parent companies in so-called CMT ('cut, make and trim') operations. A similar process, albeit on a less spectacular scale, is visible elsewhere in the world and provides much-needed employment for impoverished populations (in particular women in the case of the garment industry).[7] Overall Hummels *et al.*

---

[5] See the EU Commission's *Green Paper on Rules of Origin in preferential agreements* (CEC 2003) and part II of UNCTAD's report on trade preferences for LDCs (UNCTAD 2003).

[6] See, e.g., Ishii and Yi (1997) or Hummels, *et al.* (1998).

[7] Kenyan cut-flower exports to the EU have similarly boomed from $54 m to $139 m between 1997 and 2002. Early empirical studies (e.g. Feenstra and Hanson 1996, or Campa and Goldberg 1997) provided indirect evidence of these trends. Systematic statistical evidence of 'vertical trade' has been slower to emerge, as the necessary combination of trade and input-output data has become available only recently.

Table 1 Textile & Apparel exports under AGOA

	Exports to the US, HS61–62		AGOA util. rate 2003 (%)	Annual growth 1997–2003
	1997	2003		
Kenya	31.3	187.8	94	34.8
Lesotho	86.5	392.4	95	28.7
Mauritius	184.4	269.0	50	6.5
South Africa	70.9	231.8	54	21.8

Source: adapted from Stevens and Kennan (2004). Million US dollars.

(2001) estimate that 'vertical specialization accounts for up to 30% of world exports and has grown as much as 40% in the last twenty-five years' (p. 1).

Depending on their design, PTAs have the power to boost or hamper the development of these regional production networks. On the one hand, the experiences of Mauritius under Lomé and parts of sub-Saharan Africa under AGOA show that trade preferences can foster the emergence of North–South supply chains, in particular in the Textile and Apparel (T&A) sector (Table 1). On the other hand, stringent RoOs can prevent the smooth operation of these cross-border chains or foster the emergence of inefficient ones.

This volume brings together theoretical and empirical contributions to our understanding of how preferential RoOs affect trade flows and outsourcing decisions, how they vary across PTAs, why their legal form matters, and what political-economy forces shape them.

1. Theoretical perspectives

Pioneered by Grossman (1981),[8] the formal analysis of local-content protection is fairly recent, because it must draw on models of multistage production that are necessarily somewhat complex.[9] In the simplest possible setting, the combined effects of RoOs and tariff preferences on market access for the Southen partner of an FTA can be understood with

[8] Grossman (1982) studied so-called 'Offshore Assembly Provisions' (OAP) that, as their name indicates, grant special trade treatment to goods assembled offshore usually by domestic firms. The European Union for a while granted similar treatment to limited quantities of goods assembled in Central and Eastern Europe under the name of 'Outward Processing Treatment' (OPT) quotas. OAP and OPT have economic effects that are quite similar to those of Rules of Origin.   [9] The early work here is by Dixit and Grossman (1982).

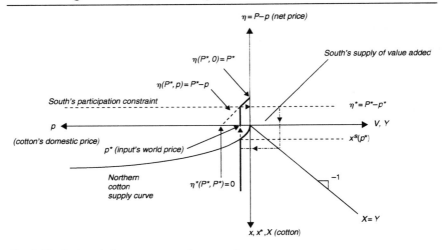

Fig. 1 Vertical trade in a two-stage framework.

the help of the four-quadrant diagram in Fig. 1. Consider a North-South FTA in which the South assembles shirts (Y) by combining value added (V) with cotton (X). The latter can be imported from either the Northern partner or the Rest of the World (ROW). The South does not produce cotton, whereas the North produces and protects both shirts and cotton, being import-competing in both sectors. Let x and x^* denote the South's use of Northern and ROW cotton respectively, so $x+x^* =X$. Southern shirt technology is Leontieff with a unit input-output coefficient, i.e. $Y=\min\{V, X\}$. In words, one shirt is made with unit of value added and one of cotton.

Value added is remunerated with what is left of sales revenue after subtracting the cost of cotton. Let P^* be the world price of a shirt and p^* that of a unit of cotton. At free trade, the 'net price' of a shirt (what is available to remunerate value added) is $\eta^* =P^* - p^*$. Let P and p be the domestic (intra-FTA) prices of shirts and cotton, respectively, and $\eta =P-p$ be the variable measured on the vertical axis of Fig. 1. Southern value added (or equivalently shirt output, as the two are by construction equal) is measured on the RHS's horizontal axis, and the curve in the first quadrant is the South's supply of value added (or, equivalently, of shirts).

Moving around clockwise, the induced demand for cotton is shown in the second quadrant as a 45° line (since $Y=X$ with a unit input-output coefficient). The vertical axis pointing downward thus measures the South's total cotton demand, from the US and from the ROW. With p, the

4

price of cotton, measured on the LHS's horizontal axis (pointing leftward), the curve in the third quadrant is the Northern supply of cotton. The quantity of Northern cotton bought by the South is just what the North can offer at world price p^*, $x^s(p^*)$, the rest being procured in the ROW. The proportion $x^s(p^*)/X$, which we will call r^* later on, is the South's *desired* regional value content.

The diagram is closed in the fourth quadrant by a line mapping the cotton price p into a net price η. To understand how it is constructed, start counterclockwise from the vertical axis by setting $P = P^*$ and $p = 0$. The net price is then $\eta = P^*$. Then raise p, i.e. slide to the left along the horizontal axis. As p goes up, the net price η goes down one-for-one, hence the downward-sloping line with slope -1 in the fourth quadrant. The line hits the horizontal axis when $p = P^*$.

The effect of tariff preferences in this diagram is straightforward (Fig. 2). Suppose that the price at which Southern shirt makers can sell in the North is now $P = P^* + \delta$, where δ is the difference between the North's MFN and preferential tariffs (the preference margin). The net price goes up by the amount of the tariff preference ($\eta = P - p^*$, so $\Delta\eta = \delta$) and the total demand for cotton goes up one-for-one with the supply of shirts. However, all the additional demand goes to ROW cotton, the price and supply of Northern cotton being unchanged at p^*. The slope of the dotted line in

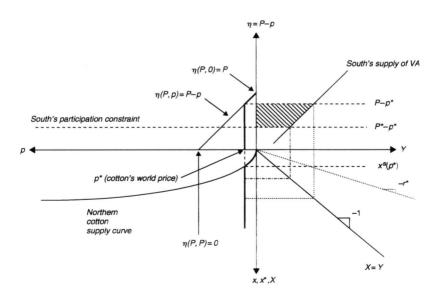

Fig. 2 The effect of tariff preferences.

the second quadrant gives the desired regional value content r^*, which has gone down as total cotton demand has gone up whereas local sourcing is unchanged. The hatched area in the first quadrant is the effect of the tariff preference on Southern producer surplus.

In this setting, a Regional Value Content (RVC), a particular form of RoO, can serve as a vehicle to force some of the additional cotton demand toward Northern suppliers (Fig. 3). Consider a new dotted line in the second quadrant with a slope $-r$ that is steeper than that of the 'desired' one (r^*). The 45° line would imply a 100% RVC, so rotating the dotted line clockwise (making it steeper) implies a more stringent RVC.

The action is now in the third quadrant, where the induced demand for Northern cotton forced by the RVC must be met at a higher domestic price p. The hatched area in that quadrant gives the additional producer surplus generated in the cotton sector by the RVC imposed in the downstream shirt sector. Abusing notation, take now the price of cotton used in the construction of the net price η on the vertical axis as the *average* price of the 'composite' cotton used by Southern producers, i.e. $\bar{p} = rp + (1 - r)p^*$. Thus $\eta = P - \bar{p}$, and the slope of η in terms of p is now $-r$ (measured leftward as before), at least as long as the RVC is binding, i.e. whenever $p > p^*$. This gives the line that closes the diagram.

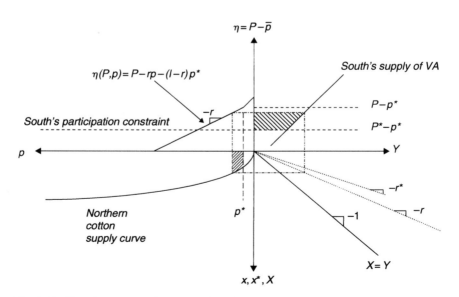

Fig. 3 Tariff preferences and RoO combined.

The interest of the diagram is that it highlights the RVC's twin effects: (i) partly offsetting the positive effect of tariff preferences on Southern producer surplus (see the reduction of the first quadrant's hatched area from Fig. 2 to Fig. 3); (ii) raising the surplus of upstream Northern producers (hatched area in the third quadrant of Fig. 3). In the extreme, the reduction in Southern producer surplus can eat up the whole benefit of tariff preferences, as indicated by the dotted 'participation constraint' line in Figs. 2 and 3.

At that point, as explained by Kala Krishna in the first chapter, a regime switch takes place and strange things happen. Drawing on her previous work with Jiandong Ju (Ju and Krishna 2002), she shows that as long as RoOs are not overly strict, tightening them raises the captive demand for local intermediates and hence their prices, as shown in Figs. 1–3. However when they become so strict as to make firms indifferent between using the preferential regime (tariff preferences cum RoO) or shipping under the MFN regime, tightening RoOs further reduces the number of exporters using the preferential regime and hence the price of intermediates, resulting in higher, not lower, imports. In her exhaustive survey of the analytics of RoOs, she also highlights several important theoretical laws; for instance the fact that they can shelter losers from the competitive effects of intrabloc trade.[10] Relatedly, she argues that the formulae upon which RoOs are based can make large differences on their impact.[11]

Matthias Thoenig and Thierry Verdier explore new territory with a game-theoretic analysis of the effect of RoOs on the outsourcing/relocation decisions of multinational companies, an issue that, as mentioned earlier, is at the heart of recent trends in international trade. Their analysis of strategic outsourcing is closely related to the classic industrial-organization literature on capacity investment. Using a model with a continuum of production stages a la Dixit–Grossman (1982), some or all of which can be outsourced, they show that competition induces oligopolistic firms to outsource too much from the point of view of their collective optimality. By putting mandatory limits on the proportion of

---

[10] This point was initially made by Krueger (1993), who noted that RoOs can 'export' trade protection from most to least protectionist FTA members. Cadot *et al.* (2001) also showed that RoOs segment the internal market of FTAs by preventing trans-shipment (and showed, incidentally, that they make it possible to generate welfare gains by selectively liberalizing member-state markets).

[11] Their legal form seems sometimes strikingly fine tuned to suit special interests. Brenton and Imagawa (forthcoming) note a particularly egregious case in which NAFTA's RoO for certain clothing products specifies that imported fabric must be 'of subheading 511111 or 511119, if hand-woven, with a loom width of less than 76 cm, woven in the United Kingdom in accordance with the rules and regulations of the Harris Tweed Association, Ltd, and so certified by the Association.' (p. 20)

7

the value chain that can be outsourced, RoOs can then act as commitment devices taking the oligopolists closer to their collusive solution. Good for them but not so, of course, for consumers. Thoenig and Verdier also show, interestingly, that in a world of incomplete contracts, RoOs can do some good by overcoming opportunism in subcontractor–client relationships.

2. The complexity of RoOs

Antoni Estevadeordal and Kati Suominen provide in chapter three a map guiding the reader through the maze of different RoOs. The difficulty of assessing the degree of stringency of this growing maze of rules explains, in part, the lack of solid empirical analysis on the economic effects of RoOs. One key distinction they make is between product-specific Rules of Origin (PSROs) and regime-wide rules. Prominent among the latter are 'cumulation' rules allowing the treatment of inputs from other PTA partners as originating. As for the former, they take myriad different forms.[12] A typical one is to require that the transformed good belong to a different tariff line or grouping than its imported inputs, but technical requirements, exceptions and so forth are plenty.[13] Estevadeordal and Suominen are able to compare the stringency of PSROs across PTAs by building on an index of PSRO restrictiveness first developed in Estevadeordal (2000) and based on a few simple classification principles.

Several observations emerge from their analysis. First and perhaps particularly strikingly, those PTAs that involve some of the most substantial intraregional trade flows, such as NAFTA and the EU's FTAs also tend to

[12] NAFTA's product-specific RoOs are so complex that Annex 301, where they are described, is over 300 pages long, whereas the Agreement itself is less than fifteen pages. The European Union's Single List of RoOs, which applies to all its preferential trade agreements (in order to make them compatible so that cumulation rules can be applied between all of them) is also quite complex. By contrast, some agreements, like the Latin American Integration Agreement (LAIA) or South & East Africa's COMESA, have simple rules applying across the board. AGOA is in the middle, with a uniform local-value-content requirement but very stiff yarn-forward rules applying to textiles and apparel (where they matter).

[13] Exceptions are often used to make RoOs selectively stringent in order to protect special interests. For instance, in her contribution to this volume Krishna cites a rule of origin of the Canada-US FTA on aged cheese according to which fresh milk is *not* an input conferring origin. Other examples are numerous. For instance, the EU's Single List confers origin to biscuits made of imported materials from any chapter *except* chapter eleven, which includes flour. Similarly, under NAFTA's RoOs, tomato ketchup qualifies as originating if it is made of imported inputs of any other chapter of the Harmonized System *except* subheading HS 200290 (tomato paste). This means that, in order to qualify, ketchup may contain imported fresh tomatoes but not imported tomato paste. This requirement is said to have been included in order to protect Mexican tomato-paste producers from Chilean competition (on this, see Brenton and Imagawa 2004 or Palmeter 1997).

have the highest restrictiveness values. Secondly, both NAFTA and the EU's PANEURO are characterized by PSROs that tend to be complex, heterogeneous, and more stringent for goods with roundabout production processes (where they do most harm).[14] This trend may become important also in most recent FTAs in Asia, where intraregional and intraindustry trade is particularly important. Meanwhile, PTAs formed among less-developed countries tend to have more uniform Rules of Origin across products and lower restrictiveness values overall.

Thirdly, they highlight, on the basis of data aggregated over all PTAs, a disturbing trend toward increasing stringency of PSROs. While the PTAs formed in the 1980s and early 1990s tended to employ relatively simple and non-restrictive PSROs and only few regime-wide rules, 'new-generation' PTAs have adopted stringent and selective regimes, although somewhat counterbalancing these features with facilitation provisions. However, recent agreements display high creativity in *ad hoc* mechanisms and instruments for the design and implementation of RoOs. For instance, the application of stringent PSROs can be temporarily suspended under 'short-supply' clauses allowing for lower regional value in cases of shortage of suitable intermediate products in the preferential area. Such clauses may bring welcome flexibility, but they may also encourage the use of otherwise stringent PSROs by creating a perception that not much damage can be done.

Estevadeordal and Suominen also develop a 'facilitation index' summarizing information on regime-wide rules. Many such rules, such as those permitting cumulation,[15] can somehow counteract the restrictiveness of

---

[14] However RoOs can also be extraordinarily complex for goods whose origin would appear at first sight straightforward to establish. The EU's RoO for fish under the Cotonou Agreement, for instance (which matters a lot for the Seychelles), requires not just that the fish be caught in the territorial waters of an eligible (ACP) country. In addition, the fish landing at an EU port should carry documentation establishing that the following criteria are met:

1. The vessel's captain, officers and at least 50% of its crew were nationals of an EU or ACP state;
2. It was registered in an EU or ACP state;
3. It sailed under the flag of an EU or ACP state;
4. It was at least 50% owned by nationals of an EU or ACP state (although under certain conditions leased or chartered vessels can qualify);
5. The chairman and the majority of the board members of the company owning the vessel were nationals of an EU or ACP state (Brenton and Imagawa 2004).

[15] 'Cumulation' can take three forms. Bilateral cumulation allows say a Mexican producer to use US inputs in the making of a product for re-export to the US. Diagonal cumulation would allow the use of Canadian inputs (third party within the preferential zone) under the same conditions. Full cumulation would allow non-originating inputs from the area (inputs themselves made from imported components *and* violating PSROs) to be treated as if they were originating provided that the last stage of transformation satisfies the PSROs.

product-specific RoO. For instance, the larger the area where a PTA member can cumulate value to its final goods subsequently exported to its PTA partners, the larger the pool of inputs and processes available for the country's producers, and the easier it becomes to comply with the product-specific RoO. This means that while restrictive product-specific RoO can be hypothesized to dampen trade, certain regime-wide RoO can compensate for it. Whereas higher values of the PSRO index mean more stringent rules, higher values of the facilitation index mean less restrictive cumulation rules.

Figure 4 shows a scatterplot of the two indices for the main PTAs currently in force. A loose correlation is apparent, suggesting that PTAs with generous cumulation rules tend, at the same time, to have stringent PSROs. This may suggest some political economy pressure by the export interests for loosening the RoO regime.

The figure, in which 'better' PTAs (characterized by light PSROs and generous regime-wide rules) lie to the Northwest, also illustrates the observation made earlier that neither NAFTA nor the EU's PANEURO look very good in terms of the mixture of PSRO and regime-wide rules they offer, by comparison with other PTAs.

Figure 4 shows the average level but not the dispersion of PSRO restrictiveness across sectors. It turns out that the most restrictive PTAs in terms of average level are also those with the greatest sectoral selectivity in PSROs. That the 'peak RoO stringency levels' tend to fall on the agricultural, food, and textile & apparel sectors suggests that RoO may not be

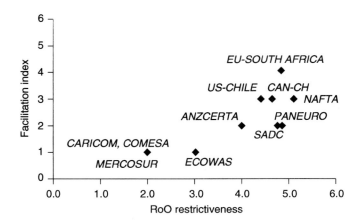

Fig. 4 PSRO restrictiveness and regime-wide facilitation, selected PTAs.

Source: Authors calculations.

RoO restrictiveness averages are simple averages.

a neutral instrument of preferential trade, but, rather, be driven by some of the same political-economy dynamics as other trade-protectionist instruments.

The issue raised by the proliferation of PTAs is not just the accompanying spread of restrictive RoO regimes around the world, but also their potential divergence. The more different regimes are from each other, the harder it will be to interlink existing PTAs with each other in the future—which, in turn, raises the risk of trade-diverting PTA blocs developing at the expense of global free trade. Abolishing RoO altogether (for example by bringing MFN tariffs to zero globally) would be the simplest means to counteract the potential negative effects of RoO. However, the politically more palatable option would be to harmonize preferential RoO at the global level. A good start might be limiting the types of RoO that can be employed in PTAs—in essence, setting RoO within a global band—and incorporating further facilitation mechanisms to the application of RoO regimes, for example, through generous cumulation provisions.

Interestingly, Americo Zampetti and Pierre Sauvé find that the RoOs applying to the producers of tradeable services tend to be less heterogeneous and opaque than those applying to goods, suggesting that rules for services have not (yet) become a battleground for special interests. However, they note that the rising importance of business-process outsourcing and other forms of service trade can quickly change the picture.

3. Rules of Origin and special interests

The value of RoOs as a protectionist device means that they can be endogenously determined by special interests. In their analysis of the political feasibility of FTAs, Grossman and Helpman (1995) focused on the exclusion of sensitive sectors and the length of phase-out periods. As noted by Duttagupta and Panagaryia (2003), RoOs are alternative instruments to win over special-interest support in favor of regional agreements.

Olivier Cadot, Antoni Estevadeordal and Akiko Suwa-Eisenmann take some of the points raised by Anne Krueger and Kala Krishna to the test of structural estimation. If RoOs provide captive markets for upstream intermediates, they reason, lobbying by producers of those intermediates should have something to do with the observed pattern of product-specific RoOs. Using the classic common-agency approach to model influence activities, they derive the relation between endogenous tariffs and RoO stringency implied by influence activities upstream. Then, combining Estevadeordal's index with input-output data, they test for this relationship and find that the stringency of NAFTA's RoOs indeed reflects a systematic pattern of influence by US producers of upstream intermediates. The benefit of tariff preferences for Mexican exporters being taken back by cost-raising RoOs, the system's beneficiaries and losers are respectively US intermediate-good makers and taxpayers. In other words, the combination of tariff preferences and RoOs replicates the effect of an export subsidy for intermediates, going around the prohibition of such subsidies under GATT rules.

The econometric evidence is, in this regard, consistent with the historical evidence on NAFTA's negotiations discussed by I. Mac Destler, who notes that NAFTA's RoOs in the automobile sector were the result of a fine balancing act between the interests of Detroit's car-makers who differed in their level of outsourcing. In textile, a 'triple transformation test' was elaborated. It required that to be treated as a North American product, a piece of apparel must have undergone three basic processes (fiber, cloth, clothing). This tight rule of origin seduced US mills in North and South Carolina by opening for them a captive market in Mexico, and thus, they gave up their traditional alliance with the domestic apparel industry.

As Destler notes, the rise of RoOs as an indirect tool of trade protection reflects both the increasing constraints weighing on the use of more traditional instruments and the slow erosion of the bipartisan consensus on free trade that dominated US postwar politics. To take the words of A. Spilimbergo, Rules of Origin are part of a Faustian pact, made to win the approval of a FTA from an originally reluctant constituency.

4. Measuring the impact of RoOs

Céline Carrère and Jaime de Melo take the econometric treatment of RoOs one step closer to what is arguably *the* key empirical question: how much do they cost? Their approach consists of extracting information on the cost of complying with RoOs by looking at preference utilization rates. Using simple assumptions on the relationship between utilization rates and compliance costs, they derive an *ad valorem* equivalent of 3.2% for NAFTA's RoOs. This may not seem terribly high but the figure is substantially higher for textile & apparel products, where tariff lines with 100% NAFTA utilization rates, which enjoy average tariff preferences of

9.7%, bear estimated RoO compliance costs of 5.6%.[16] Interestingly from a policy perspective, Carrère and de Melo's estimates suggest that technical requirements are the costliest forms of RoOs, no doubt because their opacity makes them easily to manipulate.

Pablo Sanguinetti and Eduardo Bianchi's analysis of Mercosur's RoOs is one of the few analyses available of South-South PTAs (together with the analysis of SADC by Flatters and Kirk later in this volume). The Free Trade Agreements (FTAs) signed by Chile and Bolivia with Mercosur (itself a Customs Union) provide a quasi-laboratory to analyse how FTA–CU differences affect the design of RoOs.[17] Sanguinetti and Bianchi also use the fact that external-tariff harmonization is imperfect in Mercosur to assess how external-tariff differences affect RoO stringency on the basis of an index à la Estevadeordal. As it turns out, large differences between external tariffs are associated with stiff RoOs, especially when the high-tariff country is Brazil, suggesting that the latter's political weight was prominent in the design of Mercosur's RoOs.

Joseph Francois departs from the usual analytical setting (in which inputs from different sources are perfect substitutes) by introducing a model à la Ethier in which input diversity raises productive efficiency. In this framework, RoOs reduce intra-FTA trade in final goods (because the cost of producing goods for export in the FTA is raised by RoOs) whereas the opposite is true for trade in intermediate products (because RoOs create a captive market for them). These effects are not at play in Custom Unions where RoOs are unnecessary. Francois takes these hypotheses to the data using automobile trade across a variety of PTAs, including NAFTA and the Turkey-EU Customs Union. He finds evidence that trade patterns are affected by RoOs in just the way predicted by the theory; in particular that NAFTA results in substantial trade diversion in intermediates.

Frank Flatters and Robert Kirk offer a detailed account of how the RoOs of the South African Development Community (SADC), initially simple and homogenous, have been progressively transformed by special-interest influence into a complex and *ad hoc* system. Their account of the negotiations interestingly highlights one of the running themes of this

---

[16] Carrère and de Melo's econometric estimates are in line with earlier, non-parametric estimates by Anson *et al.* (2005) that placed administrative costs at 1.8% and costs related to increased input prices at 4.4%.

[17] One of the primary justifications of RoOs is to prevent the trans-shipment of imported goods across a free-trade area's internal borders. Otherwise, member states with low external tariffs would act as ports of entry for the whole area and would deprive others of tariff revenue. However, in a CU, agreement on a Common External Tariff eliminates this problem and hence the need for RoOs. Their presence in Mercosur is thus in and by itself suggestive of other, presumably political-economy driven, motivations.

volume, namely the linkage between lobbying for RoOs and lobbying for other forms of protection (such as long tariff phase-outs). They also take argument with widespread developmental justifications for RoOs, showing for instance how SADC member countries with established processed-food manufacturers sometimes push for stiff RoOs knowing full well that other member countries have no production at all of the relevant upstream intermediates. The result is then to establish monopoly positions for the processed-food manufacturers and preclude intra-SADC trade.[18]

Finally, Paul Brenton and Takako Ikezuki examine the non-reciprocal preferences granted by the US, EU and Japan to the Least Developed Countries (LDCs). Assessing the 'value of preferences' on the basis of coverage,[19] preference margins and utilization rates, they find that it varies considerably across exporter countries and sectors. US preferences on Textile & Apparel appear most valuable to Lesotho, Kenya and Swaziland, whereas EU preferences appear most valuable to Swaziland, Malawi, Mauritius and the Seychelles, primarily on account of the sugar protocol (except for the Seychelles for which it is fish that matters). For most of the rest of sub-Saharan Africa, the value of preferences is only marginal, the reason being essentially the cost of complying with RoOs. Using an approach close to that of Anson *et al.* (2005)—namely using the average tariff-preference margin for lines with utilization rates strictly between zero and 100% as a proxy for RoO costs—they put the price tag of complying with RoOs at 6.7% in *ad valorem* equivalent for US-bound exports, 8.4% for EU-bound, and 5.6% for Japan-bound.

5. Concluding remarks

Where does this all leave us? As Destler notes, constraints weighing increasingly heavily on the use of traditional instruments of trade protection have led to a search for GATT-compatible substitutes. Those

---

[18] They cite the edifying example of ongoing negotiations on wheat flour, where South Africa is asking for a stiff local-content requirement, although this would essentially preclude flour trade among SADC members because wheat production is marginal in the area. The reason officially invoked on the South African side is to offset the high cost of local wheat, itself due to wheat protection. But, because millers have market power, they buy wheat from farmers at close to its world price. Thus, the wheat tariff as a matter of fact does *not* protect farmers and only serves as convenient justification for a stiff RoO that would reinforce the millers' market power.

[19] A preference scheme with given coverage can have very different implications for different exporting countries depending on their prior trading structures, as eligible tariff lines can be high-volume ones for a country and low-volume ones for another. Of course, once preferences are in place trading structures tend to adjust endogenously to take advantage of them.

include all forms of contingent protection (anti-dumping, safeguard and countervailing duties) but also made-to-measure Rules of Origin.

In a way, RoOs were the perfect protectionist instrument. Because their determination is a very technical exercise, it naturally calls for input from companies with interest in the outcome. The result is, unsurprisingly, often hard-wired. This has largely gone unnoticed because, for quite a while, RoOs have been allowed to grow and gain force behind the veil of technicality and expert-confined negotiations.

This book is an attempt to bring the issue closer to public scrutiny. RoOs, all contributors argue, can do substantial damage to economic efficiency; they can also make market-access promises largely empty. The evidence suggests that, pretty much as uniform tariffs were promoted in the 1980s by Washington-based institutions to put an end to the fine tuning of tariffs to suit special interests, clear, uniform and moderate RoOs should be the goal of future negotiations. The South, in particular, stands to be hurt by rules that can be easily manipulated to render vacuous market-access promises made by the North in the course of bilateral negotiations. At least for as long as regionalism stays in fashion, putting demands for clear and transparent RoOs at the center of ongoing and future market-access negotiations should be a priority for Southern countries. Conversely, negotiators in South-South agreements should resist the temptation of opening the Pandora's box of tailor-made RoOs.

References

Anson, J., O. Cadot, A. Estevadeordal, A. Suwa-Eisenmann, J. de Melo, B. Tumurchudur (2005), 'Rules of Origin in North-South Preferential Trading Arrangements with an Application to NAFTA'; forthcoming, *Review of International Economics*.

Brenton, P., H. Imagawa (2004), 'Rules of Origin, Trade Customs' in L. de Wulf, J. Sokol (ed.) *Customs Modernization: A Handbook*, World Bank.

Cadot, O., J. de Melo, M. Olarreaga (2001), Can Regionalism Ease the Pains of Multilateral Trade Liberalization?', with *European Economic Review* **45**, 27–44.

Campa, J. M., L. Goldberg (1997), 'The Evolving External Orientation of Manufacturing: A Profile of Four Countries'; *Federal Reserve Bank of New York Economic Policy Review*, 53–81.

Commission of the European Communities (2003), *Green Paper on the future of Rules of Origin in preferential trade arrangements*; COM(2003)787 final, Brussels.

Dixit, A. K., G. M. Grossman (1982), 'Trade and Protection with Multistage Production'; *Review of Economic Studies* **49**, 583–594.

Duttagupta, R., A. Panagariya (2003), 'Free Trade Areas and Rules of Origin: Economics and Politics'; IMF Working Paper 03/229.

Estevadeordal, A. (2000). 'Negotiating Preferential Market Access: The Case of the North American Free Trade Agreement.' *Journal of World Trade* 34, 1 (February).

Feenstra, R., G. Hanson (1996), 'Foreign Investment, Outsourcing, and Relative Wages'; in Feenstra, Grossman, Irwin (ed.), *The Political Economy of Trade Policy: Essays in Honour of Jagdish Bhagwati*; MIT Press.

Grossman, G. M. (1981), 'The Theory of Domestic Content Protection and Content Preference'; *Quarterly Journal of Economics* **96**, 583–603.

Grossman, G. M. (1982), 'Offshore Assembly Provisions and the Structure of Protection'; *Journal of International Economics* **12**, 301–312.

Grossman, G., E. Helpman (1995), 'The Polities of Free-Trade Agreements'; *American Economic Review* **85**, 667–690.

Hummels, D., D. Rapoport, Kei-Mu Yi (1998), 'Vertical Specialization and the Changing Nature of World Trade'; *Federal Bank of New York Economic Policy Review*, 79–99.

Hummels, D., J. Ishii, Kei-Mu Yi (2001), 'The Nature and Growth of Vertical Specialization in World Trade'; *Journal of International Economics* **54**, 75–96.

Ishii, J., Kei-Mu Yi (1997), 'The Growth of World Trade'; Federal Bank of New York Research paper 9718.

Ju, J., K. Krishna (2002), 'Regulations, Regime Switches and Non-Monotonicity when Non-Compliance is an Option: An Application to Content Protection and Preference'; *Economics Letters* **77**, 315–321.

Krueger, A. (1993), 'Free Trade Agreements as Protectionist Devices: Rules of Origin'; in *Festschrift in Honor of John Chipman*.

Palmeter, D. (1997), 'Rules of Origin in Regional Trading Agreements', in P. De Maret, F-F. Bellis, G.G. Jiminez (ed.) Regionlism and Multilaterilism after the Uruguay Round; Brussels.

Stevens, C., Kennan, J. (2004), 'Comparative Study of G8 Preferential Access Schemes for Africa; IDS.

UNCTAD (2003), Trade preferences for LDCs: an early assessment of benefits and possible improvements. UNCTAD/TCT/TSB/2003/8, United Nations: New York and Geneva.

World Bank (2005), *Global Economic Prospects*.

Part I

Rules of Origin: Theoretical perspectives

1

Understanding Rules of Origin

Kala Krishna

1.1 Introduction

The proliferation of Free Trade Areas (FTAs) in the last decade has begun to generate interest in one of its most important components: Rules of Origin or RoO for short. These specify the conditions under which a good becomes eligible for zero tariffs in an FTA. While it is tempting to think of FTAs as liberalizing, they are often not. The main reason is that RoO are in themselves hidden protection: they create what look like tariffs on imported intermediate inputs and affect the price of domestically made inputs as well. These RoO are negotiated industry by industry and there is enormous scope for well-organized industries to essentially insulate themselves from the effects of the FTA by devising suitable RoO. In this manner, RoO may even make FTAs feasible in the presence of organized interest groups. Grossman and Helpman (1995), for example, argue that being able to exclude certain sectors (which is what appropriately constructed RoO will do) can make an FTA viable.[1]

This chapter surveys the existing theoretical literature with a view to explaining in a non-technical manner what RoO do and why they are critical in determining the effects of FTAs. This is an area that has been neglected in economics[2] until quite recently, witness the absence of RoO in most books dealing with integration even as late as the book by de Melo and Panagariya (1993). Consequently, much of the work being surveyed here is quite recent.

---

[1] A recent paper that develops this idea is Duttagupta and Panagariya (2001) who argue that RoO can improve the political viability of FTAs. They do so in a menu-auction framework à la Grossman and Helpman (1995), (2001).

[2] Though not neglected in law, see, for example, Vermulst (1994).

Many analysts have tended to view *NAFTA* and other FTA arrangements as being similar to customs unions. Indeed, in some respects they are. However, RoO, which are part of both FTAs and customs union agreements, play very different roles under these two arrangements. In a customs union, members have a common external tariff so that there are no rents to be obtained from trans-shipment. Therefore, when a RoO is agreed upon, its purpose is simply to determine the extent of preferential treatment for fellow members. For example, the European Community has rules governing treatment of imports of semiconductors. In February 1989 the EU changed its practice of conferring origin based on the place of assembly. It began conferring origin based on the place of diffusion. Thus, if diffusion is undertaken within the Community, then origin is granted and importation to another *EC* country is duty-free. If, however, diffusion is undertaken abroad, then the chip is treated as having been produced outside the community, and the (common) external tariff applies. This change would promote investment in the EU by Japanese and US firms who might otherwise have only assembly operations in the EU and would grant origin to EC producers who assembled their products abroad.

In an FTA, members maintain their own external tariffs. Hence, tariffs may differ between member countries. In this setting, RoO assume a function additional to that under customs unions: RoO prevent the import of any particular commodity from entering through the country (which gets the tariff revenue) with the lowest duty on the item in question and being re-exported to other countries in the FTA. Without RoO, an FTA could be highly liberalizing as the lowest tariff would apply to each category of imports.[3] Note that such re-exports need not be a good thing. If transport costs are significant, such deflection also has real costs since trans-shipping wastes resources. RoO might prevent or reduce such waste, thereby raising welfare.[4] For example, if the trans-shipping costs are slightly below the tariff differential, welfare-reducing deflection occurs in the absence of RoO since consumer prices are essentially unchanged, resources are used in trans-shipment, while tariff revenue falls. Rules of Origin would prevent this.

Such deflection could lead to a tariff war as countries attempt to attract such trade. In the absence of transport costs, the country in the FTA with the lowest tariff on a product will be the conduit for all imports into the FTA and will reap all tariff revenues. This makes it in the interest of all

---

[3] The likelihood of such trade deflection for final goods was pointed out in Shibata (1967).

[4] In addition, standard second best arguments also apply: with many tariffs, reducing one need not raise welfare.

other countries to reduce their own tariffs in order to attract imports to their ports! Only when the lowest tariff is zero is this not an issue, suggesting that in equilibrium, all external tariffs would be competed down to zero![5] It is interesting to note that this seems to have actually happened in America after the colonies obtained independence from the British. During the Articles of Confederation period (1777–1789) the thirteen original states in America set their external tariffs independently though internal trade was essentially free. They were also Britain's largest export market. Despite this, they could not extract rents through tariffs or use the threat of tariffs to promote their own external objectives. Since British merchants landed their goods in the ports of the states offering the most favorable terms, despite independence, these states undercut one another in setting their duties resulting in very open markets. This is pointed out in McGillivray and Green (2001) and was originally mentioned in Viner (1950).

RoO can also provide an incentive for regional producers to buy intermediate goods from regional sources, even if their prices are higher than those of the identical import from outside the FTA, in order to make their product originate in the FTA and qualify for preferential treatment. This, in effect, protects FTA suppliers.[6] As a result, an FTA can profoundly affect trade patterns and the investment flows needed to sustain them. Lloyd (1993) makes the case that using a tariff on value added outside the FTA would be more efficient than using RoO.

Just because RoO may be protectionist does not prove that they are! However, RoO often account for large chunks of draft agreements (RoO took up 200 pages of the *NAFTA* agreement) and can be very contentious, suggesting that they might be strategically used. Recent work by Estevadeordal (2000) casts some light on this matter. He constructs a model with two endogenous variables: the severity of the RoO and the length of the phase in period. Both were key factors over which negotiations were conducted. Assume that the severity of the RoO is determined by exogenous factors like the difference in the (*MFN*) tariffs between the countries as well as the extent of intra-FTA trade, but does not depend on

---

[5] Richardson (1995) points out that this can happen even when there are RoO that domestic production automatically meets. As a result, domestic production is exported to the partner country and domestic consumption is imported.

[6] Krueger (1999) points out the protective effect of RoO on domestic intermediates. Krueger (1997) focuses on some political-economy implications of Free Trade Areas. Lloyd (1993) sketches out, and Rodriguez (2001) develops more formally, a model with multistage protection in the presence of such RoO. Also see Rosellon (2000), which was part of his Ph.D in 1994, and Falvey and Reed (1998).

the length of the phase in. Also, that the length of time in the phase-in period depends on the negotiated RoO, as well as other exogenous factors. Estevadeordal (2000) estimates such a model and argues that RoO are being used to prevent trade deflection as the sectors that have large differences in tariffs between the partners are those where RoO are strongest. Moreover, that protection and the extent of RoO are positively correlated. Sectors with long phase-in periods are also the sectors with high predicted RoO suggesting that the same forces drive both. The work of Cadot *et al.* (2002) also suggests that RoO are negating the effects of tariff reductions due to an FTA. They use the severity of the RoO index (as constructed in Estevadeordal (2000)) and a measure of tariff preferences in NAFTA as explanatory variables to explain Mexican exports to the US. They show that the former reduced Mexican exports, while the latter raised them, so that the net effect was close to zero.

In addition, it is worth pointing out that RoO are often quite expensive to document. As a result, even if a product satisfies origin, an importer may prefer to pay the tariff rather than bother with the documentation needed. Some idea of how extensive this is might be gleaned from the prevalence of outward processing trade (OPT) between the EU and the Central and Eastern European countries.[7] The latter have duty-free access to the EU but instead of proving origin is met, EU firms use the OPT provision, suggesting that the cost of proving origin exceeds the duty paid using the OPT provision. For example, as documented in Breton and Manchin (2002), when Albanian exports of clothing to the EU are considered, OPT provisions were used over 90% of the time. However, Turkey, which is part of the customs union (hence, it does not have any RoO to meet) used these provisions only 0.5% of the time.[8] Herin (1986) also shows that the cost of proving origin seems to have led over a quarter of EFTA exports to pay the MFN tariff.

I will argue that much of what we have learned from the literature can be summarized in four laws that are worth remembering when dealing with RoO.

Law 1: RoO can insulate an industry from the consequences of an FTA and it can provide hidden protection for intermediate inputs used by it. It may well be that the ability to insulate an industry makes FTAs easier

---

[7] OPT encourages processing overseas by *EU* firms as the duty that would have been paid on the exported inputs to be processed abroad is deducted from the duty owed on the imported product.

[8] It may also be that OPT trade allows a greater fraction of potential rent to be captured by the EU importer, an open question on the empirical side.

to pass than Customs Unions. Agents who stand to lose from an FTA can undo its effects without, for the most part, even being seen as doing so! For example, in the US-Canada Free Trade Area (FTA), the production of aged cheese from fresh milk does not confer origin.[9] This in effect prevents free trade of cheese in the FTA.

Law 2: The precise form of the RoO matters. Lawyers and trade negotiators have clearly understood this for a long time. This is evident in the importance placed on the details of the RoO negotiated. For example, great importance was placed on the treatment of interest costs by Honda when content requirements were being defined for the FTA between the US and Canada.

Law 3: The time period matters. Responses to RoO take time. Short-run partial equilibrium effects can differ greatly from long-run, general equilibrium ones. For example, in the short run the response to RoO may be primarily in terms of trade flows, while in the long run it may take the form of investment flows. Hence, it is vital to specify the time frame for analysis and to incorporate the major linkages across sectors and options available to firms.

Law 4: You can have too much of a good thing. Having more restrictive RoO may result in higher, not lower imports! This point is quite subtle and provides a warning to policy-makers and potential users that RoO may well backfire!

The chapter proceeds as follows. Section 1.2 looks at how RoO are defined. Section 1.3 examines how they affect the sourcing of inputs and hence the level of costs. Section 1.4 surveys what the literature has to say about their effects using a partial equilibrium setting. The additional complications that arise from allowing some input prices to be endogenous are outlined as well. Section 1.5 discusses extensions to general equilibrium, while Section 1.6 concludes.

1.2 Background

RoO can be defined in a variety of different ways. From a legal point of view, there appear to be four criteria used singly and in combination with each other.[10] These are (a) requirements in terms of domestic

---

[9] See Palmeter (1993) footnote 4 for details.

[10] For example, the Australia-New Zealand Closer Economic Relationship (CER) relies on a 50% value-added standard in conjunction with the requirement that the last process performed in manufacture be in the territory of the exporting member state.

content: content can be defined in terms of value added or in physical terms.[11] In addition, the required share of value added can be defined in terms of cost or price.

(b) Requirements in terms of a change in tariff heading: RoO set in terms of a change in tariff heading are specified in terms of tariff categories. To satisfy origin requirements, a product must change its tariff heading in a specified way. By making the changes needed more or less extensive, the origin requirement can be made more or less restrictive. In addition, exceptions can be explicitly made. For example, under *NAFTA*, transformation from any other chapter (2-digit classification level) of the harmonized system, to tomato ketchup, chapter 21, confers origin, *except* transformation from tomato paste that falls in chapter 20! Since the US is a larger market for ketchup than Mexico, while Mexico has a natural advantage in growing tomatoes, and hence making paste, this seems like a clear attempt to keep the production of ketchup in the US.

(c) Requirements in terms of specified processes that must be performed within the FTA or CU: in the case of American imports of apparel under *NAFTA*, the rule is one of triple transformation. Only if each step of the transformation from raw material to finished garment has been undertaken within the FTA will preferential treatment be given. American textile producers, of course, benefit from this rule.

(d) Requirements that the product has been substantially transformed. This is usually hard to pin down as it is loosely defined. In the United States the term substantial transformation has come to mean the determination of origin based on common law, reasoning from case to case. It then results in commodity-specific RoO that fall into one of the earlier three categories.

1.3 RoO and costs

From an analytical viewpoint the basic effect of RoO is to raise the production costs of the product that meets the binding RoO. In the discussion that follows I draw from Krishna and Krueger (1995). RoO specify constraints that must be met in order to obtain origin. If these constraints are binding then the choice of inputs used in production differs from the unconstrained ones and, hence, costs are higher if the RoO are met. Since

---

[11] One example of physical-content requirements is that in the cigarette industry in Australia. Cigarette manufacturers must meet a domestic content requirement on tobacco leaf use, defined by weight.

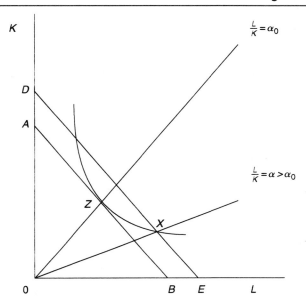

Fig. 1.1 Physical content RoO and costs.

more restrictive RoO constrain choices more than do less restrictive ones, an increase in restrictiveness raises the minimized level of costs.

This is illustrated in Fig. 1.1 that depicts a physical content requirement that has to be met to obtain origin. FTA inputs (L) and imported inputs (K) are used to make the good in question under constant returns to scale. The unit isoquant is depicted by the curve in Fig. 1.1. At existing prices for L and K, firms choose the input mix at the point labeled Z using L and K so that their ratio equals α_0. The lowest unit costs attainable are represented by the height of the line AB. A binding RoO would remove Z from the feasible set. If, for example, the RoO required L/K to be at least $\alpha > \alpha_0$, then only points below the ray from the origin with slope $1/\alpha$ and above the isoquant would be feasible. As a result, unit costs are minimized by choosing the input mix at X. Unit costs if the RoO are met are given by the height of the line DE. Note that the RoO distort the input mix in favor of the FTA made input L for any given level of output so that at any given output level, the demand for L is higher.

It is easy to see that as the RoO become more restrictive, that is, as α rises and the ray from the origin swings down, unit costs rise. Suppressing input prices in the notation for the time being, let unit costs when the RoO is met be $R(\alpha)$. Note that $R(\alpha)$ is increasing in α for $\alpha > \alpha_0$.

1.4 The effects of RoO: Partial equilibrium

The literature has by and large assumed perfect competition. The partial equilibrium setting provides three results. First, that in the long run, RoO cause large changes in investment flows due to an FTA. In the absence of RoO, there would be large changes in trade flows, not investment flows. Secondly, in the long run, RoO may raise or lower welfare relative to pre-FTA levels depending on their restrictiveness. If RoO are weak, they are likely to raise welfare,[12] while if they are stringent, they will reduce welfare. Thirdly, that in the short run, where capacity constraints exist, the form of the RoO is especially important. It is easiest to explain these three results with a particular example based on Krishna and Krueger (1995).

Suppose that the FTA is made up of countries A and B. Both countries import the final good in question from the rest of the world and take the world price of P^* as given. B also produces it domestically so that the domestic price in B equals the domestic unit cost of production, which equals the world price as we assume that the tariff in B is zero. Country A has a positive tariff on the good, and for simplicity assume A has no domestic production. All tariffs are constant across suppliers,[13] though members of an FTA get preferential treatment.

An FTA member firm interested in selling its products in the partner country has the choice of meeting the RoO and having zero tariffs levied on it, but having higher costs of production (as well as further documentation costs that the RoO has been met),[14] and not meeting it and paying the tariff. It chooses the option that has a higher payoff. Now since B imports the good and has the lower tariff, firms in A will not want to sell to B but firms in B would be interested in selling to A. Thus, the price in B is the world price, and must be not weakly lower than the price in A. Let P^A and $P^B(=P^*=C^B)$ denote domestic prices in A and B.

A firm in B exporting to A could meet the RoO and obtain $P^A - R^B(\alpha)$, or ignore it and get $P^A - C^B(1+t^A)$, where C^B and $R^B(\alpha)$ denote the unrestricted and restricted unit costs in B.[15] Hence, if $R^B(\alpha) < C^B(1+t^A)$, it is

---

[12] I say likely since in a world with multiple distortions or tariffs, a reduction in some of them may not raise welfare as indicated by the theorem of the second best.

[13] This makes sense given that most countries extend most-favored nation treatment to all their trading partners.

[14] Providing appropriate documentation to demonstrate origin can be very costly. Herin (1986) reports costs to Finnish firms of satisfying EC RoOs for entry of Finnish exports from 1.4 to 5.7 per cent of the value of shipment (Herin, p. 7). Such costs are reported to have resulted in a quarter of eligible EFTA exports to the EU paying the applied *MFN* duty rather than providing the needed documentation.

[15] Assume that tariffs are levied on price that equals domestic cost.

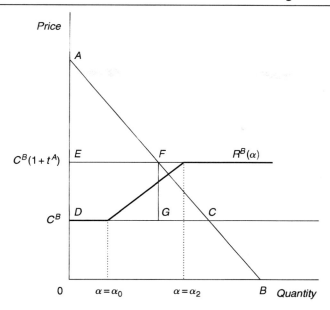

Fig. 1.2 Demand, price and cost in an FTA.

worthwhile for it to accept the restriction and otherwise it is not. The price in A is, therefore, the minimum of $R^B(\alpha)$ and $C^B(1+t^A)$. Recall that restricted costs increase in α and equal unrestricted costs for low enough levels of α. If RoO are not restrictive, i.e., α is below α_0, in Fig. 1.2 (which depicts both demand in A and costs as a function of α) then RoO are not binding and $R^B(\alpha) = C^B$. In this case the creation of an FTA will result in the effective lowering of tariffs in A on the final good to those in B. If RoO are restrictive but not too much so, i.e., α is between α_0 and α_2, then costs of supplying A exceed world costs but are below the cost of imports from outside the FTA. Thus, the price in A rises with $R^A(\alpha)$ but is still below the pre-FTA price. Once RoO are restrictive enough, i.e., α exceeds α_2, then costs of supplying A from B exceed the cost of imports from outside the FTA.

These results are in sharp contrast to those that would prevail in the absence of any RoO. In the absence of transport costs and under the same assumptions as made above, all an FTA without RoO would do would be to reduce tariffs on the final good as all imports to A would come in through B to avail of the lower tariff there. Welfare would have to rise in A due to the FTA, as the gain in consumer surplus would outweigh the loss in tariff revenue. However, production in B need not be affected. With RoO, production in B rises to the point where B supplies all A's imports and this requires large capital inflows into the sector. This is the logic of the first result.

Note that A's welfare with RoO is non-monotonic in α. Welfare is the sum of consumer surplus, producer surplus, and tariff revenue. Since there is competition and constant returns to scale, price equals cost and there are no profits in the long run. Welfare in A must, thus, increase above its pre-FTA level if $\alpha \leq \alpha_0$. This occurs as price falls so that consumer surplus rises. Although tariff revenue falls, as is usual, the consumer surplus gain (EDCF) exceeds the tariff revenue loss (EFGD) as depicted in Fig. 1.2. In the region where the RoO bind, but it remains worthwhile accepting them, that is $\alpha_1 < \alpha \leq \alpha_2$, an increase in α raises the price in A as the price equals $R^A(\alpha)$. As α approaches α_2, all consumer surplus gains vanish and since there are no tariff revenues either, welfare must be lower than prior to the FTA. In other words, as the RoO get more restrictive, the higher production costs eat away the consumer surplus gain of an FTA. At some point this makes an FTA worse than no FTA. Finally, when RoO are so restrictive that they are ignored, i.e., α exceeds α_2, the FTA has no effect on the price in A and the pre-FTA welfare prevails. This is the logic of the second result above.

All the above is valid for the long run. However, in the short run there are likely to be capacity constraints since it takes time for capacity to be built. Think of these capacity constraints as taking a very strict form so that costs are constant at $R^B(\alpha)$, until the capacity constraint where they become infinite. Thus, supply facing B when RoO are set at α consists of three distinct segments. Supply is zero when the price is below $R^B(\alpha)$. At a price of $R^B(\alpha)$ a horizontal segment exists up to B's capacity. For a price above $R^B(\alpha)$, supply equals capacity so that there is a vertical section. As world prices are given, if the price weakly exceeds $P^*(1 + t^A)$, supply is infinite. As a result, the price is given by the minimum of $R^B(\alpha)$ and $P^*(1 + t^A)$ only if capacity in B exceeds the demand at $R^B(\alpha)$. Otherwise, there are quasi-rents and the price in A exceeds production costs.

In the short run, as opposed to the long run, all imports to A do not come from B. In the short run, output, which equals exports to A from B, expands to capacity at which point marginal costs rise choking off supply. Assuming there is no change in the world price and given that B cannot meet all of A's demand, the price in A will be unchanged. All that will happen is a reallocation of A's imports from the rest of the world to B, causing a reduction in A's welfare arising from the loss in tariff revenues. In the long run, of course, assuming no changes in world prices and the price of inputs in B, investment will flow into B, leading to the long-run effects outlined above.

1.4.1 *Why details matter*

Why should the details of how RoO are defined matter to agents? Given the effort devoted to thrashing out such details, it is clear that these details are seen as being critical. The reason is simple. Even though definitions may sound alike they need not be. Some definitions may be easier to meet than others and lobbying for the most favorable definition is to be expected. For example, suppose that costs have three components: capital costs, denoted by B, FTA inputs costs denoted by A, and imported inputs costs denoted by D. Total costs are C, and $C = A + B + D$. Suppose that RoO specify the minimum share that FTA inputs must account for. Suppose that this is defined as a cost share. Now note that excluding capital costs from all costs makes any given RoO harder to meet. If capital costs are included, the share of FTA costs is given by $(A + B)/C$. If they are excluded, they are given by $A/(C - B)$. Removing B from the numerator and denominator reduces the numerator by a greater percentage than the denominator, reducing their ratio. As a result, any required share of domestic input used is harder to satisfy if capital costs are excluded.[16] The basic intuition is that including capital costs (or any other costs for that matter) raises the numerator by a greater percentage than the denominator, thus, raising their ratio, since the numerator is by definition smaller than the denominator. This might help explain why the treatment of interest costs was a bone of contention between the US and Canada and Honda in defining content requirements.[17]

Another example where details matter comes from defining shares in terms of price versus cost. In Krishna and Krueger (1995) it is argued that defining content in terms of cost or price makes no difference in the long run, basically because price equals cost in the long run. Nor would it make a difference in the long run whether a minimum share, α, of domestic inputs has to be used or whether imported inputs are restricted to the equivalent maximum share, $1 - \alpha$. However, both of these matter in the short run due to the existence of quasi-rents.

For example, consider a rule of origin defined in terms of the minimum share of domestic inputs relative to price rather than cost. Since price

---

[16] The argument is not quite tight since the choice of inputs will differ in the two cases.

[17] Some work does not look at the restrictiveness of RoO. For example, Krishna and Panagariya (2002) assume that final goods produced in the FTA using the minimum cost input mix automatically meet the RoO. Hence, all the production of the lower-tariff country is shipped to the higher-tariff one. Consumer prices differ but producer prices do not so that production efficiency is maintained. They show that, analogous to the famous Kem Wan result, there exists a Pareto-improving FTA in this setting when lump-sum transfers are permitted.

exceeds cost and an increase in the denominator makes the constraint harder to meet, the price-based scheme has a higher cost of production than the equivalent cost-based one. With this definition, for any required share, α, firms in B prefer the cost-based form to the price-based form.

Alternatively, consider a RoO defined in terms of the maximum share of foreign inputs relative to price rather than cost. Since price exceeds cost and an increase in the denominator makes the constraint easier to meet, the price-based scheme has a lower cost of production than the equivalent cost-based one! Thus, for any required share, α, firms in B prefer the price-based form to the cost-based form.

1.4.2 Going part way: allowing input price changes

There are at least two kinds of price changes that need to be allowed for: changes in the word prices of goods and changes in the prices of intermediate goods in the FTA. Incorporating the former involves dropping the small-country assumption, while incorporating the latter involves allowing for at least some general equilibrium effects to occur. Falvey and Reed (2000) argue that RoO have a role complementary to that of tariffs as RoO affect input demand. Thus, a large country could affect the terms of trade in both final and intermediate goods by using RoO as well as tariffs on the final good.

Ju and Krishna (1998) and (2002) show that allowing the price of FTA inputs to be endogenously determined results in a number of interesting insights. The discussion that follows can be found in more detail in their work. The driving force behind their results is a non-monotonicity that arises naturally in such settings and that seems to have been previously overlooked.

An intuitive explanation of what lies at the heart of their results follows. Suppose that there are two inputs, capital and intermediates. Suppose, moreover, that domestic and imported are perfect substitutes and that there are a given number of firms who have fixed capital but who can change their use of intermediates. The RoO force firms in the FTA who comply to use more of the domestic intermediate that they may wish to in order to obtain origin and, hence, qualify for zero tariffs. If the RoO are not too restrictive then all firms will wish to comply[18] and a more restrictive RoO will shift out domestic intermediate demand, making its price rise. However, once this price has risen to the point where

---

[18] This is termed the homogeneous regime.

firms are indifferent between complying and not.[19] Some firms then choose to comply while others do not, and this number changes with the level of restrictiveness to change the price of domestic intermediates so as to keep firms indifferent. In this regime, increases in restrictiveness have exactly the opposite effect on the price of domestic intermediates!

This reversal in the comparative statics results drives their model and yields their unusual results. They show that as the RoO become more restrictive, the price of intermediates and the import of final goods rise then fall, while the import of intermediates first falls and then rises. All three have a common turning point, the point where the regime switches from the homogeneous to the heterogeneous one.

Much of the concern regarding preferential trading arrangements has been with the implications of such arrangements on market access. The work of Ju and Krishna shows that effects in both final- and intermediate-good markets need to be considered as they work in opposite directions. Moreover, the work shows that it is important to look at the effect on the FTA as a whole, as well as on each member. This is because compensating flows occur in other member countries in response to changes in flows in one member country.

In the model used by Ju and Krishna the intermediate good market is the most protected (in the sense that both imports reach a minimum and the price of FTA made input reaches its maximum) when the regime switch occurs. Intermediate goods producers are best off here as this is where their product price, and hence rents, are maximized. In sharp contrast, the final good market is most open (in the sense that the imports reach their maximum) at the same point. Final-goods producers in the lower-tariff country gain the most when they have access to the higher-tariff country's markets at the least cost, that is they want the RoO to be non-distorting. Thus, these two groups are likely to lobby for different levels of RoO.

1.5 General equilibrium effects

Analysing the effects of RoO in general equilibrium seems like a rather hard thing to do in an elegant manner. Krishna (2003) develops a way of looking at the effect of conditional policies, such as RoO, in a general

---

[19] Ju and Krishna (2002) term this the heterogeneous regime.

equilibrium setting under perfect competition. A simple observation makes the problem tractable using standard duality tools in general equilibrium. Policies like RoO in an FTA have a carrot and hoop element to them. The carrot, preferential treatment, is obtained only by jumping through hoops, namely, meeting origin requirements. The basic insight used is that if, by availing itself of the policy, the firm can raise the factor prices it can afford to pay, it will be willing to do so, otherwise it will not. In other words, the paper looks at the effects of such restrictions on the factor price frontier and shows how this can be derived quite simply for certain kinds of RoO. It is shown that when RoO are set at *ex ante* binding levels, they need not be binding *ex post* nor must they result in an inflow of capital. Moreover, the paper argues, the kind of non-monotonicity seen in Ju and Krishna (1998) is likely to be prevalent in general equilibrium.

There has been some work on looking at the effects of FTAs incorporating RoOs in a partial equilibrium framework. Such back-of-the-envelope calculations are not hard and can provide very interesting results. For example, Mattoo *et al.* (2002) look at the effects of RoO in the Africa Growth and Opportunity Act recently enacted by the US and argue that restrictive conditions on market access, the most important of which are the RoO, reduce its benefits significantly: they argue that the medium-term benefits would have been almost five times greater without such conditions on access. Computable general equilibrium models can also be used to give an idea of general equilibrium effects.

1.6 Conclusion

Much of the concern felt about regional trading areas has been that they will exclude non-member countries from their markets. Much of this discussion, see, for example, Krugman (1991) and counterarguments by Bond and Syropoulos (1996), has been couched in terms of the greater market power, and hence, higher optimal tariffs of larger trade blocs. However, tariffs on most manufactured goods are bound by concessions made in successive rounds of negotiations under the auspices of *GATT*. It seems likely that RoO, which are less well understood and extremely important in practice, provide a far greater reason for concern.

While a beginning has been made in understanding the effects of RoO at a theoretical as well as empirical level, far more remains to be done and the chapters in this book are making valuable contributions in this regard.

On the theoretical side, work has been confined to partial equilibrium models and has focused on perfect competition. There are many lessons that can be learned from looking at imperfect competition and general equilibrium. Rules of Origin clearly provide a way to raise the costs of FTA rivals. The desirability of doing so has been studied in industrial organization. RoO can act to segment markets. Moreover, they can result in interesting switches in best-response functions. Many of these ideas are the subject of chapters written for this book. However, much work remains. On the political-economy side, for example, it would be fascinating to look at particular examples in more detail to see who lobbied for particular RoO, while using simple models to understand their desirability for the various interest groups.

References

Bond, E., C. Syropoulos. 1996. The Size of Trading Blocs: Market Power and World Welfare Effects. *Journal of International Economics* **40** (3–4): 411–37.

Breton, P., M. Manchin. 2002. Making EU Arrangements Work: The Role of Rules of Origin. Working Document no. 183, Center for European Policy Studies.

Cadot, O., J. de Melo, A. Suwa Eisenmann, B. Tumurchudur. 2002. Assessing the Effect of NAFTA's Rules of Origin. Mimeo.

De Melo, D., A. Panagariya. 1993. *New Dimensions in Regional Integration*, Cambridge University Press.

Duttagupta, R., A. Panagariya. 2001. Free Trade Areas and Rules of Origin: Economics and Politics. Mimeo.

Estevadeordal, A. 2000. Negotiating Preferential Market Access: The Case of the North American Free Trade Agreement. *Journal of World Trade* **34**: 141–200.

Falvey, R., G. Reed. 1998. Economic Effects of Rules of Origin. *Weltwirtschaftliches* 134 (2): 209–29.

Falvey, R., G. Reed. 2000. Rules of Origin as Commercial Policy Instruments. Research Paper no. 2000/18, Centre for Research on Globalization and Labor Markets, University of Nottingham.

Grossman, G., E. Helpman. 1995. The Politics of Free Trade Agreements. *American Economic Review* September, 667–90.

Grossman, G., E. Helpman. 2001. *Special Interest Politics*, Cambridge MA and London UK: The MIT Press.

Herin, J. 1986. Rules of Origin and Differences between Tariff Levels in EFTA and in the EC. EFTA Occasional Paper no. 13, Geneva (February).

Ju, J., K. Krishna. 1998. Firm Behavior and Market Access in a Free Trade Area With Rules of Origin. *Canadian Journal of Economics* (forthcoming) and Working Paper no. 6857, National Bureau of Economic Research.

Ju, J., K. Krishna. 2002. Regulations, Regime Switches and Non-Monotonicity when Non-Compliance is an Option: An Application to Content Protection and Preference. *Economics Letters* **77**: 315–21.

Krishna, K. 2003. Conditional Policies in General Equilibrium: Rules of Origin Revisited. Mimeo.

Krishna, K., A. Krueger. 1995. Implementing Free Trade Areas: Rules of Origin and Hidden Protection. In *New Directions in Trade Theory*, A. Deardorff, J. Levinsohn and R. Stern (ed.) University of Michigan Press.

Krishna, P., A. Panagariya. 2002. On Necessarily Welfare-Enhancing Free Trade Areas. *Journal of International Economics* **57** (2): 353–67.

Krueger, A. O. 1997. Free Trade Agreements Versus Customs Unions. *Journal of Development Economics* **54**: 169–87.

Krueger, A. O. 1999. Free Trade Agreements as Protectionist Devices: Rules of Origin. In *Trade, Theory and Econometrics: Essays in Honor of John Chipman*, J. R. Melvin, J. C. Moore and R. Riezman (ed.) 'Routledge Studies in the Modern World Economy', Routledge, London, New York.

Krugman, P. 1991. Is Bilateralism Bad? In *International Trade and Trade Policy*, E. Helpman and A. Razin (ed.) Cambridge and London: MIT Press.

Lloyd, P. J. 1993. A Tariff Substitute for Rules of Origin in Free Trade Areas. *The World Economy* **16** (6): 691–712.

Mattoo, A., D. Roy, A. Subramaniam. 2002. The Africa Growth and Opportunity Act and its Rules of Origin: Generosity Undermined? Working Paper no. 2908, World Bank Policy Research (October).

McGillivray, F., M. Green. 2001. Trading in a Free Trade Area With No Rules of Origin: The U.S. Under the Articles of Confederation. Mimeo, Yale University.

Palmeter, N. D. 1993. Rules of Origin in a Western Hemisphere Free Trade Agreement. Mimeo.

Richardson, M. 1995. Tariff Revenue Competition in a Free Trade Area. *European Economic Review* **39**: 1429–37.

Rodriguez, P. 2001. Rules of Origin with Multistage Production. *World Economy* **24** (2): 201–20.

Rosellon, J. 2000. The Economics of Rules of Origin. *Journal of International Trade and Economic Development* **9** (4): 397–425.

Shibata, H. 1967. The Theory of Economic Unions: A Comparative Analysis of Customs Unions, Free Trade Areas, and Tax Unions. In *Fiscal Harmonization in Common Markets*, C.S. Shoup (ed.). New York: Columbia University Press.

Vermulst, E. 1994. Rules of Origin in International Trade: A Comparative Study. In *Studies in International Trade Policy*, P. Waer and J. Bourgeois (ed.) Ann Arbor: University of Michigan Press.

Viner, J. 1950. *The Customs Union Issue*. New York: Carnegie Endowment for International Peace.

2

The impact of Rules of Origin on strategic outsourcing: an IO perspective

Mathias Thoenig and Thierry Verdier

2.1 Introduction

In the last decades, a number of Preferential Trading Agreements (PTA) and Free Trade Areas (FTA) have emerged in various regions of the world. Associated with them, there has been some increasing interest in one of their main trade-policy components: rules of origins (RoOs for short). These instruments consist typically of mechanisms and schemes specifying the conditions for a good to gain eligibility to face zero protection inside a FTA. Though regional agreements are generally perceived as trade liberalizing, several observers have argued, however, that instruments like RoOs are often used as hidden protection preventing the trade integration effects of FTAs (Krueger (1993), Krishna and Krueger (1995), see also the recent survey in this volume by Krishna (2005) (Chapter 1)). Negotiated on an industry-by-industry basis, RoOs indeed allow successful lobbying sectors to insulate themselves from the increased outside competition associated with the formation of the FTA. Building on the older literature on factor-content protection schemes (Grossman (1981), Vousden (1987), Hollander (1987) Mussa (1984), and Richardson (1991) and (1993)), a small theoretical economic literature has started to analyse some of the major features of RoOs (Krishna and Krueger (1995), Falvey and Reed (1998), Jiandong and Krishna (1998)). An important message of that emerging literature is the idea that RoOs may have singularly different effects depending on the degree of competition in the final-good and intermediate-good sectors on which they are applied.

Little attention, however, has been devoted to the study of the effects of RoOs in the context of multinational firms outsourcing parts of their production process and their value chain across regions. This is indeed quite surprising, given the widely cited phenomenon of increasing multinationalization of firms and international fragmentation of production processes[1]. After all, RoOs are supposed to impose constraints on the allocation and the factor content of firms' activities in international trade. It is then natural to expect some effects of RoOs on corporate decisions regarding outsourcing and international fragmentation[2]. What are the effects of RoOs in such a context? How are they influencing the boundaries of the multinational firm? What are their implications for trade flows (intra- versus interfirm flows)? Do RoOs prevent or stimulate the liberalizing impact of FTAs via these channels? What are the political economy consequences for multinationals over these rules? All these are important questions awaiting crucial answers for the design of trade policy and FTAs.

The purpose of the present work is to start to fill that gap, taking an industrial-organization perspective on the role of RoOs in the presence of multinational firms. More precisely, building on current research of our own (Thoenig and Verdier (2004a) and (2004b)), this chapter surveys two aspects of the international production fragmentation process. The first one is related to the idea that firms, in an imperfect competitive environment, have an incentive to use fragmentation or outsourcing of some intermediate input activities as a strategic variable (see, for instance, the recent work by Shy and Stenbarcka (2003a, 2003b)). In such a context, RoOs may have new and interesting implications, affecting in particular the pattern of outsourcing and interacting with the strategic behavior of firms. First, the introduction of a RoO may generate multiple equilibria in fragmentation and can be the source of important co-ordination problems in the related product market. A policy implication is the fact that RoOs in such a context, may have effects quite difficult to evaluate, if one cannot easily identify empirically which equilibrium is actually played by the firms. Secondly, RoOs in a strategic outsourcing context can fulfill the function of a commitment device to be more or less aggressive in the process of international fragmentation. This may paradoxically be beneficial to a firm foreign to the FTA at the expense of a firm domestic to the FTA. For that same reason, one may also find situations where foreign

---

[1] See Feenstra (1998) for a recent survey account of this trend.

[2] As noted by Falvey and Reed in their survey on RoOs (1998), 'The analysis of the interactions between RoOs and MNEs, is an important topic for future work' (p. 221).

and domestic firms may agree on the establishment of a particular non-liberalizing RoO.

The other aspect surveyed in this chapter concerns the impact of RoOs on the vertical chain of value-added, namely the relationships between intermediate-good producers and final-good producers. This issue becomes crucial when firm–suppliers relationships are characterized by some degree of contract incompleteness (a recurrent theme in the vertical integration and firm's boundaries literature). As emphasized by the recent literature on incomplete contracting and vertical integration (Grossman and Hart (1986)), several dimensions of social interactions between a firm and its suppliers cannot be contracted upon or verifiable *ex post* by third parties. In these relation-specific contexts, parties who need to make non-contractible investments face the well-known problem of *ex post* hold up. The final surplus between the two parties is bargained as a function of *ex post* outside options rather than *ex ante* specific investments. This, creates *ex ante* underinvestment in relation-specific assets. What is the impact of RoOs in such contexts?

RoOs, by imposing constraints on outsourcing relationships, may have important implications for the incomplete contractual problems existing between a downward foreign firm and its potential suppliers. In particular, one aspect that may be important is the way RoOs influence the outside options of the concerned parties. As a matter of fact, *ex post* sharing of the surplus between a final good producer and his intermediate inputs suppliers is generally affected by the outside options of the two parties. RoOs by constraining foreign firms to outsource intermediate inputs inside the FTA, increase the bargaining power of domestic suppliers within the FTA. Having a larger slice of the pie, suppliers may then undertake more relation-specific investments and increase the efficiency of the contractual relationship with the final-good foreign firm. Interestingly, in such a context, a RoO may be welfare improving for all parties. Moreover, this situation may actually occur without having the RoO been binding in equilibrium. Indeed, RoOs may have effects through their impact on 'potential' outcomes or, in game-theoretical terms, 'out of equilibrium' outcomes. As is well known, this in turn may determine actions and outputs that make the RoO not binding in equilibrium. An important policy implication of this is the fact that the effects of RoOs in incomplete contracting contexts cannot be solely deduced from the observation that a RoO is binding. Indeed, even when not binding, RoOs may have significant allocative and efficiency effects.

The chapter is organized in the following way. Section 2.2 considers the analysis of strategic outsourcing and the impact of RoOs in such a context. Section 2.3 discusses the impact of RoOs when firm–suppliers relationships are characterized by specific relational investments and some degree of *ex post* opportunism. A short conclusion follows.

2.2 Strategic outsourcing and RoOs

2.2.1 *A simple model of strategic outsourcing*

To investigate the issue of strategic outsourcing and the impact of RoOs in such a context, we sketch here a model of outsourcing in an imperfect competitive framework as expanded in Thoenig and Verdier (2004a). There are two firms a and b competing in a homogenous final good market. As in Dixit and Grossman (1982) or Shy and Stenbacka (2003a), the technology of production involves a continuum of tasks (stages) of production ranging over the interval $[0,1]$. To complete production of one unit of the final output, all intermediate production stages in $[0,1]$ have to be undertaken. Each firm $h \in \{a, b\}$ decides how many stages to do in-house and how many stages to outsource to outside suppliers. The cost of production task i in-house is $c_n(i)$, while the price to outsource that task is $p(i)$. Assume that production tasks can be ordered such that $p(i)$ is increasing in i and that $c_n(i)$ is decreasing in i with $p(0) < c_n(0)$ and $p(1) > c_n(1)$.[3] Hence tasks become relatively more costly to outsource when i goes up.

The unit cost of production of a given firm h outsourcing S_h stages of production is given by

$$c(S_h) = \int_0^{S_h} p(i)\mathrm{d}i + \int_{S_h}^1 c_n(i)\mathrm{d}i.$$

Note that

$$c'(S_h) = p(S_h) - c_n(S_h) \text{ and } c''(S_h) = p'(S_h) - c'_n(S_h) > 0.$$

Let S_m, defined by $p(S_m) = c_n(S_m)$, be the level of outsourcing that minimizes marginal production costs.

Co-ordination of production stages (in-house or outsourced) involves fixed headquarter costs. Let $v_0(S)$ and $v_i(1 - S)$ be, respectively, the co-ordination costs of outsourcing S stages of production (resp. producing

---

[3] In fact this assumption, made for convenience, can be relaxed. What is needed essentially is that the ratio $p(i)/c_n(i)$ is increasing in i (i.e. we can rank all intermediate tasks in terms to their relative outsourcing cost of production).

$1 - S$ stages in house). We assume $v_0(.)$ and $v_i.(.)$ to be increasing convex with $v_0(0) = v_i(0) = 0$. Let S_f such that $v_0'(S_f) = v_i'(1 - S_f)$ be the level of outsourcing minimizing the total fixed costs of production co-ordination.

To make things precise, we assume that $S_m \geq S_f$.[4] The level of outsourcing minimizing the variable costs of production is larger than that minimizing the fixed costs of co-ordination. This relationship would clearly arise when, at the margin, co-ordination costs of outsourcing are relatively more important than co-ordination costs of 'in-house' production. An assumption that appears to be quite reasonable.[5]

Firms sell the final good on a market characterized by a linear inverse demand function $p(q) = 1 - q$ with $q = q_a + q_b$ total output and q_h the final output of firm $h \in \{a, b\}$. The profit function of each firm writes as:

$$\Pi_h = p(q)q_h - c(S_h)q_h - v_0(S_h) - v_i(1 - S_h).$$

We consider then the simple following two-stage game. In the first stage, firms decide simultaneously their outsourcing levels S_h. Then, in the second stage, firms compete in quantities q_h in a standard cournot fashion. Equilibrium outputs in the second stage for each firm are readily obtained as:

$$q_a(S_a, S_b) = \frac{1 - 2c(S_a) + c(S_b)}{3}$$

$$q_b(S_b, S_a) = \frac{1 - 2c(S_b) + c(S_a)}{3},$$

and profits levels write as:

$$\Pi_h = \Pi(S_h, S_{h'}) = q_h(S_h, S_{h'})^2 - v_0(S_h) - v_i(1 - S_h) \text{ for } h, h' \in \{a, b\} \text{ and } h \neq h'.$$

The 'outsourcing' best-response function of firm h, $S_h = R_h(S_{h'})$, is easily derived from the first-order conditions of the first-stage game:

$$\frac{\partial \Pi_h}{\partial S_h} = \frac{-4c'(S_h)}{3}q_h(S_h, S_{h'}) - [v_0'(S_h) - v_i'(1 - S_h)] = 0, \qquad (2.1)$$

assuming that the second-order conditions are globally satisfied,[6] the shape of the outsourcing best-response function of firm h is easily characterized and is depicted in Fig. 2.1. When $S_{h'} < S_m$, an increase in the range of outsourced tasks by firm h', leads to a reduction in its marginal production cost. Therefore the final product market share of the other

---

[4] The alternative case $S_m \leq S_f$ is also discussed in Thoenig and Verdier (2004a).
[5] See, however, Shy and Stenbacka (2003a) for a discussion on the possibility of the alternative situation.
[6] It can be shown that this will be true when $c''(S_h), v_0''(.)$ and $v_i''(.)$ are large enough.

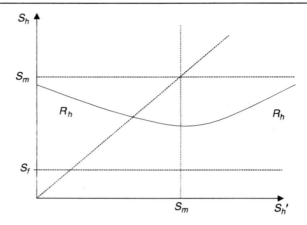

Fig. 2.1 Reaction curve of outsourcing.

firm h goes down. This, in turn, reduces firm h's marginal profitability to outsource intermediate tasks and leads to a reduction in S_h. The reverse effects occur when $S_{h'} > S_m$. From that discussion, it follows that out-sourcing decisions between firms are strategic substitutes in the range $S_{h'} < S_m$ and strategic complements when $S_{h'} < S_m$.

The characterization of the symmetric Nash equilibrium S^* is then easily obtained by the following equation

$$\frac{-4c'(S^*)}{3} \frac{1 - c(S^*)}{3} - [v'_0(S^*) - v'_i(1 - S^*)] = 0,$$

and it is immediately seen that: $S_f < S^* < S_m$.

The equilibrium in strategic outsourcing is depicted in Fig. 2.2. Inspection shows that, at the Nash equilibrium, joint profits of the two firms are increased by a global reduction in outsourcing. From a strategic point of view; each firm has an incentive to reduce its marginal cost of production in order to gain a higher market share at the expense of its competitor. In the context of the present model, this means picking up an outsourcing level as close as possible to S_m, the level minimizing variable costs of production. The incentives to do this are, however, tempered by the marginal increase in co-ordination costs (as $S_f < S_m$). Since, however, both firms undertake such strategic outsourcing, the final Nash outcome is characterized by 'over-outsourcing'.

This is best illustrated in Fig. 2.2 with the usual isoprofit curves of the two firms a and b. For instance, the isoprofit curve Π_a of firm a in the quadrant

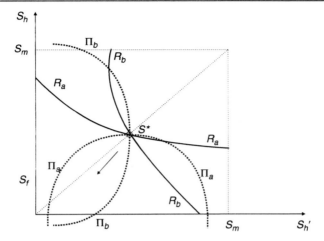

Fig. 2.2 Nash equilibrium in outsourcing.

$[0, S_m] \times [0, S_m]$ is first upward sloping below the best-response function $R_a(S_b)$ and then downward sloping above it. Further, profits of firm a in this region are increasing, as we move torward the vertical axis. Symmetrically, the isoprofit curve of the other firm b is characterized by increasing values as we move in the direction of the horizontal axis. Given that tangents of the isoprofits curves are orthogonal at the Nash equilibrium point S^*, it is clear that any point of outsourcing decisions $[S_a, S_b]$ in the shaded area southwest of S^* gives higher profits to both firms. Hence, there is 'over-outsourcing' due to the fact of strategic interactions between the two firms.

2.2.2 Introducing rules of origins

Let us now extend our previous setting to the context of an FTA with or without rules of origins (RoO thereafter). To be more specific, consider three countries A, B and C. Assume that firms a and b are, respectively, from countries A and B. For simplicity, assume also that final-good demand is only located in country B. Hence b can be viewed as the domestic firm of country B and a is a foreign firm from A competing in the home market of b. Initially, access to B's market is restricted by some trade friction reflected by a specific tariff t. Given that there is no market in country C, no tariff exists in that country for the final good produced by both firms a and b. Consider now that, for reasons outside the model, countries B and C, contemplate the formation of a FTA between themselves.

From the point of view of country B's good market in which firms a and b compete, the crucial issue is to know whether the FTA is with or without RoO. Indeed if no RoO is attached to the final good over which a and b compete, the foreign firm a can easily bypass country B's tariff t with duty-free exports to country C and re-exports from C to B inside the FTA. The tariff faced by firm a in such a case will effectively fall to 0. On the other hand, if a RoO is tied to that market, then firm a has to generate enough value added inside the FTA in order to be able to escape the external tariff t of country B. This in turn may strongly affect the pattern of outsourcing of both firms and their strategic interactions.

In the usual case where a RoO implies a constraint on the amount of intermediate activities to be undertaken inside the FTA, an important aspect therefore is related to the location of outsourced versus in-house activities of the two firms. In principle, with the previous notations, one may order these intermediate tasks such that for a given firm $h \in \{a, b\}$, the unit cost of production writes as:

$$c(S_h) = \int_0^{S_h^1} p^*(i)\mathrm{d}i + \int_{S_h^1}^{S_h^2} p(i)\mathrm{d}i + \int_{S_h^2}^1 c_n(i)\mathrm{d}i,$$

when S_h^1 activities are outsourced outside the FTA, $S_h^2 - S_h^1$ are outsourced inside the FTA and $1 - S_h^2$ are undertaken in house. $p(i)$ and $p^*(i)$ are, respectively, the cost of outsourcing activity i outside the FTA and inside the FTA. This specification indicates then two strategic variables of outsourcing, a situation that may be quite complex to analyse. To simplify matters and get some interesting insights on the interactions between RoO and strategic outsourcing, we will discuss here two polar cases. The first situation corresponds to the situation where activities can only be outsourced inside the FTA (i.e. $S_h^1 = 0$). This, for instance, corresponds to situations where all potential outside suppliers of intermediate inputs of a given firm h are necessarily located in country B or C, presumably because they have an absolute technological advantage over all other competitors in the world. The second case assumes that all activities can only be outsourced outside the FTA (i.e. $S_h^1 = S_h^2$) and will be briefly discussed at the end of this section.[7]

2.2.2.1 OUTSOURCING ACTIVITIES INSIDE THE FTA

Let us start with the case where both firms outsource all their intermediate activities inside country C or B. In order to escape the external tariff t of

---

[7] See Thoenig and Verdier (2004a) for details on this case. This other case reflects just the opposite situation in which no potential supplier of intermediate input of firm h is located in the FTA region.

country B, firm a has to produce enough intermediate production stages within the FTA. While there are several ways in which one can frame a RoO (see Krishna and Krueger (1993) for a discussion), we assume here the following simple value added RoO:

if $\int_{S_a}^{1} c_n(i)di \leq k\left[\int_0^{S_a} p(i)di + \int_{S_a}^1 c_n(i)di\right]$ then no tariff is applied

if $\int_{S_a}^{1} c_n(i)di > k\left[\int_0^{S_a} p(i)di + \int_{S_a}^1 c_n(i)di\right]$ then tariff t is applied on

$$\text{sales of } a. \qquad (2.2)$$

Consider now the following timing. First, firm a decides whether to comply or not with the RoO. Secondly, both firms choose their optimal level of outsourcing, given the regime (RoO or not). Finally, there is output competition. Note that condition (2.2) is equivalent to:

$$\int_{S_a}^{1} c_n(i)di \leq \frac{k}{1-k}\int_0^{S_a} p(i)di \quad \text{or} \quad S_a \geq S(k) \text{ with } S'(k)<0.$$

Hence a more restrictive RoO (a smaller value of k) is associated with a larger range of outsourced activities by firm a inside the FTA. Consider now the problem of that firm. If it does not comply with the RoO, it gets, after cournot competition with firm b, a profit level:

$$\Pi_a(S_a, S_b, t) = \left[\frac{1 - 2c(S_a) - 2t + c(S_b)}{3}\right]^2 - v_0(S_a) - v_i(1 - S_a).$$

If it does comply with the RoO, it gets a profit level:

$$\left\{\begin{array}{l} \Pi_a(S_a, S_b, 0) = \left[\dfrac{1 - 2c(S_a) + c(S_b)}{3}\right]^2 - v_0(S_a) - v_i(1 - S_a) \text{ when the RoO} \\[4pt] \hspace{8cm} \text{is not binding} \\[8pt] \Pi_a(S(k), S_b, 0) = \left[\dfrac{1 - 2c(S(k)) + c(S_b)}{3}\right]^2 - v_0(S(k)) - v_i(1 - S(k)) \text{ when the} \\[4pt] \hspace{9cm} \text{RoO is binding.} \end{array}\right.$$

Summarizing, the objective function of firm a writes as:

$$\Pi_a = \left\{\begin{array}{l} \Pi_a(S_a, S_b, t) \text{ when } S_a < S(k) \\[6pt] \Pi_a(S(k), S_b, 0) \text{ when } S_a \geq S(k). \end{array}\right.$$

The maximization problem of firm a is depicted in Fig. 2.3 with the two profit curves $\Pi_a^t = \Pi_a(S_a, S_b, t)$ and $\Pi_a^0 = \Pi_a(S_a, S_b, 0)$. As a tariff t is costly to firm a; $\Pi_a(S_a, S_b, t)$ is uniformly below $\Pi_a(S_a, S_b, 0)$. Also, as the tariff

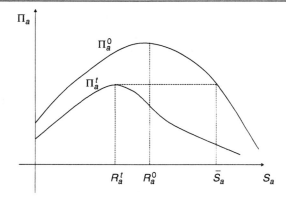

Fig. 2.3 Profit functions.

decreases the marginal incentives for firm a to undertake outsourcing, the optimal point $S_a = R_a(S_b, t) = R_a^t$ is always smaller than the optimal point $S_a = R_a(S_b, 0) = R_a^0$ of the other function $\Pi_a(S_a, S_b, 0)$. Let then $\bar{S}_a$ be the point such that $\bar{S}_a > R_a(S_b, 0)$ and satisfying:

$$\Pi_a(\bar{S}_a, S_b, 0) = Max_{S_a}\Pi_a(S_a, S_b, t) = \Pi_a(R_a(S_b, t), S_b, t). \qquad (2.3)$$

Denote the solution of eqn (2.3), $\bar{S}_a(S_b, t)$. For all outsourcing values S_a smaller than this threshold $\bar{S}_a(S_b, t)$, the regime with no tariff (i.e. $t = 0$) is preferred by firm a than the maximum that it can get under the tariff t. One can show that this threshold value is decreasing in the level of outsourcing S_b of the other firm when $S_b < S_m$ (see Thoenig and Verdier (2004a)). The intuition is quite easy. Because outsourcing decisions are strategic substitutes, an increase in S_b tends to reduce the optimal unconstrained reactions $R_a(S_b, t)$ and $R_a(S_b, 0)$ of firm a. This, in turn, implies that any constraint forcing firm a to outsource more than its optimal level is more costly in terms of profits. From this, it follows that a regime with no tariff but a constrained value of $S_a > R_a(S_b, 0)$ is less likely to dominate a tariff-unconstrained optimal regime with $S_a = R_a(S_b, t)$. Hence the threshold $\bar{S}_a(S_b, t)$ at which firm a is indifferent between these two situations will decrease.

The effective best-response function in outsourcing of firm a facing a RoO, $R_a^{roo}(S_b)$, is then easily characterized and represented in Fig. 2.4. The two downward-sloping best-response functions $R_a(S_b, 0)$ and $R_a(S_b, t)$ are shown for $S_b < S_m$. $R_a(S_b, 0)$ is above $R_a(S_b, t)$ because of $\partial^2\Pi_a/\partial t\partial S_a = 8c'(S_a)/9 < 0$ for $S_a < S_m$. Also, the downward-sloping threshold function $\bar{S}_a(S_b, t)$ is by construction always above $R_a(S_b, 0)$. For a given restrictiveness level $S(k)$ of the RoO, the effective reaction curve of firm a is then

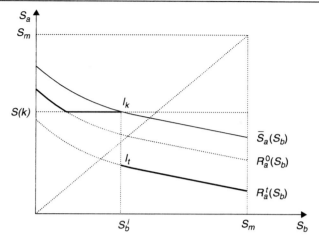

Fig. 2.4 Reaction curve under the RoO.

depicted in thick as $R_a^{roo}(S_b)$. Three regime are described. First, for values of S_b such that $S(k) < R_a(S_b, 0)$, the RoO is not binding and $R_a^{roo}(S_b)$ coincides with $R_a(S_b, 0)$. When S_b is such that $R_a(S_b, 0) \leq S(k) < \bar{S}_a(S_b, t)$, the RoO is binding and there is compliance by firm a. The reaction curve is then given by $R_a^{roo}(S_b) = S(k)$. Finally, in the last case, where S_b is such that $\bar{S}_a(S_b, t) \leq S(k)$, the RoO is binding and the firm does not comply with it. In that case, $R_a^{roo}(S_b)$ coincides with the reaction curve $R_a(S_b, t)$ of firm a when it faces the external tariff t.

Simple observation shows that, depending on the value of the restrictiveness of the RoO, this best-response function may be discontinuous. This happens at points I_k and I_t corresponding to the value $S_b = S_b^I$ of outsourcing of firm b, where firm a is just indifferent between accepting the binding RoO (at point I_k) and rejecting it and playing a best reply $R_a(S_b, t)$ under the trade regime with the external tariff t (at point I_t).

2.2.2.2 OUTSOURCING EQUILIBRIA AND RoOS

The characterization of the Nash equilibrium levels of outsourcing between the two firms a and b can be readily obtained by adding up in Figs. 2.5a–c, the best response function $R_b(S_a)$ of firm b. Inspection shows easily that the nature of the equilibrium outcomes is a function of the degree of restrictiveness of the RoO.

Figure 2.5a describes the situation where the RoO is not binding (i.e. $S(k) < S_a^0$). In that case, the outcome of the game is point $E_0 = (S_a^0, S_b^0)$

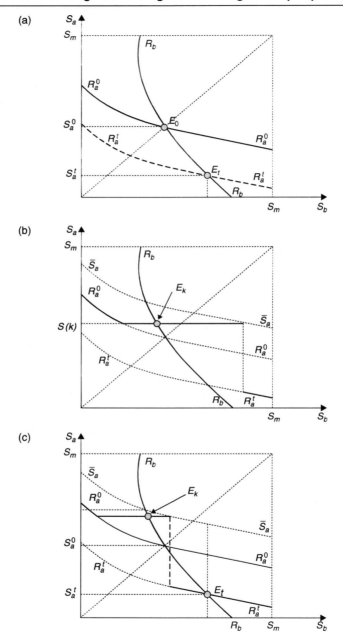

Fig. 2.5 (a) Some useful notations; (b) Equilibrium with a binding RoO; (c) Multiple equilibria in outsourcing with RoO.

intersection between the reaction curve $R_b(S_a)$ of firm b and the no tariff reaction curve $R_a(S_b, 0)$ of firm a. The effect of the FTA is obviously trade liberalizing as firm a is not constrained in terms of its outsourcing strategy and can therefore easily bypass the external tariff of country B through country C. The level of outsourcing of firm A in the FTA, S_a^0, is larger than S_a^t, namely what the firm would choose under trade protection of country B.

Figure 2.5b shows the case where the RoO becomes binding and forces firm a to outsource more activities within the FTA than it would ideally want. Whether firm a complies with the RoO or prefers to reject it and face the external tariff t of country B, depends both on the degree of restrictiveness of the RoO and the strategic outsourcing behavior of firm b. Whenever the RoO is moderately restrictive (i.e. $S(k)$ not too big), a first equilibrium occurs at point $E_k = (S(k), R_b(S(k)))$ with acompliance to a binding RoO. Indeed, in such an equilibrium, the distortion costs of complying with the RoO is less than the gain provided with the avoidance of the external tariff t. Hence, in that case firm a chooses to comply to the RoO and $S_a = S(k)$.

Figure 2.5c shows the case where the RoO becomes more restrictive: It can be seen that another equilibrium emerges at point $E_t = (S_a^t, S_b^t)$ with no RoO compliance and the imposition of the external tariff t on firm a. As a matter of fact, when the RoO becomes more restrictive, the decision for firm a to comply with it depends crucially on the level of outsourcing of the other firm b. Indeed, when firm b is expected to choose a relatively high level of outsourcing S_b, then an unconstrained firm a would ideally choose a relatively low level of outsourcing S_a. In such a situation, the distortion cost of a binding RoO forcing firm a to increase further its outsourcing activities becomes large and it is optimal for firm a not to comply with the RoO. The Nash equilibrium outsourcing level for firm a is then the one corresponding to the initial situation with external tariff $S_a = S_a^t$ and corresponds to point E_t in Fig. 2.5c.

On the contrary, when firm b is expected to choose a relatively low level of outsourcing S_b, as outsourcing decisions are strategic substitutes (for $S < S_m$), an unconstrained firm a would choose a relatively high level of outsourcing S_a. In such a situation, the distortion cost of a binding RoO forcing firm a to increase further its outsourcing activities is comparatively less important and it becomes optimal for firm a to comply with the RoO. The Nash equilibrium outsourcing level for firm a in that case corresponds to $S_a = S(k)$ at point E_k in Fig. 2.5c.

Finally, it is clear that in the case of a very restrictive RoO, it does not pay to firm a to comply with it, and this whatever the outsourcing behavior of the other firm. A unique equilibrium exists in that case and is simply given by the initial one with external tariff $E_t = (S_a^t, S_b^t)$.

From the previous discussion it follows that within a range of moderate RoOs, multiple outsourcing equilibria exist. An interesting policy implication is the fact that RoOs may create important co-ordination problems in the product market and therefore their effects may be difficult to evaluate, if one cannot identify easily which equilibrium is actually played by the firms.

2.2.2.3 WELFARE AND POLITICAL ECONOMY IMPLICATIONS

What can we say then in terms of welfare analysis and political-economy implications of the RoO in this setting? Consider then Fig. 2.6 depicting the isoprofits curves of the two firms. It is clear that firm b's profit level decreases when the equilibrium outcome shifts from point E_t to point $E_p = (S_a^p, R_b(S_a^p))$ along the reaction curve $R_b(S_a)$. Hence, the domestic firm b will always oppose a non-binding RoO as it prefers E_t to E_0. Interestingly, it will also oppose a binding RoO that generates an equilibrium outcome along $R_b(S_a)$ between E_0 and E_p. The reason is that the RoO (when accepted by firm a) provides a commitment device to the foreign firm to outsource more activities. This in turn reduces firm b's profits. It follows that firm b will only support a restrictive enough RoO that will not be accepted by

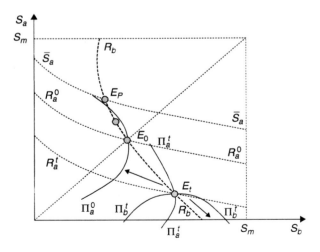

Fig. 2.6 Effects of RoO on profits.

firm a and will therefore preserve the initial situation with the external tariff t.

Conversely, it is easy to see that firm a's profits increase when the equilibrium moves from E_t to E_0 as firm a shifts to an equilibrium with external tariff t to the full trade liberalizing situation. By continuity, a moderately binding RoO corresponding to an equilibrium-like point E slightly above E_0 on the reaction curve of firm b will be even better as it stands on the left side of the isoprofit curve of a passing through E_0. The reason again is the fact that such a RoO has a positive strategic effect for firm a. Indeed the RoO provides a credible commitment for firm a to outsource aggressively. Given that outsourcing decisions are strategic substitutes, this is going to reduce the level of outsourcing of the other firm and therefore increases a's profits.

The precedent discussion tells us therefore that firm a will ideally support a FTA with no RoO or better, a moderately binding RoO. On the other hand, it will oppose a highly restrictive RoO, as one may naturally expect. It follows that the firms' interests with respect to the optimal RoO to be implemented in the FTA are opposite.

Consider finally the impact of the RoO on consumer's welfare. Note first that consumer's welfare is negatively associated with the equilibrium price p on the market:

$$p = \frac{1 - c(S_a) - c(S_b)}{3}.$$

In Thoenig and Verdier (2004a), we show that, in the space (S_a, S_b), isoprice curves are simply circular curves with higher values as we move towards point $S = (S_m, S_m)$ and crossing $R_b(S_a)$ only once from above. From this, the equilibrium price level of the initial equilibrium with external tariff p_t is certainly larger than the price level of all the other equilibria with RoOs. Hence, from the consumer point of view, an FTA with a non-restrictive RoO is always better than no FTA or a FTA with a restrictive RoO rejected by firm a.

2.2.2.4 OUTSOURCING ACTIVITIES OUTSIDE THE FTA

So far we have discussed the case where, for technological reasons, all intermediate tasks (if outsourced) had to be done within the FTA of the two countries B and C. This section discusses briefly the other polar case where all intermediate tasks can only be outsourced outside the FTA.[8] To

---

[8] Details can be found in Thoenig and Verdier (2004a).

fix ideas, suppose now that firm a is a foreign multinational having invested in a local production facility in B's market. To escape the imposition of an external tariff, firm a again has to undertake enough domestic value added inside the FTA. The RoO will now impose a maximum threshold of the fraction of outsourced activities outside the FTA. Presumably, one may also think that the same RoO will also apply to the domestic firm b if that firm outsources activities outside the FTA. To clarify the discussion and for easier comparison with the previous section, assume that the RoO only applies to the local facility of the foreign multinational firm a. Specifically, now the RoO writes as:

$$\text{if } \int_0^{S_a} p^*(i)di \leq k\left[\int_0^{S_a} p^*(i)di + \int_{S_a}^1 c_n(i)di\right] \text{ then no tariff is applied}$$

$$\text{if } \int_0^{S_a} p^*(i)di > k\left[\int_0^{S_a} p^*(i)di + \int_{S_a}^1 c_n(i)di\right] \text{ then tariff } t \text{ is applied on}$$

$$\text{sales of } a,$$

this RoO condition is now equivalent to:

$$S_a < S(k) \text{ with } S'(k) > 0.$$

Driving an analysis similar to the previous one, one can also easily compute the 'effective' outsourcing reaction function $R_a^{roox}(S_b)$ of the foreign firm a and characterize the resulting Nash equilibrium in outsourcing between the two firms. Again, depending on the restrictiveness of the RoO different regimes may occur. One interesting political economy implication of the RoO in the present context, is the fact that it can now be in the interest of both firms (domestic and foreign) to support a moderate level of RoO. The reasoning is the following. Firm b may indeed support a RoO, because the RoO provides a credible commitment inducing firm a not to outsource too aggressively. Given that outsourcing decisions are strategic substitutes, this is good from the point of view of b's profits. It is also clear that a marginally binding RoO makes firm a also better off than with the external tariff t. The reason is that the equilibrium levels of outsourcing by both firms are the same as with the tariff, while in addition; firm a saves on the tariff costs. By continuity, a moderately more binding RoO will still make firm a better off than in the situation with the external tariff t and no FTA. Hence, both firms may be likely to support the establishment of an FTA with this type of RoO compared to no FTA.

It is not difficult to see that the precedent situation is also a case where the domestic price p increases compared to the no FTA situation E_t. Hence, the gain between the two firms comes partly at the expense of the local consumers and partly through a tariff revenue loss for country *B*. From a policy point of view, one interesting implication is the fact that the formation of FTAs associated with RoOs seemingly receiving support and satisfaction from both types of firms, are in fact very likely to be costly in terms of local consumers' surplus. Indeed they may just be tools establishing implicit collusion between domestic and foreign multinationals with respect to the fragmentation game they play in/out the FTA.

2.3 RoO and outsourcing with incomplete contracts

In order to concentrate on the role of strategic interactions in outsourcing between final producers, the previous sections did assume a very standard type of relationship between the final-good firms and their potential upstream suppliers. Implicitly, outsourced intermediate tasks were supplied under competitive conditions and with no contractual problem. As emphasized by the recent literature on incomplete contracting and vertical integration (Grossman and Hart (1986)), reality is often far from such an idyllic situation. In various cases, several dimensions of market interactions between the two parties cannot be contracted upon or verifiable *ex post* by third parties. In relation-specific contexts in which parties need to make specific non-contractible investments, this leads to the well-known problem of *ex post* hold up. The final surplus between the two parties is bargained independently from what each actually contributed and the sharing of that surplus depends on the *ex post* outside options of the two parties. This, in turn creates inefficiency and *ex ante* underinvestment in specific-relation assets. In this section, we consider such issues and investigate the impact of RoO or factor-content schemes in such contexts. To simplify matters and concentrate on the new aspects it brings, we will simplify the final-good sector industrial structure and assume that it is monopolized by a foreign firm producing for the local market inside the FTA. To fix ideas, we will only consider the case where the potential outside suppliers of the foreign monopoly are located within the FTA.[9]

RoOs, by imposing constraints on suppliers–firms relationships, may affect the incomplete contractual problems existing between the downward foreign monopoly firm and its potential suppliers. In particular, RoOs may influence the outside options of the concerned parties. RoOs

---

[9] This section builds on our current work Thoenig and Verdier (2004b) in which we also discuss the case where potential external suppliers can be located outside the FTA.

by constraining foreign firms to outsource intermediate inputs inside the FTA, increase the bargaining power of suppliers within the FTA and decrease the bargaining power of suppliers outside the FTA. Having a larger slice of the pie, the FTA suppliers are then more willing to undertake relation-specific investments. This, in turn, increases the efficiency of the contractual relationship with the final-good foreign firm. Interestingly, it can be the case that establishing a RoO is welfare improving for all parties when outside suppliers are mainly established inside the FTA. Moreover, this situation may actually occur without having the RoO observed as binding in equilibrium. The reason is that the RoO will have effects through its impact on out-of-equilibrium investments and outputs.

2.3.1 *A model of outsourcing with incomplete contracts and investment*

To focus specifically on the issue of producer–suppliers relationships, consider the case of a foreign monopoly firm a selling its final-good output q on the market of a second country B that forms up a FTA with a third country C. There is no external tariff in C whereas there is an external specific tariff t in B: Hence the monopoly a may bypass the tariff by penetrating the FTA through the market of country C and then selling in B.

The monopoly may provide its inputs by producing them in-house.[10] There are also suppliers located in the FTA who can produce part of the firm a's inputs; these suppliers must engage in relation-specific investments of value only to the final good monopoly firm a: as we assume that the quality of inputs is not observable, the monopoly and the suppliers face incomplete contracting problems and *ex post* opportunism. On the one hand, vertical integration alleviates these *ex post* 'hold-up' inefficiencies. On the other hand, this strategy may impose on the firm the payment of the external tariff when RoOs in the FTA are active.

More specifically, we assume that production is made under constant return to scale: one unit of final good requires one unit of each intermediate goods j belonging to a continuum $[0,1]$. When produced in-house the unit cost of production for the monopoly is given by

$$c^*(j) = c_0 + m\,j, \qquad (2.4)$$

---

[10] Alternatively, it can purchase them abroad but with no contractual problems. We focus here on the case where all the imperfect contractual issues are only with suppliers within the FTA. Later we briefly discuss the alternative case.

while the cost of production for a local potential supplier in the FTA is given by

$$c(i) = c_0 + m\,j + \delta = c^*(j) + \delta, \tag{2.5}$$

where δ is an extra cost representing the fact that: (a) either suppliers within the FTA are assumed to produce 'standardized' or 'ill-specified' intermediates; (b) or vertical disintegration involves co-ordination costs δ.

Hence local suppliers are intrinsically less efficient than the monopoly in producing intermediate goods. However, we assume that the monopoly has to pay (iceberg-type of) transport costs $(1 + r)$ on each unit of intermediate goods that is produced in-house. As a consequence, the unit cost of in-house production is lower than production within the FTA when: $(1 + r)(c_0 + m.j) < c_0 + m.j + \delta$. Hence in-house production is more efficient than outsourcing whenever:

$$j \leq i_0 \equiv \frac{\delta - rc_0}{mr}. \tag{2.6}$$

We hereafter assume that

$$0 < i_0 < 1.$$

Finally, for a local supplier it costs a fixed design investment of value κ, to be able to produce the required quality for each intermediate j.

2.3.2 Benchmark case: FTA, no RoO and bypassing

Consider that the monopoly can pick up only one local supplier within the FTA. Later, we will discuss the case where the monopoly may outsource among a larger set of local suppliers. This strategy makes the downward firm less dependent on local suppliers. We denote s the degree of outsourcing chosen by the monopoly: the subset $[0, s]$ of the continuum of intermediate tasks are produced in-house (and abroad) and the remaining share $[s, 1]$ is produced by the local supplier within the FTA.

Consider then the following timing: In the first stage, the monopoly chooses the degree of outsourcing s and the supplier decides to commit or not some specific investment κ. In the second stage, the monopoly chooses its production level q and the amount of inputs purchased to the supplier. In the third stage, the supplier produces the intermediate inputs and enters into *ex post* bargaining over the surplus generated by this (non-verifiable) investment. A symmetric Nash bargaining provides the unit price π of inputs sold by the supplier to the monopoly. When an agreement is reached, the supplier produces the supposed range of inputs.

If an agreement is not reached, the monopoly firm must produce 'in-house' the whole production of intermediate inputs at a cost $c^*(j)$ for intermediate input j. Finally, in the last stage of the game, the monopoly firm uses 'in-house' inputs and 'outsourced' inputs to produce and sell the final good on the FTA market.

This game is solved by backward induction. In the third stage, the monopoly and the local supplier bargains over π the unit price of outsourced intermediate goods. As q, the scope of production, is chosen in the second period (i.e. before bargaining), the monopoly's revenue is independent of the issue on bargaining and given by $p(q).q$, where $p(q)$ is the inverted demand curve. When a deal is struck, the monopoly purchases inputs at the price π. In case of disagreement, the firm must produce production at a cost $(1+r)c^*(j)$ for each intermediate input. Regarding the local supplier, when an agreement is met, the supplier produces the inputs at a total cost $q. \int_s^1 c(j)dj$ and sells them for a total transfer $q.\pi$. In case of disagreement, the supplier gets zero (as the design is specific to the monopoly). The Nash bargaining solution between the firm and the local supplier is given by the following maximization problem

$$Maxq_{\pi} . \left\{ \left[p(q) - (1+r) \int_0^s c^*(j)dj - \pi \right] - \left[p(q) - (1+r) \int_0^1 c^*(j)dj \right] \right\}$$
$$\times \left\{ \pi - \int_s^1 c(j)dj \right\}.$$

This can be written as:

$$Maxq_{\pi} . \left\{ (1+r) \int_s^1 c^*(j)dj - \pi \right\} \left\{ \pi - \int_s^1 c(j)dj \right\}. \tag{2.7}$$

We get the following price level:

$$\pi(s) = \frac{1}{2} \int_s^1 c(j)dj + \frac{1}{2}(1+r) \int_s^1 c^*(j)dj. \tag{2.8}$$

From this equation we see that the input's price balances the cost of supplier's production and the cost of in-house production. In particular, the larger the transport cost r, the higher the price $\pi(s)$ as the supplier can strategically take advantage of its relatively lower cost of production in the bargaining process.

At stage 2, the firm chooses its level of production q. The total marginal cost of production γ is equal to:

$$\gamma(s) = (1+r) \int_0^s c^*(j)dj + \pi(s), \tag{2.9}$$

where π is given by eqn (2.8). Hence

$$\gamma(s) = (1+r) \int_0^1 c^*(i)di - \frac{1}{2} \int_s^1 [rc^*(i) - \delta]di. \tag{2.10}$$

The optimal output level of the firm is chosen in order to maximize the monopoly's profit $V(s)$:

$$V(s) = \arg\max_q [p(q) - \gamma(s)].q. \tag{2.11}$$

The first-order condition of this program provides the monopoly output as a decreasing function of cost of production, $q = q^m[\gamma(s)]$. As the scope of production is decreasing in $\gamma(s)$, it is obvious that $q^m(s)$ is increasing in s for $s < i_0$ and decreasing in s for $s > i_0$, where i_0 is given by eqn (2.6). Indeed the range $[i_0, 1]$ corresponds by assumption to the tasks where local production is more efficient than the foreign one. The envelope theorem tells us also that profits $V(s)$ are maximized in $s = i_0$.

At stage 1, the supplier decides to enter or not into the relationship according to the value of outsourcing s chosen by the monopoly. For a given s, the supplier's surplus is equal to:

$$W(s) = q. \left[\pi - \int_s^1 c(j)dj \right].$$

Using eqn (2.5), this may be written as:

$$W(s) = \frac{q}{2} \int_s^1 [rc^*(j) - \delta]dj. \tag{2.12}$$

The fixed cost of entering into the relationship is equal to: $\int_s^1 \kappa.dj = (1-s)\kappa$. Hence the supplier enters whenever $W(s) \geq (1-s)\kappa$. Together with eqns (2.4), (2.6) and (2.12), this condition can be written as:

$$s \geq \hat{s}(q) \equiv \frac{2\kappa/mr}{q} - (1 - i_0). \tag{2.13}$$

This condition can be interpreted as a participation constraint for the local supplier: Indeed, for a given scope of production q, $\hat{s}(q)$ corresponds to the maximum level of investment that is compatible with positive profit for the local supplier (recall that the local supplier actually produces the range $[s, 1]$). Unsurprisingly, this level is decreasing in the scope of production q (the fixed costs κ must be recovered).

Finally, the foreign monopoly chooses the degree of foreign factor content s that maximizes its profit $V(s)$ as given by eqn (2.11) under the constraint of supplier's participation eqn (2.13). The structure of

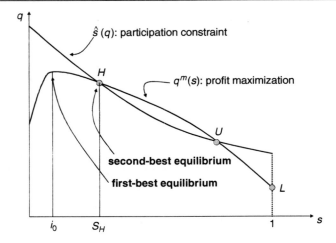

Fig. 2.7 Equilibrium in the no-RoO regime.

equilibria is depicted in Fig. 2.7 where the participation constraint $š(q)$ is a downward-sloping curve and the profit maximization curve is bell-shaped. This figure illustrates a case where there are multiple equilibria H, U, and L in foreign-factor content s and monopoly output q. The interior solution U is not stable. The two other equilibria are stable. L is with no local outsourcing ($s = 1$) for intermediate-good suppliers and low monopoly output and profits. H reflects a high equilibrium with a large local outsourcing $1 - s_H$ and high monopoly output and profits. Given the existence of multiple equilibria, it seems natural for the monopoly firm to select the high one H where the scope of production and the profits are higher.

The reasoning for these multiple equilibria is straightforward. When the expected scope of production q is large, the local supplier accepts to pay large investment's fixed costs in order to be able to produce a large range $[s, 1]$ of tasks; this enables the costs of productions $\gamma(s)$ to be reduced significantly; in turn this makes it profitable, from the monopoly point of view, to increase the scope of production q.

Finally, note that the first-best level of s that maximizes profit (i.e. $s = i_0$) may not be reached because of the *ex post* hold-up problem: This case is depicted in Fig. 2.7 where the first-best level i_0 is below $š(q)$ and is consequently not compatible with the participation constraint. This result is a standard one in the incomplete contracting theory where hold-up inefficiency generates underinvestment.

2.3.3 Introducing a RoO

The external (specific) tariff of country B is supposed to be equal to t, while there is no tariff in country C. A RoO specifies the share k of value added that must be produced within the FTA in order to escape to the tariff t. Technically this means that, to be able to penetrate market B at zero tariff, the monopoly firm has to satisfy a RoO on value added given by

$$(1 + r) \int_0^s c^*(i)\mathrm{d}i < k.\gamma^{roo}(s), \qquad (2.14)$$

where $\gamma^{roo}(s)$ is the monopoly marginal cost under the RoO; note that this cost may differ from the one derived previously (see eqn (2.10)). It can be shown that this rule on value added is equivalent to the simpler form[11]:

$$s \leq s^{roo}_{(-)}(k). \qquad (2.15)$$

Hence, the share of tasks that are produced abroad (within the monopoly) has to be smaller than $s^{roo}(k)$ for the monopoly to comply with the RoO. The modification implied by the RoO is twofold. First, it changes the *ex post* bargaining process between the monopoly and its supplier, as this later may use the RoO to improve its bargaining position. Secondly, it directly alters the monopoly's profits when the RoO is binding and the tariff must be paid.

Consider first the impact of the RoO on the bargaining solution between the firm and its supplier. Suppose first that the monopoly chooses to comply with the RoO (i.e. locally outsource a share $1 - s$ of inputs above $1 - s^{roo}(k)$, the one required under the RoO). In the case of disagreement with its supplier corresponds, the firm has no access to local inputs and needs to turn to 'in-house' production for the intermediate inputs, and the tariff must be paid. This alternative situation gives a bargaining advantage to the local supplier. It was not present in the no-RoO benchmark regime. Consequently, the sharing rule of the total surplus between the two parties will be altered in favor of the supplier. The price of the outsourced inputs will increase *ceteris paribus*. Indeed, it should now incorporate part of the tariff t saved by the monopoly because of the

---

[11] Indeed from eqn (2.16) the condition (2.14) writes as:

$$(1 + r) \int_0^s c^*(i)\mathrm{d}i < k.\left\{\frac{1}{2}1_{s<s^m}.t + (1 + r) \int_0^1 c^*(i)\mathrm{d}i - \alpha \int_s^1 [rc^*(i) - \delta]\mathrm{d}i\right\}.$$

This condition is equivalent to eqn (2.15).

agreement. From this, the unit cost of production under RoO is increased and can be shown to be equal to:

$$\frac{1}{2}t + \gamma(s).$$

Using the same arguments as in the benchmark case, one can show[12] that the supplier accepts to produce when

$$s \geq \hat{s}^{roo}(q).$$

Suppose now that the monopoly chooses not to comply with the RoO and to locally outsource a share $1 - s$ of inputs below the required threshold $1 - s^{roo}(k)$ under the RoO. Then, whatever the result of the price negociation with the local supplier, the downward firm has to pay the external tariff t. Hence, in that case the sharing rule of the total surplus between the two parties will not be biased in favor of the supplier. The price of the outsourced inputs will remain the same as in the no-RoO benchmark. The unit production cost of the monopoly is $\gamma(s)$. Using the same argument as before, the supplier will accept to produce when

$$s \geq \hat{s}(q).$$

Summarizing the preceding discussion, we can write the unit cost of production under RoO as

$$\gamma^{roo}(s, t) = \frac{1}{2}1_{s < s^{roo}}.t + \gamma(s), \qquad (2.16)$$

and the participation constraint of the local suppliers as:

$$s \geq \hat{s}^{roo}(q) = \hat{s}(q) + 1_{s < s^{roo}}(\hat{s}^{roo}(q) - \hat{s}(q)).$$

It is clear that for a given scope of production $q, \hat{s}^{roo}(q) > \hat{s}(q)$, i.e. the supplier's participation constraint when the firm decides to comply to the RoO is less stringent than the no-RoO participation constraint: Indeed, the supplier accepts to produce a larger share $(1 - s)$ of inputs as their price after bargaining is larger than in the no-RoO benchmark regime. This in turn means that, with compliance, the RoO reduces hold-up inefficiencies. By reducing the monopoly's bargaining position in favor of the supplier's one, it promotes *ex ante* investment from the supplier's side.

The whole participation condition with RoO compliance $\hat{s}^{roo}(q)$ together with the no-RoO participation constraint $\hat{s}(q)$ are depicted in Fig. 2.8. $\hat{s}(q)$ corresponds to the curve $\Phi_0\Phi_0$ and $\hat{s}^{roo}(q)$ corresponds to the curve $\Phi_1\Phi_1\Phi'_1\Phi'_0$: It coincides with $\hat{s}^{roo}(q)$ when $s \leq s^{roo}(k)$ in the RoO compliance regime and with $\hat{s}(q)$ when $s > s^{roo}(k)$ in the no-compliance regime.

---

[12] See Thoenig and Verdier (2004b) for details.

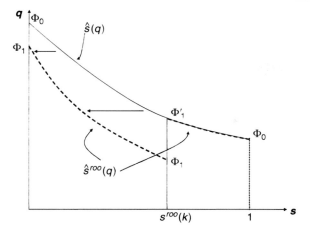

Fig. 2.8 Effect of a RoO on local supplier's investment.

Consider now the impact of the RoO on the firm's profit function. Under a RoO the problem of profit's maximization depends on the value of factor content s. Indeed when the monopoly does not comply with the RoO (i.e. $s > s^{roo}(k)$), it has to pay the specific tariff t; otherwise it can freely penetrate the FTA. Hence when $s > s^{roo}(k)$ the price perceived by the monopoly is $p - t$ where p is the market price. The problem of profit's maximization can thus be set as:

$$V^{roo}(s) = \arg\max_{q}[p(q) - 1_{s>s^{roo}}.t - \gamma^{roo}(s, t)].q.$$

The first-order condition of this program yields $p'(q).q + p(q) = \gamma^{roo}(s, t) + 1_{s>s^{roo}}.t$. The monopoly output is consequently given by: $q = q^m[\gamma^{roo}(s, t) + 1_{s>s^{roo}}.t]$. Hence the difference with the no-RoO regime is that the specific tariff is similar to an extra cost of production from the monopoly point of view.

The monopoly's output rewrites as:

$$q^{roo}(s) = q^m\left[\gamma(s) + 1_{s>s^{roo}}.t + \frac{1}{2}1_{s<s^{roo}}.t\right].$$

The monopoly's output (and profit) depends on three components. The first component reflects the cost of production of monopoly and supplier and is already present in the no-RoO output. The second component is the direct effect of a tariff that negatively impacts on profit and output: note that this effect is present only when the content of production in foreign inputs is too large, i.e. the RoO is binding with $s > s^{roo}$. The third

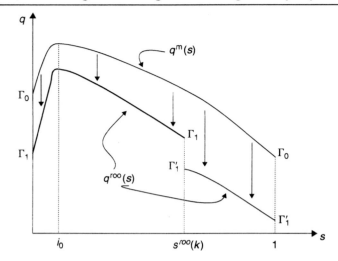

Fig. 2.9 Effect of a RoO on monopoly's output and profit.

component is the strategic effect corresponding to the fact that supplier's inputs are more expensive than in the absence of RoO. This effect is present only when the content of production in foreign inputs satisfies the level required by the RoO, i.e. the RoO is not binding with $s < s^{roo}$. Indeed the supplier enjoys an extra-strategic power under the RoO only when the supplier's contribution enables the monopoly to escape from the tariff.

It is clear that for any given level of local outsourcing s, the scope of production q and the monopoly's profits are always lower under a RoO than in absence of RoO. Monopoly's output without a RoO (i.e. $q^m(s)$) and with a RoO (i.e. $q^{roo}(s)$) are depicted in Fig. 2.9 (by, respectively, the curves $\Gamma_0\Gamma_0$ and $\Gamma_1\Gamma_1\Gamma_1'\Gamma_1'$).

2.3.4 The effect of RoO on the equilibrium value of output and factor content

Similar to the no-RoO regime, the equilibrium is determined by two equations, namely the monopoly's level of output (or equivalently profits) and the supplier's participation constraint. From this set of equations, we can see that the effect of the RoO on the equilibrium is ambiguous. On the one hand, the RoO stimulates investment by the local supplier. For a given output q, the participation constraint of the supplier is shifted down from $\Phi_0\Phi_0$ to $\Phi_1\Phi_1$, when there is compliance. On the other hand, a RoO, whether it's binding or not, degrades the monopoly's profit and output,

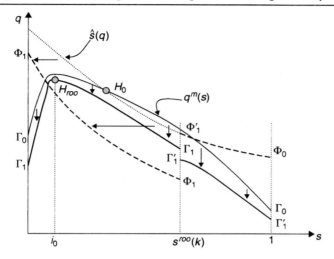

Fig. 2.10 Positive effect of a RoO on equilibrium.

(i.e. a downward shift of the profit curve from $\Gamma_0 \Gamma_0$ to $\Gamma_1 \Gamma_1 \Gamma_1' \Gamma_1'$). Depending on the relative magnitudes of both effects the value of factor content and the monopoly's output may be larger or lower than in the absence of a RoO. Figures 2.10 and 2.11 illustrate the different possibilities.

Consider a RoO where the factor-content requirement is not too large, e.g. $s^{roo}(k)$ not too far from zero. This situation is illustrated in Fig. 2.10 where the no-RoO equilibrium H_0 switches to the RoO-equilibrium H_{roo}. In particular, we see that H_{roo} pareto-dominates H_0. Indeed the degree of local outsourcing is larger than in the no-RoO equilibrium[13], i.e. $s_{roo} < s_0$, and monopoly's profits are larger, i.e. $V_{roo} > V_0$. This result arises because the pro-investment effect of the RoO dominates the profit-depressing effect; the net effect of the RoO is to reduce the hold-up inefficiencies and underinvestment by transferring bargaining power from the monopoly to the local supplier.

Moreover, inspection shows that the RoO may have such a positive impact on equilibrium even if this RoO is not stringent in the sense that it fixes a factor-content requirement that is below the one chosen *ex ante* by the monopoly (i.e. $1 - s^{roo}(k) < 1 - s_0$). This clearly stands from the fact that the RoO impacts equilibrium through affecting out-of-equilibrium options in the bargaining process.

---

[13] In the figure s_{roo} corresponds to the first-best degree of outsourcing i_0.

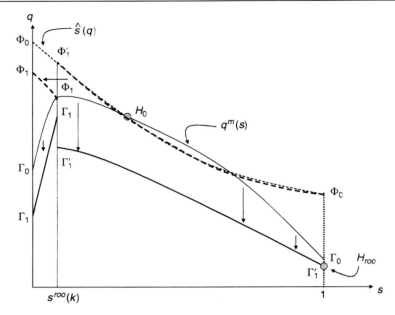

Fig. 2.11 Perverse effect of a RoO on equilibrium.

Figure 2.11 describes the alternative possibility where the factor-content requirement becomes large (i.e. $s^{roo}(k)$ getting closer to zero). The equilibrium switches from H_0 to H_{roo} that corresponds to a 'bad' equilibrium with no local outsourcing. Here, we get that a very stringent factor requirement $s^{roo}(k)$ has a strong and negative effect on the equilibrium H_0. The factor requirement becomes so stringent and depresses monopoly profits by so much that the scope of production is not compatible with any positive investment by the local supplier. Hence, the foreign monopoly has to produce the whole production 'in-house' and to pay the external tariff to sell its product inside the FTA.

2.3.5 Robustness

Finally, we may conclude this section by an informal discussion of the theoretical robustness of the setup.

2.3.5.1 MARKET POWER OF THE FOREIGN MONOPOLY

First, it is clear that the results are very sensitive to the monopoly's market power. Indeed the gap between the curves $q^m(s)$ and $q^{roo}(s)$ depends crucially on the magnitude of the price elasticity of the final good's demand. Intuitively, a very inelastic demand confers to the monopoly a strong market power and its output is not much affected by the underlying variations of unit costs and the presence of the tariff t. In that case, the curves $q^m(s)$ and $q^{roo}(s)$ are quite close. Said differently, with a small elasticity of demand the monopoly chooses a scope of production q that is relatively constant whatever the value of the underlying costs of production. In that case a RoO affects only marginally the scope of production. The profit-depressing effect of the RoO is then smaller, whereas the pro-investment effect is unchanged. The effect of the RoO is likely to be positive in the presence of strong market power as in that case the RoO reduces the hold-up inefficiency without reducing significantly the scope of production.

2.3.5.2 BARGAINING POWER AND LOCAL SUPPLIERS

Secondly, the results depend crucially on the fact that the RoO increases the bargaining power of the local supplier. In our framework, this effect is magnified because there is only one local supplier; consequently this supplier enjoys a very powerful strategic position. If the monopoly could outsource to several local suppliers, this strategic mechanism would be reduced. Still, we believe that the effects of a RoO would be partly robust to such a generalization. To see this, consider that there are n local suppliers. The average range produced by each supplier[14] is $[1 - s]/n$. In that case the RoO still has an impact on *ex ante* investment by suppliers as soon as $[s - s^{roo}(k)] < [1 - s]/n$: each supplier must have a strategic (marginal) impact on the eligibility for the RoO. Hence a RoO still has a positive impact on the equilibrium value of s if the factor requirement $s^{roo}(k)$ is not too far from the no-RoO equilibrium value of s. Finally, it is even possible that the monopoly chooses to reduce *ex ante* its number of local suppliers in order to provide them a strong strategic role. Indeed, the monopoly has no credible way for committing not to hold-up *ex post* its suppliers. By reducing the number of local suppliers, the monopoly transfers to them some *ex post* bargaining power; this in turn may be good if this promotes local suppliers' *ex ante* investment. Hence the RoO acts as an *ex ante* commitment device from the monopoly's point of view.

---

[14] This is the case if we assume that the n suppliers produce the same distribution of tasks within the range $[s, 1]$, i.e. whatever i, the n suppliers produce at least a task among $[i, i + di] \subset [s, 1]$.

2.4 Conclusion

This chapter discussed the effects of Rules of Origin in the context of multinational firms slicing up their chain value in a co-ordinated manner. We emphasized two aspects of the international production fragmentation process. The first one is the fact that final-good-producing firms, in an imperfect context environment, may use fragmentation or outsourcing of intermediate input activities as a strategic variable. In such a context, the existence of a RoO between a domestic firm in the FTA and a foreign multinational firm outside FTA, affects asymmetrically the use of that variable between the foreign and domestic firms.

First, it may trigger the existence of multiple equilibria in outsourcing and create important *co-ordination problems* in the product market. A policy implication of this is the fact that a RoO may then have effects that are difficult to evaluate, if one does not know which equilibrium is played by the firms. Secondly, from a political-economy point of view, the foreign firm paradoxically may have some interest in supporting a RoO constraining its decisions of outsourcing, while the domestic firm may have just the opposite interest. As a matter of fact, the implementation of RoO in a strategic outsourcing context can be viewed as *a commitment device* to be more or less aggressive in the process of international fragmentation. This, in turn, may be beneficial to the foreign firm at the expense of the domestic firm. For that same reason, one may also find situations where *both* firms agree on the establishment of a particular non-liberalizing RoO at the expense of local consumers and tariff revenues.

The second aspect investigated in this chapter deals with the specific impact of RoOs on the vertical chain of value added, namely the relations between intermediate-good producers and final-good producers. This issue becomes crucial when firm–suppliers relationships are characterized by some degree of contract incompleteness. We discuss one channel of interactions going through the way RoOs influence the outside options of the concerned parties. Indeed, RoOs by constraining foreign firms to outsource intermediate inputs inside the FTA, tend to increase the bargaining power of domestic suppliers within the FTA. In such a context, it can be the case that establishing a RoO is welfare improving for all parties. Interestingly, this situation may actually occur *without having the RoO observed as binding in equilibrium.*

What should then come out from this analysis for policy making? Two lessons are, we think, important. The first one is the fact that RoO may well fulfill commitment functions when the way intermediate goods affect the production process is a strategic variable of domestic firms and foreign firms. This effect may then produce counterintuitive political positions among the various firms (i.e. the foreign final-good firm in favor of the RoO, the domestic one opposing it). Also, RoOs may induce co-ordination problems and therefore trigger endogenously some strategic ambiguity in terms of market outcome.

The second lesson is probably that, once one takes into account the essential dimension of contract incompleteness of arm-length transactions, RoOs may have paradoxical effects on the nature of the international production fragmentation process. Indeed, they may be efficiency improving and have significant effects though they will not be observed as binding in reality. This, of course, raises important conceptual problems and makes the empirical evaluation of the impact of RoOs even more difficult.

References

Dixit A., G. Grossman, 1982, 'Trade and Protection with Multistage Production', *Review of Economic Studies*, XLIX, pp. 583–594.

Falvey R., G. Reed, 1998, 'Economic Effects of Rules of Origin', Weltwirtschaftliches Archiv, 134(2), pp. 209–229.

Feenstra R., 1998, 'Integration of Trade and Disintegration of Production in the Global Economy', *Journal of Economic Perspectives*, Fall 1998, 31–50.

Grossman, G., 1981. 'The Theory of Domestic Content Protection and Content Preference', *The Quarterly Journal of Economics*, 96(4), pp. 583–603.

Grossman S., O. Hart, 1986, 'The Costs and Benefits of Ownership: A Theory of Vertical and Lateral Integration', *Journal of Political Economy*, 4, pp. 691–719.

Hollander A., 1987, 'Content Protection and Transnational Monopoly', *Journal of International Economics*, November, 3/4, pp. 283–298.

Jiandong J., K. Krishna, 1996, 'Market Access and Welfare Effects of Free Trade Areas without Rules of Origin', NBER Working Papers 5480.

Krishna K., A. Krueger, 1995, 'Implementing Free Trade Areas: Rules of Origin and Hidden Protection', Chapter 6, of 'New Directions in Trade Theory', J. Levinsohn, A. V. Deardoff and R. M. Stern (ed.), University of Michigan.

Krueger A., 1993, 'Free Trade Agreements as Protectionist Devices: Rules of Origin', NBER Working Paper 4352.

Mussa M., 1984, 'The Economics of Content Protection', NBER wpn°1457.

Richardson M., 1991, 'The Effects of a Content Requirement on a Foreign Duopsonist', *Journal of International Economics*, 31, pp. 143–155.

Richardson M., 1993, 'Content Protection with Foreign Capital', Oxford Economic Papers, 45, pp. 103–117.

Shy, O., R. Stenbacka, 2003a, 'Strategic Outsourcing', *Journal of Economic Behavior & Organization*, 50(2), February, pp. 203–224.

Shy, O., R. Stenbacka, 2003b, 'Partial Subcontracting, Monitoring Costs and Market Structure', Mimeo University of Haifa.

Thoenig M., T. Verdier, 2004a, 'Strategic outsourcing and Rules of Origins', mimeo DELTA.

Thoenig M., T. Verdier, 2004b, 'An Incomplete Contracting View of Rules of Origins', mimeo DELTA.

Vousden N., 1987, 'Content Protection and Tariffs under Monopoly and Competition', *Journal of International Economics*, November, 3/4, pp. 263–282.

Part II

Rules of Origin in Regional Trade Agreements around the world

3

Mapping and measuring Rules of Origin around the world

Antoni Estevadeordal and Kati Suominen

3.1 Introduction

Preferential trading agreements (PTAs) have proliferated spectacularly around the world over the past decade.[1] The wave of PTA formation has carried with it a colorful mosaic of trade disciplines—such as provisions on market access for goods and services, standards, safeguards, government procurement, and investment—to govern economic relations between the PTA partners. These various rules dispersed through PTAs are hardly inconsequential given that more than a third of global commerce takes place within PTAs.[2] Moreover, reverberating to firms' export, outsourcing, and investment decisions around the world, PTA disciplines arbitrate both actual and potential trade and investment flows within PTAs—and between PTAs and the rest of the world (ROW).

Yet, the richness of the PTA universe notwithstanding, there are astonishingly few rigorous efforts to disaggregate PTA agreements in order to analyse the operation and effects of the various rules they carry.[3] This,

---

[1] PTAs include free trade agreements, customs unions, common markets, and single markets. Some 250 PTAs had been notified to the World Trade Organization (WTO) by the end of 2002; of these, 130 were notified after January 1995. The WTO expects the number of PTAs to soar to nearly 300 by the end of 2005.

[2] When unilateral preferential schemes such as the Generalized System of Preferences (GSP) are accounted for, no less than 60 per cent of world trade is estimated to be conducted on a preferential basis. Importantly, the unilateral preferential programs carry many of the same disciplines as PTAs.

[3] The few mappings of PTA disciplines include WTO (1998, 2002a,b), IADB (2002), and Suominen (2004) produced in tandem with this chapter. The few existing rigorous, scholarly studies on the determinants of PTA provisions (beyond the contributions on Rules of Origin

in turn, implies that (1) very little is known about the compatibility of PTA agreements with one another or with the multilateral WTO Agreements; (2) the political economy sources of the divergent contractual formats of PTAs remain unexplored; and (3) analysts have yet to disentangle the respective economic effects of the different PTA disciplines from each other, let alone from the effects of variables beyond PTAs. The lack of understanding of the various component parts of the rapidly burgeoning PTA universe severely undercuts the credibility and usefulness of the arguments of both those who view PTAs as discriminatory instruments, hostage to protectionist interests that work to obstruct global trade lib-eralization, and those who regard PTAs as containing a liberalizing logic conducive to multilateral opening.

The purpose of this chapter is to break new ground in dissecting PTAs by focusing on Rules of Origin (RoO), a crucial yet poorly understood market access discipline included in virtually every PTA. The economic justifica-tion for RoO is to curb trade deflection—to avoid products from non-PTA members from being trans-shipped through a low-tariff PTA partner to a high-tariff one. As such, RoO are an inherent feature of free trade agree-ments (FTAs) where the member states' external tariffs diverge and/or where the members wish to retain their individual tariff policies *vis-à-vis* the ROW. RoO are also widely used in customs unions (CUs), either as a transitory tool in the process of moving toward a common external tariff (CET), or as a more permanent means of covering product categories where reaching agreement on a CET is difficult, for instance due to large tariff differentials between the member countries. Thus, basically all PTAs contain rules for establishing the origin of goods.[4] RoO are not only a central facet of preferential trading today, but also at the heart of many ongoing PTA negotiations, such as the 34-country talks to establish the Free Trade Area of the Americas (FTAA), and the European Union-Southern Common Market (Mercosur) negotiations to connect the world's two largest customs unions. In addition, RoO are gaining growing policy attention at the multilateral level: in preparation for the Doha Trade Round, the WTO's Committee on Regional Trade Agreements has for the

in this volume) tend to center on a single PTA and examine intersectoral variation in its market access provisions. See Milner (1997); Kowalczyk and Davis (1998); Olarreaga and Soloaga (1998); and Estevadeordal (2000). For the effects of PTAs' market access provisions, see Estevadeordal and Robertson (2002) and Ghosh and Yamarik (2003).

[4] The Asia-Pacific Cooperation (APEC) forum is a prominent exception, with its members employing their respective domestic RoO. APEC is based on a principle of open regionalism—extending tariff preferences on an MFN basis—which renders the need for preferential RoO obsolete.

first time raised preferential RoO to a systemic issue in the negotiation agenda.

Since a failure to meet the RoO disqualifies an exporter from the PTA-conferred preferential treatment, RoO can and must be seen as a central market-access instrument reigning over preferential trade. Notably, the relevance of RoO as gatekeepers of commerce can accentuate over time: RoO remain in place even after preferential tariffs have been phased out. But what renders RoO particularly relevant is that they are hardly a neutral instrument: given that RoO can serve as an effective means to deter trans-shipment, they can tempt political-economy uses well beyond the efforts to avert trade deflection. Indeed, RoO are widely considered a trade-policy instrument that can work to offset the benefits of tariff liberalization.[5] Often negotiated at up to 8- or 10-digit levels of disaggregation, RoO, like the tariff, make a superbly targetable instrument. Moreover, that RoO are generally defined in highly technical terms rather than assigned a numerical value entails that they can be tailored for each individual product differently, and that they are not nearly as immediately quanti-fiable and comparable across products as the tariff is.

It is the use of RoO as a political economy instrument that helps account for the choice of RoO to govern preferential economic exchange—for the integrating governments' willingness to expend time and resources on the tedious, technical, and often highly contentious crafting of RoO protocols. After all, governments could completely forego using RoO by entering into a CU or by excluding the potentially trade-deflecting economic sectors from the PTA's coverage. Yet, the bulk of PTAs employ RoO, and RoO of widely different types and combinations.

Notwithstanding RoO's function of refereeing preferential market access, potential uses for distributive purposes, complexity in existing PTAs and centrality in ongoing PTA negotiations, and increasing relev-ance on the multilateral agenda, the global RoO panorama remains largely unexplored.[6] It is the task of this chapter to mend this gap. We present a

---

[5] Most prominently, RoO can be employed to favor intra-PTA industry linkages over those between the PTA and the ROW, and, as such, to indirectly protect PTA-based input producers *vis-à-vis* their extra-PTA rivals (Krueger 1993; Krishna and Krueger 1995). As such, RoO are akin to a tariff on the intermediate product levied by the importing country (Falvey and Reed 2000; Lloyd 2001), and can be used by one PTA member to secure its PTA partners' input markets for the exports of its own intermediate products (Krueger 1993; Krishna and Krueger 1995). Furthermore, given that RoO hold the potential for increasing local sourcing, gov-ernments can use RoO to encourage investment in sectors that provide high value added and/or jobs (Jensen-Moran 1996; Hirsch 2002).

[6] The exceptions are WTO (2002a), Estevadeordal and Suominen (2003), and Suominen (2004) produced in tandem with this chapter.

global mapping of the existing RoO regimes, and put forth an analytical coding scheme for the types of product-specific and regime-wide RoO employed in these regimes. The most immediate contribution of this chapter is to advance the understanding of the RoO regimes around the world. Except for Suominen (2004) produced in tandem with this chapter, there are no comparable mappings; the contribution here is the first of its kind.[7] The analytical tools developed here are already employed in empirical work, both in our efforts to capture the global trade effects of RoO,[8] and in Estevadeordal, López-Córdova and Suominen (2005). The Impact of NAFTA's Market Access Provisions on the Location of Foreign Direct Investment in Mexico. Mimeograph.] of this book that focuses on RoO's effects on investment. This chapter also strives to inspire further work aimed at disaggregating preferential trading arrangements into their component parts—a task that is absolutely crucial for understanding the implications of regionalism for the global economic system, as well as for crafting nuanced, well-informed, and fruitful policy prescriptions concerning PTAs.

The first section of this chapter presents the different types of product-specific and general RoO used in RoO regimes. The second section examines the prevalence of the different types of RoO in a hundred integration schemes in the world. Section three puts forth a methodology for developing analytical measurements of the degree of restrictiveness of product-specific RoO and flexibility provided by regime-wide RoO, and uses these measures to draw comparisons within and across RoO regimes as well as over time. The fourth section discusses the RoO innovations. Section five concludes.

3.2 Types of Rules of Origin in FTAs

There are two types of Rules of Origin, non-preferential and preferential RoO. Non-preferential RoO are used to distinguish foreign from domestic products in establishing anti-dumping and countervailing duties, safeguard

---

[7] WTO (2002a) does provide a charting of various features of RoO regimes. However, this chapter goes well beyond the WTO's study by including a greater number of regimes, analysing in much greater detail the universe of product-specific RoO, examining a broader range of regime-wide RoO, discussing RoO innovations, and, perhaps most importantly, developing methodologies for capturing the relative restrictiveness of RoO and RoO regimes.

[8] See Estevadeordal and Suominen (2004a) and Suominen (2004) for trade effects; see Estevadeordal (2000) and Suominen (2004, 2003) for the political economy of restrictiveness of RoO.

measures, origin-marking requirements, and/or discriminatory quantitative restrictions or tariff quotas, as well as in the context of government procurement. Preferential RoO, meanwhile, define the conditions under which the importing country will regard a product as originating in an exporting country that receives preferential treatment from the importing country. PTAs, in effect, employ RoO to determine whether a good qualifies for preferential treatment when exported from one member state to another.

Both non-preferential and preferential RoO regimes have two dimensions: sectoral, product-specific RoO, and general, regime-wide RoO. We discuss each in turn.

A. Product-specific RoO

The Kyoto Convention recognizes two basic criteria to determine origin: wholly obtained or produced, and substantial transformation.[9] The wholly obtained or produced-category applies only to one PTA member, and asks whether the commodities and related products have been entirely grown, harvested, or extracted from the soil in the territory of that member, or manufactured there from any of these products. The rule of origin is met through not using any second-country components or materials. Most countries apply this strict and precise definition.

The substantial-transformation criterion is more complex, involving four main components that can be used as standalone or in combinations with each other. The precision with which these components define RoO in PTAs today contrasts sharply with the vagueness of the substantial transformation-criterion as used by the United States since 1908 until the inception of the Canada-US Free Trade Agreement (CUSFTA) in 1989 and, subsequently, the North American Free Trade Agreement (NAFTA) in 1994 (Reyna 1995: 7).[10]

The first component of the substantial transformation criterion is a change in tariff classification (CTC) between the manufactured good and the inputs from extra-PTA parties used in the productive process. The CTC may require the product to alter its chapter (2 digits under the Harmonized

[9] The Revised Kyoto Convention is an international instrument adopted by the World Customs Organization (WCO) to standardize and harmonize customs policies and procedures around the world. The WCO adopted the original Convention in 1974. The revised version was adopted in June 1999.
[10] The old criterion basically required the emergence of a 'new and different article' from the manufacturing process applied to the original article. It was, however, much criticized for allowing—and indeed requiring—subjective and case-by-case determinations of origin (Reyna 1995: 7).

System), heading (4 digits), subheading (6 digits) or item (8–10 digits) in the exporting PTA member.

The second criterion is an exception attached to a particular CTC (ECTC). ECTC generally prohibits the use of non-originating materials from a certain subheading, heading, or chapter.

The third criterion is value content (VC), which requires the product to acquire a certain minimum local value in the exporting country. The value content can be expressed in three main ways: as the minimum percentage of value that must be added in the exporting country (domestic or regional value content, RVC); as the difference between the value of the final good and the costs of the imported inputs (import content, MC); or as the value of parts (VP), whereby originating status is granted to products meeting a minimum percentage of originating parts out of the total.

The fourth RoO component is technical requirement (TECH), which requires the product to undergo certain manufacturing operations in the originating country. TECH essentially prescribes or prohibits the use certain input(s) and/or the realization of certain process(es) in the production of the good.[11] It is a particularly prominent feature in RoO governing textile products.

The change-of-heading requirement is the staple of PTAs. It is used either as standalone or in tandem with other RoO criteria. Also frequently used are the import content (usually ranging from 30 to 60 per cent), value of parts, and technical requirements. Adding analytical complexity, albeit administrative flexibility, is that many RoO regimes provide two alternative RoO for a given product, such as a change of chapter or, alternatively, a change of heading plus RVC.

B. Regime-wide RoO

Besides product-specific RoO, RoO regimes vary by the types of general RoO they employ—including in the degree of *de minimis*, the roll-up principle, and the type of cumulation.

First, most PTAs contain a *de minimis* rule, which allows for a specified maximum percentage of non-originating materials to be used without affecting origin. The *de minimis* rule inserts leniency in the CTC and TECH criteria by making it easier for products with non-originating inputs to qualify.

---

[11] TECH can be highly discretional due to complicating and evaluation of sufficient transformation in the production of the good.

Secondly, the roll-up or absorption principle allows materials that have acquired origin by meeting specific processing requirements to be considered originating when used as input in a subsequent transformation. That is, when roll-up is allowed, non-originating materials are not taken into account in the calculation of the value added of the subsequent transformation.

Thirdly, cumulation allows producers of one PTA member to use materials from another PTA member (or other members) without losing the preferential status of the final product. There are three types of cumulation. Bilateral cumulation operates between the two PTA partners and permits them to use products that originate in the other PTA partner as if they were their own when seeking to qualify for the PTA-conferred preferential treatment in that partner. Basically, all RoO regimes apply bilateral cumulation. Under diagonal cumulation, countries tied by the same set of preferential origin rules can use products that originate in any part of the common RoO zone as if they originated in the exporting country. Full cumulation extends diagonal cumulation. It provides that countries tied by the same RoO regime can use goods produced in any part of the common RoO zone even if these were not originating products: any and all processing done in the zone is calculated as if it had taken place in the final country of manufacture. As such, diagonal and full cumulation can notably expand the geographical and product coverage of a RoO regime.[12] Table 3.2 illustrates the frequency of general RoO provisions around the world.

Whereas *de minimis*, roll-up, and cumulation allow for leniency in the application of RoO, there are three provisions that may have the opposite effect and increase the stringency of RoO.[13]

First, most PTAs contain a separate list indicating the operations that are in all circumstances considered insufficient to confer origin, such as preservation during transport and storage, as well as simple operations of cleaning, sorting, painting, packaging, assembling, and marking and labelling.

Secondly, many PTAs prohibit duty drawback—preclude the refunding of tariffs on non-originating inputs that are subsequently included in a

---

[12] In bilateral cumulation, the use of the partner-country components is favored; in diagonal cumulation, all the beneficiary trading partners of the cumulation area are favored. Full cumulation is more liberal than diagonal cumulation by allowing a greater use of third-country materials. However, it is rarely allowed in RoO regimes.

[13] To be sure, non-members to a cumulation area may view the cumulation system as introducing another layer of discrimination by virtue of its providing incentives to the member countries to outsource from within the cumulation zone at the expense of extra-zone suppliers.

final product that is exported to a PTA partner. Many developing countries employ drawback in order to attract investment and to encourage exports; however, drawback in the context of a PTA is viewed as providing a cost advantage to the PTA-based producers who gear their final goods to export over producers selling their final goods in the domestic market.[14] The end of duty drawback entails an increase in the cost of non-originating components for PTA-based final-goods producers. As such, the end of drawback in the presence of cumulation may encourage intra-PTA producers to shift to suppliers in the cumulation area (WTO 2002a).

Thirdly, a complex method of certifying the origin of goods can impose high administrative costs on exporters. The main certification methods are self-certification by exporters, certification by the exporting country government or an industry umbrella group to which the government has delegated the task of issuing the certificate, and a combination of the 'private' self-certification and the 'public' governmental certification. The more numerous the bureaucratic hurdles and the higher the costs for an exporter to obtain an origin certificate, the lower the incentives to seek PTA-conferred preferential treatment.

3.3 Rules of Origin around the world

This section turns to examining the great variety of combinations of product-specific and regime-wide RoO used in selected PTAs in Europe, the Americas, Asia-Pacific, Africa, and the Middle East, as well as in PTAs between these regions. We subsequently discuss the structure of non-preferential RoO. The latter part of this section presents an analytical, comparative assessment of (1) the relative restrictiveness of the product-specific RoO governing different economic sectors in the different RoO regimes; and (2) the degree of flexibility instilled in the various RoO regimes by the regime-wide RoO.

A. Comparing the structure of RoO regimes in five regions

i. Europe: expansion of the PANEURO system

The RoO regimes employed across the EU's FTAs are highly uniform *vis-à-vis* each other. This is due largely to the European Commission's recent

---

[14] Cadot *et al.* (2001) show that duty drawback may have a protectionist bias due to reducing the interest of producers to lobby against protection of intermediate products.

drive to harmonize the EU's existing and future preferential RoO regimes in order to facilitate the operations of EU exporters dealing on multiple trade fronts, and to pave the way for particularly the EU's East European FTA partners to draw greater benefits from the EU-provided preferential treatment via diagonal cumulation—that was previously precluded by the lack of compatibility among the EU's RoO regimes. The harmonization efforts pertained to product-specific and regime-wide RoO alike. They extended to EU's RoO protocols with the European Free Trade Association (EFTA) countries that dated from 1972 and 1973, as well as across the EU's FTAs forged in the early 1990s in the context of the Europe Agreements with Bulgaria, Czech Republic, Estonia, Hungary, Latvia, Lithuania, Poland, Slovakia, and Romania.[15] The work culminated in 1997 in the launch of the Pan-European (PANEURO) system, which established identical RoO protocols and product-specific RoO across the EU's existing FTAs, thereby providing for diagonal cumulation among the participating countries. The Commission's regulation 46 of January 1999 reiterates the harmonized protocols, outlining the so-called single-list RoO. Overall, the PANEURO RoO are highly complex, combining CTC mainly at the heading level with exceptions, VC, and TECH, and varying markedly across products.[16]

Since 1997, the PANEURO model has become incorporated in the EU's newer FTAs, including the Euro-Mediterranean Association Agreements, the Stabilization and Association Agreements with Croatia and the Former Yugoslav Republic of Macedonia, the EU-Slovenia FTA, as well as the extra-regional FTAs with South Africa, Mexico, and Chile. Also, the RoO of the EU's generalized system of preferences (GSP) and the 2000 Cotonou Agreement with the African, Caribbean, and Pacific (ACP) developing countries approximate the single-list, PANEURO model. EFTA's recently concluded FTAs with Mexico and Singapore follow the PANEURO model, albeit providing an additional alternative rule in selected sectors—such as plastics, rubber, textiles, iron and steel products, and some machinery products.

---

[15] See Driessen and Graafsma (1999) for a review.

[16] The harmonized RoO do not represent a dramatic break with those of the pre-1997 era. For example, the RoO in nearly 75 per cent of the products (in terms of tariff subheadings) in PANEURO and the original EU-Poland RoO protocol published in 1993 are identical. Both the new and the old versions combine CTC with VC and/or TECH. Indeed, EU RoO feature remarkable continuity: the RoO of the European Community-Cyprus FTA formed in 1973 are strikingly similar to the PANEURO model used today. One notable difference between the older and the newer protocols is that the latter allow for an optional way of meeting the RoO for about 25 per cent of the products, whereas the former specify mostly only one way of meeting the RoO. The second option, alternative RoO, much like the first option RoO, combines different RoO criteria; however, the most frequently used alternative RoO is a standalone import-content criterion.

Importantly, the EU's eastward enlargement 1 May 2004 terminated the FTAs forged among the 10 new member states and also between them and the EU. The new members became incorporated in the EU customs union; as such, they set out to apply the EU's CET, with their overall external tariffs dropping from nine to four per cent, and also assumed the rights and obligations of the FTAs that the EU has in place with non-member countries.

ii. The Americas: four RoO families

There is much more variation across RoO regimes in the Americas. Nevertheless, distinct RoO families can be identified (Garay and Cornejo 2002). One extreme is populated by the traditional trade agreements such as the Latin American Integration Agreement (LAIA), which uses a general rule applicable across the board for all tariff items (a change in tariff classification at the heading level or, alternatively, a regional value content of at least 50 per cent of the FOB export value of the final good). The LAIA model is the point of reference for RoO used in the Andean Community (CAN) and Caribbean Community (CARICOM). At the other extreme lie the so-called new-generation PTAs such as NAFTA, which is used as a reference point for the US–Chile, US–Central America and Dominican Republic (CAFTA), Mexico–Costa Rica, Mexico–Chile, Mexico–Bolivia, Mexico–Nicaragua, Mexico–Northern Triangle (El Salvador, Guatemala, and Honduras), Chile–Canada, and Mexico–Colombia–Venezuela (or G-3) FTAs. The RoO regimes in these agreements may require a change of chapter, heading, subheading or item, depending on the product in question. In addition, many products combine the change of tariff classification with an exception, regional value content, or technical requirement. The NAFTA model, particularly the versions employed in the US–Chile FTA and CAFTA, is also widely viewed as the likeliest blueprint for the RoO of the Free Trade Area of the Americas (FTAA).

Mercosur RoO, as well as RoO in the Mercosur–Bolivia and Mercosur–Chile FTAs fall between the LAIA–NAFTA extremes. They are mainly based on change of heading and different combinations of regional value content and technical requirements. The Central American Common Market's (CACM) RoO regime can be seen as being located between those of the Mercosur and NAFTA: it uses chiefly change in tariff classification only, but in more precise and diverse ways than Mercosur due to requiring the change to take place at either the chapter, heading, or subheading level, depending on the product in question. The recently concluded CAFTA will, once ratified by all parties, coexist with the CACM's market access mechanisms under the so-called multilateralism principle, which allows

Central American producers to choose between the CACM and CAFTA market access regimes when exporting to the other Isthmus markets.

Notably, unlike the EU's extra-European FTAs that follow the PANEURO system, US bilateral FTAs with extra-Hemispheric partners—Jordan and Israel—diverge markedly from the NAFTA model, operating on VC alone. However, the RoO of the US–Singapore FTA are again more complex, resembling the NAFTA RoO. Similarly, the RoO of the recently forged Chile–South Korea FTA also feature a high degree of sectoral selectivity à la NAFTA, and, indeed, the US–Chile FTA. Nonetheless, the RoO of the Chile–Korea regime are overall less complex than either NAFTA or US–Chile RoO, and also more reliant on the change in heading criterion than NAFTA, which has an important change in chapter component, and US–Chile FTA, which features an important change in subheading component.

iii. Africa, Asia, Middle East: toward sectoral selectivity?

The relative complexity of RoO in Europe and the Americas stands in contrast to the generality of RoO in many Asian, African, and Middle Eastern PTAs. Some of the main integration schemes in these regions—the ASEAN Free Trade Area (AFTA), Australia–New Zealand Closer Economic Relations Trade Agreement (ANZCERTA), Singapore–Australia Free Trade Agreement (SAFTA), and South Pacific Regional Trade and Economic Cooperation (SPARTECA) in Asia–Pacific; the Economic Community of West African States (ECOWAS), Common Market for Eastern and Southern Africa (COMESA), and Namibia–Zimbabwe FTA in Africa; and the Gulf Cooperation Council (GCC) in the Middle East—are based on an across-the-board VC rule that, when defined as RVC, ranges from 25 per cent (in Namibia–Zimbabwe FTA) to 50 per cent (ANZCERTA). Some of the agreements allow, or, indeed, require, RoO to be calculated on the basis of import content. Most of these regimes also specify an alternative RoO based on the CTC criterion; most often the alternative involves a change in heading or, in the case of ECOWAS that has a relatively low RVC requirement of 30 per cent, change in subheading.

However, the more recent RoO regimes in both Africa and Asia-Pacific carry RoO of high degrees of sectoral selectivity. The Southern African Development Community (SADC) RoO approximate the PANEURO model both in the types of sectoral RoO and in sectoral selectivity. Moreover, there have been some initiatives to renegotiate COMESA RoO; such attempts may well eventually lead to regimes of greater complexity. On the Asian front, the RoO of the Japan-Singapore Economic Partnership Agreement (JSEPA) are also complex, as evinced by the more than

200-page RoO protocol. However, much like in the Chile-Korea FTA, nearly half of JSEPA RoO are based on a simple change in heading criterion, which makes the regime much less complex than the PANEURO and NAFTA models. Furthermore, for many products JSEPA introduces an alternative, usually PANEURO-type, free-standing VC rule, which instills generality and flexibility to the agreement.

The intercontinental RoO regimes of the US–Singapore and Chile–Korea FTAs have delivered additional complexity to the Asia–Pacific RoO theater. RoO in these agreements tend to follow the NAFTA model yet be notably less complex overall, featuring a strong change of heading component. The future Mexico–Singapore, Canada–Singapore, Mexico–Korea, Mexico–Japan, and US–Australia FTAs, among others, will likely compound this trend. Meanwhile, further European overtures to the Asian front will likely bring the PANEURO model to accompany the NAFTA model in the region.

B. Non-preferential RoO

Non-preferential RoO are used for purposes distinct from those of preferential rules. Even if a country did not use preferential RoO, it would still apply some type of non-preferential RoO. Unlike preferential RoO that have thus far escaped multilateral regulation, non-preferential RoO have been under a process of harmonization since 1995 as mandated by the Uruguay Round's Agreement on Rules of Origin (ARO). The harmonization work, propelled precisely by growing concerns about the divergent national RoO's effects on trade flows, has been carried out under the auspices of the Committee on Rules of Origin (CRO) of the World Trade Organization (WTO) and the Technical Committee on Rules of Origin (TCRO) of the Brussels-based World Customs Organization. The latter has been responsible for the technical part of the work, including discussions on the RoO options for each product.

The harmonization drive was initially scheduled for completion by July 1998. However, the deadline has been extended several times since then. The Technical Committee's work was concluded in 1999, with about 500 pending issues that could not be solved at the technical level being sent to the CRO in Geneva. As of July 2003, the process at the WTO had yet to reach a solution to 94 core policy issues; these affect an estimated fifth of the tariff subheadings of the entire tariff universe. The General Council at the time extended the deadline for completion of the issues to July 2004, and agreed that following resolution of these core policy issues, the CRO would complete its remaining work by the end of 2004. In their current structure, the non-preferential RoO approximate the PANEURO and NAFTA models in sectoral specificity, yet are less demanding than either of the two main RoO regimes. However, since several issues are still contested at the WTO, the final degree of complexity and restrictiveness of the non-preferential RoO remains to be gauged.

C. Depicting product-specific RoO around the world

Figure 3.1 focuses on the first RoO component, the CTC criterion, in the RoO regimes of 29 PTAs around the world. These are three of the EU's PTAs (PANEURO—where the RoO are basically fully identical to those of the EU–South Africa FTA—and the EU–Mexico and EU–Chile FTAs); EFTA-Mexico FTA where RoO approximate the EU–Mexico RoO model; seven FTAs drawing on the NAFTA RoO model that is gaining prominence in the Western Hemisphere (NAFTA, US–Chile, CAFTA, Group of Three, and Mexico–Costa Rica, Mexico–Bolivia, and Canada–Chile FTAs); CACM-Chile FTA; Mercosur–Chile and Mercosur–Bolivia FTAs; LAIA; seven PTAs in Asia–Pacific (ANZCERTA, SAFTA, SPARTECA, AFTA, Bangkok Agreement, JSEPA, and Chile–Korea FTA); four PTAs in Africa (ECOWAS, COMESA, Namibia–Zimbabwe FTA, and SADC); the Gulf Cooperation Council in the Middle East; and US extrahemispheric FTAs with Jordan and Israel. The two final sets of bars depict two potential outcomes of the harmonization process of the non-preferential RoO (as set to their 'lowest' and 'highest' levels of stringency, which will be discussed in the next section).[17]

The change-of-heading criterion dominates EU RoO, whereas the RoO built upon the NAFTA RoO regime are based on change of heading and change of chapter criteria at relatively even quantities. The US–Chile FTA and CAFTA stand somewhat apart from the NAFTA format for requiring only change in subheading for a substantial number of tariff lines. Meanwhile, the Chile-CACM FTA diverges from the NAFTA model due to its marked change in heading-component, as do the Japan–Singapore and Chile–Korea FTAs. The other Asian PTAs considered here stand out for their generality—for using an across-the-board value-content requirement exclusively. Except for the SADC, African RoO regimes are also marked by general, across-the-board CTC RoO, as are LAIA and Mercosur's FTAs with Chile and Bolivia that employ the change-of-heading criteria across the RoO universe. In contrast to the PANEURO and NAFTA models, non-preferential RoO feature also a prominent change-of-subheading component.

---

[17] The figure is based on the first RoO only when two or more possible RoO are provided for a tariff subheading.

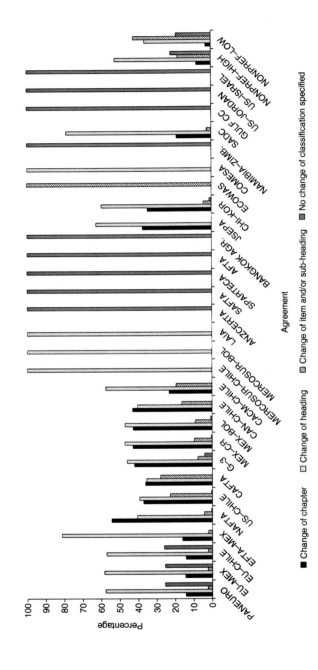

Fig. 3.1 Distribution of CTC criteria by agreement.

Source: Authors' calculations on the basis of PTA texts.

Another notable difference between the various PTAs is that some, such as ANZCERTA, employ the VC criterion across sectors, completely foregoing the use of the CTC-criterion. The EU does this in about a quarter of its RoO; the bulk (more than 80 per cent) of these RoO are based on the wholly obtained criterion used particularly in agricultural products, or on the import-content rule that imposes a ceiling of 40–50 per cent to non-originating components of the ex-works price of the final product. The standalone import content RoO are used particularly frequently for optics, transportation equipment, and machinery and electrical equipment. Another idiosyncrasy of the EU RoO, yet one that escapes the figure here, is the use of the so-called 'soft RoO' in more than a quarter of the RoO requiring a change of heading and about a sixth of the RoO requiring a change of chapter. Soft RoO allows the use of inputs from the same heading (or chapter) up to a certain share of the price of the final product even when the RoO requires a change of heading (or change of chapter). The share is generally between 5 and 20 per cent.

Table 3.1 centers on the tariff subheadings governed by VC (including combinations of VC with CTC, and VC when employed as an alternative to a CTC criterion) in various RoO regimes, and, in particular, on the level of the VC criterion. The most usual level of VC is 40–50 per cent, whether defined as MC or RVC. However, in the US–Chile FTA, CAFTA, and Chile–CACM FTA, RVC is generally set at lower levels of 30–35 per cent; at the other extreme, for some products in the PANEURO and SADC regimes, the permitted value of non-originating inputs of the price of the final product is as low as 15–30 per cent. The table also displays the various bases for calculation of the VC. Differences in the method of calculation can have crucial implications to the exporters' capacity to meet the RoO. The PE model that is separated here for analytical purposes essentially involves the same product-specific RoO as the PANEURO model, while diverging somewhat from the PANEURO in the regime-wide RoO. It applies to a handful of European FTAs, particularly to those forged by the EU and East European countries with Israel (WTO 2002a).

Capturing the full scale of variation in the RoO regimes requires a look at the various combinations of RoO components. Table 3.2 displays the RoO combinations in selected FTAs around the world. It considers the entire tariff universe in each RoO regime, and shows the percentage shares of all possible RoO types and combinations thereof in each respective regime. Particularly notable is the high degree of selectivity of PANEURO, NAFTA, and non-preferential RoO.

Table 3.1 VC criteria by agreement

PTA	Value-content criterion (%)		Basis for calculation
	MC	RVC	
PANEURO	50–30		Ex-works price[i]
PE	50–30		Ex-works price
EU–South Africa	50–30		Ex-works price
EU–Mexico	50–30		Ex-works price
EU–Chile	50–30		Ex-works price
EFTA–Mexico	50–30		Ex-works price
NAFTA		50–60	50 net cost; 60 transaction value[ii]
US–Chile		35–45	35 build-up; 45 build-down[iii]
CAFTA		35–45	35 build-up; 45 build-down
Canada–Chile		50–60	50 net cost; 60 transaction value
G–3		50–55[iv]	Transaction value
Mexico–Costa Rica		41.66–50	41.66 net cost; 50 transaction value
Mexico–Bolivia		41.66–50	41.66 net cost; 50 transaction value
Mexico–Chile		40–50	40 net cost; 50 transaction value
CACM		N/A	Transaction value
CACM–Chile		30	Transaction value
Mercosur	40	60	Fob export value[v]
Mercosur–Chile	40		Fob export value[vi]
Mercosur–Bolivia	40		Fob export value
Andean Community	50[vii]		Fob export value
Caricom–Dom. Rep.		N/A	Transaction value
LAIA	50		Fob export value
ANZCERTA		50	Factory cost[viii]
SAFTA		30–50	Factory cost
SPARTECA		50	Factory cost
AFTA		40	Value of content
Bangkok Agreement		40	Ex-works[ix]
Japan–Singapore	40	60	Export value[x]
US–Singapore		30–65	30–35 build-up; 45–65 build-down
Chile–Korea		30–45	30 build-up; 45 build-down
COMESA	60	35	60 value of materials; 35 ex-factory cost[xi]
ECOWAS		30	Factory cost
Namibia–Zimbabwe		25	N/A
SADC	70–35		Ex-works price
Gulf Coop. Council		40[xii]	Ex-works price
US–Jordan		35	Value of materials/processes[xiii]
US–Israel		35	Value of materials/processes
Mexico–Israel		35–45	35 net cost; 45 transaction value
Non-preferential RoO	60–40		Ex-works price

Source: Authors' classification based on PTA texts.

D. Regime-wide RoO

Besides sectoral RoO, the different RoO regimes can be compared by their regime-wide RoO. Table 3.3 contrasts the various RoO regimes by their general, regime-wide RoO—*de minimis*, roll-up, cumulation, and drawback.

First, EU's RoO regimes feature a higher *de minimis* (at 10 per cent) than NAFTA and many other FTAs in the Americas; the exceptions are US–Chile FTA and CAFTA, where *de minimis* is the same as in PANEURO. Meanwhile, there is no *de minimis* rule in Mercosur's FTAs and various FTAs in Asia and Africa. However, the principle does have exceptions in most regimes: for example, EU's *de minimis* does not apply to textiles and apparel, except for allowing an 8 per cent *de minimis* of the total weight of textile materials in mixed textiles products. In the EU–South Africa FTA, *de minimis* is set at 15 per cent but excludes fish and crustaceans, tobacco products, as well as certain meat products and alcoholic beverages. NAFTA *de minimis* does not extend to the production of dairy produce; edible products of animal origin; citrus fruit and juice; instant coffee; cocoa products, and some machinery and mechanical appliances, such as air conditioners and refrigerators (Reyna 1995: 115–117).

Secondly, the roll-up principle is widely used around the world. For example, in NAFTA, a good may acquire originating status if it is produced in a NAFTA country from materials considered as originating (whether such materials are wholly obtained or have satisfied a CTC or RVC criterion) even if no change in tariff classification takes place between the intermediate material and the final product. Similarly, the EU–Mexico FTA stipulates that 'if a product which has acquired originating status by fulfilling the conditions . . . is used in the manufacture of another product, the conditions applicable to the product in which it is incorporated do not apply to it, and no account shall be taken of the non-originating materials which may have been used in its manufacture.'

Thirdly, the EU's Pan–European system of cumulation applied since 1997 draws a clear distinction between the EU RoO regimes on the one hand, and most RoO regimes elsewhere in the world, on the other. The foremost diagonal cumulation regime in the world, the Pan–European system incorporated 16 partners and covered no fewer than 50 FTAs prior to the EU's eastward enlargement.[18] In concrete terms, the system enables producers to use components originating in any of the participating countries without losing the preferential status of the final product. The European Economic Association (EEA) agreement between EU and EFTA permits full cumulation. The EU–South Africa FTA allows both parties to cumulate diagonally with the ACP states. In addition, it incorporates the

---

[18] The participants in the PANEURO system of cumulation prior to the eastward enlargement were the EU, Bulgaria, Czech Republic, Estonia, Hungary, Iceland, Latvia, Liechtenstein, Lithuania, Norway, Poland, Romania, Slovak Republic, Slovenia, Switzerland, and Turkey. Eight of these countries—Czech Republic, Estonia, Hungary, Latvia, Lithuania, Poland, Slovak Republic, and Slovenia—entered the EU in May 2004.

Table 3.2 Distribution of RoO combinations, selected PTAs (1st RoO only)

Requirement	EUROPE					AMERICAS								
	PANEURO	EU-MEX	EU-CHI	EU PRE-97	EFTA-MEX	NAFTA	US-CHI	G3	MEX-CR	MEX-BOL	CAN-CHI	CACM-CHI	MERC-CHI	LAIA
NC	0.39	0.39	0.39	0.20		0.54	0.51	4.05	0.55	0.95	0.04			
NC + ECTC	2.39	2.04	2.39	2.36										
NC + TECH	1.39	1.39	1.39	0.72			0.02							
NC + ECTC + TECH														
NC + VC	11.46	10.91	11.90	11.08				0.02						
NC + ECTC + VC	1.57	1.57	1.57	1.61										
NC + VC + TECH	0.08	0.20	0.20											
NC + WHOLLY OBTAINED CHAPTER	7.62	7.62	7.62	3.24										
NC + WHOLLY OBTAINED HEADING	0.70	0.70	0.70	0.70										
SUBTOTAL	*25.60*	*24.82*	*26.16*	*19.91*	*0.00*	*0.54*	*0.53*	*4.05*	*0.54*	*0.95*	*0.04*	*0.00*	*0.00*	*0.0*
CI											0.99			
CI + ECTC						0.02				0.04	0.23			
CI + TECH					2.17						0.02			
CI + ECTC + TECH														
CI + VC														
CI + ECTC + VC						0.02								
CI + VC + TECH														
SUBTOTAL	*0.00*	*0.00*	*0.00*	*0.00*	*2.17*	*0.04*	*0.00*	*0.00*	*0.04*	*0.00*	*1.24*	*0.00*	*0.00*	*0.0*
CS	0.20	0.20	0.20	0.12		1.29	16.56	1.54	2.99	2.94	10.52	19.16		
CS + ECTC						2.52	5.57	0.73	2.14	1.32	4.13	0.20		
CS + TECH	1.90	1.90	1.78	1.89		0.04	0.14	0.10		0.02	0.11			
CS + ECTC + TECH						0.40	0.04	0.04	0.23	0.43	0.26			
CS + VC	0.27	0.27	0.27	0.37			0.42	4.60	4.25	4.24	0.06	0.03		
CS + ECTC + VC						0.10	0.04				0.10			
CS + VC + TECH								0.04		0.26				
CS + ECTC + VC + TECH								0.83						
SUBTOTAL	*2.37*	*2.37*	*2.25*	*2.38*	*0.00*	*4.35*	*22.77*	*7.88*	*9.66*	*9.21*	*15.18*	*19.39*	*0.00*	*0.0*
CH	32.99	32.99	32.86	38.00	58.79	17.09	23.70	16.45	24.32	7.00	17.42	57.15	46.00	100.0
CH + ECTC	4.60	5.13	4.56	4.10	7.22	19.18	11.19	13.45	19.66	4.27	18.72	0.26		
CH + TECH				0.86		0.02	0.34	0.97		0.22	0.17		20.04	
CH + ECTC + TECH	6.66	6.66	6.66	6.66	9.04	0.14	0.44	0.26		1.74	0.09			
CH + VC	13.01	12.68	12.78	13.56	6.1	3.54	3.25	2.01	2.67	2.17	3.52		9.99	
CH + ECTC + VC	0.37	0.86	0.37	0.42	0.08	0.58	0.48		0.52	0.85	0.52			
CH + VC + TECH						0.10		0.06	0.02	0.01			23.97	
CH + ECTC + VC + TECH	0.02	0.02	0.02	0.02	0.03			4.82		0.89				
SUBTOTAL	*57.65*	*58.34*	*57.25*	*63.62*	*81.26*	*40.65*	*39.40*	*46.02*	*47.19*	*47.15*	*40.44*	*57.41*	*100.00*	*100.0*
CC	2.16	2.16	2.16	2.28		30.95	23.18	21.09	31.05	21.80	29.20	22.94		
CC + ECTC	1.02	1.02	1.02	0.74	0.7	17.71	5.83	5.90	5.65	5.67	8.08	0.26		
CC + TECH	0.04	0.04	0.04	0.04	0.05	0.02	0.06	5.43		6.30	0.04			
CC + ECTC + TECH	11.02	11.25	11.02	11.02	15.41	5.76	8.08	6.65	5.81	6.24	5.74			
CC + VC							0.06	0.14	0.26	0.43				
CC + ECTC + VC														
CC + VC + TECH								2.67		1.24				
CC + ECTC + VC + TECH								0.20						
SUBTOTAL	*14.24*	*14.47*	*14.24*	*14.08*	*16.16*	*54.44*	*37.21*	*42.08*	*42.77*	*42.68*	*43.06*	*23.20*	*0.00*	*0.0*
TOTAL	100	100	100	100	100	100	100	100	100	100	100	100	100	100

Notes: NC = No change in tariff classification required; CI = Change in tariff item; CS = Change in tariff subheading; CH = Change in tariff heading; CC = Change in tariff chapter; ECTC = Exception to change in tariff classification; VC = Value content; TECH = Technical requirement. Calculations at 6-digit level of the Harmonized System.
Source: Author's calculations on the basis of PTA texts.

ASIA/PACIFIC						AFRICA					MIDDLE EAST			NON-PREF	
ANZCERTA	SAFTA	SPARTECA	AFTA	BANGKOK	JSEPA	CHI-KOR	ECOWAS	COMESA	NAM-ZIMB	SADC	GULF CC	US-JORDAN	US-ISRAEL	HIGHEST	LOWEST
						0.51									
														0.72	9.62
100	100	100	100	100		0.78			100		100	83.94	100	11.48	0.06
														0.34	0.5
												10.06		9.39	3.7
					0.42										
100.00	100.00	100.00	100.00	100.00	0.42	1.29	0.00	0.00	100.00	0.00	100.00	100.00	100.00	21.93	18.88
														3.54	6.18
														0.12	0.12
											1.39			0.03	3.09
0.00	0.00	0.00	0.00	0.00	0.00	0.00	0.00	0.00	0.00	0.00	1.39	0.00	0.00	3.84	9.39
						1.68	100				1.16			13.53	30.42
					0.05	0.47								0.64	0.92
															1.41
						2.11									
						0.16									
0.00	0.00	0.00	0.00	0.00	0.05	4.42	100.00	0.00	0.00	0.00	1.16	0.00	0.00	14.17	32.75
					45.81	46.87		100			58.65			40.13	33.88
					14.46	9.12					3.35			11.64	2.22
					0.58	0.17								0.36	
											6.52				
					1.66	2.95					0.13				
					0.10	0.49									
											0.03				
0.00	0.00	0.00	0.00	0.00	62.61	59.57	0.00	100.00	0.00	0.00	78.65	0.00	0.00	52.13	36.10
						22.49					0.68			7.86	2.78
					37.35	4.71								0.1	0.1
						0.08									
						5.67					18.09				
						1.80									
0.00	0.00	0.00	0.00	0.00	37.35	34.75	0.00	0.00	0.00	0.00	18.77	0.00	0.00	7.96	2.81
100	100	100	100	100	100	100	100	100	100	100	100	100	100	100	100

Table 3.3 Regime-wide RoO in selected PTAs

PTA	De minimis (percentage)	Roll-up	Cumulation		Drawback allowed?[vi]
			Bilateral	Diagonal	
PANEURO (50)	10	Yes	Yes	Yes (full in EEA)	No
PE (15)	10	Yes	Yes	Yes	No[xiv]
EU–South Africa	15	Yes	Yes	Yes with ACP (full with SACU)	Not mentioned
EU–Mexico	10	Yes	Yes	No[xv]	No after 2 years
EU–Chile	10	Yes	Yes	No	No after 4 years
EFTA–Mexico	10 (not chs. 50–63)	Yes	Yes	No	No after 3 years
NAFTA	7 (exceptions in agric. and ind. products; 7% of weight in chs. 50–63)	Yes except automotive	Yes	No	No after 7 years
US–Chile	10 (excep. in agric. and processed agric. products)	Yes	Yes	No	No after 12 years
CAFTA	10 (excep. in agric. and ind. products; 7% of weight in chs. 50–63)	Yes	Yes	Yes (in ch 62 w/Mexico & Canada)	Not mentioned
G3	7 (7% of weight in chs. 50–63)	Yes	Yes	No	Not mentioned
Mexico–Costa Rica	7 (excep. in chs. 4–15 and headings 0901, 1701, 2105, 2202)	Yes	Yes	No	No after 7 years
Mexico–Chile	8 (excep. in agric. and ind. products; 9% of weight in chs. 50–63)	Yes	Yes	No	Not mentioned
Mexico–Bolivia	7 (not chs. 1–27 unless CS; not chs. 50–63)	Yes	Yes	No	No after 8 years
Canada–Chile	9 (excep. in agric. and ind. products; 9% of weight in chs. 50–63)	Yes	Yes	No	Not mentioned
CACM–Chile	8 (not chs. 1–27 unless CS)	Yes	Yes	No	Not mentioned
CACM	10 until 2000; 7 from 2001 on (7% of weight in chs. 50–63)	N/A	Yes	No	Yes

Mercosur	Not mentioned	Yes except automotive	Yes	No	Yes (except automotive imports from Arg. and Braz.)
Mercosur–Chile	Not mentioned	Yes	Yes	No	No after 5 years
Mercosur–Bolivia	Not mentioned	Yes	Yes	No	No after 5 years
Caricom	Not mentioned	Not mentioned	Yes	No	Possibly[xvi]
Caricom–DR	7	Not mentioned	Yes	No	Not mentioned
ANZCERTA	2	Yes	Yes	Yes (full)	Yes
SAFTA	2	Yes	Yes[xvii]	No	Not mentioned
SPARTECA	2	Yes	Yes	Yes (full)	Yes
AFTA	Not mentioned	Not mentioned	Yes	No	Yes
Bangkok Agreement	Not mentioned	Yes	Yes[xviii]	No	Possibly[xix]
Japan–Singapore	To be determined	Yes	Yes	No (OP allowed)	Not mentioned
US–Singapore	10 (excep. in various agric. products; 7% of weight in chs. 50–63)	Yes	Yes	No (OP & ISI allowed)	Not mentioned
Chile–Korea	8 (not chs. 1–24 unless CS; 8% of weight in chs. 50–63)	Yes	Yes	No	Not mentioned
COMESA	2[xx]	Yes	Yes	No	No after 10 years
ECOWAS	Not mentioned	Not mentioned	Yes	No	Not mentioned
SADC	10 (not chs. 50–63, 87, 98)	Yes	Yes	No	Not mentioned
Gulf CC	Not mentioned	Not mentioned	Yes	No	Not mentioned
US–Jordan	Not mentioned	Not mentioned	Yes	No	Not mentioned
US–Israel	Not mentioned	Yes	Yes	No	Yes
Canada–Israel	10 (excep. in agric. and ind. products; 7% of weight in chs. 50–63)	Yes	Yes	Yes (w/ a 3rd party with which both have FTA)[xxi]	Not mentioned
Mexico–Israel	10 (excep. in agric. and ind. products; 7% of weight in chs. 50–63)	Yes	Yes	No	Not mentioned

Source: Authors' classification on the basis of PTA texts.

'single territory' concept, whereby South Africa can calculate working or processing carried out within the Southern Africa Customs Union (SACU) area as if these had been performed in South Africa (but not in the EU).

Other cumulation schemes include the ANZCERTA model, which provides for full cumulation, and the Canada–Israel FTA, which permits cumulation with the two countries' common FTA partners, such as the United States. Singapore's FTAs incorporate the outward processing (OP) concept tailored to accommodate Singapore's unique economic features and its access to low-cost processing in neighboring countries. The US–Singapore FTA also incorporates the integrated sourcing initiative (ISI), which provides further flexibility for outsourcing. OP and ISI will be detailed in Section 3.4. CAFTA stands out in the Americas for providing for diagonal cumulation with Canada and Mexico. However, the clause covers only materials used for producing goods in chapter 62, and so only up to a limited amount of imports to the US market and only after Canada and Mexico agree on the clause.

Fourthly, EU's FTAs and FTAs in the Americas tend to explicitly preclude drawback. Nonetheless, both have allowed for phase-out periods during which drawback is permitted. For instance, the EU–Mexico FTA permitted drawback for the first two years, while the EU–Chile FTA allows drawback through 2007, the fourth year of the FTA. NAFTA allowed for drawback for the first seven years; however, drawback in the bilateral trade between Canada and the United States under the agreement was valid for only two years. Importantly, NAFTA does provide leniency in the application of the no-drawback rule by putting in place a refund system, whereby the producer will be refunded the lesser of the amount of duties paid on imported goods and the amount of duties paid on the exports of the good (or another product manufactured from that good) upon its introduction to another NAFTA member. AFTA, ANZCERTA, SPARTECA, the US–Israel FTA, CACM, and Mercosur's FTAs stand out for not prohibiting drawback. However, in Mercosur *per se*, there is a no-drawback rule governing Argentine and Brazilian imports of intermediate automotive products when the final product is exported to a Mercosur partner; this should help place Paraguay and Uruguay at a par with the two larger economies in attracting investment in the automotive sector.

E. Administration of RoO

The various RoO regimes diverge in their administrative requirements, particularly in the method of certification (Table 3.4).

Table 3.4 Certification methods in selected PTAs

PTA	Certification method
PANEURO	Two-step private and public; limited self-certification
PE	Two-step private and public; limited self-certification
EU–South Africa	Two-step private and public; limited self-certification
EU–Mexico	Two-step private and public; limited self-certification
EU–Chile	Two-step private and public; limited self-certification
NAFTA	Self-certification
US–Chile	Self-certification
CAFTA	Self-certification
G3	Two-step private and public
Mexico–Costa Rica	Self-certification
Mexico–Bolivia	Self-certification (two-step private and public during first 4 years)
Canada–Chile	Self-certification
CACM–Chile	Self-certification
CACM	Self-certification
Mercosur	Public (or delegated to a private entity)
Mercosur–Chile	Public (or delegated to a private entity)
Mercosur–Bolivia	Public (or delegated to a private entity)
Andean Community	Public (or delegated to a private entity)
Caricom	Public (or delegated to a private entity)
Caricom–DR	Public (or delegated to a private entity)
LAIA	Two-step private and public
ANZCERTA	Public (or delegated to a private entity)
SAFTA	Public (or delegated to a private entity)
SPARTECA	Not mentioned
AFTA	Public (or delegated to a private entity)
Bangkok Agreement	Public (or delegated to a private entity)
Japan–Singapore	Public (or delegated to a private entity)
US–Singapore	Self-certification
Chile–Korea	Self-certification
COMESA	Two-step private and public
ECOWAS	Public (or delegated to a private entity)
SADC	Two-step private and public
US–Jordan	Self-certification

Source: Authors' classification on the basis of PTA texts.

The EU RoO regimes require the use of a movement certificate, EUR.1, that is to be issued in two steps—by the exporting-country government once application has been made by the exporter or the exporter's competent agency, such as a sectoral umbrella organization. However, the EU regimes provide for an alternative certification method, the invoice declaration, for 'approved exporters' who make frequent shipments and are authorized by the customs authorities of the exporting country to make invoice declarations.

Meanwhile, NAFTA and a number of other FTAs in the Americas as well as the Chile–Korea FTA rely on self-certification, which entails that the exporter's signing the certificate suffices as an affirmation that the items covered by it qualify as originating. In CAFTA, the importer rather than the exporter claiming preferential tariff treatment is the party ultimately responsible for seeing that the good is originating.[19] In Mercosur, Andean Community, Caricom, AFTA, ANZCERTA, SAFTA, the Bangkok Agreement, JSEPA, and ECOWAS require certification by a public body or a private umbrella entity approved as a certifying agency by the government. However, unlike in the two-step model, the exporter is not required to take the first cut at filling out the movement certificate, but, rather, to furnish the certifying agency with a legal declaration of the origin of the product.[20]

The self-certification model can be seen as placing a burden of proof on the importing-country producers; as such, it arguably minimizes the role of the government in the certifying process, entailing rather low administrative costs to exporters and governments alike. In contrast, the two-step system requires heavier involvement by the exporting-country government and increases the steps—and likely also the costs—that an exporter is to bear when seeking certification.

3.4 Analytical coding methodology for RoO Rules of Origin in FTAs

This section presents a methodology for measuring (1) the relative restrictiveness of the product-specific RoO governing different economic sectors in the different agreements; and (2) the degree of flexibility instilled in the various RoO regimes by the various regime-wide RoO, such

[19] The CAFTA certification of origin can be prepared by the importer, exporter, or the producer of the good; alternatively, the importer can claim origin through his/her 'knowledge that the good is an originating good'. Verification of origin can be made via written requests or questionnaires to the importer, exporter, or producer, or by visits by an importing-country authority to the exporting-party territory. Similarly, in the US-Chile FTA, the importer is to declare the good as originating and can also certify origin; however, verification can be made by the customs of the importing member 'in accordance with its customs laws and regulations.' In contrast, in NAFTA, the exporter or producer are parties in charge of certifying origin, and verification of origin is conducted through written requests or visits by one NAFTA member to the premises of an exporter or a producer in the territory of another member.

[20] The certificate in NAFTA, G3, and CACM-Chile FTA will be valid for a single shipment or multiple shipments for a period of a year; in ANZCERTA and SAFTA, the certificate will be valid for multiple shipments for two years. In ECOWAS, the certificate is not required for agricultural, livestock products and handmade articles produced without the use of tools directly operated by the manufacturer. In ANZCERTA, SAFTA, and Mercosur–Chile, Mercosur–Bolivia, and CARICOM-DR FTAs, the certificate needs to be accompanied by a legal declaration by the final producer or exporter of compliance with the RoO. In CAN and CARICOM, declaration by the producer is required. In CARICOM, the declaration can be completed by the exporter if it is not possible for the producer to fill it.

as *de minimis* and drawback. We subsequently compare RoO regimes by the values yielded by these two analytical measures.

A. A comparative analysis of the levels of restrictiveness of product-specific RoO

The NAFTA RoO family is based on the change of chapter rules, whereas the change of tariff heading component figures prominently in the EU and most Asian and African RoO models. As such, these regimes will entail somewhat divergent demands on exporters. However, understanding the implications of membership in the different types of regimes for an exporter operating in a particular industry requires both (1) a measure of the restrictiveness of RoO that allows for a more nuanced sectoral analysis of the requirements imposed by RoO; and (2) an indicator of the overall flexibility instilled in a RoO regime by the various regime-wide RoO. This section presents two such measures: a restrictiveness index, and a facilitation index.

i. Restrictiveness of RoO

The manifold RoO combinations within and across RoO regimes present a challenge for cross-RoO comparisons. This chapter seeks to draw such comparisons through an index grounded on the plausible restrictiveness of a given type of RoO. Estevadeordal (2000) constructs a categorical index ranging from 1 (least restrictive) to 7 (most restrictive) on the basis of NAFTA RoO. The index can be conceptualized as an indicator of how demanding a given RoO is for an exporter. The observation rule for the index is based on two assumptions: (1) change at the level of chapter is more restrictive than change at the level of heading, and change at the level of heading more restrictive than change at the level of subheading, and so on; and (2) VC and TECH attached to a given CTC add to the RoO's restrictiveness (see Appendix I for details).[21]

Figure 3.2 reports the restrictiveness of RoO as calculated at the six-digit level of disaggregation in selected FTAs. The EU RoO regimes are again strikingly alike across agreements. The RoO regimes based on the NAFTA model, such as the G-3, are also highly alike. The Mercosur model pertinent to Mercosur–Chile and Mercosur–Bolivia FTAs is more general, yet

---

[21] Given that the degree of restrictiveness is a function of *ex ante* restrictiveness rather than the effective restrictiveness following the implementation of the RoO, the methodology—much like that of Garay and Cornejo (2002)—is particularly useful for endogenizing and comparing RoO regimes. The methodology allows RoO to be analysed in terms of their characteristics rather than their effects.

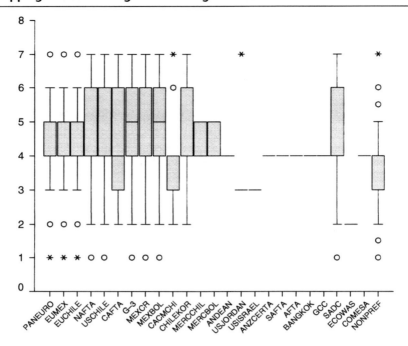

Fig. 3.2 Restrictiveness of RoO in selected PTAs.

Note: Boxplots represent interquartile ranges. The line in the middle of the box represents the median 50th percentile of the data. The box extends from the 25th percentile to the 75th percentile, or through the so-called inter-quartile range (IQR). The whiskers emerging from the boxes extend to the lower and upper adjacent values. The upper adjacent value is defined as the largest data point less than or equal to $x(75) + 1.5$ IQR. The lower adjacent value is defined as the smallest data point greater than or equal to $x(25) + 1.5$ IQR. Observed points more extreme than the adjacent values are individually plotted (outliers and extreme values are marked using '*' and 'o' symbols, respectively).

Source: Authors' calculations on the basis of codes generated per methodology in Appendix I.

still exhibits more cross-sectoral variation in the restrictiveness of RoO than the LAIA model marked by the across-the-board change of heading RoO. The generality of the LAIA model is replicated by most Asian and African RoO regimes. However, some newer PTAs—such as Chile–Korea FTA and SADC—feature high levels of cross-sectoral variation in RoO.

ii. Comparing the restrictiveness of sectoral RoO

To what extent does the restrictiveness of RoO vary across economic sectors? Are some sectors more susceptible to the potential negative trade and investment effects of restrictive RoO than others?

We explore these questions by focusing on twelve RoO regimes with intersectoral variation in RoO. Table 3.5 reports the restrictiveness values in these regimes, as aggregated from 6-digit values by section of the Harmonized System. The average restrictiveness and the standard deviation values at the bottom of the table are based on calculations at the 6-digit level.

The data reveal that agricultural products and textiles and apparel are marked by a particularly high restrictiveness score in each regime, which suggests that the restrictiveness of RoO may be driven by the same political economy variables that arbitrate the level of tariffs particularly in the EU and the United States. Non-preferential RoO exhibit similar patterns across sectors, communicating the operation of political economy dynamics also at the multilateral level. Weighting the sectoral restrictiveness values with trade produces very similar results— which may in and of itself be an indication that stringent RoO stifle commerce.

B. Comparing regime-wide RoO: a facilitation index

Product-specific RoO in complex PTAs—PTAs not carrying across-the-board RoO—can impose highly divergent requirements to the exporters of different goods. Even an across-the-board rule will undoubtedly have more striking implications in some sectors than in others, depending on the product-specific features. However, as discussed above, RoO regimes employ several mechanisms to add flexibility to the application of the product-specific RoO. We strive to capture the combined effect of such mechanisms by developing a regime-wide 'facilitation index'. The index is based on five components: *de minimis*, diagonal cumulation, full cumulation, drawback, and self-certification. The maximum index value of 5 results when the permitted level of *de minimis* is 5 per cent or higher and when the other four variables are permitted by the RoO regime in question.

Figure 3.3 graphs the 'facil index' values for PTAs. The PANEURO and NAFTA models are nearly on a par; the difference here is produced by coding NAFTA as allowing drawback, as it did for the first seven years. The EU–South Africa and the Canada–Israel are the most 'permissive' regimes, the former thanks to drawback and diagonal and full cumulation, and the latter because of self-certification, drawback and cumulation with any of the party's common FTA partners. Meanwhile, many regimes with an across-the-board RoO neither provide for

Table 3.5 Sectoral restrictiveness of sectoral RoO in selected PTAs

HS Section	PAN-EURO	EFTA-MEX	NAFTA	US-Chile	CAFTA	CR-MEX	G-3	Chile-CACM	JSEPA	Chile-Korea	SADC	Non-pref. avg.
1. Live Animals	7.0	5.3	6.0	6.0	6.0	6.0	5.4	5.9	7.0	6.0	7.0	6.2
2. Vegetable Products	6.6	4.0	6.0	6.0	5.9	6.0	6.7	5.6	7.0	6.1	6.6	6.6
3. Fats and Oils	4.7	4.0	6.0	6.0	6.0	6.0	3.5	3.0	7.0	7.0	7.0	4.0
4. Food, Bev. & Tobacco	5.0	4.4	4.7	5.7	5.7	5.4	4.8	3.7	6.8	5.2	5.4	4.6
5. Mineral Products	3.5	3.5	6.0	3.9	4.0	5.7	5.7	5.3	6.6	5.4	4.0	4.8
6. Chemicals	3.9	3.8	5.3	2.6	2.5	3.8	3.9	2.6	3.7	4.0	4.0	2.5
7. Plastics	4.9	4.9	4.8	3.7	3.6	4.2	4.2	3.2	4.0	4.1	4.7	4.0
8. Leather Goods	3.3	3.5	5.6	5.0	4.5	5.5	5.5	3.7	4.0	4.9	3.8	3.4
9. Wood Products	2.9	2.9	4.0	4.1	4.1	4.7	4.6	3.2	4.0	4.1	4.8	3.3
10. Pulp and Paper	4.4	4.6	4.8	4.9	4.9	6.0	6.2	4.1	4.0	4.3	4.3	3.9
11. Textile and App.	6.1	6.1	6.9	5.9	5.9	5.8	5.8	4.5	6.0	5.5	6.1	3.4
12. Footwear	2.8	4.1	4.9	4.8	3.8	4.8	4.3	3.5	4.3	4.7	2.6	3.7
13. Stone and Glass	3.7	3.7	4.9	4.4	4.4	4.9	5.0	4.2	4.0	5.0	3.7	3.5
14. Jewellery	3.7	3.7	5.3	5.2	4.9	5.4	5.4	4.0	4.0	5.4	3.7	3.4
15. Base Metals	4.2	4.2	4.6	4.6	4.6	4.6	4.7	3.8	4.0	4.5	3.9	3.4
16. Mach. & Elec. Eq.	4.8	4.0	3.2	2.9	2.8	3.7	4.5	4.3	6.0	3.8	4.1	3.6
17. Transportation Eq.	4.7	4.2	4.8	4.2	3.7	4.2	3.3	3.4	4.0	4.3	3.8	3.8
18. Optics	5.0	4.4	4.0	4.5	4.1	3.8	4.8	4.0	4.0	4.3	3.9	3.5
19. Arms & Ammun.	4.0	4.0	4.7	5.5	5.5	5.5	5.9	4.0	4.0	4.8	3.1	4.0
20. Works of Art, Misc.	4.1	4.1	5.1	5.3	5.2	5.8	6.0	3.6	4.6	4.7	4.0	3.3
Average	4.5	4.2	5.1	4.8	4.3	4.8	4.9	4.0	4.9	4.9	4.5	3.9
Complexity (Stand. Dev.)	1.4	1.2	1.2	1.6	1.6	1.3	1.5	1.4	1.4	1.4	1.4	1.4

Source: Authors' calculations on the basis of codes generated per methodology in Appendix I.

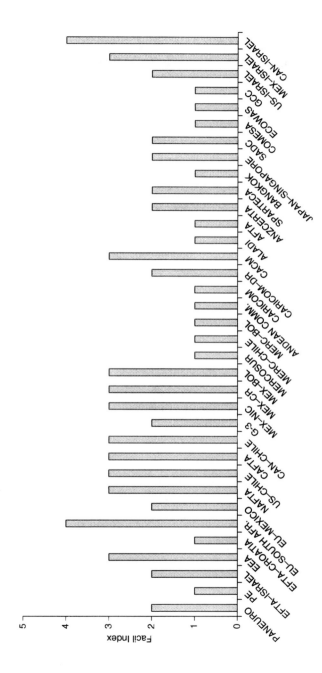

Fig. 3.3 Facilitation index for selected PTAs.

Source: Authors' calculations on the basis of coding scheme above.

de minimis nor feature many regime-wide provisions of flexibility; the most usually occurring regime-wide rule in these PTAs is drawback. Indeed, that regimes with the most stringent RoO and the highest degree of sectoral selectivity in RoO feature the highest facilitation values may evince counterlobbying by producers jeopardized by stringent product-specific RoO.

3.5 RoO 'innovations': *ad hoc* mechanisms for flexibility

This section provides a look at some further dimensions of RoO regimes that go beyond the more traditional and prevalent components included in the restrictiveness and facilitation indices in this study, but that alleviate the impact of stringent RoO: (1) a phase-in period for a stringent value content RoO; (2) permanent deviations for a country or a set of countries from the RoO regime that would otherwise apply; (3) flexibility in the ways of calculating value content; and (4) tariff preference levels (TPLs) employed when the partner lacks intermediate product industries. While most regimes employing these provisions make them applicable to all members, some regimes provide them asymmetrically, for instance to accommodate some country-specific idiosyncrasies in production structures or to provide greater leniency to a developing member country when the parties' development levels differ. These provisions can be of great importance particularly to countries with limited production base and/or in the absence of relatively cheap inputs and production processes in the PTA area.

A. RoO phase-ins

Some regimes have adopted what are in many cases highly detailed product-specific provisions that allow for phasing in of the RoO. Mercosur–Chile FTA provides a seven-year adjustment period for Paraguay to start applying the FTA's import content RoO of 40 per cent in selected headings across a host of sectors such as food products, chemicals, plastics, textiles, apparel, footwear, base metals, and machinery. During the period, Paraguay applies a 60 per cent import content rule. Mercosur–Bolivia FTA allows Bolivia to export to Mercosur some selected goods at 50 per cent import content for the first five years, and others at 60 per cent for three years as opposed to the 40 per cent that will subsequently take effect. For its part, Paraguay can export to Bolivia at 60 per cent import content for the first three years.

Also, the EU's extra-European agreements with Mexico and Chile allow for some product-specific deviations from the PANEURO standard for a certain period of time.[22] In the case of the EU–Mexico FTA, these pertain to one whole chapter (knitted apparel) and to 25 headings (or subheadings) in chemicals, textiles, footwear, machinery, and vehicles, and endure from two to six years prior to converging to the benchmark RoO. In footwear, the RoO is more restrictive for the EU than in its other FTAs: the same RoO applies as in the FTAs with Chile and South Africa up to a certain quota, while the rest of the EU exports to the Mexican market are regulated by much more stringent RoO. The RoO phase-ins are fewer in the case of the EU–Chile FTA, pertaining to textiles and bicycles for the first three years of the agreement.

B. Permanent reductions in the level of RVC

A second means to add leniency to the RoO protocol are permanent deviations for a country or a set of countries from the RoO regime that would otherwise apply. The RoO of the Andean Community allows the less-developed members, Bolivia and Ecuador, to use non-originating components up to 60 per cent of the value of the final good, as opposed to the 50 per cent applicable to the other members. LAIA allows the less-developed partners to use non-originating components of up to 60 per cent of the value of the final good, as opposed to 50 per cent applying to the rest of the members. In COMESA, products of importance to economic development to the partners (selected headings in mineral products, chemicals, machinery, and optical instruments) enjoy a 25 per cent RVC, as opposed to the across-the-board 35 per cent RVC that otherwise applies.

Also, the EU–Mexico and EU–Chile FTAs allow for permanent deviations from the single list, PANEURO model. The deviations are rather minor and apply only to selected industrial products.[23] Nonetheless, they indicate that Mexico and Chile did achieve some favorable sectoral outcomes in the RoO bargaining with the EU.

C. Options for calculating value content

Some regimes have created innovative optional means of calculating value content. In SADC, the more-developed members may allow the less-developed members to count as originating processes that are usually left outside the value-content calculation. Regimes modelled after NAFTA

---

[22] For a detailed treatment, see Estevadeordal and Suominen (2003).
[23] See Estevadeordal and Suominen (2003).

provide a number of optional ways of calculating RVC in vehicles when the producer uses pre-defined intermediate goods from chapters 40 and 84, as well as for calculating the RVC for these intermediate goods.[24]

However, it is Singapore's FTAs that incorporate perhaps the most innovative and comprehensive mechanisms to add flexibility to the calculation of the value content. These are designed to help the many Singaporean industries that have extensive outsourcing ties especially in South-East Asia to qualify for the preferential treatment provided by its FTA partners. The two key mechanisms are outward processing (OP) and integrated sourcing initiative (ISI). OP is recognized in all of Singapore's FTAs, while ISI is incorporated in the US–Singapore FTA. The concept of OP enables Singapore to outsource part of the manufacturing process, usually the lower value-added or labor-intensive activities, to the neighboring countries, yet to count the value of Singaporean production done prior to the outsourcing activity toward local, Singaporean content when meeting the RoO required by the export market. Table 3.6 illustrates the process.

Although the OP concept applies only to products with a value-added rule, it is credited to have encouraged outsourcing of labor-intensive and low-value processes and retaining higher-value activities in Singapore.

For its part, ISI operating in the US-Singapore FTA applies to non-sensitive, globalized sectors, such as information technologies. Under the scheme, certain IT components and medical devices are not subject to RoO when shipped from either of the parties to the FTA partner. ISI is designed to reflect the economic realities of globally distributed production linkages, and to further encourage US multinationals to take advantage of outsourcing opportunities in the ASEAN countries.

D. Tariff Preference Levels

The fourth *ad hoc* mechanism to add leniency to a RoO regime is Tariff Preference Levels (TPLs). TPLs allow goods that would not otherwise satisfy the RoO protocol to qualify for the preferential treatment up to

---

[24] The producer of a vehicle can calculate the RVC by averaging the calculation over the fiscal year by using any one of the following categories: (a) the same model line of vehicles in the same class of vehicles produced in the same plant in the territory of a party; (b) the same class of motor vehicles produced in the same plant in the territory of a party; and (c) the same model line of motor vehicles produced in the territory of a party. Meanwhile, the producer can calculate the RVC intermediate goods for vehicles by (a) averaging the calculation over the fiscal year of the motor vehicle producer to whom the good is sold, over any quarter or month, or over its fiscal year, if the good is sold as an aftermarket part; (b) calculating the average separately for any or all goods sold to one or more motor vehicle producers; or (c) calculating separately those goods that are exported to the territory of the other party.

Table 3.6 Operation of outward processing in Singapore's FTAs

Stage1	Stage 2	Stage 3
Singapore →	Foreign Country →	Singapore → Exported
Conventional RoO →	Stage 3 = Local Content	
Recognition of OP →	Stage 1 + Stage 3 = Local Content	

some pre-specified annual quotas. Above these levels, non-originating goods become subject to the importer's MFN tariff. Most commonly applying to textiles and apparel, TPLs are employed particularly in the NAFTA-model RoO regimes. They are generally extended by all parties to all other parties, made available by any given party on a 'first-come, first-served' basis.

NAFTA provides TPLs for such non-originating products as cotton and manmade fiber apparel, wool apparel, manmade fiber fabrics, and fiber spun yarn. Depending on the product category, they reach up to 80 million square meters equivalent (SMEs) for Canadian and 45 million SMEs for Mexican exports to the US market, and 12 million for selected US exports to Mexico. The most recent RoO regime signed by the US, CAFTA, offers TPLs for only two of the Central American countries, Costa Rican and Nicaragua, and phases them out quickly. In the case of Costa Rica, TPLs are set at 500 000 SMEs, limited to wool, and due to expire in two years. Nicaragua's TPLs start at 100 million SMEs and are phased out in equal annual cuts over five years.

Still other regimes employ what could be viewed as a modified form of TPLs, allocating the quotas not fully free of RoO, but against some more lenient product-specific RoO. For instance, SADC provides quotas at more lenient RoO for the textile and apparel exports of Malawi, Mozambique, Tanzania, and Zambia (MMTZ countries) to the SACU region for a period of five years.

3.6 Policy recommendations: counteracting restrictive RoO and the splintering of the global RoO panorama

While RoO are not necessarily bad for sound economic decisions, restrictive RoO can be. Furthermore, the existing differences in the product-specific and regime-wide RoO *across* the different RoO regimes can even in a simplified bi- or tripolar RoO world make a difference in economic decisions and limit exporters' opportunities for diversifying markets.

How can the potential frictions created by stringent RoO and cross-regime differences in RoO be reduced? How can entrepreneurs import inputs from the cheapest sources, firms exploit cross-border economies of scale at lowest costs, and multinational companies make sweeping investment decisions based on economic efficiency rather than distortionary policies? What are the best ways to counter the development of trade- and investment-diverting hubs in favor of a globally free flow of goods, services, and investment?

Abolishing RoO altogether would certainly be the best and simplest means to counteract the impact of RoO. Another way to relegate RoO to irrelevance is by bringing MFN tariffs to zero globally. However, since these options are hardly politically palatable in the near future, a third possibility is to harmonize preferential RoO at the global level. Establishing a small set of RoO combinations—a 'RoO band'— would be a good start. This would ensure that at least the required production methods in a given sector would remain relatively similar across export markets—and enhance the prospects of linking agreements with each other in the future. Measures to accompany the harmonization work could involve (1) the incorporation of the various mechanisms of flexibility to RoO regimes during the transition to a global RoO regime; and (2) the establishment of a multilateral mechanism to monitor the member states' implementation of preferential and non-preferential RoO.

To be sure, harmonization would not be a simple endeavor given the differences in the types of RoO around the world. Even slight differences can be difficult to overcome due to political resistance by sectors benefiting from status quo. Meanwhile, it is not clear that a strong global exporter lobby would materialize to voice demands for harmonization. Perhaps most importantly, both the EU and the US would likely in principle be reluctant to adopt each other's RoO. Both parties would likely also be concerned of the counterpart's striving for a RoO regime that would allow it to trans-ship via the parties' common PTA partners, such as Mexico, to the other party's market.

However, adopting global regulations for preferential RoO regimes is not necessarily all that daunting. There are five sources of optimism.

First, the WTO members have already been able to sit down and compromise on harmonized non-preferential RoO, which not only evinces a reservoir of political will to tackle RoO, but also provides an immediately available blueprint for harmonizing preferential RoO. And not only are non-preferential RoO negotiated and readily available as a model, but they make a good model: overall, they are less restrictive and complex than either the NAFTA- or PANEURO-type RoO.

Secondly, preferential RoO would likely prove easier to negotiate than non-preferential RoO. Non-preferential RoO involve tracking the production process all the way to the country in which the good originates, while preferential RoO simply require a determination that the final exporter country is also the country of origin: the good either originates in the PTA area or it does not, with the 'true' and very initial origin being immaterial. Preferential RoO talks would thus likely engage a smaller number of interested parties to contest a given rule. Moreover, unlike non-preferential RoO that are employed in the application of numerous other trade-policy instruments, preferential RoO have few purposes beyond refereeing the market access of goods to the PTA space. As such, their negotiation would probably not involve as much consideration of the other WTO agreements as the harmonization of non-preferential RoO does.

Thirdly, the growing attention at the WTO on PTAs in general and preferential RoO, in particular, should propel constructive proposals as to the types of RoO that are most conducive to the march toward unfettered global flow of commerce. For the first time in its history, the WTO Committee on Regional Trade Agreements (CRTA) has decided to consider RoO a 'systemic' issue, as opposed to both individual PTA issues such as prior considerations of the PANEURO system, and issues that—whether systemic or individual—are not being prioritized by the CRTA.

Fourthly, advances in Trade-Related Investment Measures (TRIMS) can help advance the harmonization of RoO, if RoO are viewed, as they rightfully can and should be, as policy instruments affecting investment decisions (Thorstensen 2002). Like TRIMS, RoO can be employed strategically as an incentive to attract investment and encourage exports— *and* exports with high local value. A sturdier multilateral regulatory framework on investment policies could help curb the strategic, trade- and investment-distorting uses of RoO.

Harmonization of preferential RoO—and harmonization toward a flexible-regime model—provides at present the most attainable means to counteract RoO's negative effects on global trade and investment. The negotiators of the Doha Trade Round should decisively tackle RoO as a distortionary trade and investment policy instrument, and do so in four concrete ways.

First, they should provide a forceful push for completing the task of harmonizing non-preferential RoO. Completing the harmonization process is all the more compelling in the face of the growth of global commerce and the increasing fragmentation of global production, both of which would thrive under a clear and uniform set of rules.

Secondly, the Doha negotiators should launch a process of *de jure* harmonization of preferential Rules of Origin. The relatively high levels of restrictiveness of the main RoO regimes and the differences between regimes pose unnecessary policy hurdles to rational economic decisions, limiting the opportunities for exporters to operate on multiple trade fronts simultaneously, and hampering consumers' access to the best goods at the lowest prices.

Thirdly, the Doha Round should forge in a multilateral mechanism to monitor and enforce the transparent application of both preferential and non-preferential RoO. And fourthly, RoO should be incorporated in the TRIMs negotiations.

Preferential RoO matter only as long as there are MFN tariffs. Thus, the ultimate key to counteracting preferential RoO's negative effects lies in the success of multilateral liberalization. Should multilateral trade rounds result in deep MFN tariff lowerings and the proliferation of PTAs engender a dynamic of competitive liberalization worldwide, the importance of preferential RoO as gatekeepers of commerce would automatically dissolve.

3.7 Conclusion

This chapter has sought to present a novel descriptive and analytical mapping of the global Rules of Origin panorama. We have (1) reviewed the types of RoO used around the world; (2) drawn comparisons between the structure of RoO across a host of PTAs; (3) presented methodologies for constructing generalizable measurements for (a) the degree of restrictiveness and selectivity of product-specific RoO, and (b) the level of flexibility provided by the various regime-wide RoO; and (4) explored the behavior of RoO over time. We have also sought to chart some of the main *ad hoc* measures in RoO regimes, and offer policy recommendations for reducing the actual restrictiveness of RoO and the proliferation of divergent types of RoO regimes around the world.

We have provided precursory evidence that RoO are to an important extent driven by political-economy dynamics. The analytical tools developed here can be employed to evaluate the politics behind the definition of RoO as well as the economic effects of RoO. On a broader level, we have striven to help pave the way for further efforts to disaggregate PTAs by the various disciplines they prescribe. Such a task is central for developing a full understanding of the extent of contractual diversity in the rapidly proliferating PTA universe. It is also crucial for moving the debate on the effects of PTAs on the multilateral trading system toward PTA-PTA comparisons—and, ultimately, for making recommendations for designing PTAs in ways that are conducive to unfettered global commerce.

References

Cadot, O., J. de Melo, M. Olarreaga. 2001. 'Can Duty Drawbacks Have a Protectionist Bias? Evidence from Mercosur.' World Bank Working Paper 2523. Washington, DC: The World Bank.

Driessen, B., F. Graafsma. 1999. 'The EC's Wonderland: An Overview of the Pan-European Harmonised Origin Protocols.' *Journal of World Trade* 1999, 33 (4).

Estevadeordal, A. 2000. 'Negotiating Preferential Market Access: The Case of the North American Free Trade Agreement.' *Journal of World Trade* 34, 1 (February).

Estevadeordal, A., R. Robertson. 2002. 'Do Preferential Trade Agreements Matter for Trade? The FTAA and the Pattern of Trade.' Paper prepared for the IDB-INTA/Harvard University Conference on *FTAA and Beyond: Prospects for Integration in the Americas*. Punta del Este, Uruguay, 15–16 December.

Estevadeordal, A., K. Suominen. 2004a. 'Opening the PTA Universe: Trade Effects of Rules of Origin.' Journal article (in progress).

Estevadeordal, A. 2004b. 'Rules of Origin: What Impact on Development?' Journal article (in progress).

Estevadeordal, A. 2003. 'Rules of Origin in FTAs in Europe and in the Americas: Issues and Implications for the EU-Mercosur Inter-Regional Association Agreement.' In Valladão, Alfredo G.A. and Roberto Bouzas (ed.), *Market Access for Goods & Services in the EU-Mercosur Negotiations*, Paris: Chaire Mercosur de Sciences Po.

Estevadeordal, A., E. Lopez-Córdova, K. Snominen. 2005. Rules of Origin and Investment Effects—Inter-American Development Bank (mimo).

Falvey, R., G. Reed. 2000. Rules of Origins as Commercial Policy Instruments. Research Paper No 2000/18. Centre for Research on Globalization and Labor Markets, University of Nottingham.

Garay, L., R. Cornejo. 2002. Metodología para el Análisis de Régimenes de Origen: Aplicación Jen el Caso de las Américas. INTAL-ITD-STA. Documents de Trapajo 8. Washington, DC: Inter-American Development Bank.

Ghosh, S., S. Yamarik. 2003. 'Does Trade Creation Measure Up? A Re-Examination of the Effects of Regional Trading Arrangements.' Draft (February).

Hirsch, M. 2002. 'International Trade Law, Political Economy and Rules of Origin: A Plea for a Reform of the WTO Regime on Rules of Origin.' *Journal of World Trade* 36, 2 (April).

Inter-American Development Bank (IADB). 2002. *Beyond Borders: The New Regionalism in Latin America*. Economic and Social Progress in Latin America, 2002 Report. Washington, DC: IADB.

Jensen-Moran, J. 1996. 'Trade Battles as Investment Wars: The Coming Rules of Origin Debate.' *The Washington Quarterly* 19, 1 (Winter).

Kowalczyk, C., D. Davis. 1998. 'Tariff Phase-Outs: Theory and Evidence from GATT and NAFTA.' In Jeffrey Frankel (ed.) *The Regionalization of the World Economy*. Chicago: University of Chicago Press.

Krishna, K., A. O. Kruger. 1995. 'Implementing Free Trade Areas: Rules of Origin and Hidden protection.' In Alan Deardorff, James Levinsohn and Robert Stern (eds.) *New Directions in Trade Theory*. Ann Arbor: University of Michigan Press.

Krueger, A. O. 1993. 'Free Trade Agreements as Protectionist Devices: Rules of Origin.' NBER Working Paper No. 4352. Cambridge, MA: NBER.

Lloyd, P. J. 2001. 'Rules of Origin and Fragmentation of Trade.' In Leonard K. Cheng and Henryk Kierzkowski (ed.) *Global Production and Trade in East Asia*. Boston, MA: Kluwer Academic Publishers.

Milner, H. V. 1997. 'Firms, States and Regional Trade Blocs.' In Edward D. Mansfield, and Helen V. Milner (ed.) *The Political Economy of Regionalism*. New York: Columbia University Press.

Olarreaga, M., I. Soloaga. 1998. 'Endogenous Tariff Formation: The Case of MERCOSUR.' *World Bank Economic Review* 12, 2: 297–320.

Reya, J. V. 1995. *Passport to Northern American Trade: Rules of Origin and Customs Procedures under NAFTA*. Colorado Springs: Shephard's/McGraw-Hill, 1995.

Suominen, K. 2003. 'Selective Liberalization in Response to Globalization: Rules of Origin as Determinants of Market Access Provisions in PTAs.' *Integration & Trade* 19, 7 (July–December).

Suominen, K. 2004. *Rules of Origin in Global Commerce*. PhD Dissertation, University of California, San Diego.

Thorstensen, V. 2002. Regras de origem: as negociações e implicações para a política de comércio exterior. *Revista Brasileira de Comércio. Exterior*. 15, 73 (outubro-dezembro).

World Trade Organization (WTO). 1998. 'Inventory of non-Traffic Provisions in Regional Trade Agreements.' Committee on Regional Trade Agreements (5 May).

World Trade Organization (WTO). 2002a. 'Rules of Origin Regimes in Regional Trade Agreements.' Committee on Regional Trade Agreements (5 April).

World Trade Organization (WTO). 2002b. 'Coverage, Liberalization Process and Transitional Provisions In Regional Trade Agreements.' Committee on Regional Trade Agreements (5 April).

Appendix I

The observation rule yields a RoO index as follows:

$$y = 1 \text{ if } y^* \leq CI$$
$$y = 2 \text{ if } CI < y^* \leq CS$$
$$y = 3 \text{ if } CS < y^* \leq CS \text{ and } VC$$
$$y = 4 \text{ if } CS \text{ and } VC < y^* \leq CH$$
$$y = 5 \text{ if } CH < y^* \leq CH \text{ and } VC$$
$$y = 6 \text{ if } CH \text{ and } VC < y^* \leq CC$$
$$y = 7 \text{ if } CC < y^* \leq CC \text{ and } TECH$$

where y^* is the latent level of restrictiveness of RoO (rather than the observed level of restrictiveness); CI is change of tariff classification at the level of tariff item (8–10 digits), CS is change at the level of subheading (6-digit HS), CH is change at the level of heading (4 digits), and CC is change at the level of chapter (2 digits HS); VC is a value-content criterion; and TECH is a technical requirement.

We make three modifications to the observation rule in the case of RoO for which no CTC is specified in order to allow for coding of such RoO in the PANEURO, SADC and other regimes where not all RoO feature a CTC component. First, RoO based on the import content rule are equated to a change in heading (value 4) if the content requirement allows up to 50 per cent of non-originating inputs of the ex-works price of the product. Value 5 is assigned when the share of permitted non-originating inputs is below 50 per cent, as well as when the import content criterion is combined with a technical requirement. Secondly, RoO featuring an exception alone is assigned the value of 1 if exception concerns a heading or a number of headings, and 2 if the exception concerns a chapter or a number of chapters. Thirdly, RoO based on the wholly obtained criterion are assigned value 7.

To be sure, the observation rule is somewhat crude (1) for accounting for the restrictiveness of a standalone TECH RoO, which is likely more demanding than a coding of 1–2 allows; and (2) for capturing subtleties of the EU RoO as it does not account for the 'soft' CTC criterion used by the EU. However, it does allow for establishing useful cross-regime comparisons.

Appendix IIa PTAs around the world, by year of entry into force and full name

PTA	ENTRY YR	FULL NAME/TYPE
EU–ICELAND	1973	PANEURO
EU–NORWAY	1973	PANEURO
EU–SWITZERLAND	1973	PANEURO
BANGKOK AGREEMENT	1976	
LAIA	1981	Latin American Integration Association
SPARTECA	1981	South Pacific Regional Trade and Economic Cooperation Agreement
ANZCERTA	1983	Australia-New Zealand Closer Economic Relations Trade Agreement
GULF CC	1983	Gulf Cooperation Council
US–ISRAEL	1985	
ECOWAS Trade Liberalisation Scheme	1990	Economic Community of West African States
MERCOSUR	1991	Southern Common Market
NAMIBIA–ZIMBABWE	1992	
EFTA–CZECH REPUBLIC	1992	PANEURO
EU–CZECH REPUBLIC	1992	PANEURO
EU–HUNGARY	1992	PANEURO
EU–SLOVAK REPUBLIC	1992	PANEURO
EFTA–SLOVAK REPUBLIC	1992	PANEURO
EFTA–TURKEY	1992	PANEURO
EU–POLAND	1992	PANEURO
EU–BULGARIA	1993	PANEURO
AFTA	1993	ASEAN Free Trade Area
CEFTA	1993	Central European Free Trade Area/PANEURO
EFTA–BULGARIA	1993	PANEURO
EFTA–ISRAEL	1993	PANEURO
EFTA–HUNGARY	1993	PANEURO
EFTA–POLAND	1993	PANEURO
EFTA–ROMANIA	1993	PANEURO
EU–ROMANIA	1993	PANEURO
BAFTA	1994	Baltic Free Trade Agreement/PANEURO
COMESA	1994	Common Market for Eastern and Southern Africa
EEA	1994	European Economic Area/PANEURO
NAFTA	1994	North American Free Trade Agreement
G3	1995	Group of Three
EFTA–SLOVENIA	1995	PANEURO
EU–LATVIA	1995	PANEURO
EU–LITHUANIA	1995	PANEURO
EU–ESTONIA	1995	PANEURO
MEXICO–BOLIVIA	1995	
MEXICO–COSTA RICA	1995	
EFTA–ESTONIA	1996	PANEURO
EFTA–LATVIA	1996	PANEURO
EFTA–LITHUANIA	1996	PANEURO
SLOVENIA–LATVIA	1996	PANEURO
SLOVENIA–FYROM	1996	PE
MERCOSUR–CHILE	1996	
CZECH REPUBLIC–LITHUANIA	1997	PANEURO
POLAND–LITHUANIA	1997	PANEURO
SLOVAK REPUBLIC–ISRAEL	1997	PANEURO
SLOVENIA–ESTONIA	1997	PANEURO
CZECH–ISRAEL	1997	PANEURO
CZECH–LATVIA	1997	PANEURO
SLOVAK REPUBLIC–LATVIA	1997	PANEURO
SLOVAK REPUBLIC–LITHUANIA	1997	PANEURO
SLOVENIA–LITHUANIA	1997	PANEURO
EU–FAROE ISLANDS	1997	PE

Appendix IIa (*Continued.*)

PTA	ENTRY YR	FULL NAME/TYPE
TURKEY–ISRAEL	1997	PE
CAN–CHILE	1997	
CAN–ISRAEL	1997	
MERCOSUR–BOLIVIA	1997	
CZECH–ESTONIA	1998	PANEURO
HUNGARY–TURKEY	1998	PANEURO
ROMANIA–TURKEY	1998	PANEURO
SLOVAK REPUBLIC–ESTONIA	1998	PANEURO
SLOVAK REPUBLIC–TURKEY	1998	PANEURO
TURKEY–LITHUANIA	1998	PANEURO
CZECH REPUBLIC–TURKEY	1998	PANEURO
HUNGARY–ISRAEL	1998	PE
POLAND–ISRAEL	1998	PE
SLOVENIA–CROATIA	1998	PE
SLOVENIA–ISRAEL	1998	PE
EU–TUNISIA	1998	
EU–SLOVENIA	1999	PANEURO
POLAND–LATVIA	1999	PANEURO
CHILE–MEXICO	1999	
TURKEY–BULGARIA	1999	
EFTA–MOROCCO	1999	
HUNGARY–LITHUANIA	2000	PANEURO
POLAND–TURKEY	2000	PANEURO
TURKEY–LATVIA	2000	PANEURO
TURKEY–SLOVENIA	2000	PANEURO
HUNGARY–LATVIA	2000	PANEURO
BULGARIA–FYROM	2000	PE
TURKEY–FYROM	2000	PE
EU–ISRAEL	2000	PE
SADC	2000	Southern African Development Community
EU–MEXICO	2000	
EU–SOUTH AFRICA	2000	
MEXICO–ISRAEL	2000	
EU–MOROCCO	2000	
US–JORDAN	2001	
EFTA–MEXICO	2001	
EFTA–CROATIA	2002	PANEURO
EU–CROATIA	2002	PANEURO
CACM–CHILE	2002	
JSEPA	2002	Japan–Singapore Economic Partnership Agreement
SAFTA	2003	Singapore–Australia Free Trade Agreement
EU–CHILE	2003	
EFTA–SINGAPORE	2003	
CHILE–SOUTH KOREA	2003	
US–CHILE	2003	
US–SINGAPORE	2004	
CAFTA	Yet to be ratified	US–Central America Free Trade Agreement

Appendix IIb Selected PTAs by member states

	PTA	MEMBERS
AFTA		Brunei, Darussalam, Cambodia, Indonesia, Laos, Malaysia, Myanmar, Philippines, Singapore, Thailand, Vietnam
ANZCERTA		Australia, New Zealand
BAFTA		Estonia, Latvia, Lithuania
BANGKOK AGREEMENT		Bangladesh, China, India, Republic of Korea, Laos, Sri Lanka
CACM		Costa Rica, El Salvador, Guatemala, Honduras, Nicaragua
CAFTA		Costa Rica, El Salvador, Guatemala, Honduras, Nicaragua, United States and Dominican Republic
CARICOM		Antigua and Barbuda, the Bahamas, Barbados, Belize, Dominica, Grenada, Guyana, Haiti, Jamaica, Montserrat, St. Lucia, St. Kitts and Nevis, St. Vincent and the Grenadines, Suriname, Trinidad and Tobago
CEFTA		Bulgaria, Czech Republic, Hungary, Poland, Romania, Slovak Republic, Slovenia
COMESA		Angola, Burundi, Comoros, Democratic Republic of Congo, Djibouti, Egypt, Eritrea, Ethiopia, Kenya, Madagascar, Malawi, Mauritius, Namibia, Rwanda, Seychelles, Sudan, Swaziland, Uganda, Zambia, Zimbabwe
EEA		EU, Iceland, Liechtenstein, Norway
EFTA		Iceland, Liechtenstein, Norway, Switzerland
ECOWAS		Benin, Burkina Faso, Cabo Verde, Ivory Coast, Gambia, Ghana, Guinea, Guinea Bissau, Mali, Liberia, Niger, Nigeria, Senegal, Sierra Leone, Togo, Namibia, Zimbabwe
FSRs		Belarus, Kazakhstan, Kyrgyz Republic, Russia
G3		Mexico, Colombia, Venezuela
GULF CC		Bahrain, Kuwait, Oman, Qatar, Saudi Arabia, United Arab Emirates
JSEPA		Japan, Singapore
LAIA		Argentina, Bolivia, Brazil, Chile, Colombia, Cuba, Ecuador, Mexico, Paraguay, Peru, Uruguay, Venezuela
MERCOSUR		Argentina, Brazil, Paraguay, Uruguay
NAFTA		US, Canada, Mexico
SADC		Angola, Botswana, Lesotho, Malawi, Mauritius, Mozambique, Namibia, South Africa, Swaziland, Tanzania, Zambia, Zimbabwe
SAFTA		Singapore, Australia
SPARTECA		Australia, New Zealand, Cook Islands, Fiji, Kiribati, Marshall Islands, Micronesia, Nauru, Niue, Papua New Guinea, Solomon Islands, Tonga, Tuvalu, Vanuatu, Western Samoa

Notes for tables

[i] Ex-works price means the price paid for the product ex works to the manufacturer in the Member States in whose undertaking the last working or processing is carried out, provided the price includes the value of all the materials (the customs value at the time of importation of the non-originating materials used, or the first ascertainable price paid for the materials in the member state concerned) used, minus any internal taxes that are, or may be, repaid when the product obtained is exported.

[ii] The transaction method is:

$$RVC = (TV - VNM/TV) \times 100,$$

where RVC is the regional value content, expressed as a percentage; TV is the transaction value of the good adjusted to a FOB basis; and VNM is the value of non-originating materials used by the producer in the production of the good.
The net cost method is

$$RVC = [(NC - VNM)/NC] \times 100,$$

where RVC is the regional value content, expressed as a percentage; NC is the net cost of the good; and VNM is the value of non-originating materials used by the producer in the production of the good.

[iii] The build-down method is

$$RVC = [(AV - VNM)/AV] \times 100;$$

the build-up method is:

$$RVC = (VOM/AV) \times 100,$$

where RVC is the regional value content, expressed as a percentage; AV is the adjusted value; VNM is the value of non-originating materials used by the producer in the production of the good; and VOM is the value of originating materials used by the producer in the production of the good.

[iv] The initial VC for chs. 28–40 is 40 per cent for the first three years, 45 per cent during the fourth and fifth years, and 50 per cent starting in year six. For chs. 72–85 and 90, VC is 50 per cent for the first five years, and 55 per cent starting year six.

[v] The Mercosur RoO is 60 per cent RVC, and, additionally, change in tariff heading (Garay and Cornejo 2002). When it cannot be determined that a change in heading has taken place, the CIF value of the non-originating components cannot exceed 40 per cent of the FOB value of the final good. Special RoO apply to selected sensitive sectors, including chemical, some information technology, and certain metal products.

[vi] The requirement is that the CIF value of the non-originating materials does not exceed 40 per cent of the FOB export value of the final good.

[vii] A 50 per cent MC rule applies to Colombia, Peru and Venezuela; products from Bolivia and Ecuador are governed by a 60 per cent MC rule.

[viii] The value-added test and is based on the formula: Qualifying Expenditure (Q/E)/Factory Cost (F/C), where Q/E = Qualifying expenditure on materials + qualifying labor and overheads (includes inner containers); and F/C = Total expenditure on materials + qualifying labor and overheads (includes inner containers). The factory or works cost are essentially the sum of costs of materials (excluding customs, excise or other duties), labor, factory overheads, and inner containers.

[ix] The agreement requires the value added ensuing from their production in member states be not less than 40 per cent of their final value 'at the termination of

the production phase'. In addition, the share owned by the citizens of the member states of the producing plant cannot be less than 51 per cent.

[x] The MC criterion is calculated from CIF and FOB as follows:

$$NOM = (MCIF/FOB) \times 100.$$

where NOM is the value content of non-originating materials, MCIF is the CIF value on non-originating materials, and FOB is the free on-board value payable by the buyer to the seller.

[xi] The origin protocol requires that either the CIF value of non-originating materials does not exceed 60 per cent of the total cost of the materials used in the production of the goods; or that the value added (the difference between the ex-factory cost of the finished product and the CIF value of the materials imported from outside the member states and used in the production) resulting from the process of production accounts for at least 35 per cent of the ex-factory cost (the value of the total inputs required to produce a given product) of the goods.

[xii] Besides the 40 per cent RVC rule, the share of member states' citizens of the plant that produced the product must be at least 51 per cent.

[xiii] The RVC is calculated as the sum of (i) the cost or value of the materials produced in the exporting Party, plus (ii) the direct costs of processing operations performed in the exporting party. It cannot be less than 35 per cent of the appraised value of the article at the time it is entered into the other party.

The cost or value of materials produced in a party includes: (i) the manufacturer's actual cost for the materials, (ii) when not included in the manufacturer's actual cost for the materials, the freight, insurance, packing, and all other costs incurred in transporting the materials to the manufacturer's plant, (iii) the actual cost of waste or spoilage (material list), less the value of recoverable scrap, and (iv) taxes and/or duties imposed on the materials by a party, provided they are not remitted upon exportation. When a material is provided to the manufacturer without charge, or at less than fair market value, its cost or value shall be determined by computing the sum of: (i) all expenses incurred in the growth, production, or manufacture of the material, including general expenses, (ii) an amount for profit, and (iii) freight, insurance, packing, and all other costs incurred in transporting the material to the manufacturer's plant.

Direct costs of processing operations mean those costs either directly incurred in, or that can be reasonably allocated to, the growth, production, manufacture, or assembly, of the specific article under consideration. Such costs include, for example, (i) all actual labor costs involved in the growth, production, manufacture, or assembly, of the specific article, including fringe benefits, on-the-job training, and the cost of engineering, supervisory, quality control, and similar personnel, (ii) dies, molds, tooling and depreciation on machinery and equipment that are allocable to the specific article, (iii) research, development, design, engineering, and blueprint costs insofar as they are allocable to the specific article; and (iv) costs of inspecting and testing the specific article.

xiv Drawback is not mentioned in Hungary–Israel, Poland–Israel, Slovenia–Croatia, Slovenia–FYROM FTAs. Drawback allowed for the first two years in EU–Palestinian Authority, two and one half years in EFTA–Palestinian Authority, three years in EFTA–FYROM, one year in Bulgaria–FYROM, three months in Turkey–FYROM, and two years in Israel–Slovenia.

xv Joint Declaration I of the FTA opens the possibility for full cumulation, stating that 'or that purpose, the Parties will examine the parameters to be considered in evaluating the economic conditions needed to eventually implement full cumulation. This process will begin no later than three years after entry into force of this Decision.'

xvi The Revised Treaty of Chaguaramas Establishing the Caribbean Community, including the CARCIOM Single Market and Economy stipulates that any member state needs to justify the need to apply an export drawback Council for Trade and Economic Development (COTED). COTED is mandated to review the use of drawback by members on an annual basis.

xvii When products from the South Pacific Islands that are exported to New Zealand are cumulated with Australian inputs, a minimum of 25 per cent of 'qualifying expenditure' from South Pacific Islands is required.

xviii Requires the expenditure on goods produced and labor performed *within the territory of the exporting* member state in the manufacture of the goods to not less than 50 per cent of the ex-factory or ex-works cost of the goods in their finished state.

The agreement stipulates that 'With respect to drawbacks within one year from the date of entry into force of this Agreement, the Standing Committee shall consider whether drawbacks on goods imported from third countries should be permitted in relation to products used in the manufacture of finished products for which concessions have been exchanged by the Participating States.'

xx Mentioned in the section on trade remedies. One of the criteria for imposing a countervailing duty is that the targeted subsidy is not less than the 2 per cent *de minimis*.

xxi The FTA stipulates that 'Where each Party has entered separately into a free trade agreement under Article XXIV of the GATT 1994 with the same non-Party before this Agreement enters into force, a good, which, if imported into the territory of one of the Parties under such free trade agreement with that non-Party, would qualify for tariff preferences under that agreement, shall be considered to be an originating good under this Chapter when imported into the territory of the other Party and used as a material in the production of another good in the territory of that other Party.'

4

Rules of Origin for services: economic and legal considerations

Americo Beviglia Zampetti and Pierre Sauvé[1]

4.1 Introduction

The proliferation of preferential trade and investment agreements has spawned a rich and lively debate over the design and economic effects of Rules of Origin. Yet, even as the most recent wave of bilateral and regional trade pacts typically feature comprehensive rules on services trade and investment, little analytical attention has so far been devoted to the issue of Rules of Origin in a services and investment context. This chapter wades into this largely uncharted territory by advancing a few thoughts on a range of economic and legal considerations arising from the way in which various trade and investment agreements seek to determine and condition who gets to benefit from services trade and investment liberalization. To gain a more solid foothold in this nascent policy area, the chapter focuses on the practice of preferential and non-preferential services trade liberalization as found in various bilateral and regional trade and investment agreements as well as the World Trade Organization's (WTO) General Agreement on Trade in Services (GATS). Interest in determining the origin of services traded internationally as well as the nationality of globally active service providers has acquired greater salience of late in the context of the debate over the labor-market effects

[1] The views expressed in this chapter are personal and should not be attributed to the United Nations or its Member countries. The authors are grateful to Julian Arkell, Antoni Estevadeordal, Aaditya Mattoo, Carsten Fink and Brian Staples for useful discussions and to participants at the conference on 'Rules of Origins' organized by the Inter-American Development Bank in Washington, D.C. on January 20–21, 2004.

of growing recourse to sourcing various input services, in particular non-core business processes, from service providers located in developing countries.[2]

The rest of this chapter is divided into three sections. Section 4.2 addresses a range of conceptual issues relating to services trade that impinge upon the design and implementation of Rules of Origin for services. The discussion draws attention to a number of salient characteristics of trade in services that limit the usefulness of concepts and approaches to origin developed in the context of trade in goods. Attention is also drawn to a number of economic considerations that should inform the design of Rules of Origin for services trade so as to minimize the potentially adverse effects of trade and investment diversion and maximize the economy-wide gains in allocative efficiency that well-designed services liberalization can entail.

Section 4.3 turns its attention to the practice of Rules of Origin for services and investment. It discusses the various means that governments have taken to determine the origin or nationality of those natural (i.e. people) and juridical (i.e. firms) persons that stand to benefit from preferential or non-preferential liberalization and to deny such benefits to non-participants. The discussion focuses in turn on bilateral investment agreements (BITs), Regional Trade Agreements, as well as the GATS. Section 4.4 offers a few concluding thoughts.

4.2 Conceptual issues

Rules of Origin define the criteria used to determine the national origin of a product. Origin rules are necessary because products may be subject to different measures and treatment depending on their origin or nationality. In a completely open world economy, there would be no demand for such rules because it would be immaterial where goods and services originated. Even in a less than fully open world economy, 'the prominence of Rules of

---

[2] See 'The Great Hollowing Out Myth', in *The Economist*, 21 February 2004; Friedman, T., 'The silver lining of outsourcing overseas', in *New York Times*, 27 February 2004; 'No need to moan about services', in *Financial Times*, 31 December, 2003; Schumer, C. and P. C. Roberts, 'Exporting jobs is not free trade', in *International Herald Tribune*, 7 January 2004; Luce, E. and K. Merchant, ' "The logic is inescapable": why India believes commercial imperatives will help it beat the offshoring backlash', in *Financial Times*, 28 January 2004; Irwin, D., 'Outsourcing' is good', in *Wall Street Journal*, 29 January 2004.

Origin would be limited as long as trade-restrictive measures were applied across-the-board, i.e. on a non-discriminatory basis.'[3]

Rules of Origin were originally established to determine the treatment, especially customs duties and associated non-tariff restrictions, connected to the importation of goods. Still today such treatment typically varies according to the origin of an imported product. Rules of Origin are thus used for a number of purposes, including to determine whether imported products shall receive autonomous, most-favored nation (MFN) or preferential treatment; to implement measures and instruments of commercial policy such as anti-dumping duties and safeguard measures; for the application of labelling and marking requirements; and for administering government procurement contracts.

In principle, Rules of Origin are (or should be) merely definitional in character. They ought to help determine the scope of application of a legal instrument, such as a country's tariff legislation or an international trade agreement. In the most straightforward case of a multiple column tariff schedule, Rules of Origin should indicate which tariff rate applies to which goods, once the tariff line to which the product belongs has been established.

However, Rules of Origin have evolved into a very complex and subtle body of law, which today transcends definitional purposes and is more often than not meant to reinforce or at least support broader policy goals well beyond customs law.[4] This is particularly the case with respect to preferential Rules of Origin, which are increasingly designed as instruments to induce foreign direct investment into the host country that applies the rules and to establish and/or deepen linkages with local suppliers. In so doing, Rules of Origin serve a clear industrial-policy function as instruments of investment promotion and as surrogate local-content requirements.

In a world where products are increasingly assembled through multi-country production networks (using inputs such as physical components, labor and other services that are themselves sourced from various locations), conferring origin to a product has become an increasingly difficult task. Most often, products acquire the origin of the country where the last substantial transformation has occurred, which usually leads to a change in tariff classification. Origin may also be conferred in specific cases on the basis of local value-added or local content.

---

[3] See E. Verlmust, 'Rules of Origin as Commercial Policy Instruments—Revisited', in *Journal of World Trade*, December 1992, p. 61.

[4] For instance, in the case of anti-dumping duties, a finding that a product has not changed origin but has retained the origin of a country against which duties are in place may mean enlarging the coverage of such duties without a need to go through a new investigation.

In the case of preferential trade agreements, including unilateral schemes (such as the Generalized System of Preferences or GSP) and reciprocal (e.g. Free Trade Areas (FTAs)) as well as non-reciprocal agreements (such as the Cotonou Agreement[5] or the Caribbean Basin Initiative[6]), Rules of Origin can aim to induce foreign direct investment flows into the preference-receiving county. In order to benefit from the trade preference, usually a lower tariff or a quota allocation, foreign producers/exporters need to see the origin of the beneficiary country being accepted by the preference-granting country as the origin of their goods. This means, in particular when Rules of Origin are based on value-added or local content, performing activities locally or using domestic inputs to the extent specified by the applicable origin rule.

The preceding discussion illustrates how an otherwise relatively straight-forward operation—determining the origin of a product—has become increasingly difficult in a globalizing environment, raising a number of complex economic and legal ramifications. Such difficulties are arguably compounded when policy attention turns to determining the origin of services.

Indeed, a number of salient characteristics of services and of trade in services can affect and at times render quite complex the matter of determining the origin or nationality of a traded service. Such characteristics include: the intangible nature of various transactions and the associated difficulty of measuring them; the importance of network-based service delivery and the difficulty of assigning value added along various parts of the network; the strong recent growth in services traded remotely over electronic networks; the need for physical proximity between seller and consumer and the associated mobility of factors of production (capital and labor) such proximity entails; as well as the desirability (and often greater practical feasibility) of conducting trade through an established presence (i.e. foreign direct investment).

4.2.1 *Rules of Origin for services: do the key characteristics of services and services trade matter?*

As noted earlier, the literature on Rules of Origin has focused almost exclusively on merchandise trade flows and hence on policies for

---

[5] See Partnership Agreement between the Members of the African, Caribbean and Pacific Group of States of the one part, and the European Community and its Member States, of the other part, 23 June 2000.

[6] See Caribbean Basin Economic Recovery Act (CBERA, also known as the Caribbean Basin Initiative, or CBI) first enacted in 1984.

117

determining the origin or nationality of tangible *products*. Much less attention has been devoted to the increasingly important issue of how to determine the origin of *producers*, which is primarily what the study of Rules of Origin in services trade and investment is concerned with. Since contesting service markets often requires the physical presence of suppliers in the territory of consumers, either in the form of individual service providers performing cross-border transactions on a temporary (i.e. contract) basis or as entities servicing a foreign market on the basis of a commercial presence in that market, governments that are signatories of trade and investment agreements may need to ascertain whether suppliers originate in other countries, with a view to extending or denying the benefits foreseen under such agreements. Determining the origin of a service and/or the nationality of a service provider relates to the 'subject-matter' coverage of an agreement, which defines the activities and the persons (natural and juridical) to which the provisions of an agreement apply.[7]

Services differ from goods in a number of ways that may have implications for the design and implementation of Rules of Origin. First, because many services transactions take place behind national borders, domestic regulation—both that which is overtly discriminatory in content or that restricts market contestability on a non-discriminatory basis—is the preferred means of protection in services trade. While tariffs are typically not levied on services transactions, the need to determine the origin of services and of service providers arises as soon as an international agreement providing for differential treatment between parties and non-parties is entered into. This is particularly important in the case of preferential bilateral or regional integration agreements, which have proliferated in recent years and have as one of their main rationales the granting of special treatment to members of economic integration schemes.

An additional difficulty encountered in determining the origin of a service stems from the fact that most service sectors differ from goods in that one cannot easily evaluate the different components or inputs that make up a service. Many services, such as telecommunications, multimodal transport, energy, water distribution and other environmental services, are indeed network based, and the question arises of whether it is possible to assess and measure value added at each point over the network.[8]

---

[7] However, a similar need would arise in the context of domestic legislation, which may differentiate treatment according to origin or nationality. Definitions would then be equally crucial.

[8] See Kingston, E. I. (1993), 'The Economics of Rules of Origin', in Vermlust, E., P. Waer and J. Bourgeois (ed.), *Rules of Origin in International Trade: A Comparative Study*, Studies in International Trade Series, Ann Arbor: University of Michigan Press, pp. 19–21.

Rules of Origin for goods trade often focus on processing activities. What matters is not only where value was added (i.e. where the processing occurred), but also how much value was added to a specific product. Beyond the statistical challenges posed by attempts at measuring the contribution of services to domestic economic activity or to international trade, the intangible nature of many types of service transactions, and the fact that they are often embodied in other goods or services, present additional challenges if one wishes to determine their origin relying on value added. Many tradable services either constitute processing activities or add value to goods via distribution, marketing and after-sales service. Furthermore, criteria such as the substantial transformation and changes in tariff headings that are the hallmark of Rules of Origin for trade in goods are clearly not workable in a services context. For one, as just noted in the case of network-based services, insufficient information may be available regarding the structure of production for most services and the inputs involved in final service offerings. More fundamentally, most traded services will involve 'substantial transformations' of whatever inputs are used, simply because the service will not have existed before it was sold and consumed. The non-storability of many services thus makes traditional approaches to origin determination impractical. The same may be said of physical-content requirements, as services tend to be both intangible and indivisible.[9]

This chapter's survey of Rules of Origin found in various agreements covering services trade and investment (see Section 4.3) suggests that Rules of Origin applied to producers are generally less restrictive than those often applied to products. Unlike goods trade, where such rules tend to display considerable cross-sectoral variance (and thus may serve as highly targeted and efficient instruments of trade and investment diversion), Rules of Origin applied to producers tend to be more transparent and uniform across sectors of activity. In many instances, a legal and (especially) natural person will be able to demonstrate origin or nationality in a relatively straightforward manner. Such relative simplicity stands in marked contrast to Rules of Origin for goods. Compared to the detailed and intricate descriptions of origin regimes for traded products, services and investment provisions dealing with the origin of producers afford no equivalent detail. Such differentiated treatment draws attention to one of the salient characteristics of services trade noted earlier: the

---

[9] See Hoekman, B. (1993), *op. cit.*, p. 89.

need for physical presence and proximity to clients will likely entail that foreign suppliers add significant value locally.

However, recent technological changes have greatly enhanced the tradability of services, lessening, in the process, the need for physical presence and progressively breaking down the need for simultaneity in production and consumption arising from the non-storability of services. The growing technological sophistication of services production, the spread of global production networks involving the segmentation of the service production value chain; the strong recent spread of 'off-shoring' or outsourcing service activities that used to be performed in-house to distant locations abroad, can all complicate the task of assigning an origin or nationality to services and service providers.[10] An interesting policy question that arises in this regard is whether such difficulties could imply that the relatively liberal (or less overtly protectionist) bias in Rules of Origin for producers might also extend to services products themselves, thereby further widening the differences between the treatment accorded to goods relative to that applied to services.[11]

Similar challenges arise from spectacular recent growth of e-commerce, which at the time of the Uruguay Round and the NAFTA was not yet a commercial reality commanding the attention of trade-policy officials but is today an important feature of newer-generation trade agreements as various Internet-based applications are vastly increasing the scope for remote supply of services.[12] The growth of transactions in cyberspace, and the territorial uncertainties such trade can entail from the perspective of regulatory oversight, notably in terms of the protection of consumers, public morals, or intellectual property, illustrate well the challenges noted

---

[10] 'Dubbed "non-tradables", services have long been perceived as having to be delivered in person, on site. That's no longer the case. Offshore outsourcing of services is now occurring up and down the value chain—from low value-added transactions processing and call centres to activities with high intellectual capital content, such as software programming, engineering, design, accounting, actuarial expertise, legal and medical advice, and a broad array of business consulting functions.' See Roach, S. (2004), 'How global labour arbitrage will reshape the world economy', *Global Agenda, The Magazine of the World Economic Forum Annual Meeting*, No. 2, p. 90. For an informed discussion of how IT applications are enhancing the tradability of services see Mann, C. L. (2003), Globalization of IT Services and White Collar Jobs: The Next Productivity Growth, *International Economics Policy Briefs*, Number PB03-11, (December), Washington, D.C.: Institute for International Economics. On the growing importance of outsourcing, see, for instance, Auguste, B. G., *et al.* (2002), 'The Other side of Outsourcing', *The McKinsey Quarterly*, Number 1. On business process outsourcing services, see UNCTAD, *E-Commerce and Development Report 2003*, Chapter 5, United Nations, New York and Geneva.　　　　　　　　　　　　　　　　[11] See Hoekman, B. (1993), *op. cit.*, p. 97.
[12] See Wunsch-Vincent, S. (2003), 'The Digital Trade Agenda of the U.S.: Parallel Tracks of Bilateral, Regional and Multilateral Liberalization', in *Aussenwirtschaft*, No. 58, pp. 7–46.

above. The hypothetical examples below draw attention to some of the complexities involved in determining the origin or nationality of services in a globalizing environment with regard to:

- composite services featuring elements of telecommunications and audiovisual production (e.g. Internet-based video on demand services) from different countries;
- remotely supplied architectural, engineering or interior design services from professionals and firms based in various countries that are incorporated in a construction project realized in a third country;
- cross-border M&A advice supplied by an investment bank featuring elements of legal, accounting, auditing, regulatory and banking services produced within and outside the bank in various jurisdictions;
- insurance policies sold on a cross-border basis, for instance, to Canadian consumers by the wholly owned US subsidiary of a German insurance company operating a call center in the Caribbean.

The examples above suggest how governments might be tempted, including on grounds of regulatory precaution, to apply stricter Rules of Origin for cross-border transactions with a view to possibly shifting incentives towards supplying e-commerce offerings through a commercial presence. In such instances, a restrictive rule of origin could be likened to a surrogate local-presence requirement.

To be sure, while the challenge of assigning origin in the context of global production networks is not new, the debate surrounding 'corporate nationality' is certainly as old as the multinational corporation itself. Yet, as is revealed both by the still limited level of cross-border liberalization commitments achieved under existing agreements (be they bilateral, regional or multilateral)[13] and by the dominant share (an estimated 60 per cent) of services 'trade' taking the form of establishment-related transactions (so-called Mode 3 trade in GATS-speak), the question of origin rules for services is closely related to the treatment of investors and their investments under various agreements.

The issue of corporate nationality has been salient in domestic as well as international law for some time. No single test of corporate nationality is universally applied. In international law, the issue of corporate

---

[13] For a cogent discussion of hurdles to cross-border trade in services and of various means of reducing the establishment bias of liberalization commitments in services, see Mattoo, A. and S. Wunsch-Vincent (2004), 'Securing Openness of Cross-Border Trade in Services: A Possible Approach', Mimeo, Washington, D.C.: World Bank and Institute for International Economics.

nationality arises in a number of contexts, particularly when a State formally seeks to exercise diplomatic protection over a company[14] or invokes relevant provisions of international treaties.

The criteria most commonly used, separately or in combination, to determine a company's nationality are its place of incorporation, the location of the 'seat' or head office of the corporation, and the nationality of the shareholders who exercise effective 'control' over the corporation. In the national legal systems derived from Anglo-American common law, the State of incorporation is the main test of nationality.

The criterion of incorporation has been deemed inadequate in a number of circumstances. For example, it may accord nationality to corporations that are incorporated in a country for tax-avoidance or related purposes, but do no business or have no assets in that country. The example of flags of convenience in international shipping is perhaps the most obvious case in point. The limitations of incorporation-based criteria are hardly limited to shipping, and have been found to arise in air transport, banking, insurance and, most recently, in a range of services conducted over electronic networks in cyberspace. For this reason, the requirement that a company carries out substantial economic activities—i.e. not be a mere 'shell' or 'letter-box' entity—in the country granting nationality is commonplace.

In most civil-law systems of continental Europe and those influenced by them, the test is often that of the company's 'seat', i.e. the place where the direction and central administration are located. The two tests lead to similar results in the many cases where the seat formally provided for in the corporation's statutes is the place of incorporation. Where the statutory seat does not coincide with the place from which direction is actually exercised, the latter (the 'real seat' as distinguished from the

---

[14] The *locus classicus* is the 1970 decision of the International Court of Justice in the Barcelona Traction Case, which established a rather restrictive test, according to which only 'the State under the laws of which [the corporation] is incorporated and in whose territory it has its registered office' has the ability to exercise diplomatic protection (Barcelona Traction, Light and Power Company, Limited (New Application: 1962) (Belgium v. Spain) *I.C.J. Reports 1970*, 3). In some of the judges' opinions in this case, and in the extensive analysis of it, other criteria were proposed and discussed (see, *inter alia*, L. Caflisch, 'The Protection of Corporate Investments Abroad in the Light of the Barcelona Traction Case', in *Zeitschrift für ausländisches öffentliches Recht und Völkerrecht*, vol. 31, 1971, pp. 162–196). In the 1989 ELSI Case (*I.C.J. Reports 1989*), the Court recognized the right of the national state of shareholders to exercise diplomatic protection on their behalf, in the frequent case where the company in which the interest is held is a national (because incorporated in) of the respondent state. See B. Stern, 'La Protection Diplomatique des Investissements Internationaux. De Barcelona Traction à Elettronica Sicula ou les glisserments progressifs de l'analyse', in *Journal Du Droit International*, 1990, p. 897 et seq.

statutory one) prevails in many continental legal systems. However, there is also no clear definition of the concept of 'seat'. If in some jurisdictions this refers to the place of a firm's central administration and direction, in others it refers to the location of the firm's (main) production facilities. Even as regards the location of a firm's central administration, it may refer to the meeting place of the directors or that of its shareholders.

The third test, focusing on 'control', has tended to generate greater controversy. Such a test is essentially political in origin, since in many countries it was first used in wartime to deal with locally incorporated companies whose shareholders were enemy aliens.[15] The test is used in a variety of regulatory contexts to distinguish between domestic and foreign corporations, in order to restrict the access of foreign companies to particular industries (e.g. air transport, coastal shipping) or to provide privileged treatment to local firms. It is also sometimes used by home countries to establish jurisdiction over aspects of the activities of foreign affiliates of corporations owned by their nationals.

4.2.2 Economic considerations[16]

The above discussion shows that, as in the case of Rules of Origin for goods, different means can be used to determine the nationality of service providers. Unlike goods trade, however, there is considerably less experience in the use of rules aimed at determining the origin or nationality of services. Still, when countries grant differential treatment to services or service providers on the basis of origin or nationality, an important question remains, as with trade agreements governing trade in goods: whether Rules of Origin (or nationality) principally serve a definitional role and are thus subordinated to the fulfilment of the stated aims of the legal instrument to which they belong or, whether, instead, they can be used as instruments to pursue broader policy goals (including that of trade or investment protection and the attainment of industrial policy objectives).

As with goods trade, and despite their greater uniformity across sectors, experience shows that Rules of Origin for services and investment can play a significant role in determining the degree to which regional trading

---

[15] For instance, at the outbreak of World War I English courts held the Daimler Company Ltd., a wholly owned subsidiary of the German Daimler Company, to be an enemy for the purpose of appointing a custodian for its assets, in spite of being established and registered in England as a limited company under English law.

[16] This section benefitted from discussion with Aaditya Mattoo.

arrangements discriminate against non-member countries, and hence the extent of potentially costly trade and investment diversion. When levels of protection differ between participating countries, the effective preference granted to a trading partner will depend on how restrictive the applied rule of origin is. In the extreme, if one participant has a fully liberalized market, the adoption of a liberal rule of origin by the other participants can be likened to MFN liberalization, as services and service suppliers can enter or establish themselves in the liberal jurisdiction and from there move to—or service—the other partner countries. Indeed, under a liberal rule of origin for services and investment (aimed at ensuring that established foreign operators are not mere shell companies), third-country investors and service providers can take full advantage of the expanded market opportunities afforded by the creation of a Regional Trade Agreement (RTA) by establishing a commerial presence within the integration area.[17] Not surprisingly, participants who seek to benefit from preferential access to a protected market and deny benefits to third-country competitors are likely to argue for the adoption of restrictive Rules of Origin. This could be the attitude, in particular, of regionally dominant but non-globally competitive service providers towards third-country competition within a regionally integrating area.[18]

The decision to favor a particular type of origin rules for services trade and investment will typically involve two conflicting considerations. On the one hand, the adoption of a liberal rule of origin will tend to minimize the costs of trade and investment diversion and will thus be economically optimal. Yet such an approach suffers from the known bargaining downsides of MFN-based liberalization: it can lessen the incentive for anyone to negotiate a preferential agreement, and it can also reduce an insider country's negotiating leverage *vis-à-vis* third (non-participant) countries.

Defensive concerns pleading in favor of more restrictive Rules of Origin may be expected to arise in the case of regional agreements that link countries with marked differences in levels of openness towards services trade or foreign direct investment. In such instances, the country with a

[17] See Sauvé, P. (2003), 'Services', in OECD, *Regionalism and the Multilateral Trading System*, Paris: OECD, pp. 23–43.

[18] For instance, in the current discussion within the Common Market of Eastern and Southern Africa (COMESA) on the establishment of a COMESA Common Investment Area, the issue of the definition of 'COMESA investor' has been characterized by the concern that 'foreign multinational investors may use smaller countries as a way to circumvent national pre-investment screening in other countries.' See presentation by W. Mkandawire, 'Towards the Creation of the COMESA Common Investment Area', mimeo, Geneva, 2004.

more restricted market may fear that the adoption of a liberal rule of origin would bestow liberalization benefits on a *de facto* MFN basis to third-country competitors, such that any service provider established in a partner country could benefit from the integration scheme on a non-discriminatory basis.

Because a number of key service sectors—particularly the core infra-structural sectors of telecommunications, energy, finance, transport, water supply, distribution services—possess dynamic, growth-enhancing properties, securing access to the most efficient provider of such services may be of considerable importance to a country's longer-term growth and development prospects.[19] The policy stance taken with regard to Rules of Origin for services and investment in an RTA can thus play in important role promoting or inhibiting access to the most efficient suppliers of services. In many service sectors the most efficient (or globally compet-itive) suppliers will tend to be either developed-country firms or firms originating outside an integrating area. Accordingly, the adoption of Rules of Origin that restrict benefits to nationals of member states can exert detrimental effects by potentially locking in integrating partners into suboptimal patterns of production and consumption.

The above problem may be compounded, and generate longer-term deadweight losses, to the extent that many services, particularly network-based services, involve significant location-specific sunk costs, such that first movers (even if relatively inefficient) can exert long-term dominance and extract monopolistic rents. The problem with location-specific sunk costs is that a country may be stuck with inferior suppliers for a long time even if it subsequently liberalizes on an MFN basis.[20] Indeed, because of the importance of sunk costs in many service industries, sequential entry (which preferential liberalization with restrictive Rules of Origin can easily promote) can produce very different results from simultaneous entry. If entry is costly, an incumbent may indeed be able to fully deter entry, leading to greater market concentration and a reduction in consumer welfare.

Two important qualifications to the above reasoning can nonetheless be made. First, subsequent entry by a more efficient firm can take place

---

[19] For a comprehensive discussion of the growth-enhancing properties of infrastructural services, see Chapters 4 and 5 in World Bank (2002), *Global Economic Prospects and the Developing Countries 2002: Making Trade Work for the Poor*, Washington, D.C.: The World Bank. See also Mattoo, A., R. Rathindran, and A. Subramanian. 2001. 'Measuring Services Trade Liberalization and its Impact on Economic Growth: An Illustration', *World Bank Policy Research Working Paper No. 2380*, World Bank, Washington, D.C.

[20] See Mattoo and Fink (2002), *op. cit.*

through the acquisition route, thus circumventing some of the problems linked to first-mover advantages. This has been the experience of a number of countries in the financial sector, especially those where first movers may have overbid or sunk excessive costs in setting up their operations in the early stages of privatization-led liberalization.

Secondly, in certain service sectors, firms could learn by doing: the experience acquired by established operators during a previous period may reduce their current costs, enhancing their profitability and discouraging others from entering. In such circumstances, entry deterrence, including that conferred through restrictive Rules of Origin, may paradoxically promote welfare. Caveats aside, a country needs to carefully evaluate not just the static costs of granting preferential access to a particular country, but also determine how the (greater) eventual benefits from multilateral liberalization are likely to be affected.[21]

As with goods trade (and its strong links to domestic manufacturing activity), restrictive Rules of Origin for services trade and investment can be motivated by broad (i.e. non-sector-specific) industrial policy considerations. Indeed, one rationale for RTAs covering services to feature restrictive Rules of Origin may be looked upon as a variant of the infant-industry argument. South-South RTAs, in particular, are often seen as a form of gradual liberalization. Exposure to competition first in the more sheltered confines of a regional market may help firms prepare for global competition. This approach improves on traditional infant-industry protection because some degree of international competition is fostered as a result of the integration process. There is also the possibility that firms that have gained competitiveness and achieved economies of scale by operating in an enlarged regional market may be less prone to resist broader-based liberalization. The latter may even lend support to subsequent MFN liberalization as they begin to reap the benefits of open markets and run up against the constraints of a regional market. In this sense, RTAs can be seen as 'building blocks' towards multilateral liberalization.[22]

The risk does exist, however, that regional liberalization might create a new constellation of vested interests that could resist further market opening, raising the concern that regionalism can become a 'stumbling block' to further multilateral liberalization. The GATS offers a way out of

---

[21] See Mattoo and Fink (2002), *op. cit.*

[22] See Bhagwati, J. (1990), 'Multilateralism at Risk: The GATT is Dead, Long Live the GATT,' *The World Economy*, 13(2):149–69 and Lawrence, R. Z. (1991), 'Regional Trade Agreements: Building Blocks or Stumbling Blocks?', in O'Brien, R. (ed.), *Finance and the International Economy: 5*, London: Oxford University Press.

this dilemma by allowing Member countries to pre-commit to future multilateral liberalization, signalling a time frame over which regional preferences may be progressively eroded and/or eliminated.

Furthermore, the adoption of restrictive Rules of Origin on service providers, which may take the form of temporary entry privileges that are limited to nationals of Member countries (as is the case under NAFTA) or through recognition arrangements whose benefits may be denied to non-national residents hailing from third countries (as is the case of professional services), may exert negative effects on an integration area's overall labor-market performance. Such rules can wind up driving up wages and scarcity rents in some professional or skill categories, deny access to workers who otherwise meet local standards and qualification requirements and thus reduce the overall supply of human capital in an integrating area.

4.3 Current practice in the area of services

International transactions involving services go back a long way. Their systematic regulation at the international level, however, is a more recent affair, at least if one is to abstract from the practice—dating back to the nineteenth century (and before)—of concluding Treaties of Commerce and Navigation, which elaborated on the legal rights of aliens already existing under customary international law. By defining the rights of private traders and investors, some services transactions were, at least in part, covered by such treaties.[23]

Up until the Uruguay Round, the multilateral trading system did not address trade in services. It could be said that the audiovisual sector was the only one addressed to some extent (albeit in an indirect manner) in the original GATT(1947). Indeed, Article IV of the GATT(1947) provided a special, and unique, exception for cinematograph films to GATT national treatment rules and duty concessions have been made in relation to films. In recognition of the difficulty that domestic film producers faced

---

[23] See, for instance, the Treaty of Friendship, Commerce and Navigation between the United States of America and the Italian Republic, of 2 February 1948, Art. I.2: '*The nationals of either High Contracting Party shall, within the territories of the other High Contracting Party, be permitted, without interference, to exercise, in conformity with the applicable laws and regulations, the following rights and privileges upon terms no less favourable than those now or hereafter accorded to nationals of such other High Contracting Party: (a) to engage in commercial, manufacturing, processing, financial, scientific, educational, religious, philanthropic and professional activities except the practice of law . . .*'.

in finding adequate screen time to exhibit their films in the immediate post-World War II period, GATT founders authorized the continuation of existing screen-time quotas. The special regime provided that a Contracting Party might maintain or establish quantitative regulations requiring the exhibition of films of national origin during a specified minimum portion of the total screen time in the commercial exhibition of all films of whatever origin; such screen quotas were to be subject to negotiations for their limitation, liberalization or elimination. However, the GATT did not provide any further rule on how to determine the national origin of cinematograph films.[24]

A much richer set of practices can instead be found in bilateral investment treaties (BITs), regional and bilateral trade agreements and other plurilateral instruments. These will be reviewed in turn, before examining how the issue of origin for services has been dealt with in the GATS. On the basis of this review a few policy conclusions will be drawn in the final section.

4.3.1 *The practice of BITs*

Since the second half of the 1960s, BITs have proliferated, encompassing an increasing number of countries. As is well known, BITs are designed to protect, promote and facilitate foreign investment and constitute to date the most widely used instrument for such purposes.[25] BITs have traditionally been negotiated between developing countries seeking to attract international investment and developed countries as the principal homes to foreign investors. The network of BITs has expanded markedly since the 1990s, as more developing countries and economies in transition concluded treaties with a wider range of developed countries and started to sign BITs between themselves.

---

[24] The nationality of films remains a controversial issue, in particular when it is the condition for the granting of subsidies. For instance, in France, a film is considered as French once it has been agreed (*agréé*) by the Centre National de la Cinématographie (CNC), a procedure that makes the film eligible for receiving French subsidies. The CNC agreement procedure requires that a minimum number of points should be collected by a film in order to be considered of French nationality. These points are assigned on the basis of such factors as the hiring of French actors or workers and the use of the French language in the film and during its making.

[25] The content of BITs has become increasingly standardized over the years. Their main provisions typically deal with the scope and definition of foreign investors and their investments; admission of investments; national and most-favored-nation treatment; fair and equitable treatment; guarantees and compensation in respect of expropriation; guarantees of free transfer of funds and repatriation of capital and profits; and dispute-settlement provisions, both State-to-State and investor-to-State.

In current BIT practice there is a marked tendency to use broad, asset-based definitions of investment, which include movable and immovable property, intellectual property as well as equity and other interests in companies. Hence, most BITs do not distinguish between direct and portfolio investment. Investment in services activities is generally covered, unless specifically excluded. As such, the BIT practice is relevant for the present investigation.

Within BITs the part dealing with scope and definition is the most useful for a review of international practice on how nationality is determined, both for natural and juridical persons. In general, the main objective of BITs is to protect the investments made by investors of one party in the territory of the other party. Hence, treaties must define which investors have a sufficient link with the respective signatories to merit protection. In particular, the capital-importing country may be reluctant to grant the benefits of a BIT to persons and companies having only a tenuous relationship with its treaty partner (e.g. so-called 'shell' or 'mailbox' companies). Establishing the nationality of the investor is thus fundamental to taking full advantage of the substantive provisions set out in a treaty.

The definition of the term 'investor' usually includes natural persons and juridical entities, often referred to generically as 'companies'. Some BITs do not use the term 'investor' and refer directly to natural persons and companies. With respect to natural persons, most BITs give protection to persons who are 'nationals' of each of the contracting countries concerned. The general practice is then to provide that a natural person possesses the nationality of a State if the law of that State so provides. For instance, the 1999 BIT between the United States and El Salvador states that ' "national" of a Party means a natural person who is a national of that Party under its applicable law'[26]; the 1992 BIT between Argentina and the Netherlands refers, with regard to either Contracting Party, to 'natural persons having the nationality of that Contracting Party in accordance with its law.'[27]

Some BITs, perhaps inspired by the customary international law doctrine of effective nationality,[28] require the existence of a genuine link

[26] See Treaty between the Government of the United States of America and the Government of the Republic of El Salvador concerning the Encouragement and Reciprocal Protection of Investment, of 10 March 1999, Art. I (c).

[27] See Agreement on encouragement and reciprocal protection of investments between the Kingdom of the Netherlands and the Argentine Republic, of 20 October 1992, Art. 1 (b)(i).

[28] The principle of effective nationality has long been applied to resolve conflicts of nationality in international adjudication. See, for instance, the Nottebohm Case, (Liechtenstein v. Guatemala) Second Phase, Judgment, *I.C.J. Reports 1955*, Rep 4, also on the concept of the *'genuine and effective link'*.

between the individual and the country granting nationality, in the form of residence or domicile.[29] However, in general, BITs do not resolve the problem of treatment of natural person investors with dual or multiple nationalities.

With regard to legal persons, BITs generally take an expansive approach in terms of the kinds of entities that are meant to be covered. Some treaties, in defining the term 'investor', include legal persons constituted under the law of a party, thus covering companies, as well as other legal entities. Other BITs define the term 'company' quite broadly to comprise, as in the case of the 1991 BIT between Tunisia and Turkey *'any kind of juridical entity, including any corporation, company, business association or other organization that is duly incorporated, constituted or otherwise duly organized under the applicable laws and regulations of a Party'*.[30]

BITs extend protection to companies that are deemed to have the nationality of one of the signatories. Problems arise because in most cases, and increasingly with the spread of multinational corporations and international production networks, places of incorporation, the location of business activities and/or the nationality of ownership and control often involve multiple jurisdictions. In most instances a multinational corporation operates in a host state through a subsidiary incorporated therein. Such a subsidiary acquires the nationality of the host state and could not avail itself of the diplomatic protection of its home state. A multinational corporation could also choose to do business through an entity incorporated in a third state, whose corporations may not be entitled to the same treatment as the home-state companies in the host state.

BITs have in recent years tried to respond to these complications, by using—often in combination—the traditional nationality tests or criteria, namely the place of incorporation; the location of the 'seat' of the corporation (sometimes referred to as the *siège social*, real seat, or the principal place of management); and the nationality of the shareholders who own or control the corporation.

---

[29] See, for instance, the 1976 BIT between Germany and Israel (article I (3) (b)) and 1968 BIT between Denmark and Indonesia (article I (a)).

[30] Art. I (1)(h). See, also for instance, Art. I (a) of the El Salvador-U.S. BIT, cit., which states that: ' *"company" means any entity constituted or organized under applicable law, whether or not for profit, and whether privately or governmentally owned or controlled, and includes a corporation, trust, partnership, sole proprietorship, branch, joint venture, association, or other organization.'*

The place of incorporation, organization or constitution of a company is a widely used criteria to determine nationality thanks to its ease of application. For instance, the 1996 Foreign Investment Protection Agreement (FIPA) between Canada and Panama provides that an investor means: *'In the case of Canada: ... ii. any enterprise incorporated or duly constituted in accordance with applicable laws of Canada ... In the case of the Republic of Panama: ... ii. any enterprise incorporated or duly constituted in conformity with the laws of the Republic of Panama.'*[31]

However, such a test lends itself to granting nationality to a company that has only a formal link with the country of incorporation and does not engage in any economic activity there. Indeed, the place of incorporation could be chosen exclusively to enjoy treaty advantages reserved to nationals of signatories.

Such a situation has prompted two types of responses. Some BITs combine the place of incorporation test with criteria focusing on a company's 'seat'. This test attributes the nationality of the place where the *siège social* is located. The 'seat of a company' often refers to the place of effective management decision making, and as such, while more difficult to determine, reflects a more significant economic relationship between the corporation and the country granting nationality. For instance, the 1992 BITs between Argentina and the Netherlands considers investors of either Contracting Party *'legal persons constituted under the law of that Contracting Party and actually doing business under the laws in force in any part of the territory of that Contracting Party in which a place of effective management is situated.'*[32]

Other BITs instead include a denial of benefits clause meant to prevent, under certain circumstances, nationals of third countries from obtaining BIT treatment by incorporating in one of the signatory countries. This approach is typical in the practice of the United States. For instance, the 1995 Honduras-US BIT provides that *'Each Party reserves the right to deny to a company of the other Party the benefits of this Treaty if nationals of a third country own or control the company and (a) the denying Party does not maintain normal economic relations with the third country; or (b) the company has no*

---

[31] See Treaty between the Government of Canada and the Government of the Republic of Panama for the Promotion and Protection of Investments, of 12 September 1996, Art. I.h.

[32] See Art.1 (b) (ii). A similar approach can be found in the Acuerdo entre el Gobierno de la Republica de Venezuela y el Gobierno de la Republica Argentina para la promocion y proteccion reciprocas de inversiones, of 16 November 1993, which provides, at Art. 1.1, that *'El término "inversor" designa: (a) toda persona jurídica constituida de conformidad con las leyes y reglamentaciones de una Parte Contratante y que tenga su sede en el territorio de dicha Parte Contratante ...'.*

substantial business activities in the territory of the Party under whose laws it is constituted or organized.'[33] Similar language is also included in the 2003 Japan-Korea BIT.[34]

The country of the seat is sometimes, albeit more rarely, used as the sole criterion. For instance, in 1990 BIT between Germany and Swaziland: *'The term "companies" means (a) in respect of the Federal Republic of Germany: any juridical person as well as any commercial or other company with or without legal personality having its seat in the German area of application of this Treaty, irrespective of whether or not its activities are directed at profit ... '.*[35]

The country of ownership or control is the most difficult test to administer, but also the most significant in terms of the economic links it pre-supposes between the company and the country of nationality. It is especially complex in the case of public companies with shares traded in stock exchanges. In such cases, the nationality of the owner or of the controlling investor may change quite frequently or easily. This is why the ownership or control test is often employed in conjunction with one of the other two main criteria. According to such a test, the subsidiary, albeit incorporated in the host country, is considered for the purpose of the treaty a foreign national. It acquires the nationality of the parent company. For instance, the 1999 BIT between Costa Rica and the Netherlands defines the term 'nationals' as comprising *'with regard to either Contracting Party the following subjects: ... (ii) legal persons constituted under the law of that Contracting Party which have their seat or domicile in the territory of that Contracting Party; (iii) legal persons constituted under the law of the other Contracting Party but controlled, directly or indirectly, by natural persons as defined in (i) or by legal persons as defined in (ii) above.'*[36] The terms

[33] See Treaty between the Government of the United States of America and the Government of the Republic of Honduras concerning the Encouragement and Reciprocal Protection of Investment, of 1 July 1995, Art. XII.

[34] See Agreement between the Government of Japan and the Government of the Republic of Korea for the Liberalisation, Promotion and Protection of Investment, 22 March 2003, Art. 22.   [35] See Art, 1 (4).

[36] See the Agreement on encouragement and reciprocal protection of investments between the Republic of Costa Rica and the Kingdom of the Netherlands of 21 May 1999, Art. 1 (b). See also the Accord entre le Conseil fédéral Suisse et le Gouvernement de la République d'Afrique du Sud concernant la promotion et la protection réciproque des investissements, of 27 June 1995, Art. 1 (3), which reads: *'Le terme "investisseur" désigne, en ce qui concerne chaque Partie Contractante, (a) les personnes physiques qui, d'après la législation de cette Partie Contractante, sont considérées comme ses nationaux; (b) les sociétés, y compris les sociétés enregistrées, les sociétés de personnes et autres organisations, qui sont établies conformément à la législation de cette Partie Contractante, et ont leur siège sur le territoire de cette même Partie Contractante; (c) les sociétés qui ne sont pas établies conformément à la législation de cette Partie Contractante mais qui sont effectivement contrôlées par des personnes physiques ou par des sociétés, respectivement selon les lettres (a) et (b) du présent alinéa.'*

'ownership' or 'control' are not commonly defined in BITs. Some treaties, however, do so in a Protocol.[37]

4.3.2 The experience of regional and other agreements

The practice under bilateral trade agreements, regional integration agreements as well as other regional or plurilateral instruments is relevant both with regard to determining the origin of services and to attaching a nationality to service providers, particularly companies. In this latter regard, the practice with respect to the nationality of investors (which, in many cases, would also cover investors active in the supply of services) is again important. Significant examples will be reviewed in turn. However, there are also a number of bilateral and Regional Trade Agreements that closely follow the GATS model, such us, for instance, the 2000 US–Vietnam Bilateral Trade Agreement or the 1997 Mercosur Protocol of Montevideo.[38] These will not be considered in this section.

With regard to the origin of a 'service' in particular, many bilateral and regional agreements are either silent on the matter or follow the GATS lead in considering, in the case of cross-border transactions, *'service of another Member'* a service that is supplied from the territory of that other Member. Thus origin coincides with the place of supply, regardless of the nationality of the service supplier. There are agreements, such as the 1994 North American Free Trade Agreement (NAFTA) or the 2003 Singapore-US FTA,[39] that do not consider the issue as the treatment provisions of the agreement are only directed towards service suppliers.[40] Interestingly,

---

[37] See the Treaty between the United States of America and the Arab Republic of Egypt concerning the Reciprocal Encouragement and Protection of Investments, of 11 March 1986, Protocol, paragraph 2: ' *"Control" means to have a substantial share of ownership rights and the ability to exercise decisive influence.'* See also the Acuerdo entre el Gobierno de la República de Venezuela y el Gobierno de la República Argentina para la promoción y protección recíprocas de inversiones, 16 November 1993, Annex, where it says that with regard to effective control ' ... *las personas jurídicas que deseen invocar el presente Acuerdo podrían ser obligadas a proporcionar la prueba de dicho control. Serán aceptados entre otros, a título de prueba, los hechos siguientes: 1. El carácter de filial de una persona jurídica de una de las Partes Contratantes. 2. Un porcentaje de participación en el capital de una persona jurídica que permita un control efectivo, tal como en particular, una participación superior a la mitad del capital. 3. La posesión directa o indirecta de derechos de voto, que permitan tener una posición determinante en los órganos directivos de la persona jurídica o influir de otro modo de manera decisiva sobre su funcionamiento.'*

[38] See Mercosur/CMD/DEC No. 13/97 - Anexo: Protocolo de Montevideo sobre el Comercio de Servicios del Mercado Comun del Sur.

[39] See United States–Singapore Free Trade Agreement, 6 May 2003, Art. 8.3 (National Treatment), 8.4 (Most-Favoured-Nation Treatment) and 8.5 (Market Access).

[40] There are agreements, such as the Free Trade Agreement Between the Government of the Republic of Korea and the Government of the Republic of Chile, 15 February 2003, which, while granting national treatment also to services of the other Party (Article 11.3 (National Treatment)), do not define the term.

the 2003 Chile-US FTA contains footnotes in the articles dealing with national treatment, MFN treatment and market access indicating that the Parties understand that 'service suppliers' has the same meaning as 'services and service suppliers' as in the respective GATS articles. Thus, even if there is no specific definition of how to determine the origin of services, the GATS approach is adopted.[41] The 1998 Andean Community Decision 439 restricts instead the category of services originating in the subregion to those provided by natural and juridical persons themselves originating in the subregion.[42] Thus, only such services and/or service providers benefit from the preferential treatment afforded by the instrument.

In as far as the nationality of service providers is concerned, be they natural or legal entities, the practice of regional and other agreements is rich but tends to parallel the approaches reviewed in the context of BITs. With regard to service providers that are natural persons, most instruments fall back on the definition of citizen (and also very often permanent residents) of signatory countries, in order to grant nationality for the purpose of the application of the instrument's substantive provisions. The NAFTA is one example among many.

The issue of dual nationality is generally not addressed. One exception is the MIGA Convention, which provides that '*[i]n case the investor has more than one nationality[. . .], the nationality of a member shall prevail over the nationality of a non-member and the nationality of the host country shall prevail over the nationality of any other member*'.[43]

With respect to legal persons the criteria of incorporation, place of the seat, substantive business operations and ownership or control are those mainly used to determine nationality. These criteria are rarely used in isolation. One example, with regard to incorporation, is the 1981 Agreement

---

[41] See Free Trade Agreement Between the Government of the United States of America and the Government of the Republic of Chile, 6 June 2003, Art. 11.2 (National Treatment), Art. 11.3 (Most-Favored-Nation Treatment) and Art. 11.4 (Market Access).

[42] See Andean Community Decision 439: General Framework of Principles and Rules and for Liberalizing the Trade in Services in the Andean Community, of 11 June 1998, Chapter IX (Origin of the Services), Article 23, '*The following shall be considered as services originating in the sub-region, for purposes of enjoying the benefits stemming from this General Framework: 1) Those furnished by natural or physical persons with permanent residence in any of the Member Countries, in accordance with the respective national regulations; 2) Services provided by juridical persons incorporated, authorized or residing according to domestic law in any of the Member Countries, which effectively carry out substantial operations in the territory of any of those Countries, or by Andean Multinational Enterprises; and 3) In the case of the cross-border provision of services, such services that are produced and furnished directly from the territory of a Member Country by natural or physical persons or by juridical persons as stipulated in paragraphs 1 and 2 above.*' In case of doubts Art. 24 provides for a consultation and investigation procedure.

[43] See Convention Establishing the Multilateral Investment Guarantee Agency, 11 October 1985, Art. 13 (Eligible Investors).

on the Promotion, Protection and Guarantee of Investment among Member States of the Organisation of the Islamic Conference.[44]

More often the criteria are combined and/or the agreements feature a denial of benefits clause. This latter approach is used, for instance, in the NAFTA. Under the NAFTA, services can be supplied by service providers and investors. Indeed, the Agreement's chapter (11) setting out the regulation of investment covers all sectors. Service providers and investors can be natural persons or enterprises. Under the NAFTA, an enterprise (and a branch of an enterprise) must be constituted or organized under the law of a Party.[45] There is no requirement that the enterprise be controlled by nationals of a NAFTA country. However, if the enterprise is controlled by persons of a non-NAFTA country, benefits can be denied if the enterprise has no substantial business activities in the territory of the Party under whose laws it is constituted. Various bilateral and regional agreements in the Americas have adopted a similar approach. These include, *inter alia*, the 1994 Costa Rica-Mexico FTA,[46] the 1994 Mexico, Colombia, and Venezuela FTA,[47] the 1994 Bolivia-Mexico FTA[48] and 1996 Canada-Chile FTA.[49] A similar model is also adopted in agreements reached outside the region, such as the 2003 Singapore-US FTA, the 2003 China-Panama FTA,[50] and the 2003 Chile-Korea FTA.[51]

[44] See Art. 1 (6): '...*Nationality shall be determined as follows:...(b) Legal personality: Any entity established in accordance with the laws in force in any contracting party and recognized by the law under which its legal personality is established.*' Reproduced in UNCTAD, *International Investment Instruments: A Compendium*, New York and Geneva, vol. II, 1996, p. 243.

[45] 'Enterprise means any entity constituted or organized under applicable law, whether or not for profit, and whether privately-owned or governmentally-owned, including any corporation, trust, partnership, sole proprietorship, joint venture or other association.' See NAFTA, Art. 201.

[46] See Tratado de Libre Comercio entre México y Costa Rica of 5 April 1994, Artículo 9–01: (Definiciones) '*Para efectos de este capítulo, se entenderá por:... empresa de una Parte: una empresa constituida u organizada de conformidad con la legislación de una Parte y que tenga su domicilio en el territorio de esa Parte; y una sucursal ubicada en el territorio de una Parte que desempeñe actividades comerciales en la misma;...*' And Artículo 9–15: (Denegación de beneficios) '*Cada Parte podrá denegar los beneficios derivados de este capítulo a un prestador de servicios de otra Parte, previa notificación y realización de consultas, cuando la Parte determine que el servicio está siendo prestado por una empresa que no realiza actividades de negocios importantes en territorio de esa otra Parte, y que, de conformidad con la legislación de cada Parte, es propiedad o está bajo control de personas de un país que no es Parte.*'

[47] See the Free Trade Agreement of the Group of Three among Mexico, Colombia, and Venezuela of 13 June 1994, Art. 10-01 and 10-15.

[48] See Tratado de Libre Comercio México–Bolivia, 10 September 1994, Art. 9-01 and 9-13.

[49] See Free Trade Agreement between the Government of Canada and the Government of the Republic of Chile, 5 December 1996, Art. H-11 and H-12.

[50] See Free Trade Agreement between the Republic of China and the Republic of Panama, 6 May 2003.

[51] See, Chile-Korea FTA, Chapter 10 Investment, Art. 11.1 (Definitions) and Art. 10.17 (Denial of Benefits); Chapter 11 Cross-Border Trade in Services, Art. 11.1 (Definitions) and Art. 11.11 (Denial of Benefits).

The 1994 Energy Charter Treaty follows a comparable approach. It considers investors, natural persons that are citizens or permanent residents, and companies and other organizations, which are organized according to the laws of the host country.[52] Such a provision is accompanied by a denial of benefits clause for legal entities owned or controlled by third-state nationals, with no substantial business activities in the contracting party in which it is organized.[53] A denial of benefits article is also included in the 1995 ASEAN Framework Agreement on Services.[54]

The country of incorporation is combined in a number of cases with other criteria not through the denial of benefits clause but at the level of definitions or as part of the substantive rules. For example, the EC Treaty states that 'Companies or firms formed in accordance with the law of a Member State and having their registered office, central administration or principal place of business within the Community shall, for the purposes of this Chapter [Chapter 2 (Right of establishment)], be treated in the same way as natural persons who are nationals of Member States.'[55] The same approach is followed in the 1992 EEA Agreement,[56] and the 2001 EFTA Agreement.[57] Many Association and Cooperation Agreements to which the EC and its Member States are parties, as well as the 2000 ACP-EC Cotonou Agreement,[58] combine the incorporation and location of the

---

[52] See the Energy Charter Treaty of 17 December 1994, Art. 1 (7), ' "*Investor" means: (a) with respect to a Contracting Party: (i) a natural person having the citizenship or nationality of or who is permanently residing in that Contracting Party in accordance with its applicable law; (ii) a company or other organization organized in accordance with the law applicable in that Contracting Party.*' Reproduced in UNCTAD, *cit.*, vol. II, 1996, p. 549.

[53] See Energy Charter Treaty, Art.17.

[54] See ASEAN Framework Agreement on Services of 15 December 1995, Art. VI (Denial of Benefits) '*The benefits of this Framework Agreement shall be denied to a service supplier who is a natural person of a non-Member State or a juridical person owned or controlled by persons of a non-Member State constituted under the laws of a Member State, but not engaged in substantive business operations in the territory of Member State(s).*' Reproduced in UNCTAD, *cit.*, vol. IV, 2000, p. 45.

[55] See Consolidated Version of the Treaty Establishing the European Community, Art. 48 (ex Art. 58). The right of establishment includes the establishment for the purpose of providing services. Furthermore 'Freedom of establishment shall include the right to take up and pursue activities as self-employed persons and to set up and manage undertakings, in particular companies or firms within the meaning of the second paragraph of Article 48, under the conditions laid down for its own nationals by the law of the country where such establishment is effected, subject to the provisions of the chapter relating to capital.' (Art. 43 (ex Art. 52) second paragraph.

[56] See Agreement on the European Economic Area, 2 May 1992, Art. 34.

[57] See the Vaduz Convention, 21 June 2001, amending and updating the original Stockholm Convention of 1960, Art 23 (Principles and scope). Paragraph 2 of this article adds: '*in order to be considered as a company or firm of a Member State, the company or firm shall have a real and continuous link with the economy in that Member State.*'

[58] See Partnership Agreement, *cit.*, Annex II (Terms and Conditions of Financing), Art. 14 (Definition of 'companies and firms') '*1. For the purpose of this Agreement, "companies or firms of a Member State or an ACP State" mean companies or firms constituted under civil or commercial law,*

seat criteria, with the requirement of the existence of a 'real and continuous link with the economy' of the party granting nationality.[59] The 2000 EFTA States-Mexico FTA also follows this model.[60]

A combination of the incorporation and corporate seat criteria is used also by the 1987 ASEAN Agreement for the Promotion and Protection of Investments that provides that '*[t]he term "company" of a Contracting Party shall mean a corporation, partnership or other business association, incorporated or constituted under the laws in force in the territory of any Contracting Party wherein the place of effective management is situated*'.[61] The 1994 Colonia Protocol on the reciprocal promotion and protection of investment within Mercosur uses the incorporation as well as the seat and control criteria.[62] The 2001 Revised Treaty Establishing the Caribbean Community, is an example of the cumulation of the three main criteria—country of incorporation, of the seat and of ownership/control—compounded by the requirement that, in order to be deemed a national, the legal entity must carry on 'substantial activity' in the country of nationality.[63]

including corporations, whether public or otherwise, cooperative societies and other legal persons and partnerships governed by public or private law, save for those which are non-profit-making, formed in accordance with the law of a Member State or an ACP State and whose statutory office, central administration or principal place of business is a Member State or an ACP State. 2. However, a company or firm having only its statutory office in a Member State or an ACP State must be engaged in an activity which has an effective and continuous link with the economy of that Member State or ACP State.'

[59] See, for instance, Decision No 2/2001 of the European Union and Mexico Joint Council of 27 February 2001 implementing Articles 6, 9, 12(2)(b) and 50 of the Economic Partnership, Political Coordination and Cooperation Agreement, in *Official Journal of the European Communities*, L 70, 12 March 2001, pp. 7–50, Art. 3(e): '*a "Community juridical person" or a "Mexican juridical person" means a juridical person set up in accordance with the laws of the State of the Community or of Mexico, respectively, and having its registered office, central administration, or principal place of business in the territory of the Community or of Mexico, respectively; Should the juridical person have only its registered office or central administration in the territory of the Community or Mexico, respectively, it shall not be considered as a Community or a Mexican juridical person, respectively, unless its operations possess a real and continuous link with the economy of the Community or Mexico, respectively*.'

[60] See Free Trade Agreement between the EFTA States and the United Mexican States, 27 November 2000, Art. 20 (Definitions). Reproduced in UNCTAD, *cit.*, vol. IX, 2002, p. 198.

[61] See Art. I (2). *Id.*, p. 294.

[62] See the Protocolo de Colonia para la promocion y proteccion reciproca de inversiones en el Mercosur (Intrazona), of 17 January 1994, Art. 1.2 '*El término "inversor" designa ... b) toda persona jurídica constituída de conformidad con las leyes y reglamentaciones de una Parte Contratante y que tenga su sede en el territorio de dicha Parte Contratante. c) las personas jurídicas constituídas en el territorio donde se realiza la inversión, efectivamente controladas, directa o indirectamente, por personas físicas o jurídicas definidas en a) y b)*.' Similar language is also contained in the Protocolo sobre promocion y proteccion de inversiones provenientes de estados no partes del Mercosur, of 5 August 1994, Art. 2.2. These texts are reproduced in UNCTAD, *cit.*, vol. II, 1996, pp. 514–515 and 529.

[63] See Revised Treaty of Chaguaramas Establishing the Caribbean Community Including the Caricom Single Market and Economy, Art. 32 providing that '*a person shall be regarded as a national of a Member State if such person [...] is a company or other legal entity constituted in the*

On the other hand, the 2002 Singapore-Japan Economic Partnership Agreement considers a juridical person of the other Party as any entity constituted therein, which, even if owned or controlled by persons of non-Parties, is engaged in substantive business operations in the territory of either Party.[64] The same liberal approach is followed in the 2002 EFTA States-Singapore FTA.[65] Unlike the Singapore-Japan Agreement, the EFTA-Singapore one does not include denial of benefit provisions.[66] The 2003 Singapore-Australia FTA deems *'legal persons of the other Party'* those constituted or otherwise organized under the law of such Party, with no further requirement. In case of services provided through locally established legal entities, these are deemed *'of the other Party'*, if they are owned or controlled by a natural or legal person of the other Party. This approach is balanced, only with respect to service suppliers, by a denial of benefits clause.[67]

Member State in conformity with the laws thereof and which that State regards as belonging to it, provided that such company or other legal entity has been formed for gainful purposes and has its registered office and central administration, and carries on substantial activity, within the Community and which is substantially owned and effectively controlled by persons mentioned in subparagraphs (i) [dealing with citizens] and (ii) [dealing with residents] of this paragraph .... a company or other legal entity is: (i) substantially owned if more than 50 per cent of the equity Interest therein is beneficially owned by nationals [citizens and residents]; (ii) effectively controlled if nationals [citizens and residents] have the power to name a majority of its directors or otherwise legally to direct its actions.' Reproduced in UNCTAD, *cit.*, vol. VIII, 2002, pp. 44–45.

[64] See Agreement between Japan and the Republic of Singapore for a New-Age Economic Partnership, of 13 January 2002, Art. 58 (Scope and Definitions under Chapter 7) *'the term "juridical person of the other Party" means a juridical person which is either: (i) constituted or otherwise organised under the law of the other Party and, if it is owned or controlled by natural persons of non-Parties or juridical persons constituted or otherwise organised under the law of non-Parties, is engaged in substantive business operations in the territory of either Party; or (ii) in the case of the supply of a service through commercial presence, owned or controlled by: (A) natural persons of the other Party; or (B) juridical persons of the other Party identified under sub-paragraph (i) above.'* See also Article 62 (Service Suppliers of Any Non-Party) *'Each Party shall also accord treatment granted under this Chapter to a service supplier other than those of the Parties, that is a juridical person constituted under the laws of either Party, and who supplies a service through commercial presence, provided that it engages in substantive business operations in the territory of either Party.'* Reproduced in UNCTAD, *cit.*, vol. VIII, 2002, p. 166 and 170.

[65] See Free Trade Agreement between the EFTA States and Singapore, 26 June 2002, Art. 22 (Definitions). Reproduced in UNCTAD, *cit.*, vol. X, 2002, pp. 224–25.

[66] Similarly, the Free Trade Agreement Between the EFTA States and the Republic of Chile, 26 June 2003, includes a definition of *'judicial person of a Party'* based on incorporation and substantial business operations and on ownership or control in case of provision of services through locally established presence (Art. 23 (Definitions)). The agreement does not include a denial of benefit clause.

[67] See Singapore-Australia Free Trade Agreement, 17 February 2003, Chapter 7 (Trade in Services), Art. 1 (Definitions) and Art. 17 (Denial of Benefit): 'Subject to prior notification and consultation, a Party may deny the benefits of this Chapter to a service supplier of the other Party where the Party establishes that the service supplier is owned or controlled by persons of a non-Party and that it has no substantive business operations in the territory of the other Party.'

An interesting case is also the 2003 China-Hong Kong Closer Economic Partnership Arrangement. It stipulates that a service supplier of any WTO Member, which is constituted under the laws of one signatory and engaged there in substantive business operations, is entitled to treatment granted by the other signatory under the Arrangement.[68] An Annex specifies in great detail the requirements for incorporation and substantive business engagement necessary to be considered a Hong Kong service supplier.[69]

The country of ownership or control test is adopted as the sole test by a few instruments. These include the 1975 Multinational Companies Code of the Central African Customs and Economic Union,[70] and the 1991 Decision 291 of the Commission of the Cartagena Agreement.[71] The 1998 Framework Agreement on the ASEAN Investment Area contains an elaborate definition of ASEAN investor based on a minimum ASEAN equity requirement.[72]

---

[68] See Mainland and Hong Kong Closer Economic Partnership Arrangement, 29 July 2003, Art. 12 (2).

[69] See Annex 5 (Definition of 'Service Supplier' and Related Requirements), 29 September 2003. In general, a 'juridical person' means any legal entity duly constituted or otherwise organized under the applicable laws of Hong Kong and has engaged in substantive business operations in Hong Kong. The criteria for determining that an enterprise has engaged in substantive business operations in Hong Kong include the years of substantive business operations in Hong Kong (for most services, at least three years; for construction, banking and insurance services, at least five); payment of profit tax; owning or renting of premises for business operations in Hong Kong, commensurate with the scope and the scale of the enterprise's business; share of employment (more than 50 per cent of employees engaged in the substantive business operations in Hong Kong should be residents staying in Hong Kong without limit of stay and employees from the Mainland staying in Hong Kong on One Way Permit).

[70] See Art. 6 (b) '*foreign investors: natural persons and corporate bodies of foreign nationality, as well as companies in whose capital national participation is less than 50 per cent.*' Reproduced in UNCTAD, *cit.*, vol. II, 1996, p. 177.

[71] See Decision 291 (Regime for the Common Treatment of Foreign Capital and Trademarks, Patents, Licensing Agreements and Royalties), of 21 March 1991, Art. 1: '*Foreign Enterprise: an enterprise incorporated or established in the recipient country, in which national investors own less than fifty-one percent of the equity capital or, if more than that, in the judgment of the competent national agency that percentage is not reflected in the technical, financial, administrative and commercial management of the enterprise.*' *Id.*, p. 447. Members of the Cartagena Agreement are: Bolivia, Colombia, Ecuador, Peru, and Venezuela.

[72] See The Framework Agreement on the ASEAN Investment Area, of 7 October 1998, '*"ASEAN investor" means: i. a national of a Member State; or ii. any juridical person of a Member State, making an investment in another Member State, the effective ASEAN equity of which taken cumulatively with all other ASEAN equities fulfills at least the minimum percentage required to meet the national equity requirement and other equity requirements of domestic laws and published national policies, if any, of the host country in respect of that investment. For the purpose of this definition, equity of nationals or juridical persons of any Member State shall be deemed to be the equity of nationals or juridical persons of the host country. "Effective ASEAN equity" in respect of an investment in an ASEAN Member State means ultimate holdings by nationals or juridical persons of ASEAN Member States in that investment. Where the shareholding/equity structure of an ASEAN investor makes it difficult to establish the ultimate holding structure, the rules and procedures for determining effective equity used by the Member State in which the ASEAN investor is investing may be applied.*' Reproduced in UNCTAD, *cit.*, vol. IV, 2000, p. 228.

In conclusion, the practice of bilateral and regional agreements is rather consistent with the one developed in the context of BITs. The nationality of service providers as natural person investors is generally regulated by the national law of the signatories and often covers both citizens and permanent residents. The nationality of service providers as corporate investors is determined on the basis of a combination of various criteria, most typically the place of incorporation, the place of the corporate seat, the carrying out of substantial business operations and the nationality of the owner or controller of the legal person.

There is no clear trend in terms of the combination and cumulation of the various criteria. However, some instruments are distinctly more 'liberal' in extending their coverage to entities that have a less strict relation with the economies of the parties. Others show a preference to afford the preferential treatment only to companies clearly and effectively linked to the signatories. The origin of services as such is generally not addressed in any detail.

4.3.3 *The approach of the GATS*

In a legal system such as the WTO that is fast approaching universality, the issue of origin should in principle be of lesser relevance. However, attaching an origin to services and service providers remains an important issue even in a non-preferential context. The same is indeed true also in the area of goods trade as the continuing relevance of non-preferential Rules of Origin clearly suggests.

With regard to services an additional reason for the continued relevance of multilateral Rules of Origin is the existence of a list of MFN exceptions lodged under Article II of the GATS, which, in order to be applied, require a determination of origin or nationality. Furthermore, in a system where, unlike BITs and a large number of regional agreements, there is no private right of action for investors, the nationality of service providers may also be of particular concern in the field of dispute settlement.

The GATS does not depart substantially from the practice under bilateral and regional agreements. In so far as the origin of a service is concerned, Art. XXVIII (Definitions) provides that ' *"service of another Member" means a service which is supplied, . . . from or in the territory of that other Member*'. This means that for cross-border supply of services, or 'Mode 1', the territory from which a service is supplied to the consumer confers origin. It also means that for consumption abroad or 'Mode 2' the territory in which the service is supplied to the consumer confers origin. This result obtains in both cases even if such a territory is that of the last (and potentially less significant) stage in a multicountry production process or that from which the service was only retailed. Art. XXVIII also provides that, for a service that is supplied through commercial presence (i.e. the presence of a juridical person, or 'Mode 3') or through the presence of a natural person (or 'Mode 4'), ' "*service of another Member" means a service which is supplied, . . . by a service supplier of that other Member.*' This means that for Modes 3 and 4 the origin of a service is identical to the nationality of the service supplier that provides that particular service.

A ' "*service supplier" means any person that supplies a service*'. A person can either be a natural or a juridical person. With regard to natural persons the GATS adopts the approach common to many BITs and bilateral and regional agreements of considering '*natural persons of another Member*' both its nationals and permanent residents on the basis on the domestic law of each Member.[73] With respect to juridical persons,[74] the GATS again adopts the familiar criteria of incorporation, substantial business operations and ownership and control. In general a '*juridical person of another Member*' means a juridical person who is '*constituted or otherwise organized under the law of that other Member, and is engaged in substantive business operations in the territory of that Member or any other Member*'.[75] Thus the country of incorporation confers nationality also in the case where the substantive business operations are carried out in another Member country. However, when a juridical person is constituted in a Member country for the purpose of supplying services, such an entity retains the nationality of the natural or juridical person who owns or controls it.[76] A '*juridical person*' is considered to be either owned by nationals of a particular Member if

---

[73] See Art. XXVIII (k): ' "*natural person of another Member" means a natural person who resides in the territory of that other Member or any other Member, and who under the law of that other Member: (i) is a national of that other Member; or (ii) has the right of permanent residence in that other Member, in the case of a Member which: 1. does not have nationals; or 2. accords substantially the same treatment to its permanent residents as it does to its nationals in respect of measures affecting trade in services, as notified in its acceptance of or accession to the WTO Agreement, provided that no Member is obligated to accord to such permanent residents treatment more favourable than would be accorded by that other Member to such permanent residents. Such notification shall include the assurance to assume, with respect to those permanent residents, in accordance with its laws and regulations, the same responsibilities that the other Member bears with respect to its nationals*'.

[74] The category of juridical persons is broad as it includes '*any legal entity duly constituted or otherwise organized under applicable law, whether for profit or otherwise, and whether privately-owned or governmentally-owned, including any corporation, trust, partnership, joint venture, sole proprietorship or association*'. See Art. XXVIII (l). Unincorporated entities are also covered as footnote 12 provides that '*Where the service is not supplied directly by a juridical person but through other forms of commercial presence such as a branch or a representative office, the service supplier (i.e. the juridical person) shall, nonetheless, through such presence be accorded the treatment provided for service suppliers under the Agreement. . . .*' [75] See Art. XXVIII (m) (i).

[76] See Art. XXVIII (m) (ii): '*in the case of the supply of a service through commercial presence, owned or controlled by: 1. natural persons of that Member; or 2. juridical persons of that other Member identified under subparagraph (i)*'.

they held more than 50 per cent of its equity, or controlled by nationals of a Member if they had the power to name a majority of its directors or otherwise to legally direct its actions.[77]

Again adopting a well-known approach, the GATS also contains a denial of benefits clause. Such a clause, embodied in Article XXVII, allows a Member to deny benefits under the agreement to services originating in the territory of a non-Member, as well as to service suppliers that are juridical persons. In this latter case, benefits can be denied if the denying Member *'establishes that it [such service supplier] is not a service supplier of another Member'*.[78] This means that benefits can be denied to service suppliers owned or controlled by natural persons of, or legal entities incorporated in, non-WTO Member countries.

Finally, in the area of preferential trade, the GATS contains two important provisions. Art. V (Economic Integration) states in mandatory language that a juridical person service supplier of any WTO Member, once it is constituted under the laws of a party to an economic integration agreement,[79] 'shall be entitled to treatment granted under such agreement, provided that it engages in substantive business operations in the territory of the parties to such agreement.'[80] This is tantamount to saying that a service provider incorporated in a country member to a preferential agreement, even if owned or controlled by nationals of a (WTO Member) third party, such as a subsidiary, will have to be treated in an identical way as a service provider of any of the preferential agreement's signatories (i.e. it will be treated as a national). The only requirement being that such juridical person engages in substantial business operation in any of the parties. If the economic integration agreement is composed only of developing countries some flexibility applies, as 'more favourable treatment may be granted to juridical persons owned or controlled by natural persons of the parties to such an agreement.'[81]

4.3.4 Ranking the rules?

The diversity of practices with regard to Rules of Origin for services and investment across BITs and regional agreements complicate attempts

---

[77] See Art. XXVIII (n): *'a juridical person is: (i) "owned" by persons of a Member if more than 50 per cent of the equity interest in it is beneficially owned by persons of that Member; (ii) "controlled" by persons of a Member if such persons have the power to name a majority of its directors or otherwise to legally direct its actions; (iii) "affiliated" with another person when it controls, or is controlled by, that other person; or when it and the other person are both controlled by the same person'.*

[78] Art. XXVII also adds that benefits can be denied to *'a service supplier of a Member to which the denying Member does not apply the WTO Agreement.'*

[79] As defined in GATS Art. V(1).   [80] See Art. V (6).   [81] See Art. V(3)(b).

at comparative assessment. First, actual practice with regard to the determination of the origin of any particular service is very limited. What prevails is the GATS-inspired approach of conferring as origin the country from which or in which the service is supplied or the country of nationality of the service supplier. Such an approach, while having the advantage of simplicity, may prove unsuited to the evolving reality of technologically sophisticated services that are increasingly traded electronically and made up of inputs sourced from various locations.

An assessment of origin or nationality rules for service providers can rely instead on a much broader experience. If one were to rank existing approaches in terms of how much they increase or decrease the coverage of any agreement's substantive rules (i.e. to how many natural and in particular juridical persons an agreement's (preferential) treatment provisions apply), a few considerations could be advanced. Under current practice, recourse to four main corporate nationality criteria—place of incorporation, location of the seat, substantive business operation and ownership or control—is rather consolidated. The place of incorporation is the criterion that would probably yield the most expansive coverage, as it appears to be the easiest and cheapest for investors to meet. The location of a company's seat or headquarters also does not seem unduly burdensome so long as the seat is interpreted to refer to a company's 'statutory' seat. However, if such a test refers to the place of the enterprise's central administration and direction, then such a requirement could certainly restrict the granting of nationality for many companies (in particular subsidiaries), which could then be deemed as assuming the nationality of their parent corporation. The criterion of substantial business operations aims to exclude from coverage all companies that operate primarily as nameplates for taxation or other (e.g. regulatory) purposes. Finally, a test of control and even more so, of (full) ownership can be likened to a citizenship requirement applied to the licensing of a professional, as it essentially excludes all foreign companies, even if fully integrated into the domestic economy of a signatory, from the benefits of an integration scheme. However, as the notions of 'substantial business operation' as well as 'ownership' and 'control' remain very often undefined, these tests could be contentious.

Such a ranking, albeit hard and fast, tends to be complicated by the usual combination and cumulation of criteria. Very often, more than one test is used and thus their impact cumulates. Furthermore, the selected criteria are in various instances accompanied by a denial of benefits rule that allows for flexibility in the application of the chosen criteria, in particular the most restrictive one relating to ownership and control. The discretion such an approach entails obviously complicates any assessment of the potential impact of agreed rules of nationality.

In general, recourse to more 'restrictive' criteria as well as the cumulation of different criteria tend to be used in those instances where parties aim at limiting the benefits of an agreement to those legal entities that effectively have economic ties with the signatories and at preventing free riding by companies that are nationals of third parties. On the contrary, when free riding is of less concern and the objective is to broaden an agreement's scope of application and reduce the incidence for trade and investment diversion, agreements provide for the possibility of applying more liberal rules, notably those relating to a company's place of incorporation or to the need to show the existence of substantial business operations.

4.4 Concluding remarks

Rules of Origin and nationality for services and investment are substantially different from those applicable to goods. A number of salient characteristics of how services are produced and traded internationally help to explain key differences in rule design. Tests of substantial transformation and value added, even if conceivable in theory, would be quite difficult to apply to services in practice. This is especially so given the predominance of commercial presence as the most frequent mode of supplying services in foreign markets.

Unlike goods trade, current practice in the area of services and investment focuses on producers, rather than products (services). This plays a large role in explaining their relative simplicity, and also the fact that, unlike goods-related rules, they are not sector or service specific but tend to be applied across the board. Such uniformity tends to lessen their potential protectionist incidence as instruments of targeted industrial-policy activism.

However, information technologies are greatly enhancing the scope for cross-border tradability, and the advent of manufacturing-like production chain features will likely complicate determination of the origin of many types of services in the future. Whether such a trend will heighten the risk of restrictive, product-specific, Rules of Origin (for outsourced services, for instance, given current concerns over white collar job loss in OECD countries) or *a contrario* provide incentives for the adoption of more liberal rules given the difficulty of assigning origin to hybrid, composite product offerings, remains to be seen. For the most part, experience with conferring origin to services remains too modest at this stage to allow any analytically discernable trend to emerge.

Practice in terms of corporate nationality is, however, far richer. On this basis, it is already possible to note how various types of nationality or origin rules can exert differing economic effects. From an economic efficiency standpoint, a liberal rule of origin—a substantial business operation test that allows any established firm, regardless of its nationality of ownership, to partake in the benefits of an integration scheme—is preferable to more restrictive tests that emphasize control and/or ownership, as the latter can far more easily (and effectively) respond to protectionist and national champion or other industrial-policy yearnings.

Because of the first-mover advantages that come with incumbency in some (especially network-based sectors) services, and the economy-wide growth properties of a number of core infrastructural services, securing access to the most efficient service suppliers is important for development purposes. Accordingly, a restrictive rule of origin that denies investment benefits to firms owned and controlled by nationals of non-parties, as well as rules that deny labor market or temporary entry access to non-nationals, are most likely to be second best.

However, other considerations are also at play in the creation of preferential schemes. Parties to such schemes may aim at fostering regional service providers on traditional infant industry rationales. They may try to induce investment from third-party providers in the region in order to capture the benefits that such investment may generate. In such instances, Rules of Origin and nationality that are less expansive and require the existence of significant economic linkages in the territories of the parties may be deemed preferable by the integrating partners. Furthermore, liberal Rules of Origin suffer from the negotiating dynamic downsides of MFN-based liberalization, notably its associated free-riding dimension.

While at present less detailed and complex than in the area of goods, Rules of Origin and nationality for services can nonetheless be designed, like their goods brethren, to meet various policy objectives. One can only hope that they remain primarily instrumental in scope rather than mutating into yet another instrument in the protectionist toolbox of countries.

Part III

The political economy of Rules of Origin

5

Rules of Origin as export subsidies[†]

Olivier Cadot, Antoni Estevadeordal, and Akiko Suwa-Eisenmann

5.1 Introduction

With the proliferation of preferential trading agreements over the last two decades, considerable attention has been devoted to assessing their effect on market access. Notwithstanding the fact that GATT Article XXIV, para. 8(b) requires the removal of trade barriers on 'substantially all trade' in Free-Trade Agreements (FTAs), in reality numerous barriers to intrabloc trade are often left intact or even erected as part of the agreements.[1] Rules of Origin (RoOs) feature prominently among those barriers.

In principle, RoOs are meant to prevent the trans-shipment of goods imported from the rest of the world, via member states with low external tariffs, into those with higher ones. In practice, these rules often have the effect of 'exporting protection' from high-tariff members to low-tariff ones, as pointed out by Krishna and Krueger (1995) and Krueger (1997).

In North-South FTAs, in particular, the combination of tariff preferences and RoOs can affect trade flows in ways that are not conducive to economic efficiency. Suppose that the production of final goods involves two stages: the capital-intensive production of components, and labor-intensive assembly. If goods are entirely produced in the North early on

† We are thankful to Celine Carrere, Jon Haveman, Jim de Melo, Marcelo Olarreaga, Pablo Sanguinetti, Maurice Schiff, and participants at the IIIrd Workshop of the Regional Integration Network, Punta Del Este, December 2003, the joint IDB/CEPR workshop, Paris, April 2003, the IDB/CEPR/INRA/DELTA conference,Washington, February 2004, and a seminar at GREQAM, University of Aix, for useful comments and suggestions on previous versions. All errors remain ours, and the views expressed in this chapter do not necessarily reflect those of the institutions to which the authors are affiliated. Special thanks go to Kati Suominen and to David Colin for superb research assistance.

1 See Serra *et al.* (1996) for a review of shortcomings in the application of Article XXIV.

in their product cycle, preferential tariff reductions may accelerate the process of assembly relocation in the South, leading to what Hanson (1996) called 'regional production networks'.[2] Suppose, however, that component manufacturing could profitably be relocated to another Northern country outside of the preferential trading bloc. Rules of Origin, by forcing Southern assemblers to source a minimum fraction of their components in the area, prevent the ultimate relocation of the whole value chain in the world's most efficient location. In other words, RoOs, when they bind, organize trade diversion by creating captive markets for relatively inefficient Northern intermediate-good producers.

While the potentially trade-diverting effect of RoOs has been widely recognized in the literature (see, for instance, Falvey and Reed, 2000), the recent political-economy literature has also highlighted the fact that RoOs can sometimes make preferential agreements politically feasible in circumstances where they wouldn't be otherwise (Duttagupta, 2000; Duttagupta and Panagaryia, 2002). As Grossman and Helpman (1995) showed that trade-diverting FTAs are, *ceteris paribus*, more likely than others to be politically acceptable, Duttagupta and Panagariya's result is quite consistent with RoOs acting as 'trade diverters'.

While the theoretical analysis of RoOs has made considerable strides since Krueger's pioneering work, their empirical analysis is still in its infancy, partly because their complex legal nature makes measurement difficult. Estevadeordal (2000) recently proposed a way of overcoming this difficulty by devising a qualitative index of RoO strictness. Using the fact that most RoOs are—at least in recent agreements—expressed as a required change in tariff heading at various levels of aggregation, Estevadeordal's index takes values that increase in the level of aggregation of the required change, the idea being that a change at a more aggregate level is 'wider' and hence a more stringent transformation requirement. On the basis of his index, he identified a strong negative effect of NAFTA's RoOs on Mexican market access. Using the same index, Anson *et al.* (2003) showed that the effect of NAFTA's tariff preferences is systematically reduced by RoOs.

Although Anson *et al.*'s results are qualitatively unambiguous, they suffer from the fact that the potential endogeneity of RoOs is not treated. If there is little doubt that, as pointed out by Estevadeordal (2000) and

---

[2] However, Hanson also shows that the emergence of vertical trade between Mexico and the United States largely pre-dates the formation of NAFTA, as assembly plants operating under the older 'maquiladora' regime already accounted for 53% of Mexico's manufactured exports in 1992.

Sanguinetti (2003), RoOs are the result of a political bargaining process that is itself likely to be affected by trade patterns, it is not entirely clear, short of a full political-economy model, what exactly they are endogenous to. If they are endogenous to Mexican final-good exports, clearly there is a simultaneity problem. If, however, RoOs are endogenous to trade flows that are related to Mexican exports only through an indirect, non-linear relationship, for estimation purposes the relevant system may be recursive rather than truly simultaneous.

In this chapter, we take the endogeneity problem as a starting point for an exploration of the political-economy forces that are likely to shape RoOs. Although many assumptions must be made along the way, we show that in a model of endogenous RoO determination à la Grossman–Helpman (1994), the key determinant of RoOs in terms of trade flows is a product of US intermediate-good exports to Mexico and input-output coefficients. The model generates results both in terms of interpretation of what RoOs do and in terms of what the estimation strategy should be.

As for interpretative results, the key one is that whereas RoOs create captive markets for US intermediate goods, tariff preferences needed to make them acceptable to Mexican exporters along their participation constraint constitute a transfer—albeit a modest one—from US taxpayers.[3] The combination of RoOs and tariff preference is then equivalent to an export subsidy on US intermediate goods. The model thus proposes a tentative answer, in this particular context, to a question arising frequently in trade policy—namely, why inefficient indirect instruments are used to redistribute income or favor particular activities when more direct instruments would achieve the same results at lower welfare costs. Here, RoOs substitute for a prohibited instrument, as export subsidies would be in violation of the US's obligations under the GATT.

Our analysis of Rules of Origin requires a model with multiple stages of production. In contrast to Lloyd (1993), Rodriguez (2001) and Carrère and de Melo (2004) who use a multistage production model due to Dixit and Grossman (1982), our analysis requires only a two-stage Leontieff production technology whose analytics are very simple.

As for the estimation, the model suggests, as the key determinant of NAFTA's RoOs, a vector product of input-output coefficients multiplied by US intermediate-good exports upstream of the good to which RoOs apply. Our estimation strategy thus consists of regressing RoOs on steady-state

---

[3] By participation constraint, we mean that the rate of effective protection granted to Mexican final-good producers by the combination of tariff preferences and Rules of Origin is just zero.

tariff preferences (equal, at the end of the phase-out period, to the US MFN tariff adjusted for exceptions) and the upstream variable just described, the functional form being the political-economy model's first-order condition. This generates a vector of predicted RoOs that are then used in the market-access equation. As for tariff preferences, we do not model their endo-geneity directly as intra-NAFTA tariffs smoothly converge to zero over a fixed phase-out period. A fuller model would recognize, as Estevadeordal (2000) did, that the length of the phase-out may itself be endogenous, but the model we use does not lend itself easily to taking this into account.

NAFTA, on which we test the model's main predictions, is a good testing ground for the effect of RoOs. It is the quintessential example of the North-South agreement due to the comprehensive tariff liberalization built in the agreement and the fact that member countries share borders, eliminating the need to account for distance as in traditional gravity exercises. From 1989 to 1994, Mexico's exports to the United Stated benefitted from the Generalized System of Preferences (GSP), after which this regime was overhauled by NAFTA. We construct a panel dataset with information dating back to 1994 on commodity exports from Mexico to the United States under different preferential programs. The data was compiled mostly from USITC sources at the 6-digit HS disaggregation level and contains information on tariff preferences (GSP and NAFTA rates) granted by the United States to Mexico. The data on Rules of Origin comes from Estevadeordal (2000).

The results are in striking conformity with the model's predictions. All variables are significant—most of them at the 1% level—and have the expected signs. Tariff preferences and RoOs exert positive and negative influences respectively on Mexican exports, and the key variable influ-encing endogenously determined RoOs—a product of input-output coefficients and US intermediate exports to Mexico—has the predicted sign and is significant at the 1% level.

The chapter is organized as follows. Section 5.2 sets out the political-economy model and characterizes its equilibrium. Section 5.3 presents the empirical methodology and results, and Section 5.4 concludes.

5.2 Politically determined RoOs

This section uses a simple, stripped-down political-economy model to illustrate the simultaneous determination of tariff preferences and RoOs. Although the model borrows from Grossman and Helpman (1994) the appearance of a general-equilibrium model, it is best thought of as a partial-equilibrium one as interindustry linkages are non-existent except for the vertical linkages around which the discussion is centered.

5.2.1 *The economy*

Consider a PTA formed by two small economies, North (N) and South (S). The North produces, under increasing cost, an intermediate good denoted by the subscript I and exports it to the South that uses it to assemble a final good denoted by the subscript F. Southern supply of the final good is not enough to cover the North's consumption at its tariff-ridden price, so the North also imports from the rest of the world. The South imports all its own consumption of the final good from the rest of the world and exports all its production to the North.[4]

Households in both countries consume the final good and an aggregate of all other goods, which also serves as numeraire, under identical and quasilinear preferences. Let c_F and c_0 denote, respectively, the quantities of final and 'other' goods consumed by a representative consumer in either country. The utility function is

$$U = c_0 + u(c_F), \tag{5.1}$$

where $u' > 0$ and $u'' < 0$.

The final good sold in the free-trade area is produced by combining value added and the intermediate good. Value added is created with inter-sectorally mobile labor ℓ and specific capital κ under a technology $f(\ell, \kappa)$. The technology producing the final good, into which the value-added production function is nested, is of the Leontieff type with input-output coefficient a_{IF}. Letting y_F and x_I stand, respectively, for the final-good output and quantity of intermediate good consumed in the process,

$$y_F = \min\{f(\ell, \kappa); x_I/a_{IF}\}. \tag{5.2}$$

Let p_I^* and p_F^* be, respectively, the intermediate and final goods' world prices. Under free trade, given the technology postulated, the 'net price' out of which a Southern producer can remunerate value added (wages and profits) is

$$p^* = p_F^* - a_{IF} p_I^*. \tag{5.3}$$

With the stock of specific capital fixed, the technology f that generates value added displays diminishing returns on labor. The supply of value

---

[4] This is shown to arise endogenously as a result of tariff preferences, perfect competition, and the non-market saturation assumption in Cadot *et al.* (2001).

added is therefore upward sloping in its net price p^*, and economic rents accrue to owners of specific capital, who are assumed to be the industry's residual claimants.

A similar good is sold in the rest of the world, and the marketing mix between the free-trade area and the rest of the world is determined by a Constant Elasticity of Transformation (CET) technology (see the footnote in Section 5.3) that provides the functional form for the market-access equation estimated in the empirical part.

The rest of the economy uses only labor under constant returns to scale, which fixes the wage rate. Given this assumption, the model becomes a quasi-partial equilibrium one. In this setting, the Southern final-good producers' surplus under free trade, π_F^*, is a monotonic increasing function of p^*:

$$\pi_F^* = p^* y_F - w_S \ell_F.$$

Letting p be the *domestic* net price, $(p - p^*)/p$ is the effective rate of protection granted to Southern producers when selling on the Northern market.[5]

The intermediate good is produced in the North with 'value added only' (no intermediate consumption) under a technology similar to f (i.e. a CRS combination of labor and specific capital). Letting y_I be its output, the producer surplus is

$$\pi_I = p_I y_I - w^N \ell_I. \qquad (5.4)$$

Finally, we will treat the intermediate-good's supply elasticity in the North, $\varepsilon_I \equiv p_I y_I'/y_I$, as a constant.

5.2.2 The preferential regime

In order to keep things simple, we will treat MFN (external) tariffs on the final and intermediate goods as pre-determined to the PTA and hence parametric. Northern tariffs are, respectively, t_F^N and t_I^N and Southern ones t_F^S and t_I^S. In order to focus on the effects of Northern tariffs and RoOs, we will set $t_F^S = t_I^S = 0$. Extensions to other cases are straightforward but add little to the analysis.[6]

---

[5] To see this, it suffices to observe that p is unit value added.

[6] First, note that endogenous determination of MFN tariffs would yield $t_I^S = t_F^N = 0$ given that the South does not produce the intermediate good and the North does not produce the final one. However, if specialization is a result of the PTA and MFN tariffs are pre-determined to it (say, because they are negotiated in multilateral rounds and thus constitute valuable bargaining chips), they will not be eliminated after the PTA's formation.

The model's endogenous political-economy variables are the preferential tariff applied, as part of the PTA, on Southern exports of the final good, τ, and the regional value content of the RoO, r. Let x_I^N be the amount of intermediate good sourced in the North (as opposed to imported from the rest of the world), and let $\delta = t_F^N - \tau$ be the rate of preference (in specific form). The price at which Southern final-good producers—we will henceforth use the term 'assemblers' for brevity—can sell in the North is

$$p_F = \begin{cases} p_F^* + \delta & \text{if } x_I^N \geq rx_I \\ p_F^* & \text{otherwise.} \end{cases} \tag{5.5}$$

That is, Southern assemblers can sell under the PTA's preferential regime if they satisfy the RoO. If not, they sell under the MFN regime, i.e. at the world price.

Given the RoO, Southern assemblers selling under the preferential regime source a proportion r of their intermediate good in the North. The price of the 'composite' intermediate good is thus $rp_I + (1 - r)p_I^*$, and the net price faced by Southern assemblers is

$$p = p_F^* + \delta - a_{IF}[rp_I + (1 - r)p_I^*]. \tag{5.6}$$

5.2.3 The politics

We assume no bargaining between the Northern and Southern partners: the North makes a take-it-or-leave-it offer to the South that the South accepts as long as its participation constraint is not violated. This is admittedly a rather crude description of negotiations between Northern and Southern preferential partners but perhaps not an unrealistic one judging from ample anecdotal evidence about US-Mexico or EU-Eastern Europe negotiations.

Thus, the political action is in the North, where the RoO's RVC content r and the rate of preference δ are simultaneously determined. Our analysis is concerned with a transition phase during which preferences are partial. In the long run, after intrabloc tariffs have been phased out the rate of preference is automatically equal to the rate of MFN tariffs, so the participation constraint suffices to determine the RoO's RVC content. During

---

Secondly, even if $t_F^S > 0$, is level is inconsequential. To see this, observe that if $t_F^S < t_F^N$, the South's entire output is sold in the North and the analysis is as if t_F^S was zero. If $t_F^S > t_F^N$, the South's output is sold in priority on the Southern market. But if some of it is also exported to the Northern market (which is, of course, necessary for RoOs to have any effect at all) then the South's output being larger than its consumption, the Southern price is 'competed down' to the level of the Northern tariff-ridden price, and the analysis proceeds as before.

the transition phase, however, both are determined simultaneously. As a further simplification, whereas intrabloc tariffs are phased out progressively in a continuous manner, we assume that the phase-out is done in two steps: from MFN tariff to 'the' preferential rate (on which our analysis focuses), and hence to zero.

The politics is described by a Grossman–Helpman game in which the intermediate producers lobby faces the government with a contribution schedule $C(\delta, r)$ conditioned on the policy variables of interest to it, δ and r. The function C has the 'truthfulness' property that

$$\left.\frac{\partial C}{\partial r}\right|_{r^e, \delta^e} = \left.\frac{\partial \pi}{\partial r}\right|_{r^e, \delta^e} \quad \text{and} \quad \left.\frac{\partial C}{\partial \delta}\right|_{r^e, \delta^e} = \left.\frac{\partial \pi}{\partial \delta}\right|_{r^e, \delta^e},$$

where the superscript e designates equilibrium values. With only one lobby, the common agency degenerates into a simple principal-agent relationship.[7] Without hidden action, the principal (the lobby) is then able to appropriate the entire protection rents, and any equilibrium will have the property that the government is just indifferent between implementing the lobby's preferred policy and the default one (free trade).[8] Put differently, the lobby's contribution just compensates the government for the (subjective) monetary equivalent of the efficiency loss generated by trade protection. The government determines δ and r to maximize a linear combination of welfare (valued at a constant monetary equivalent a) and the lobby's contribution:

$$G^N \equiv C(\delta, r) + aW(\delta, r).$$

The pair (δ, r) is set to leave the FTA's Southern partner on its 'participation constraint'. Given that the South's consumption of the final good is

[7] The model ignores lobbying by Northern final-good producers, if any. There are several reasons for this. First, in terms of modelling issues, competitive final-good producers would be concerned about prices only, not market shares. As the Northern MFN tariff on the final good is unchanged, their profits would be unchanged as long as the area is not self-sufficient at the Northern tariff-ridden price. Secondly, even if the market is not competitive, as long as the South is on its participation constraint (more on this below) Southern exports to the North are unchanged.

Empirically, as far as NAFTA is concerned, a substantial proportion of the companies doing assembly work in Mexico for re-export into the US are either subsidiaries of US companies or non-competing subcontractors. Cases in which Mexican companies compete head on with US assemblers (either independent or vertically integrated) are, arguably, sufficiently marginal to assume that reducing such competition was *not* a key consideration for US negotiators.

[8] This assumption about rent sharing is in conformity with the empirical observation that small contributions seem to buy 'large' policies in terms of redistributive effects (Ansolobehere *et al.*, 2002). Any alternative assumption would imply larger contributions, which would go against the evidence.

always priced at p_F^*, consumer surplus is unaffected by changes in either τ or r. Thus, the only change in Southern welfare—or any political objective function combining welfare and producer surplus—is in assemblers' profits, and the South's participation constraint is completely characterized by $p = p^*$.

5.2.4 Equilibrium

RoOs have the effect of segmenting the intermediate good's market in the trading bloc. Southern assemblers selling on the Northern market must comply with the RoO if they are to benefit from the preferential regime. The market on which they buy the intermediate good is then a closed-economy market where Northern supply must match the RoO-induced Southern demand. We now determine p_I, the price prevailing on that market.

Price determination As already noted, with their home market unprotected, Southern assemblers sell all their output on the protected Northern market where they enjoy preferential access. Suppose that p_I is greater than p_I^*. In an interior solution, it has to be. The RoO's domestic content is then binding, which means that a proportion r of the South's intermediate-good demand will be sourced 'locally' (in the North). The market-clearing condition determining the intermediate good's domestic price is thus that the local demand induced by the RoO, $r a_{IF} y_F(p)$, be equal to its supply, i.e.

$$r a_{IF} y_F(p) = y_I(p_I), \tag{5.7}$$

where, as before, y_F is the South's final-good production and y_I is the North's intermediate-good production.

Let p_I satisfy eqn (5.7). If $p_I \leq p_I^* + t_I^N$, the RoO is not binding, which means that the North's supply of the intermediate good is sufficient to satisfy the South's needs and more. We will henceforth disregard this case and suppose that the intermediate good's price determined by eqn (5.7) is larger than its tariff-ridden price in the North.

Using eqns (5.3) and (5.6), the South's participation constraint can be written as

$$p_F - a_{IF}[r p_I + (1 - r)p_I^*] = p_F^* - a_{IF},$$

or, using eqn (5.5) and simplifying,

$$\delta = r a_{IF} \Delta p_I, \tag{5.8}$$

where $\Delta p_I = p_I - p_I^*$. Expression (5.8) says that the degree of effective protection given to Southern assemblers by the combination of r and δ is zero.

In conformity with the agency literature, we will assume that when just indifferent, Southern assemblers choose to use the preferential regime. Moreover, we assume homogeneity of firms, so *all of them* use the preferential regime. With compliance-cost heterogeneity among Southern assemblers, the preferential regime's utilization rate would be less than one and a decreasing function of the rate of effective protection conferred by the mix of preferences and RoOs, as in Carrere and de Melo (Chapter 7). As this would add substantial complication to the analysis, we leave it for further research.

Under compliance-cost homogeneity, the Northern government's maximization problem under the South's participation constraint and the intermediate-good market-clearing condition is

$$\max_{\delta,r} G^N \equiv C_I(\delta, r) + aW^N(\delta, r)$$

s.t.

$$\delta = ra_{IF}\Delta p_I \tag{5.9}$$

$$ra_{IF}y_F(p) = y_I(p_I)$$

$$0 \le r \le 1, 0 \le \delta \le t_F^N.$$

As an intermediate step before solving problem (5.9), we now calculate two useful derivatives treating r as pre-determined: dp_I/dr and $d\delta/dr$. The first measures the marginal effect of the RoO, expressed as a regional value content (RVC) r, on the intermediate good's internal price. The second measures the substitutability between the RoO's RVC rate r and the tariff preference rate δ along the South's participation constraint. Both apply only to interior solutions, i.e. when the inequality constraints (5.9) are not binding.

Differentiating totally eqns (5.7) and (5.8) with respect to p_I, δ and r and rearranging gives

$$d\delta = a_{IF}\Delta p_I dr + ra_{IF}dp_I$$

$$a_{IF}y_F dr = y_I' dp_I.$$

The second line gives directly

$$\frac{dp_I}{dr} = \frac{a_{IF}y_F}{y_I'} = \frac{p_I}{r\varepsilon_I} > 0, \tag{5.10}$$

where ε_I is the intermediate good's supply elasticity—treated as constant—and the second part of the equation comes from eqn (5.7). As can be read directly from eqn (5.10), the elasticity of the intermediate good's internal price to the RoO's RVC rate is just the inverse of its supply elasticity. As the latter goes to infinity, as expected the price becomes totally insensitive to a tightening of the RoO.

Moreover, eqn (5.10) shows that, as long as tariff preferences can be adjusted, the ambiguity of the RoO's effect on the intermediate-good's price noted by Ju and Krishna (1998, 2000) does not apply except at corners. The reason is that, by construction, along the South's participation constraint value added in the final-good sector cannot go down, so (given the Leontieff technology) nor can output. In other words, here RoOs cannot become so stiff as to become self-defeating because any tightening of r is met by an offsetting increase in δ. In order to see what happens at corners, solve eqn (5.8) for r at $\delta = t_F^N$ and define $\bar{r} \equiv t_F^N / a_{IF} \Delta p_I$ as the RVC that just satisfies the participation constraint at full preferences. Ju and Krishna's argument applies in the semi-open interval $(\bar{r}, 1]$ if $\bar{r} < 1$. With homogenous firms in the South (in terms of their compliance costs), beyond $\bar{r}$ the participation constraint is violated and the preferential regime's utilization rate jumps down to zero.

Upon rearrangement, the first line of eqn (5.10) gives

$$\begin{aligned}
\frac{d\delta}{dr} &= a_{IF} \Delta p_I + r a_{IF} \frac{dp_I}{dr} \\
&= a_{IF} (\Delta p_I + \frac{p_I}{\varepsilon_I}) > 0.
\end{aligned} \tag{5.11}$$

Thus, the compensation required by a tightening of the RoO's RVC rate, in terms of tariff preferences, has two components. The first is just the difference between the internal and world prices of the intermediate good multiplied by the input-output coefficient. The second reflects the fact that as the RoO's RVC rate is tightened, costs go up for Southern assemblers not just because they must source a higher proportion of intermediate goods in the area where they are more expensive, but in addition, doing so puts upward pressure on their internal price. This last effect is inversely proportional to its supply elasticity.

We are now in a position to solve problem (5.9). Combining the inequality constraint on δ with the participation constraint gives

$$r a_{IF} \Delta p_I \leq t_F^N.$$

Letting λ and μ be two Lagrange multipliers, we have

$$\pounds = G[\delta(r), r] + \lambda(1 - r) + \mu(t_F^N - r a_{IF} \Delta p_I),$$

and the Kuhn–Tucker conditions are

$$\frac{dG}{dr} \leq 0, r \geq 0, r\frac{dG}{dr} = 0;$$
$$1 - r \geq 0, \lambda \geq 0, \lambda(1 - r) = 0;$$
$$t_F^N - ra_{IF}\Delta p_I \geq 0, \mu \geq 0, \mu(t_F^N - ra_{IF}\Delta p_I) = 0.$$

We now construct the expression for dG/dr that will be set equal to zero under the first-order condition. It has two components: a contribution effect and a welfare effect.

Contribution effect Using Hotelling's lemma and the contribution function's truthfulness property, we have, in the neighborhood of the equilibrium,

$$\frac{dC}{dr} = \frac{d\pi_I}{dr} = y_I \frac{dp_I}{dr} = \begin{cases} p_I y_I/r\varepsilon_I & \text{if } r < \bar{r} \\ 0 & \text{if } r > \bar{r}, \end{cases} \tag{5.12}$$

and the derivative is undefined at $r = \bar{r}$ because p_I jumps down to one at that point (because the preferential regime's utilization rate falls to zero). Thus, left to itself—i.e. absent any welfare consideration—the Northern intermediate-good lobby would be willing to push RoOs to $\bar{r}$, the level of RoO strictness that makes Southern assemblers just indifferent between using the preferential regime or not given tariff-free access ($\delta = t_F^N$).[9]

Combining eqns (5.12) and (5.11), it is apparent that the Northern intermediate-good lobby is willing to contribute in favor of 'deep' tariff preference in the downstream sector because, along the South's participation constraint, tariff preference buys stiffer RoOs, which in turn are to its advantage.

Welfare effect Let m_F and m_F^* be the North's imports of final goods from the South and from the rest of the world, respectively. As the North does not produce the final good, $m_F + m_F^* = c_F$. Under quasi-linear preferences, Northern welfare is the sum of income—from profits, wages and tariff revenue—and consumer surplus, which by eqn (5.1) comes only from consumption of the final good. Formally,

$$W^N = \pi_I + w^N\ell_I + \tau m_F + t_F^N m_F^* + u(c_F) - p_F c_F.$$

As $m_F = y_F$ (the South exports its entire final-good output to the North), $m_F^* = c_F - m_F = c_F - y_F$, so

$$W^N = \pi_I + w^N\ell_I + t_F^N c_F - \delta y_F + u(c_F) - p_F c_F. \tag{5.13}$$

[9] We are grateful to Maurice Schiff for helping to clarify this discussion.

Along the South's participation constraint, p is constant and hence so is y_F. Thus, treating p_I and δ as endogenous variables along the problem's constraints,

$$\frac{dW^N}{dr} = y_I \frac{dp_I}{dr} - y_F \frac{d\delta}{dr}$$
$$= \frac{p_I y_I}{r\varepsilon_I} - a_{IF} y_F (\Delta p_I + \frac{p_I}{\varepsilon_I}).$$

Using the fact that, by eqn (5.7), $a_{IF} y_F = y_I/r$, this becomes

$$\frac{dW^N}{dr} = \frac{y_I}{r} \left\{ \frac{p_I}{\varepsilon_I} - (\Delta p_I + \frac{p_I}{\varepsilon_I}) \right\}$$
$$= -\frac{y_I}{r} \Delta p_I < 0.$$

(5.14)

Combining the contribution and welfare effects gives

$$\frac{dG^N}{dr} = \frac{dC}{dr} + a \frac{dW^N}{dr}$$
$$= \frac{p_I y_I}{r\varepsilon_I} - a \frac{y_I}{r} \Delta p_I$$
$$= \frac{p_I y_I}{r} (\frac{1}{\varepsilon_I} - \frac{a\Delta p_I}{p_I}).$$

Under the first-order condition, this expression is set equal to zero, so

$$\frac{p_I}{\Delta p_I} = a\varepsilon_I.$$

(5.15)

The second-order condition requires $a\varepsilon_I > 1$, which we assume to hold.[10]

It can be shown by algebraic manipulation that, along the first-order condition, r is a decreasing function of δ. However, the equilibrium value of r that is observed in the data is not determined just by the model's first-order condition but by its intersection with the participation constraint along which r is an increasing function of δ. Using eqn (5.8) to substitute for Δp_I in eqn (5.15) gives

$$r = \frac{\delta a\varepsilon_I}{a_{IF} p_I}.$$

(5.16)

[10] This assumption is not innocuous. The parameter a is, in our setting, the dollar amount that the intermediate-good lobby must contribute per equivalent-dollar of welfare reduction. As contributions are typically small relative to the distortionary costs of trade policies, a is likely to be less than one. Then ε_I, the elasticity of supply of intermediate goods, must be above one. When this assumption is violated, a corner solution occurs at either $r = 0$ (no RoO) or $r = \bar{r}$.

Reintroducing the inequality constraints, the solution is thus

$$r = \begin{cases} t_F^N/a_{IF}\Delta p_I & \text{if } \delta a \varepsilon_I \Delta p_I/p_I \geq t_F^N \\ 0 & \text{if } \delta a \varepsilon_I/a_{IF}p_I \leq 0 \\ \delta a \varepsilon_I/a_{IF}p_I & \text{otherwise.} \end{cases}$$

With several inputs indexed by i and one output indexed by j, it is easily verified that eqn (5.16) becomes

$$r_j = \frac{a\delta_j}{\sum_i a_{ij}p_i/\varepsilon_i}. \tag{5.17}$$

This expression will guide the empirical analysis in the section that follows.

5.3 Market access and RoO determination

5.3.1 The data

The estimation is carried out on a panel dataset covering the period from 1994 to 2001 and containing information on commodity trade and tariffs between Mexico to United States under MFN and preferential regimes. The data was compiled mostly from USITC sources at the 6-digit HS level of disaggregation. The data on Rules of Origin comes from Estevadeordal (2000). Descriptive statistics are shown in Table 5.1.

5.3.2 Empirical estimation

We estimate two equations: a market-access one and a political one. Let j stand for a tariff line (at the HS6 level) and t for time measured in years. The estimated system has a peculiar structure in the time dimension.

Table 5.1 Descriptive statistics

Variable	Obs	Mean	Std. Dev.
log RoO restrict. index	41 944	1.5753	0.3380
log pref. margin	41 834	0.0255	0.0500
log Mex. NAFTA exp.	21 041	13.093	3.090
log Mex.exports to ROW	33 706	11.819	2.959
agriculture	41 944	0.1024	0.3032
final	41 944	0.2530	0.4347
Chge of Chap.	41 944	0.5208	0.4996
Chge of Heading	41 944	0.3863	0.4869
Dhge of Sub-head	41 944	0.0411	0.1986
Exception	41 944	0.4439	0.4968
Technical req.	39 873	0.0651	0.2466
Regional value content	41 723	0.2713	0.445

Mexican exports to the US (y_{jt}) and to the world (x_{jt}) vary over time. So does the rate of preference (δ_{jt}), as NAFTA's tariff reductions were phased in progressively over a transition period (on this, see Estevadeordal, 2000). By contrast, Rules of Origin (r_j) were negotiated once and for all in the early 1990s. Thus, the market-access equation must be estimated on panel data, whereas the political determination of RoOs must be estimated on a cross-section of tariff lines with the variables suggested by the model as likely determinants of RoOs, as of the 1990s.

We measure RoOs in two alternative ways. First, we use a vector of binary variables, each marking the presence of a specific RoO instrument (change of tariff heading, technical requirement, etc.). Secondly, we use Estevadeordal's synthetic index. Using both proxies provides a check on the construction of Estevadeordal's index, as estimated coefficients should be larger in absolute value for instruments assigned a higher value in his index.

Thus, the market-access equations to be estimated is either

$$\ln y_{jt} = \alpha_{0t} + \alpha_1 \ln x_{jt} + \alpha_2 \ln \delta_{jt} + \alpha_3 r_j + u_{jt}, \tag{5.18}$$

where x_{jt} stands for Mexican exports of good j to the rest of the world, δ_{jt} is the rate of preference granted to good j in year t under NAFTA, r_j is Estevadeordal's (2000) index of RoO strictness, and u_{jt} is an error term. Alternatively,

$$\ln y_{jt} = \alpha_{0t} + \alpha_1 \ln x_{jt} + \alpha_2 \ln \delta_{jt} + \sum_{k=1}^{n} \tilde{\alpha}_k r_{kj} + u_{jt}, \tag{5.19}$$

with a vector of n binary variables for the n legal forms of RoOs.

We control for serial correlation in the time dimension by time effects and for unobserved industry characteristics by fixed effects at the section level. As the estimation is carried out at the hs6 level of aggregation, we control for heteroskedasticity by using weighted least squares, the weight being Mexico's total exports. Expected signs and magnitudes in eqn (5.18) are $\alpha_1 > 1, \alpha_2 > 0, \alpha_3 < 0$, and, in eqn (5.19), $\tilde{\alpha}_{k+1} < \tilde{\alpha}_k < 0$ if RoO type $k + 1$ is assigned a higher value than RoO type k in Estevadeordal's index.[11]

---

[11] This equation can be justified as follows. Consider a Mexican final-good exporter maximizing profits by choice of a mixture of export destinations. Let y stand for the value added of exports to the US, x for the value added of exports to the rest of the world, and let p be the relative net price in the US. Assume that the firm produces out of a fixed pool of resources R under a Constant Elasticity of Transformation technology (Powell and Gruen, 1962), i.e. $x^\alpha + y^\alpha = R$, where α is the inverse of the elasticity of transformation. The value of R is itself determined in the previous stage of a two-stage optimization problem. The second-stage problem is thus

$$\max_{x,y} x + py \text{ s.t. } x^\alpha + y^\alpha = R.$$

The political equation is based on eqn (5.17) in log form. As values of δ during the phase-out period were determined simultaneously with Rules of Origin, we instrument for δ using its steady-state value $\bar{\delta}_j$, the US MFN tariff (the value for 2001), and other variables s_j dummies signalling an agricultural good or a consumption good rather than intermediate good.[12] Thus,

$$\ln r_j = \beta_0 + \beta_1 \ln\left(\sum_i a_{ij}p_i/\varepsilon_i\right) + \beta_2 \ln\bar{\delta}_j + \beta_3 s_j \qquad (5.20)$$

Alternatively, noting that, by eqn (5.10)

$$\frac{p_i}{\varepsilon_i} = \frac{ra_{ij}y_j}{y_i'} = \frac{y_i}{y_i'},$$

it follows that

$$\sum_i \frac{a_{ij}p_i}{\varepsilon_i} = \sum_i \frac{a_{ij}y_i}{y_i'},$$

so letting $z_j = \sum_i a_{ij}y_i/y_i'$, the equation to be estimated becomes

$$\ln r_j = \beta_0 + \beta_1 \ln z_j + \beta_2 \ln\bar{\delta}_j + v_j, \qquad (5.21)$$

where $\beta_0 = \ln a < 0$ (if $a < 1$), $\beta_1 < 0$, $\beta_2 = 1$, v_j is an error term, and $z_j = \sum_i a_{ij}y_i/y_i'$ is proxied (with measurement errors since y_i' is unobserved) by $\sum_i a_{ij}y_i$, the sum, over all goods i upstream of j, of the product of US exports of good i to Mexico, y_i, times the share a_{ij} of good i in good j's output.

Note that there is no endogeneity bias from the fact that z_j is a linear combination of intermediate-good exports from the US to Mexico that

---

The FOC yield $y/x = p^{1/(\alpha-1)}$ or

$$\ln y = \frac{1}{\alpha-1}\ln p + \ln x,$$

a functional form close to eqn (5.18). If this equation is roughly invariant across tariff lines, the elasticity of transformation between the US and the ROW can be retrieved from the parameter estimate on the tariff-preference term, whereas the parameter estimate on exports to the ROW should be insignificantly different from one.

The interest of this formulation is that because of the curvature of the transformation surface, the export mixture is an interior solution even when the participation constraint is binding (i.e. when $p = 1$), an observation that is largely true at the tariff line (although not necessarily true at the firm level). This framework can be easily extended to a three-dimensional choice in which exports to the US can be made under either the preferential regime or the MFN one. If the choice between legal regimes for exports to the US involves no efficiency consideration, the transformation surface can be represented as

$$x^\alpha + (y_{NAFTA} + y_{MFN})^\alpha = R.$$

[12] We also tested an alternative formulation, namely $\bar{\delta}_j = \sum_{t=0}^{\infty} \beta^t \delta_{jt}$ with $\beta = 0.9$. The results were similar.

may be affected by final-good exports from Mexico to the US because z_j is calculated as an average for three years before NAFTA's entry into force, so the link between the two types of trade flows is tenuous at best. Thus, the system is recursive and estimated as such.

As Estevadeordal's RoO index is a categorical variable that takes on integer values between one and seven, the political equation is estimated as an ordered probit. As a result, direct quantitative interpretation of parameter estimates in terms of eqn (5.21) is not possible. As the model assumes that RoOs take the form of a continuous RVC, whereas actual ones are combinations of discrete instruments, there is no way around this difficulty.

5.3.3 Results

Estimation results are shown in Tables 5.2 and 5.3.

Column (1) of Table 5.2a shows results for eqn (5.21). The dependent variable is the log of Estevadeordal's index. The regressor called 'upstream' is z_j averaged out over 1989–93. Its coefficient is negative as predicted and significant at the one per cent level. The coefficient on the log of the US MFN tariff is positive as predicted, and also significant at the one per cent level. The coefficients are robust to other specifications where additional

Table 5.2a Regression results, RoO equation

dep. var (log) Procedure	(1) RoO index WLS	(2) RoO index WLS	(3) RoO index WLS
upstream	−0.198 [0.007]**	−0.194 [0.007]**	−0.339 [0.066]**
US MFN tariff 2001	4.039 [0.119]**	4.233 [0.124]**	−2.006 [0.743]**
Mex. MFN tariff 93		−2.147 [0.177]**	
Agriculture		0.156 [0.623]	
Final		0.066 [0.017]**	
Constant			7.823 [0.919]**
Observations	34 927	33 993	39 440
R-squared	0.34		

Notes:
All regressions with section, year dummy and weighted bytotal Mex.exports. standard-errors in parenthesis.
*significant at 5% level, **significant at 1% level.
(1) and (2): ordered probit. pseudo R2
(3): ordered probit; heterogeneity by HS section.

Table 5.2b Regression results, RoO equation

dep. var (log) Procedure	(4) pref.marg. WLS	(5) pref.marg. WLS	(6) RoO index SURE	(7) pref.marg. SURE
upstream			−0.069 [0.002]**	0.001 [0.000]**
predicted RoO	−0.006 [0.001]**	−0.004 [0.0004]**		
US MFN tariff 2001	0.868 [0.004]**	0.835 [0.003]**	0.634 [0.032]**	0.843 [0.002]**
Mex. MFN tariff 93	0.011 [0.003]**	0.011 [0.003]**	−1.785 [0.045]**	0.011 [0.003]**
Constant	−0.015 [0.010]	0.014 [0.010]	2.753 [0.140]**	−0.015 [0.010]
Observations	33 993	33 993	33 993	33 993
R-squared	0.85	0.85	0.48	0.85

Notes:
All regressions with section, year dummy and weighted by total Mex.exports. standard-errors in parenthesis.
*significant at 5% level, **significant at 1% level.
(4): RoO predicted in (1)
(5): RoO predicted in (3) –with heterogeneity-
(6) and (7): SURE equations. Correlation of residuals: −0.0001. Independence rejected (Breush–Pagan test)

variables are thrown in. In column (2), the coefficient of the log of initial Mexican MFN tariff is negative and significant, which supports the view that Rules of Origin are meant to avoid the trade-deflection effect. The easier it is to enter into the Mexican market, the higher the rule of origin. As expected, a final good is associated with a more restrictive rule of origin.[13] The relatively low explanatory power of the regression is not a surprise given that it is very parsimonious, that the data is only a cross-section, and that the dependent variable is itself a constructed one. Column (3) takes into account heterogeneity in the coefficient of the RoO index. Allowing for heteregeneity (at the section level in the HS classification), the sign of the US MFN tariff becomes negative, but the coefficient of the 'upstream' variable that stems from the political-economy model seems quite robust.

Columns (4) and (5) of Table 5.2b show an *ad hoc* regression of tariff preferences on the log of the 2001 value of the US MFN tariff (equal to the steady-state value of NAFTA tariff preferences), the log of the Mexican MFN tariff, and the predicted value of the RoO index from eqn (5.21):

$$\ln{(1 + \delta_{jt})} = \gamma_0 + \gamma_1 \ln{(1 + \overline{\delta}_j)} + \gamma_2 \ln{(1 + t_{j0}^{Mex})} + \gamma_3 \widehat{r}_j + v_{jt}. \qquad (5.22)$$

---

[13] We used the BEC's classification rather than the WTO's because the latter classifies all goods in automobile and machinery and equipment as final ones, whereas vertical trade in those sectors is particularly important for Mexico.

Table 5.3a Regression results, market-access equation

Dep. Var.: log Mex. pref. exports	(1)	(2)	(3)
Exports to ROW	0.611	0.577	0.5761
	[0.006]**	[0.006]**	[0.006]**
RoO restrict.	−0.395		
	[0.031]**		
Pref. margin	2.828	1.887	
	[0.199]**	[0.193]**	
Chge of Chap.		−1.095	
		[0.131]**	
Chge of Head.		−0.751	
		[0.115]**	
Chge of Sub-head.		−0.773	
		[0.112]**	
Exception		0.506	
		[0.036]**	
Reg. Value Content		−0.432	
		[0.032]**	
Tech. req.		1.000	
		[0.055]**	
Upstream			0.226
			[0.012]**
US MFN tariff 2001			3.128
			[0.189]**
Mex MFN tariff 93			2.696
			[0.305]**
Pref.margin=0			−0.147
			[0.268]
US MFN=0			0.722
			[0.280]*
Constant	7.094	7.925	3.748
	[0.573]**	[0.555]**	[0.377]**
Observations	19 951	19 032	19 343
R-squared	0.70	0.72	0.71

Notes:
Dependent variable : log of Mexican exports under Nafta regime
All regressions are weighted. Standard-errors in parentheses. *significant at 5% level;
**significant at 1% level.

Tariff preferences are influenced by the US MFN tariff and, to a lesser extent, by the initial Mexican tariff. Although δ and r are negatively related along the model's FOC condition, the negative coefficient of the RoO index's predicted value has no direct interpretation as observed pairs (r, δ) are determined jointly by the FOC and the participation constraint. The last two columns—(6) and (7)—of Table 5.2b show the results of seemingly unrelated regressions, where the RoO restrictiveness index and the preferential margin are assumed to depend on the same variables. Independence between the two equations is rejected though the residuals correlation is low.

Table 5.3b Regression results, market-access equation

Procedure	(4) I.V.	(5) I.V.	(6) I.V.	(7) OLS	(8) OLS	(9) OLS
Exp. to ROW	0.597	0.586	0.625	0.604	0.604	0.607
	[0.006]**	[0.006]**	[0.005]**	[0.006]**	[0.005]**	[0.006]**
RoO restrict.	−1.527	−2.219		−1.14	−0.689	−1.57
	[0.110]**	[0.091]**		[0.061]**	[0.037]**	[0.116]**
Pref. margin	3.318	3.517	3.06	7.986	0.849	3.525
	[0.233]**	[0.244]**	[0.224]**	[0.359]**	[0.242]**	[0.229]**
RoO restrict*1994			−0.078			
			[0.010]**			
RoO restrict*1995			−0.043			
			[0.009]**			
RoO restrict*1996			−0.065			
			[0.009]**			
RoO restrict*1997			−0.054			
			[0.009]**			
RoO restrict*1998			−0.03			
			[0.009]**			
RoO restrict*1999			0.007			
			[0.009]			
RoO restrict*2000			−0.005			
			[0.009]			
Constant	9.351	10.852	6.755	6.15	8.855	9.399
	[1.265]**	[0.708]**	[0.635]**	[0.628]**	[0.643]**	[0.670]**
Observations	19 343	19 343	19 343	19 343	19 343	19 343
R-squared	0.68	0.65	0.7	0.7	0.7	0.7

Notes:
(4) and (6): pref.margin and RoO index instrumented. Instruments are upstream, US mfn tariff 2001, Mex mfn tariff 1993, section, year
(5) pref.margin and RoO index instrumented (same variables as (4) + agriculture, final)
(7) RoO index predicted with an ordered probit (Table 5.2, eqns (5.2) and (5.4))
(8) RoO index predicted with an ordered probit with heterogeneous effects by section (Table 5.2, eqns (5.3) and (5.5)).
(9) RoO and pref.margin predicted in SURE equations (Table 5.2, eqns (5.6) and (5.7))

Table 5.3 shows estimation results for the market-access equations (5.18 and 5.19).

Columns (1)–(3) of Table 5.3a report estimation results of Mexican exports ignoring the endogeneity issue. Column (1) shows the results of eqn (5.18). The coefficient on the log of Mexican exports to the ROW is 0.61 (and is quite stable across equations). The coefficient of the preference margin is positive, as expected, and significant at the one per cent level. The sign of the coefficient of RoO restrictiveness is negative, as expected. The explanatory power of the regression is quite high (with an unadjusted R-square of 0.7). In column (2), Estevadeordal's synthetic index is replaced by a vector of binary variables that code if the RoO requires a change at different levels of tariff classification or a technical specification, a regional value content and if it allows any exception to the rule. The coefficients on RoO instruments are all significant at the one per cent level. Concerning the changes in tariff classification, their ranking is consistent with Estevadeordal's index: the more demanding the change in classification, the more negative is the impact of preferential imports. The coefficient of regional value content is also negative. However, the coefficient of dummies associated with the requirement of a technical specification or the existence of an exception are positive. Perhaps, this might be explained by the fact that a technical requirement is always associated with a change in classification. Column (3) runs the same regression, where both the RoO index and the preferential margin are replaced by explicative variables used in Table 5.2. All coefficients are positive, including the upstream variable. The only exception is a dummy that records if the preferential margin for that good is equal to 0. In that case, as can be expected, exporting under Nafta is of no interest.

Columns (4) and (5) of Table 5.3b take into account the endogeneity problem by using instrumental variables for both the RoO index and the preferential margin. As a result, the order of magnitude of the coefficient of the RoO index increases to a level comparable to the coefficient of preferential margin. Column (6) tests for the evidence of a learning curve, by interacting the coefficient on RoO with year effects. The order of magnitude of the coefficients of the interaction terms is indeed decreasing over time and is not significant after 1999. A test of equality of coefficients shows that the coefficients are significatively different only in 1997 compared to 1996 (and again in 2000 compared to 1999). The learning curve is thus not as marked as for Central and Eastern European countries (Tumurchudur, 2004).

Columns (7) and (8) of Table 5.3b show estimation results where the preferential margins and the RoO index are replaced by their predicted values from the sequential eqns (5.21) and (5.22) reported in Table 5.2. Finally, column (9) reports the estimation results of Mexican exports on preferential margin and RoO index predicted in the seemingly unrelated regressions. Signs and levels of significance are unaffected, suggesting that qualitative conclusions hold irrespective of the handling of endogeneity issues. However, the magnitudes of point estimates are seriously affected, especially if one takes into account a possible heterogeneity of the impact of RoO across sectors, suggesting that quantitative conclusions must be drawn carefully.

5.4 Concluding remarks

Two messages come out of our results. One is empirical, the other conceptual. First, at the empirical level, NAFTA's Rules of Origin seem to dilute the benefits generated by preferential trade liberalization, in terms of market access, for Mexico. This result, which is in conformity with the findings of the recent literature, suggests that RoOs should indeed be viewed as an economically sensitive item rather than a technical one in the agenda of bilateral trade negotiations. Moreover, the effect seems to be stronger for final goods than for intermediate ones, in conformity with what one would expect in a multistage production model where each stage is located according to the production stage's factor intensity and the host-country factor abundance. This result begs the question, why do Northern partners create policy instruments that put hurdles in a process that is economically efficient? One reason might be that RoOs are the price to pay for the acquiescence of Northern final-good producers threatened by Southern competition. However, many of the final-good assemblage activities undertaken by Southern 'maquiladoras' are non-competing, making this explanation less than satisfactory.

The second point of our chapter is about this issue. We use a standard model of endogenous trade policy—Grossman and Helpman's common-agency model—to explore an alternative logic, namely that RoOs reflect political pressure by Northern intermediate-good producers interested in creating captive markets for their goods in the South. The logic is as follows. On the assumption that the Mexican side is on its 'participation constraint', i.e. that the rate of effective protection conferred to Mexican final-good producers by the simultaneous use of tariff preferences and RoOs is just about zero, tariff preferences are the price to be paid for Mexican assemblers' acquiescence to a system that forces them to buy US intermediate goods. Seen in this way, as the model shows, preferences-cum-RoOs amount to a pure transfer from US taxpayers to intermediate-good producers, i.e. to a hidden export subsidy. Because export subsidies are in violation of any country's obligations under the GATT, recourse to an indirect and inefficient substitute instrument—RoOs—makes sense.

Empirically, the model suggests the inclusion, among the right-hand side variables of the second equation (RoO determination), of the product of input-output coefficients by US intermediate sales to Mexico. This somewhat unintuitive prediction provides a test of the approach's validity, since it is difficult to think of an alternative theoretical approach that would lead to the inclusion of that particular algebraic term. Empirical results are in striking conformity with the model's predictions. In sum, they suggest that the use of NAFTA to create a captive market for US intermediates was indeed one of the forces shaping the agreement's Rules of Origin.

References

Ansolobehere, S., J. de Figuereido, J. Snyder (2002), 'Why is There So Little Money in U.S. Politics?'; NBER working paper #9409.

Anson, J., O. Cadot, A. Estevadeordal, J. de Melo, A. Suwa-Eisenmann, B. Tumurchudur (2003), 'Rules of Origin in North-South Preferential Trading Arrangements with an Application to NAFTA', mimeo, University of Lausanne.

Cadot, O., J. de Melo, M. Olarreaga (2001), 'Can Regionalism Ease the pains of Multilateral Trade Liberalization?' *European Economic Review* **45**, 27–44.

Carrère, C., J. de Melo (2004), 'A Free-Trade Area of the Americas: Any Gains for the South?'; mimeo, University of Geneva.

Dixit, A., G. Grossman (1982), 'Trade and Protection with Multistage Production'; *Review of Economic Studies* **49**, 583–594.

Duttagupta, R. (2000), *Intermediate Inputs and Rules of Origin—Implications for Welfare and Viability of Free Trade Agreements*, Ph.D dissertation, University of Maryland.

Duttagupta, R., A. Panagariya (2002), 'Free Trade Areas and Rules of Origin: Economics and Politics', mimeo, University of Maryland.

Estevadeordal, A. (2000), 'Negotiating Preferential Market Access: The Case of the North American Free Trade Agreement', *Journal of World Trade* **34**, 141–166.

Falvey, R., G. Reed (2000), Economic Effects of Rules of Origin, *Weltwirtchafliches Archiv* **143**, 209–229.

Grossman, G., E. Helpman (1994), 'Protection for Sale', *American Economic Review* **84**, 833–850.

Grossman, G., E. Helpman (1995), 'The Politics of Free-Trade Agreements', *American Economic Review* **85**, 667–690.

Hanson, G. (1996), 'Localization Economies, Vertical Integration, and Trade', *American Economic Review* **86**, 1266–1278.

Ju, J., K. Krishna (1998), 'Firm Behaviour and Market Access in a Free Trade Area With Rules of Origin', NBER Working Paper 6857.

Ju, J., K. Krishna (2002), 'Regulation, Regime Switches and Non-Monotonicity when Non-Compliance is an option: An Application to Content protection and Preference', forthcoming, *Economics Letters*.

Krishna, K., A. Krueger (1995), 'Implementing Free Trade Areas: Rules of Origin as Hidden Protection', in A. Deardorff, J. Levinsohn, R. Stern eds. *New Directions in Trade Theory*, 149–187.

Krueger, A. (1997), 'Free Trade Areas versus Customs Union', *Journal of Development Economics* **54**, 169–197.

Lloyd, P. (1993), 'A tariff Substitute for Rules of Origin in Free-Trade Areas'; *World Economy* **16**, 699–712.

Powell, A.A., F.H.G. Gruen (1962), 'The Constant Elasticity of Transformation Production Frontier and Linear Supply System', *International Economic Review* **9**, 315–328.

Rodriguez, P. (2001), 'Rules of Origin with Multistage Production', *World Economy* **24**, 201–220.

Sanguinetti, P. (2003), 'Implementing Rules of Origin in the southern cone PTAS in Latin America', paper presented at the IADB/CEPR workshop on Rules of Origin, Paris, April 2003.

Serra, J., G. Aguilar, C. Hills (ed.) (1996), *Reflections on Regionalism: Report of the Study Group on International Trade*; Washington, D.C.: Carnegie Endowment for International Peace Press.

Tumurchudur, B. (2004), 'Rules of Origin and market access in the EU's agreements with the CEECs', mimeo, University of Lausanne (Ph.D dissertation work in progress).

6

Rules of Origin and US trade policy

I. M. (Mac) Destler

Traditional, autarkic, producer-based protectionism has long been declining in the United States, and is now weaker than at any time since Alexander Hamilton's *Report on Manufactures*.[1] But the same globalization that has rendered it obsolete has generated a broad political backlash against new reciprocal market-opening agreements. Part of that backlash has embodied controversial demands, resisted by many 'free-traders' at home and abroad, that future negotiations lead to enforceable labor and environmental obligations. These social issues have undercut the longstanding, pro-liberalization consensus in the US Congress.[2] And division over these issues has been exacerbated by increasing partisan polarization in the Congress generally, and the House of Representatives in particular.[3]

If the domestic politics of trade has therefore become a hard slog, the international side has become forbidding as well. Progress on global trade issues has been painfully slow since completion of the Uruguay Round ten years ago. The breakup of the Doha Round talks at Cancun in September 2003 gave graphic illustration to the difficulty. A herculean effort by developed and developing countries alike succeeded in putting these talks back on track at Geneva in July 2004, but the road to final agreement remained filled with pitfalls. Hence, more than ever, on both the domestic and the international front, the lot of the US Trade Representative is not a happy one.

[1] I present evidence for this in 'The Decline of Traditional Protectionism,' Chap. 9 in my *American Trade Politics*, 4th edn (Institute for International Economics, 2005).
[2] 'New Issues, New Statements,' Chap. 10 in *American Trade Politics*, 4th edn.
[3] 'Partisan Rancor and Trade Politics in the New Century,' Chap. 11 in *American Trade Politics*, 4th edn.

In order to keep the trade bicycle rolling, the present incumbent—Robert Zoellick—has raised the banner of 'competitive liberalization,' accelerating the pursuit of bilateral and regional agreements with willing partners. FTAs have been negotiated with Singapore, Chile, Australia, Morocco, and Central America, with the first four approved by Congress in 2003 and 2004Mu. Negotiations with a range of other trading partners are underway: Southern Africa, Thailand, Colombia, etc., etc.

But if the international political process of negotiating FTAs has proved easier than Doha or FTAA, the path domestically has not always been smooth. The majority of agreements have sailed through Congress—those with Israel, Canada, and Jordan as well as the first four of those listed above. But the fight for enactment of the North American Free Trade Agreement (NAFTA) was anything but easy, and resistance to the Central American Free Trade Agreement (CAFTA) (now including the Dominican Republic), completed in early 2004, led to postponement of a Congressional vote until after the November elections and then approval in July 2005 by a very narrow margin (217–215).

How can the USTR line up the necessary business support for such agreements? One important device has been a mechanism that has operated largely below the public radar screen—the negotiation of Rules of Origin (RoOs) that build advantages for influential industries into the text of the agreements.

6.1 Background

'Rules of Origin' are regulations, often quite detailed, that determine which products (and hence, which producers) will gain the benefits of discriminatory trade agreements. They are made necessary, of course, by trade policies that discriminate among supplier nations. In a pure MFN (aka NTR) world, where a product comes from is of no consequence, except for the compilation of trade statistics (and perhaps the satisfaction of labelling requirements). Those who move it across a national border must pay the same required tariff to the importing country, and once it crosses that border it is treated, in most respects, identically with those produced within that importing country. But though MFN remains the governing rule for most trade, there are important occasions when we want to know the origin of a product. One is to enforce trade remedy laws—think of all the country distinctions (legal and illegal) that the Bush administration made on its steel safeguards during the limited period

(March 2002–December 2003) that they were in effect. Two others have been particularly prominent.

One of these, presumably diminishing in importance, arises from the implemention of country-specific export restraint or quota agreements, such as those that proliferated under the Multi-Fiber Arrangement (MFA) of 1973 and its successors. If Hong Kong is allowed to sell the United States X number of men's shirts, for example, and does not fill the quota for economic reasons, its exporters are not allowed to make up the shortfall with shirts produced on the Chinese mainland. But they have a strong incentive to do so, or to undertake token reprocessing (sewing on a few buttons) in Hong Kong. US textile and apparel producers have regularly denounced such circumvention of course, insisted on rules to prevent it, and urged tighter monitoring and enforcement of these country-of-origin rules. But with the scheduled phase-out of the MFA at the end of 2004, and the broader Uruguay Round prohibition against Voluntary Export Restraint agreements (VERs), the incidence and importance of this source of RoOs is evidently diminishing.

By contrast, free trade agreements (FTAs), the second major source of RoOs, are clearly on the increase. If two or more countries agree to eliminate barriers on products sold within their group, but still maintain their own varied schedules of restrictions against imports from countries outside the group, they risk circumvention. Exporters will move a product into the nation with the lowest tariff, for example, and then trans-ship it across the now-duty-free boundary to a higher-tariff group member. The FTA member nations could avoid the need for RoOs, of course, if they took the next step and established a customs union with common external trade barriers, as provided in Europe's Treaty of Rome. But assuming they do not, and most do not, they need rules to prevent outside producers' going around members' higher tariff rates.

It is this second driver of RoOs that is the focus of this chapter and this volume. And it gains salience from the globalization of production. If a product is crafted entirely within one country, then the identity of that country determines whether or not the product gets into an FTA member country duty-free. But the product may in fact be 'multinational'—its main raw material from country A, its locus of final assembly in country B, with inputs brought in from countries C and D, etc. Again, a simple rule would be to define its origin as country B, where it is assembled. But for some products, the value added in the final assembly process is small. In fact, a firm could build a sort of sham factory in an FTA-member country that would simply join two elsewhere-constructed parts together, or sew a few buttons on a shirt, a process adding minuscule value to the final product but enabling it to benefit from duty-free treatment when shipped to another FTA member.

So if the benefits to FTA members are to be preserved, we need a rule, or rules, distinguishing goods that receive favored status from those that do not. We need to have a way to know what is a 'North American product,' to take the largest and most successful of the new generation of FTAs. How much value must be added within the free trade area for it to qualify? Or what manufacturing processes must it undergo? The basic rule could be very simple: in the Canada-US Free Trade Agreement, for example, an automobile could be shipped duty free across the border if 50 per cent or more of its value was generated within the two member countries: if not, then it could not. The US-Jordan agreement has a similar general rule: an article is eligible for duty-free entry into the United States, for example, if the value added in Jordan 'is not less than 35 per cent of the [total] appraised value.'[4] This would seem to be a reasonable, even Solomonic, general standard. Why not simply apply it across the board and be done with it?

The answer, of course, is that rules matter a great deal to competing producers. Those within the contracting nations wish to maximize the degree to which they benefit from the agreement at the expense of competitors—particularly those based outside of the FTA. In the case of autos, US manufacturers thought the Canada agreement standard insufficient for their fierce international competitive battle. So when it came time to negotiate the North American Free Trade Agreement (NAFTA), they went for a more demanding percentage. As Frederick W. Mayer describes it,

All three [US] automakers had an interest in a reasonably high rule of origin to make it more difficult for European and Japanese competitors to locate assembly plants in Canada or Mexico and thereby ship finished automobiles to the United States duty free. But GM differed from Ford and Chrysler. . . . Because of [its] joint venture with Izuzu in Canada, GM favored a lower rule of origin, around 60 per cent. For reasons that reflected their own patterns of production and competitive position, Ford and Chrysler preferred a higher rule, approximately 70 percent. Autoparts makers had every incentive to push for as high a percentage as possible, since high percentages protected them from foreign competition.[5]

---

[4] Section 102(a)(1)(B)(I), Public Law 107-43 (September 28, 2001), the United States-Jordan Free Trade Area Implementation Act.

[5] F. W. Mayer, *Interpreting NAFTA: The Science and Art of Political Analysis* (Columbia University Press, 1998), pp. 157–58.

Balancing these preferences, US negotiators sought a 65 per cent RoO. Canada and Mexico preferred a number closer to the 50 per cent of Canada-US, to accommodate Japanese and European transplant producers within their borders.[6] In the end, agreement was reached on 62.5 per cent, reflecting the particular strength of the US 'Big Three' automakers. As Mayer notes in his analysis, 'In this bargain...the negotiation begins to look less like a deal among three nations than a deal among a collection of private interests, many of whom span national borders.'[7]

Why? The answer is not subtle. US negotiators required Congressional support in the forthcoming legislative battle. Without the backing of the most important and powerful US manufacturing industry, they did not believe they could win that battle. And at a time of maximum competitive threat from across the Pacific, automakers were looking for every advantage they could get in buttressing their position in the North American market.

6.2 Business and government in a new trade game

Autos was the largest US industry involved in the tailoring of RoOs for NAFTA, but its leaders were anything but alone. Annex 401 to the North American Free Trade Agreement contains 150 pages of 'specific Rules of Origin' divided into twenty 'sections' (and 97 'chapters'), from 'live animals' to 'mineral products' to 'wood and articles of wood' to 'textile and textile articles,' to name but a few. Why this wildly complex elaboration of rules in an agreement that was supposed to be for 'free trade?' George Will once noted that a true FTA would not require a text of more than two or three pages. So why did NAFTA need two thousand pages?

The answer lies, of course, at the intersection of business economics and trade politics. Because they affect 'who gets what, when, and how,'[8] RoOs are intrinsically political, and interests try to have them crafted to their advantage. But why do they often do so well in the United States? Here we must explore two converging, if contradictory-seeming trends—the decline of traditional, producer-based protectionism, and the erosion of the US political consensus in support of trade liberalization.

---

[6] The numbers are not strictly comparable, as NAFTA employed a method of calculation different from that in the bilateral pact.   [7] *Interpreting NAFTA*, p. 162.

[8] This is the classic definition by Harold D. Lasswell and the title of his book: *Politics: Who Gets What, When and How*. A recent publisher is Peter Smith (January 1990).

6.3 The globalization of US business

Over recent decades, the international engagement of US producers has multipled. Goods production has declined as a share of the total economy, from 43 per cent in 1970 to 35 per cent in 2000. But over the same period *trade in goods* has grown—from 4 per cent to 10 per cent of GDP.[9] Thus the ratio of goods production to trade (average of exports and imports) has risen even faster—from 0.09 to 0.29. Producers export a larger share of their output. They also import a larger share of their products' final value. And those who lag in exploiting gains from trade face uphill competition from those who do exploit them.

In this context of a globalizing economy, a pure protectionist position becomes harder and harder to maintain. And so we find fewer US industries seeking new protection. The middle 1980s and late 1990s saw similar surges in the volume of US imports, for example.[10] And during the former period, a parade of industries sought (and usually, received) new protection—autos, steel, machine tools, shoes, semiconductors, and last but not least, textiles. During the latter import surge, however, only steelmakers launched a serious campaign for new import restrictions.

Did the others become free-traders? Not exactly. But they did seek ways to come to terms with the more open US economy. They abandoned a strategy of opposition to all new international trade agreements and instead looked for ways to gain advantage *within* these agreements.

6.4 The erosion of bipartisan trade consensus

Over the same period, US government officials continued to pursue market-opening trade agreements. And they continued to need producer support to win Congressional approval of such agreements. Industry interests had shifted, on average, in the pro-trade direction, but this did not mean that business would regularly, on its own, supply the political muscle needed. For most firms, the gains *to them* from foreign-barrier-reduction remained uncertain, conjectural, speculative. And the rise of

[9] Trade here is the average of exports and imports, or $(X+M)/2$. Properly speaking, trade/ goods production should be seen as a ratio, not a percentage, since trade statistics represent final value of goods bought and sold and GDP represents just the value added to goods in the United States. All statistics are calculated from *Economic Report of the President*, February 2004, Tables B-1, B-8, and B-103 (all are current dollar statistics).

[10] The quantity of US merchandise imports rose by 65 per cent between 1982 and 1986, an exceptionally sharp rate of increase. The same indicator rose by 63 per cent between 1996 and 2000.

social issues, plus partisan polarization in Congress, weakened the broad bipartisan consensus that had been critical to past legislative successes. The narrow political margin for trade policy in the twenty-first century was illustrated (perhaps exaggerated) by the dearly bought, single-vote House margin by which the House approved Trade Promotion Authority (TPA) in December 2001.[11]

The problem of mobilizing support was particularly acute in regional agreements, where it was plausible for the United States to demand serious labor and environmental provisions. Clinton had needed side agreements on such issues to win his uphill battle for NAFTA approval in 1993; nothing comparable was necessary in the overwhelming vote to approve the Uruguay Round/WTO agreements the following year. When House Democrats drafted their alternative TPA bill in 2001, they included a separate and much more demanding set of labor/environment negotiating objectives for regional and bilateral agreements. And the Bush administration's Central America Free Trade Agreement (CAFTA) faced vociferous opposition in 2004 because supporters of labor–environment linkage for its provisions weak in these spheres.[12]

So trade negotiators look for particularized benefits they can offer important industries in exchange for their support. Industries look for ways to gain advantage within the new economics of globalization. Rules of Origin can meet the needs of both. Because they are often detailed and technical, their politics tends to be asymmetric: those who benefit directly are deeply engaged, while others affected only marginally tend to stay on the sidelines. And while, by their very nature, they tilt the balance of advantage in FTA agreements away from producers in the partner nation, these foreign producers typically find restrictive RoOs a tolerable price to pay for assured, preferential overall access to the US market.

6.5 Rules of Origin in practice and theory

In some cases, the impact of a RoO may be less than originally apparent. The 62.5 per cent North-American content rule for autos is, on its face,

---

[11] For an interpretation of that vote, stressing in particular the deep partisan bitterness in the House in general and the Ways and Means Committee in particular, see my 'Partisan Rancor and Trade Politics in the New Century,' Chap. 11 in *American Trade Politics*, 4th edn (Institute for International Economics).

[12] For an argument on why bilateral and Regional Trade Agreements are particular susceptible to social issue linkage, see my 'Congress and Foreign Trade,' in R. A. Pastor and

exceptionally restrictive. The 'Big Three' executives lobbied hard for it, and gave every appearance of needing and valuing it in 1991–92. Despite major restructuring in the 1980s, and several years of protection from 'voluntary' Japanese export restraint, US manufacturers were still viewed as losers in the market battle with their trans-Pacific adversaries. And they acted like they saw themselves in that way. Their plight was symbolized, albeit exaggerated, by President George H.W. Bush's ill-fated trip to Tokyo accompanied by the Big Three executives, with the United States seeming to be deploying political strength to offset economic weakness.

As Mayer illustrates in detail, the auto executives deployed that political strength in the NAFTA talks as well. The US government adopted their objective as its own, and once the deal was struck, the auto industry joined the broad coalition of supporters that turned the political tide in the fall of 1993. But their gains were limited because the underlying MFN tariff was very low. This was reflected in US negotiator Jules Katz's reply to the outrage expressed by Ford's CEO at the US agreement to drop the percentage from its original goal of 65 per cent: 'We're talking about a 2.5 percent difference on a 2.5 percent tariff.'[13]

Textiles is an even more interesting, and economically more consequential story. For more than half a century, the politically potent mills, concentrated in the states of North and South Carolina, had aligned themselves with the geographically dispersed US apparel makers to win broad and oft-growing trade protection, over a period when most other import-impacted industries were losing theirs. The economic logic of the alliance was simple: the US apparel industry was the main market for the mills' cloth. The political logic was simple as well: they threatened to block general trade-expansion legislation if their needs for protection were not met. Working both ends of Pennsylvania Avenue, the textile industry got administration after administration to negotiate a comprehensive regime of quotas, first bilateral restraint agreements under Dwight D. Eisenhower, then a general 'arrangement' on cotton cloth and products under John F. Kennedy, broadened to include synthetics and wool products in the Multi-Fiber Arrangement negotiated under Richard M. Nixon. Between 1985 and 1990, they also succeeded in getting Congress to pass,

R. F. de Castro, *The Controversial Pivot: The United States Congress and North America* (Brookings Institution Press, 1998), pp. 121–46.

[13] Quoted in Mayer, *Interpreting NAFTA*, p. 143.

on three separate occasions, bills that would have embedded such quotas in US law, in gross violation of the nation's GATT commitments.[14]

But they couldn't get enough House votes to override any of the anticipated three Presidential vetoes that followed. And their negotiated protection was proving leaky—imports rose substantially, particularly in the 1980s, and particularly of labor-intensive apparel products. So after pushing for quota legislation beyond the time when it had any chance of enactment, the textile manufacturers reviewed their position. The Uruguay Round negotiations were pointing clearly towards an MFA phase-out. Assuming such an agreement, fewer and fewer domestic apparel firms were likely to survive to use the mills' fiber and fabric. Indeed, many were already going out of business or shifting production overseas. So the textile industry shifted its stance: if a growing share of clothing sold in the United States was to be imported, they would look for ways to have that imported clothing made with their fabric.

So they parted company with the remaining domestic apparel producers. They could live with NAFTA—with the likely flood of apparel imports from lower-wage Mexico—if 'North American' clothing had to be made with North-American cloth.[15]

For USTR negotiators knowing that NAFTA was politically controversial and looking to broaden its support, this was an offer they could not refuse. So officials and the industry negotiated a particularly ingenious RoO centered on the so-called 'triple transformation test' (also known as the 'yarn-forward rule'). This required that for a piece of apparel to be treated as a North American product, it had to go through three basic processes— the making of fiber, then cloth, then clothing—within the NAFTA region. Since clothing made in Mexico would avoid both MFA quotas and the relatively high US tariffs, it was likely to significantly displace, in the US market, imports from East Asia. If that clothing used NAFTA-made fiber and fabric, US mills stood to gain enormously, since they had comparative advantage on textile production within the NAFTA region.

By liberal-trade criteria, the triple transformation test is an abomination. In their comprehensive rating of RoO provisions for twenty product

---

[14] For details, see my *American Trade Politics*, esp. pp. 29–30 and 191–90. And those who *really* want detailed history may wish to read I. M. Destler, H. Fukui and H. Sato, *The Textile Wrangle: Conflict in Japanese-American Relations, 1969–1971* (Cornell University Press, 1979).

[15] For a comprehensive analysis of the fundamental shift in textile industry trade strategy, see C. VanGrasstek, 'U.S. Policy in Textile and Apparel Trade: From Managed Protection to Managed Liberalization,' October 23, 2003, http://www.asiatradeinitiative.org/docs/2004-Feb/44.%20US%20Policy%20in%20Textile%20and%20Apparel%20Trade.pdf.

sectors in five separate FTAs, Antoni Estevadeordal and Kati Suominen find the NAFTA textile and apparel rules the most restrictive of all.[16] These rules are literally one in a hundred!

But to win the support of a major, traditionally protectionist industry for a trade-expanding agreement was a major political achievement. And the RoO clearly garnered Carolina votes for NAFTA. In the 1991 vote extending fast-track rules that was a *de facto* authorization for the Bush administration to pursue the NAFTA negotiations, Representatives from North Carolina had voted 9–2 in the negative. But this was before the Rules of Origin were negotiated. Once the triple transformation test was embedded in the treaty, and it came before the House for its dramatic final vote in 1993, legislators from that state shifted to 8–4 in favor.

Of course, the textile firms did not rest on their laurels, but worked to enact similar rules elsewhere. The African Growth and Opportunity Act was enacted in 2000 to provide broad preferential access to the US market for exports from that generally low-trading continent. But easing its enactment path were similar textile RoOs. For the poorest, they are in fact somewhat less stringent—thirty particularly poor sub-Saharan African countries could sell their apparel in the United States duty-free regardless of where the fabric originated, up to a certain ceiling.[17] On the other hand, a restrictive RoO hurts Africa more than Mexico, since apparel is, for many African nations, the primary growth opportunity in manufactures trade. An IMF Working Paper projecting AGOA's impact estimates that the increase in exports would be 'nearly five times [$400 million] greater' if the law had included 'a rule of origin that requires only assembly in the beneficiary countries—as under the MFA,' rather than the more restrictive, NAFTA-type rule actually incorporated.[18]

The textile industry has also pressed for tightening of rules within the Western Hemisphere, to incorporate provisions that require dyeing of the cloth in the region as well. An opportunity came in December 2001, when Republican leaders—having alienated many swing Democrats—were desperate for votes to pass President George W. Bush's TPA bill. A textile

---

[16] 'Rules of Origin in FTAs: A World Map,' Table 7. *http://www.iadb.org/intal/foros/ LAestevadeordal.pdf*

[17] For a good discussion of textile-apparel RoOs in AGOA and some proposals for reform, see W. R. Cline, *Trade Policy and Global Poverty* (Center for Global Development and Institute for International Economics, 2004), esp. p. 103.

[18] A. Matoo, D. Roy, and A. Subramanian, 'The Africa Growth and Opportunity Act and Its Rules of Origin: Generosity Undermined?' *IMF Working Paper*, September 2002, p. 2.

Congressman who normally opposed trade-expanding legislation was available—provided the President would promise to get the rules for Andean nations' trade preferences revised to include the dyeing requirement. The promise was made, the vote was switched, and the gavel came down, locking in the 215–214 margin.

Trade economists have properly highlighted the degree to which RoOs reduce the welfare gains from FTAs, particularly those of the less-wealthy nations party to them. Kala Krishna and Anne Krueger were pointing to 'hidden protection' from such rules as early as 1995.[19] In the eyes of scholars like Richard Cooper, a key drawback of free trade agreements is that 'the need for Rules of Origin creates a playground for protectionist interests'—RoOs tend to escape public notice because they are 'arcane and technical.'[20] With the goal of putting some limits on such perceived abuses, his Harvard colleague Robert Z. Lawrence has suggested, citing Richard H. Snape, that there should be a single rule for all products: 'the use of sector-specific Rules of Origin should be illegal in free trade areas.[21]

Those specializing in trade politics have been slower to focus on the issue. Kenneth A. Oye, however, has addressed the broader phenomenon of how the particularity of FTAs can strengthen their political viability, Writing at a time when discriminatory trade arrangements were increasing and the global, GATT-based MFN trade regime appeared to be weakening, he argued that the negotiating of discriminatory agreements could have, and has had, 'liberalizing effects' by 'providing export-oriented sectors with a narrow interest in campaigns against protection of import-competing sectors.'[22] More generally, such non-MFN agreements contributed to a more open national and global economy by giving particularized benefits to interests that were therefore given a direct stake in trade expansion—even though the agreements inevitably created trade diversion as well. Economists Rupa Duttagupta and Arvind Panagariya have modelled the rules-of-origin issue specifically and found that, under their assumptions, 'an FTA that, , ,was voted down in the absence

---

[19] 'Implementing Free Trade Areas: Rules of Origin and Hidden Protection,' NBER Working Paper No. 4983, January 1995.

[20] 'Comment,' in J. J. Schott, (ed.), *Free Trade Agreements: US Strategies and Priorities*, Institute for International Economics, April 2004, p. 22.

[21] R. Z. Lawrence citing R. H. Snape, 'Regionalism and the WTO: Should the Rules Be Changed?' in J. J. Schott, (ed.), *The World Trading System: Challenges Ahead* (Institute for International Economics, 1996), p. 51.

[22] K. A. Oye, *Economic Discrimination and Political Exchange: World Political Economy in the 1930s and 1980s* (Princeton University Press, 1992), p. 170.

of...Rules of Origin may become feasible in the presence of these rules,' even though they reduce overall welfare.[23]

There is a parallel here in the political role of US trade remedy laws. RoOs helped NAFTA in the same way that incorporating a restrictive interpretation of the Uruguay Round anti-dumping agreement helped smooth the enactment of its implementing legislation. And as in the case of the so-called 'unfair trade' statutes, advocates of RoOs have also imposed their normative vocabulary on the debate. They have legitimacy because, in their basic form, they address a clear apparent problem of enforcing the rules of an FTA. Just as critics of skewed dumping rules risk can be charged with wanting 'to weaken our protections against unfair trade,'[24] those who oppose restrictive Rules of Origin can be accused of advocating 'circumvention' of the agreement by producers in non-member states. RoOs surely offer political cover for some outrageous specifics. Yet often their advocates can also claim the high moral ground.

For the most part, however, the RoO debate has been among specialists—it has largely escaped public notice—and WTO scrutiny. As one particularly cogent and informative summary of the relevant issues puts it,

Because most people had the misconception...that the formulation and application of Rules of Origin result from a technical and objective process, few people paid attention to, much less scrutinized, the process of defining and applying Rules of Origin. The lack of transparency was heightened by the complex, technical nature of Rules of Origin, which would have made it difficult to realize that they were being used for restrictive purposes. Furthermore, while the GATT increasingly restricted the ability of countries to use tariffs or traditional non-tariff barriers to protect domestic industry from foreign competition, it did not regulate Rules of Origin. Therefore...By taking advantage of the fact that formulations of the rules and determinations of origin are not technically objective exercises but rather policy-influenced decisions, governments were able to protect domestic industries in a hidden, effective manner.[25]

[23] 'Free Trade Areas and Rules of Origin: Economics and Politics,' January 2, 2001. [*http://www.bsos.umd.edu/econ/panagariya/apecon/Technical%20Papers/FTA-RoO-rd-ap-pub13.pdf*]
[24] Research that I conducted jointly with John S. Odell and Kimberly Ann Elliott found that there was less resistance to trade protection in cases where it came in the context of charges of unfairness and enforcement of the anti-dumping laws. The normative framing of the issue seems to matter. See *Anti-Protection: Changing Forces in United States Trade Politics* (Institute for International Economics, Policy Analysis No. 21, 1987), pp. 73–74.
[25] *Free Trade Agreements and Rules of Origin*, Policy Brief 0012, Middle East and Africa Program, International Center for Economic Growth, no author, no date. [The brief is described as a 'verbatim' synthesis of studies by: Olivier Cadot, Jaime de Melo, and Marcelo Olarreaga (1999); Kala Krishna and Anne Krueger (cited above, 1995); Joseph A. LaNasa III (1996); and Mariana Silveira (n.d.).] The web address is: *http://www.iceg.org/NE/policybriefs/P_B%28E%2912.PDF*

6.6 Concluding thoughts

For free-traders, restrictive Rules of Origin—like anti-dumping laws—represent a sort of pact with the devil. The backing of their supporter-beneficiaries is often needed for an FTA to become law. So the Lawrence–Snape remedy—outlawing industry-specific rules—could prove worse than the disease—if one believes that the resulting FTAs still represent a net welfare gain.

But if RoOs seem politically necessary in the short run, they are pernicious in the longer run. So the question for pragmatic trade-expanders is the ancient one: Can one dicker with the devil without joining him in Hell? The long experience with textiles in general suggests that the answer can be yes: quota protection for that industry eased enactment of generations of liberalizing legislation, and in the end it was the quotas that eroded, not market-opening trade policy. Experience with anti-dumping legislation is less encouraging, however—these rules have not, on balance, eroded, and their utilization and impact have not discernably declined.[26]

For free-traders, the need is to yield only what one has to, when one has to, and recoup when one can. The aim of the particularized interests, by contrast, will be to pocket what they have and go for more: to tighten Rules of Origin, to close 'loopholes,' to broaden definitions to their advantage—just as some have done persistently with the anti-dumping laws. The House vote of 2001 is a case in point.

How can one limit such concessions, or at least limit their impact on trade? There are essentially three approaches: one direct and two indirect.

6.7 Seek constraints on RoOs in the WTO

Just as the WTO has extensive, enforceable rules bounding the use of contingent protection, it could establish binding constraints on Rules of Origin in FTAs. The WTO does address Rules of Origin generally, but the general descriptive language from the organization's website is revealing:

The Rules of Origin Agreement requires WTO members to ensure that their Rules of Origin are transparent; that they do not have restricting, distorting or disruptive effects on international trade; that they are administered in a consistent, uniform,

---

[26] Research on anti-dumping cases for *American Trade Politics*, 4th edn, finds no statistically significant trend in numbers of anti-dumping cases or outcomes, up or down, over the period beginning in 1980. There is also no significant difference before vs. after the Uruguay Round agreements of 1994. See pp. 237–42.

impartial and reasonable manner; and that they are based on a positive standard (in other words, they should state what does confer origin rather than what does not).

For the longer term, the agreement aims for common ('harmonized') Rules of Origin among all WTO members, *except in some kinds of preferential trade—for example, countries setting up a free trade area are allowed to use different Rules of Origin for products traded under their free trade agreement* [emphasis added].[27]

An effort to fill this loophole might be part of a broader elaboration of the seldom-enforced Article 24 that permits FTAs and provides loose guidelines, including one that an FTA should 'not raise barriers to the trade of other [WTO] members.'[28] Possible new rules range from an outlawing of FTAs that are not customs unions (this would largely eliminate the RoO problem) to limits on the content of RoOs, like allowing just 'one rule for all products,' such as 'a certain percentage of value added.'[29] One might also imagine other devices to modify pernicious rules: like a sunset or review provision for RoOs, requiring their reanalysis and redrafting every 5 to 10 years. At this later point, industry leverage might not be so great, since the agreement itself would not hang in the balance.

Under present political circumstances, however, the United States government would surely oppose such constraints. The USTR *needs* flexibility on RoOs to build support for FTAs. Hence the first *indirect* means of constraining Rules of Origin:

6.8 Broaden domestic support for open trade

Textile people had leverage in the NAFTA negotiations because the ratification vote was expected to be excruciatingly close. They had leverage in 2001 because the TPA vote *was* close. And it was close because other potential sources of support had been alienated, particularly on-the-fence Democrats. So the way to constrain restrictive Rules of Origin is the same way to avoid a Free Trade Area of the Americas being hostage to the Florida orange growers: by broadening the base of support.[30] This means, among other things, responsiveness to social issues Democrats care about,

---

[27] See *http://www.wto.org/english/thewto_e/whatis_e/tif_e/agrm9_e.htm#origin.*

[28] Lawrence, p. 51. [29] *Ibid.*, p. 52.

[30] Similarly, the narrowness of the political base was a key reason that the just-negotiated FTA with Australia excludes sugar entirely from its provisions, though Presidential electoral politics seem to have played a role as well. See the front-page story in *Inside U.S. Trade*, February 13, 2004.

effective implementation (and further broadening) of newly expanded trade adjustment programs for workers, and engaging now-minority Democrats in the House legislative process on trade, rather than circumventing them as was the Republican strategy in 2001.

Success in this approach would in turn contribute to the second *indirect* means of addressing RoOs:

6.9 Reduce the value of RoOs through overall reduction of MFN tariffs

The auto RoO in NAFTA was of mainly symbolic value because the tariff relief it granted was so modest. By contrast, textile and apparel tariffs remain high, so RoOs convey substantial rents to US-based producers. So the most effective, long-term way to mute their impact is to reduce these tariffs. Of course, bringing down those tariffs that remain is no easy task politically—the height of these 'tariff peaks' is not an accident. But if, to repeat the words of Katz, fights over RoOs could be reduced to 'a 2.5 percent difference on a 2.5 percent tariff,' RoOs would go the way of the Smoot–Hawley Act of 1930—still on the books, but lacking serious relevance and impact.

Part IV

Measuring the impact of Rules of Origin

7

Are different Rules of Origin equally costly? Estimates from NAFTA[†]

Céline Carrère and Jaime de Melo

7.1 Introduction

Rules of Origin (RoO) are a key ingredient in any preferential trading agreement (PTA) short of a customs union, as well as in any preferential market access scheme such as the Generalized System of Preferences (GSP) or the more recent 'Everything But Arms' (EBA) and Africa Growth Opportunity Act (AGOA) initiatives. Low rates of utilization have led many observers to question the extent of market access, not only because of lower Most Favored Nation (MFN) tariffs worldwide or because there may be significant learning effects that contribute to low utilization rates in the early years of implementation, but mostly because of the presumed cost-raising effects of these seemingly 'made-to-measure' RoO. Yet, there is little systematic direct evidence documenting the cost-raising effects of RoO. This chapter provides more systematic evidence for NAFTA.

Useful anecdotic evidence abounds. For example, there is ample documentation of the stringent requirements that must sometimes be satisfied to meet origin (i.e. the definition of 'vessel' under the EBA (Brenton 2005), the description of the triple-transformation rule widely applied in textiles or the detailed description of RoO in SADC (Flatters and Kirk 2005)). Several contributions have used gravity trade models with dummy variables or synthetic indices to capture the effects of RoO. These studies

† We thank conference participants, our discussant Ana Maria Mayda, and Olivier Cadot, Alberto Portugal-Pérez, Marcelo Olarreaga, Pablo Sanguinetti, and Ernesto Stein for helpful comments.

typically conclude that, after controlling for other factors, trade volumes are indirectly related either to indices of the presence of RoO or of their levels of restrictiveness (see, e.g., Augier *et al.* 2005; Estevadeordal and Suominen 2005; Cadot *et al.* 2005).[1]

Another promising approach, inspired from earlier work on EFTA (Herin 1986) has used revealed preference to estimate upper and lower bounds on the cost of RoO. The assumption here is that for sectors with utilization rates close to 100%, the utilization rate would give an upper bound on the costs of RoO, while for sectors with close to zero utilization rates, preference rates would provide a lower bound of the costs associated with RoO. Under the assumption that transitional adjustment to the administrative requirements of the RoO has taken place, this non-parametric method is a useful way to obtain bounds on the costs of RoO when one has data on utilization rates (see, e.g., Anson *et al.* 2005 and below).

While useful, these comparisons of utilization rates do not exploit the variance in the types of RoO used across sectors. Estevadeordal (2000) was the first to recognize explicitly the importance of different RoO in terms of their potential cost-raising effects by constructing a synthetic index, r_i, that explicitly accounted for differences in types of RoO.[2] The appeal of a synthetic index is potentially of great practical use since, like suitably constructed effective rates of protection that provide a summary description of a country's trade regime, a synthetic index describing the set of RoO that accompany a preferential agreement could also provide an overall idea of the restrictiveness of the system of RoO.

As explained below, the observation rule is not confronted with the data. For example broad categories of sectors (raw materials, intermediates and final goods) may not be affected in the same way by a given RoO (say a

---

[1] Other contributions have sought to provide more direct estimates. For example, in the context of The Europe Agreements, Brenton and Manchin (2003) have observed that several East-European partners have preferred to enter the EU market under overseas processing trading (OPT) arrangements than under the presumably more generous market access provided by the FTA. More recently, in an assessment of market access provided by the EU under the EBA and the GSP, Brenton (2005) concludes that the low take-up of preferences under the EBA must at least partly be due to costs associated with the accompanying RoO.

[2] Estevadeordal built an observation rule that relied on this assumption: a RoO requiring a change of chapter heading would be more restrictive than one requiring a change of classification at the tariff line (HS-8) level, and (other things being equal), adding a regional value-content requirement or a technical requirement would make the RoO more restrictive (and hence more costly), resulting in an ordinal integer index at the HS-8 level, r_i, in the range $[1 < r_i < 7]$, with the property that larger values of r_i would correspond to a more restrictive RoO. This synthetic index was constructed on the same data for Mexican exports to the US under NAFTA.

change of chapter). Nor is its usefulness as a measure of restrictiveness of RoO under NAFTA systematically analysed. Within the limits imposed by data availability (the effects of different types of RoO can only be captured by dummy variables and firm heterogeneity accounting for observations at the tariff line cannot be controlled for), this chapter provides a more direct estimate of the costs of the three important categories of RoO under NAFTA: change of tariff classification, existence or not of a regional value content (RVC) scheme, and the presence or not of a technical (TECH) requirement. Our estimates also allow us to check the reasonableness of the assumptions used in building the Estevadeordal's r_i index described above. Finally, for sectors subject to a RVC, we provide illustrative simulations of the cost-raising effects of these RoO.

The remainder of the chapter is organized as follows. Section 7.2 discusses the particular characteristics of the RoO map negotiated under NAFTA that are relevant for the econometric estimates that follow, and present non-parametric estimates that can be obtained by the use of a synthetic index. Section 7.3 presents a simple model leading to econometric estimates that take into account differences across broad categories of goods and across types of RoO. Results from estimating this model are presented in Section 7.4. How these cost estimates compare with Estevadeordal's index is discussed in Section 7.5. Section 7.6 then carries out illustrative cost calculations in the case where RoO take the form of a RVC. Conclusions follow in Section 7.7.

7.2 NAFTA RoO map, and non-parametric cost estimates

Section 7.2.1 describes briefly the main RoO in NAFTA, along with utilization rates in 2001, a year when NAFTA was just about in full force, since the average preferential rate of 4.1% for Mexican exports was almost equal to the average US MFN tariff (4.3%). Section 7.2.2, then turns to non-parametric cost estimates for 2000 and 2001, based on the r_i index.

7.2.1 Preferences and utilization rates under NAFTA

Table 7.1 describes the data used in the calculation of the compliance cost estimates for Mexican exporters of RoO under NAFTA. All data are for 2001, when NAFTA was in full force, and are defined at the HS-6 level of aggregation, only for tariff lines with positive exports to the US. This

Table 7.1 RoO map, preferences and utilization rates

Section	Obs	%	Export to US %	u_i Mean	τ_i Mean	CC %	CH %	CSI %	E %	TECH %	RVC %	r_i Mean	Interm %	Final %
1 Live Animals	80	2.3	0.71	30.7	4.1	100	0	0	15	0	0	6	6.3	23.8
2 Vegetable Prod.	150	4.2	2.17	70.3	3.6	100	0	0	0	0	0	6	12.7	8
3 Fats & Oils	27	0.8	0.02	77.9	5.1	100	0	0	0	0	0	5.9	0	100
4 Food. Bev. & tob.	123	3.5	1.75	76.6	7.6	79.7	18.7	1.6	17.1	0.8	0	5.6	11.4	86.2
5 Mineral Products	86	2.4	7.17	11.8	0.3	80.2	19.8	0	19.8	0	0	5.6	16.3	4.7
6 Chemicals	430	12.1	1.35	62.3	3.4	75.4	20	4.7	84.7	1.2	0.9	5.5	73.5	26.3
7 Plastics & Rubber	175	4.9	1.36	71.7	3.8	11.4	88	0.6	26.3	5.7	64	4.9	60.6	30.9
8 Leather Goods	52	1.5	0.18	51.3	4	61.5	38.5	0	42.3	0	0	5.5	32.7	46.2
9 Wood Products	55	1.5	0.24	37.3	2.1	7.3	92.7	0	7.3	0	0	4.2	43.6	45.5
10 Pulp & Paper	97	2.7	0.52	56.2	0.7	57.7	42.3	0	42.3	0	0	5.2	39.2	55.7
11 Textiles & Apparel	618	17.4	7.35	79.9	10.4	80.3	19.7	0	97.9	41.6	0	6.0	40.9	53.9
12 Footwear	47	1.3	0.28	67.6	6.8	19.2	80.9	0	72.3	0	48.9	4.9	0	100
13 Stone & Glass	129	3.6	1.15	60.1	3.2	54.3	43.4	2.3	43.4	0	0	5.0	10.1	89.9
14 Jewellery	35	1	0.37	45.5	2.7	60	40	0	40	0	0	5.2	34.3	40
15 Base Metals	430	12.1	3.56	67.9	2	42.6	56.1	1.4	45.4	1.2	0	4.8	50.5	48.1
16 Mach. & Elec. Eq.	631	17.7	39.52	35.5	1.5	0	81.3	18.7	31.9	4.6	1.4	3.8	0	100
17 Transp. Equip.	85	2.4	20.38	56.4	3.4	2.4	91.8	5.9	14.1	0	22.4	4.2	0	100
18 Med. Instruments	170	4.8	3.69	45.2	2.1	15.3	76.5	8.2	14.7	0	3.5	4.2	0	100
19 Arms & Ammunition	8	0.2	0.02	13.4	0.5	62.5	37.5	0	0	0	0	5.3	0	100
20 Misc. Manufact.	127	3.6	8.2	40.4	3.1	82.7	11.8	5.5	0.8	0	0	5.4	0	100
Total	**3555**	**100**	**100**	**58**	**4.1**	**50**	**45.1**	**5**	**47**	**8.6**	**4.9**	**5.1**	**29.5**	**61.2**
Raw	330	9.3	9.4	34.2	1.8	95.2	4.5	0.3	10.3	0.9	0	5.9	-	-
Interm.	1048	29.5	4.1	74.2	4.8	58.4	39.4	2.2	68.4	0.2	8.7	5.2	-	-
Final	2177	61.2	86.6	53.9	4.2	39.1	53.9	7	42.2	13.9	3.8	4.9	-	-

Notes: total Mexican exports to US under NAFTA=$131 million

All calculations are at the 6-digit level of the HS (so the table presents simple *average* by sector and category and not the *aggregate* indicator. i.e. weighted by the imports values of each line).

u_i = utilization rate of the NAFTA regime; τ_i = tariff preference margin; r_i = the Estevadeordal (2000) index of Rules of Origin ($1 < r_i < 7$, a higher value indicating a more restrictive RoO. see text).

CC = Change in Chapter / CH = Change in Heading / CS = Change in Subheading / E = Exception to Change of Tariff Classification / RVC = Regional Value Content / TECH = Technical Requirement.

represents 3555 observations[3], 99 chapters and 20 sectors. Utilization rates, denoted u_i, are defined as the ratio of USA imports from Mexico under US-NAFTA preferential tariffs to total USA imports from Mexico (at the 6-digit HS-level). Tariff preference margins, $\tilde{\tau}_i$ are also calculated at the product line level and are defined as:

$$\tilde{\tau}_i = \frac{t_i - \tau_i}{1 + \tau_i}; \quad (t_i = t^{us}_{i,\text{mfn}}; \tau_i = t^{us}_{i,\text{mex}}), \tag{7.1}$$

where world prices are set equal to one by choice of units. Table 7.1 also reports the average value of Estevadeordal's index (which takes values in the range $1 < r_i < 7$). All data in Table 7.1 are simple (unweighted) averages at the HS-2 level, i.e. for 20 sectors (with the number of HS-6 level tariff lines in each sector for 2001).

In Table 7.1, all data on RoO refers to percentage of tariff lines subject to the corresponding RoO. Take for example sector 11 (textiles and apparel, henceforth T&A) with 618 observations at the HS-6 level, and that represents 7.35% of the total Mexican exports to US in 2001. T&A has an average utilization rate of 79.9% and an average tariff preference margin of 10.4%, with 54% and 41% of the observations falling under the final and intermediate good, respectively. Within that sector, 80% [19.7%] of observations had to satisfy a change of classification at the chapter [heading] levels, and 42% of the tariff lines had technical requirements.

Only T&A has an average tariff preference margin above 10%. Note also that some sectors with a substantial number of observations (i.e. over 100) have relatively high utilization rates in spite of low preference margins (e.g. stone and glass, sector 13).

According to stages of processing, raw materials are the least important sector, since about 30% of observations fall under the intermediate category (which represents only 4% of the total exports) and the remainder falls under the final good category (61% of the observations accounting for 87% of Mexican exports to the US). Finally, in spite of large dispersions within sectors, on average, tariff preference margins are the same for final- and intermediate-goods-producing sectors, even though average utilization rates are much higher for the intermediate-goods sectors (74% vs. 54%). If indeed, Mexico has a comparative advantage in final-goods-producing activities, it would appear that RoO that are only slightly more

---

[3] In view of the econometric estimates that follow, we have eliminated 5 outliers with $\tilde{\tau}_i > 100\%$, 3 belonging to Chapter 24 (Tobacco) and 2 to Chapter 12 (Vegetables). These 5 outliers are classified as 'raw materials' according to the WTO, and faced only a Change of Chapter, without exception, technical requirement or regional value content. The utilization rates for these five products are 100%.

restrictive according to the r_i synthetic index for final-goods-producing activities, have a greater impact on utilization rates than for intermediate-producing activities.

Turn next to the distribution of types of RoO, recalling that their effects can only be captured by the use of dummy variables in the statistical analysis below. About 45% of the tariff lines have to meet a Change of Heading (CH) with the remainder (50%) having to meet a Change of Chapter (CC). This means that it would be futile to attempt to capture the effects of both types of changes in tariff classification since the dummy variables would be almost quasi-perfectly collinear. Along the same lines, note that exceptions (whose effects on costs are difficult to interpret anyway), denoted E, cover about half of the tariff lines, being present for 98% of the lines in T&A (sector 11) and 85% in chemicals (sector 6). Turning to the technical requirements (TECH) that cover only 8.6% of the lines and 6 sectors, they are concentrated in sector 11. Regional value content (RVC) is prevalent in four sectors, and covers 5% of the observations.

Finally, we look at the cumulative frequency distribution of the two variables of interest, utilization rates, u_i, and preference margins, $\tilde{\tau}_i$. Utilization rates are evenly distributed around three groups of values: one-third of the total sample with u_i equal to zero, one quarter with u_i equal to 1 and the remainder in-between. As to preference rates, the sample average preference is 4.11% with the following quartile distribution: [25%:0%]; [50%:2.58%] and [75%:5.5%].

The distribution of utilization rates and preference margins are quite different between intermediate and final goods: zero utilization rates ($u_i = 0\%$) apply for 20% [34%] for intermediate [final] goods. Full utilization rates ($u_i = 100\%$) apply for 50% [16%] for intermediate [final] goods. As to the extent of preferential access, the distribution of $\tilde{\tau}_i$, the average for the intermediate goods sample is around 4.81% and the quartile repartition are: [25%: 0.6%]; [median or 50%: 3.7%] and [75%: 7.36%], whereas for the final goods the average is 4.13% and the quartile distribution: [25%: 0%]; [median or 50%: 2.5%] and [75%: 5.0%]

7.2.2 Non-parametric estimates

Based on data for 2000 (very close to the data reported in Table 7.1), Anson *et al.* (2005) used revealed preference arguments and Estevadeordal's (2000) synthetic index, r_i, to estimate the total compliance costs for Mexican exporters to NAFTA. As a starting point, we carry out the same exercise here with 2001 data when the average margin of preference was almost the same (4.11% in 2001 vs. 4.10% in 2000) and the average utilization rate slightly higher (58% vs. 57%). We also compare these estimates with those for 2000 to see if one can detect any learning effects through time.

As a first step, we reproduce for 2001, the non-parametric estimates of compliance costs of RoO, c_i, expressed as a percentage of unit price, of Anson *et al.* carried out for 2000. This involves comparing preference margins and utilization rates for selected values of the index of restrictiveness, r_i. By revealed preference, for headings with $u_i = 100\%$, the preference margin is an upper-bound for compliance costs (as c_i cannot be greater than the benefit conferred by $\tilde{\tau}_i$). Likewise, for headings with $u_i = 0\%$, the preference margin gives a lower-bound estimate. For the remaining sectors with $0\% < u_i < 100\%$, assumptions must be made. Anson *et al.* (2005) assumed that firms were indifferent to export to the US under the NAFTA or the MFN regimes (heterogeneity of firms notwithstanding). Then, an approximation of compliance costs would be given by the average rate of tariff preference computed for the remaining sectors, i.e. on the sample $0\% < u_i < 100\%$. Applying this reasoning, we obtain for 2000, [2001], $c = \tilde{\tau} = 6.11\%, [c = \tilde{\tau} = 6.16\%]$.

Anson *et al.* further break down total compliance costs, c_i, into an administrative component, δ_i, and a distortionary component, σ_i:

$$c_i = \delta_i + \sigma_i, \tag{7.2}$$

where all variables expressed as a percentage of unit price. To come up with an estimate of administrative costs, they assume that administrative costs would be negligible for firms on their participation constraint, $(0\% < u_i < 100\%)$, provided that they would also have low values of r_i, i.e. values corresponding to a change of tariff classification at the heading level, CH, i.e. when $r_i \leq 2$ (not much paperwork is involved in 'proving' a change of heading). Hence, calculating preference margins for utilization rates close to 100% (say $u_i = 95\%$) when $r_i \leq 2$, gives an upper bound of the distortionary component, σ_i. These average preference margins for 2000, [2001] are $\tilde{\tau} = 4.30\%$ [$\tilde{\tau} = 4.44\%$]. Recalling that the average total compliance costs for 2000, [2001] are $c = \tilde{\tau} = 6.11\%, [c = \tilde{\tau} = 6.16\%]$ we get average administrative cost estimates for δ of $\delta = 6.11\% - 4.30\% = 1.81\%$ [$\delta = 6.16\% - 4.44\% = 1.72\%$].

Both estimates are close, though interestingly the administrative cost estimate for 2001 is less than that for 2000 both in absolute terms and in relative terms, as it falls from 45% to 42% of the total compliance costs (by assumption equal to the average preference margin). These non-parametric estimates confirm the hunch that there may be significant learning effects that could explain low utilization rates in early years of preferential access (see, e.g., Brenton 2005 in his explanation of low take-up under EBA).

7.3 A simple model

The above non-parametric cost estimates are averages across sectors, rely entirely on values taken by the r_i index, and potentially gloss over differences across types of RoO.[4] If one is ready to assume that utilization rates provide some information on the stringency of RoO and to make a few additional assumptions, one can sketch a simple model that improves along these two dimensions.

Assume first that aggregation from the firm to the tariff line level does not introduce systematic biases (which we can't check for anyway in the absence of firm-level data). Assume next that the utilization rate of NAFTA for product line i is a positive function of the difference between the tariff preference rate, $\tilde{\tau}_i$, and (unobserved) total compliance costs, c_i, again expressed as a percentage of unit price, associated with applying the RoO criteria, i.e.:

$$u_i = f(\tilde{\tau}_i - c_i); f'(.) > 0, \tag{7.3}$$

where $\tilde{\tau}_i$ is defined in eqn (7.1). This assumption is only defensible in the absence of firm-level information (see Appendix) that would recognize that the utilization rate is a zero–one decision for the firm. So think of eqn (7.3) as a specification for costs at the aggregated HS-6 level that circumvents the problems associated with heterogeneous behavior associated with firm heterogeneity (see Ju and Krishna 2003 and Krishna 2005).

For compliance costs associated with the RoO, c_i, assume a linear relation with each of the set of relevant RoO, i.e.:

$$c_i = \delta + \beta' RoO_i + v_i. \tag{7.4}$$

Here, RoO_i is a vector of dummies capturing the RoO described in Table 7.1 and δ captures the administrative cost of RoO. For reasons discussed below, we will include dummy variables for tariff classification change at the chapter level (CC_i), regional value content (RVC_i), and technical requirement ($TECH_i$).

---

[4] Spreads in utilization rates are also assumed to reflect differences in administrative costs rather than firm heterogeneity. Unfortunately, we have no data to control for firm heterogeneity, so this source of bias in the model presented here, cannot be controlled for.

Equations (7.3) and (7.4), lead to the following reduced form for estimation:[5]

$$u_i = \alpha(\tilde{\tau}_i - \delta - \beta' RoO_i) + (\mu_i - \alpha v_i). \tag{7.5}$$

Hence we estimate the following equation:

$$u_i = \lambda + \alpha\tilde{\tau}_i + \theta RoO_i + \varepsilon_i. \tag{7.6}$$

Estimation of (7.6) yields estimates of $\hat{\alpha}$ and $\hat{\theta}$ that can then be used to approximate the distorsion costs generated by RoO, $\hat{c}_i$, i.e.:[6]

$$\hat{c}_i = \frac{\hat{\theta}}{\hat{\alpha}} RoO_i. \tag{7.7}$$

Equation (7.7) states that the costs of a RoO will be proportional to the responsiveness of the utilization rate to the RoO (just like the costs of protection are an increasing function of the elasticity of import demand) and inversely proportional to the responsiveness of the utilization rate to the preference margin.

Since the dependent variable (the utilization rate) takes a value of only between zero or one, the appropriate estimation procedure for the reduced form (7.6) is a two-limit (or double-censored) Tobit (see, Appendix and e.g., Maddala 1983, Chap. 6).[7]

In this model setup, it is assumed that preferential rates and RoO are both exogenous. In reality, RoO are negotiated knowing that the preference margin will be the MFN tariff (unless it is also under negotiation multilaterally). So there is a potential multicollinearity between the RoO and $\tilde{\tau}_i$ variables in eqn (7.6). An endogeneity problem would arise if a second equation can explain RoO as a function of $\tilde{\tau}_i$ and another variable that would also influence the endogenous variable u_i. While this may be the case, in any event we do not have at our disposal a good variable to instrument the RoO variable. Moreover, instrumenting would be difficult anyway since it would take place over dummy variables.

---

[5] See details in Appendix.

[6] We do not estimate total compliance costs of RoO, i.e. $\hat{c}_i = (\hat{\lambda}/\hat{\alpha}) + (\hat{\theta}/\hat{\alpha}) RoO_i$ because it is difficult to give an economic interpretation for the regression constant term (notably due to the econometric procedure used and to the introduction of dummy variables for section and stage of production—see Section 7.4).

[7] The use of the maximum likelihood Tobit estimates of the linear model coefficients is preferred to the standard OLS estimates using the White correction for heteroskedacity, because the Tobit model makes expected values of the dependent variable conditional on the probability of censoring in the sample. Since there is censoring, we will usually report double-censored estimates.

In general (and certainly in the case of NAFTA as explained by Estevadeordal 2000) negotiations can be viewed as a 'game' played by three parties in which negotiation is over two instruments: speed of preferential tariffs *phase-in* and RoO criteria. Moreover, in our NAFTA application, we use data for 2001, a year quite late in the NAFTA process of preferential tariff liberalization (the preference margin for Mexican imports was equal to the US MFN tariff for 3215 tariff lines out of 3555 at HS-6 level). Finally, the US MFN tariff cannot be suspected of endogeneity with the NAFTA RoO. Nonetheless, a more ambitious assessment of RoO would rely on a political-economy approach as in Cadot *et al.* (2005).

7.4 Cost estimates by type of RoO and category of activities

The usefulness of costs estimates obtained from eqn (7.7) depends on the plausibility of the first-stage results for the reduced-form estimation, and should satisfy the revealed-preference criterion used in the non-parametric estimates above. Estimation is carried out for the whole sample and for broad categories of goods (intermediates and final goods[8]) adding sector dummy variables, D_k, to control for sector-specific heterogeneity:

$$u_i = \lambda + \alpha\tau_i + \theta RoO_i + \sum_k D_k + \varepsilon_i, \qquad (7.8)$$

where $i = 1,\ldots, 3225; k = 1,\ldots, 20; RoO_i = CC_i, TECH_i, RVC_i.$[9]

Expected signs in eqn (7.8) are $\hat{\alpha} > 0, \hat{\theta}_1 < 0, \hat{\theta}_2 < 0, \hat{\theta}_3 < 0$.

Note the bounds on the estimated coefficient values in eqn (7.8). Since all variables are in the interval [0,1] (we have eliminated the five preference rates above one), when plugging values obtained from eqn (7.8) into eqn (7.7), one should obtain reasonable cost estimates provided that measurement errors and biases for the coefficients in the numerator and denominator are not systematic. One would also expect different coefficient values for the dummy variables across broad category of goods: for example a change of chapter should have a greater negative impact on utilization rates for final than for intermediate goods.

---

[8] Adding raw materials does not affect overall results as this category represents only 9% of the sample. Furthermore, the only RoO component for these products is a CC. However, as previously explained, we eliminated this part of the sample because all the outliers in terms of tariff preference margins belonged to this category.

[9] For multicollinearity reasons (see Section 7.2), we could not add a dummy for CH and for E in addition to CC_i. Note also that the vector RoO_i depends on the category considered, since some categories of goods do not face certain types of RoO (e.g. intermediates do not face technical requirements).

Table 7.2 Determinants of utilization rates and total costs of RoO

u_i	Total sample		Intermediate goods		Final goods	
	OLS	Tobit	OLS	Tobit	OLS	Tobit
$\bar{\tau}_i$	2.2757**	4.3683**	3.0389**	9.0450**	2.0910**	3.9310**
	(0.41)	(0.20)	(0.47)	(0.54)	(0.45)	(0.21)
CC_i	−0.0684**	−0.1676**	−0.0604**	−0.2122**	−0.0801**	−0.1447**
	(0.02)	(0.04)	(0.03)	(0.09)	(0.02)	(0.04)
$TECH_i$	−0.2088**	−0.4975**	−	−	−0.2288**	−0.4391**
	(0.03)	(0.08)			(0.04)	(0.09)
RVC_i	−0.1065**	−0.1517**	−0.2850**	−0.4058*	−0.1147**	−0.1811*
	(0.05)	(0.04)	(0.12)	(−0.24)	(0.05)	(0.11)
Obs.	3225	3225	1048	1048	2177	2177
R^2-adj	0.39		0.38		0.40	
Log likelihood		−2995.5		−959.8		−2024.8

Notes:
Constant and dummy variables for section and stage of production are included but not reported in order to save space
OLS: coefficients estimate with Ordinary Least Squared with White correction.
TOBIT: coefficients estimate with the Two-Limit Tobit Model.
Standard deviations in parenthesis.
** and *, respectively, significant at the 5% and 10% level.

We start with the results for the two broad categories of sectors (intermediates and final goods), then comment briefly on results for the T&A sector. Table 7.2 reports the results of the OLS and two-limit Tobit estimates of eqn (7.8). For the entire sample (3225 observations) all coefficients are strongly significant with the expected sign: the tariff preference margin influences positively the utilization rate and the sign of the dummy variables relative to RoO are all negative, indicating that these requirements reduce the use of the NAFTA regime. In this linear specification, in terms of magnitude, the strongest negative impact on utilization rates comes from the TECH requirement, a plausible result if one recalls that these requirements are added when it is felt that a change of tariff heading is 'insufficient'.

Turning to the comparison of estimates for final and intermediate goods, note that TECH is only present for final goods (and applied mostly to the T&A sector), but RVC is present and significant for both categories.[10]

Turn now to the magnitudes of the coefficients on RoO dummies, recalling that only 5% of the tariff lines have an RVC, and less than 9% a TECH requirement. Model shortcomings deserve to be mentioned. First, according to eqn (7.3), the coefficient for $\bar{\tau}_i$ in eqn (7.6) represents the

[10] When the reduced form is estimated for raw materials, the tariff preference margin is positive and strongly significant (due to some outliers). But CC, the only RoO faced by this category is not significant. This is not surprising, and conforms with *a priori* expectations.

impact of the difference between $\tilde{\tau}_i$ and c_i on the utilization rate. If so, a given increase in $(\tilde{\tau}_i - c_i)$ has an impact on u_i about three times as large for intermediates than for final goods. Secondly, differences in coefficient values on the RoO variables (which combine the impact of the RoO variables on the cost c_i and the impact of the difference $(\tilde{\tau}_i - c_i)$ on u_i discussed above), cannot be easily interpreted within the model. This said, all coefficient values have the expected signs and are significant at the 5% level, justifying turning to the compliance cost estimates obtained by plugging estimates of eqn (7.8) into eqn (7.7). The contributions to costs of the different RoO are reported in Table 7.4, columns 3 and 4, and will be discussed later.

For the estimates to be useful, they should meet the revealed preference criterion used in the non-parametric estimates reported in Section 7.2.2. This means that the estimated compliance costs should, on average, be lower [greater] than the average preference margin for products with an utilization rate of NAFTA of 100% [0%], whatever the category (total, final or intermediate). This is indeed the case for all product categories, for utilization rates of 100% [0%]. As to the products with $0\% < u_i < 100\%$, the estimated compliance costs are systematically inferior to the tariff preference margin, often by non-negligible margins. Given that the preference margins are almost at the same level for sectors with non-zero utilization rates, it could be that the absence of variation in the data prevents identifying costs, so that even with sector dummies, there is too much uncontrolled firm heterogeneity.

Unfortunately, the problem of uncontrolled firm heterogeneity cannot be alleviated by turning to sector-level estimates, because plausible results could only be obtained for one sector. Indeed, among the 2-digit sectors with more than 100 observations and average preference margins above 4% (an estimate of total compliance costs of 3% of which there are 6 sectors if one omits the misc. manuf. category), only the largest sector (the T&A sector with 618 observations) gives significant and plausible results. Since this is an important sector for Mexico in NAFTA and for developing countries engaged in preferential market access with Northern countries (e.g. under EBA and AGOA, or under other FTAs by the EU and US), estimates are reported in the last column of Table 7.3.[11]

---

[11] The estimation of eqn (7.8) for T&A sample (618 observations) by the two-limit Tobit model, yields the following first stage results:

$$u_i = \underset{(0.06)}{1.15} + \underset{(0.32)}{3.11}\,\tau_i - \underset{(0.06)}{0.21}\,CC_i - \underset{(0.05)}{0.37}\,TECH_i.$$

with standard errors in parenthesis and associated compliance cost estimates reported in the last column of Table 7.3.

Table 7.3 Costs and preference rates

	Total sample			Intermediate goods			Final goods			Textiles and apparel		
	Obs	$\bar{\tau}_i$	$\hat{c}_i^{TOBIT}$	Obs	$\bar{\tau}_i$	$\hat{c}_i^{TOBIT}$	Obs	$\bar{\tau}_i$	$\hat{c}_i^{TOBIT}$	Obs	$\bar{\tau}_i$	$\hat{c}_i^{TOBIT}$
$0\% < u_i < 100\%$	1410	5.92%	3.86%	322	5.28%	2.04%	1088	6.10%	4.17%	337	11.82%	13.01%
$u_i = 0\%$	954	0.38%	1.71%	211	0.76%	1.69%	743	0.27%	1.43%	34	1.87%	6.63%
$u_i = 100\%$	861	6.32%	3.01%	515	6.17%	1.61%	346	6.55%	3.69%	247	9.71%	5.65%

Notes:
Computed from coefficients estimated in eqn (7.8) applied to eqn (7.7).
$\hat{c}_i^{TOBIT}$: cost obtained from Two-Limit Tobit Model estimations.

Comparing the estimates for the T&A sector with those for larger categories of activities, it is clear that both CC and TECH criteria represent larger costs (respectively 6.7% vs. 3.01% and 11.8% vs. 9.17%) which reflects the fact that utilization rates are not much higher than average in the T&A sector in spite of high preferential margins. In interpreting these results, one should be cautious since the CC and TECH coefficients must capture some of the effects associated with 'exceptions' (98% of the lines face an exception in sector 11!). Also according to the distribution of TECH requirements, these are mostly on production processes (33% of technical requirements) with the remaining (9%) on both product and process.

To summarize, among the significant results, the revealed preference criterion is satisfied and the data classification of the RoO components in terms of estimated compliance costs is reasonable since $CC < RVC < TECH$. This is precisely the ranking assumption about restrictiveness used by Estevadeordal (2000) in setting up his observation rule to construct his synthetic index.

Perhaps more importantly, estimates conform to *a priori* expectations with respect to the costs of RoO across broad categories of goods. For instance, the costs of each component are found to be different across the stages of production with CC and RVC representing a greater cost for final-goods producing sectors than for intermediate-goods producing sectors. Since final-goods producers also faced technical requirements, it is not surprising to find total compliance costs (on average over all product lines) that are greater for final-goods-producing sectors than for inter-mediate-goods-producing sectors (3.2% vs. 2.0%). And given that the tariff preference margin is lower for final goods than for intermediate (4.3% vs. 4.8%), we can also expect (still in average terms over all product lines), a lower utilization rate for final-goods-producing sectors, than for intermediate-goods-producing sectors. This is indeed confirmed in Table 7.2 (utilization rates are 53.9% and 74.3%, respectively).

7.5 Evaluating Estevadeordal's synthetic index

Can synthetic indices of RoO regimes serve the same summary descriptive roles as effective rate of protection for trade regimes? We raise this question for Estevadeordal's index, constructed from the same data set, and subsequently used by Estevadeordal and Suominen (2005) to summarize RoO for several FTAs.

Consider first the following calculation. Take US sectors with tariff peaks, i.e. 3 times or more the 2001 average US tariff around 4% and compare the corresponding average value of r_i in those sectors with the corresponding values in the low-tariff sectors (less than one-third the average tariff). Values for the index (number of observations in each group in parenthesis) are in decreasing order of protection: $r_i = 6.0(257)$, and $r_i = 4.8(1432)$. Since tariff escalation according to the stage of processing is widely observed across all countries, tariff peaks are concentrated in the final-goods sectors. It follows that, at least according to this index of restrictiveness, under NAFTA, RoO would protect final-goods-producing sectors.

Are costs similar across types of RoO? Recall from eqn (7.7) that the costs of a given RoO are assumed to depend on how utilization rates react to the RoO and to the response of utilization rates to preferential rates. Computations of the costs of each type of RoO (when it applies) according to eqn (7.7) are reported in columns 3 and 4 of Table 7.4. RVC criteria have similar effects for intermediate and final goods: the imposition of an RVC on a product generates a cost estimated at 4.5% [4.6%] for intermediate [final] goods. As one would expect, a change of classification at the chapter level (CC) generates a higher cost for final (3.7%) than for intermediate goods (2.3%).[12] Finally, again according to intuition, the greatest cost for final products results from technical requirements, with an impact of 11% on total compliance costs.

To evaluate Estevadeordal's index, we make the necessary assumptions to come up with a lexicographic ordering suggested by our estimates, then compare it with his constructed from the observation rule used to construct the r_i index.[13] Both rankings are summarized in Table 7.4. On the one hand, Estevadeordal's (2000) is built around a finer distinction for the type of change of classification heading (CH, CS, CI levels), which was

---

[12] This result still holds when one replaces the CC_i dummy by a CH_i dummy.

[13] We have assumed that for the RoO not included in our econometric indices, they would have taken a value of 1. This is probably plausible though one may question that CH would take a value of 1 (our justification for this ranking is that cost estimates for CC are low). However, we use question marks to indicate that the rankings are assumed rather than estimated.

Table 7.4 Comparison of Estevadeordal's index and costs estimates

RoO criteria	obs.	Estevadeordal's index	Costs estimates[a]		
			Total	Final	rank
CI	9	1	N.A.	N.A.	1(?)
CS	134	2	N.A.	N.A.	1(?)
CS + RVC[b]	2	3	3.84%	4.61%	3
CS + TECH[b]	30	3	11.39%	11.17%	4
CH	1400	4	N.A.	N.A.	1(?)
CH + RVC[b]	167	5	3.84%	4.61%	3
CH + TECH[b]	16	5	11.39%	11.17%	4
CH + RVC + TECH	4	5	15.23%	15.77%	6
CC	1209	6	3.47%	3.68%	2
CC + TECH	254	7	14.86%	14.85%	5

Notes:
a/ Estimates obtained from substituting values obtained in eqn (7.7) and in eqn (7.8).
b/ No distinction between CH and CS in econometric estimates (See text).
N.A. Not applicable (See text).

impossible to carry out in the econometric estimates due to quasi-perfect multicollinearity between the CC and CS dummy variables. On the other hand, for the more restrictive RoO (e.g. for the combination of RoO with values equal to or greater than 5), our cost estimates allow for a finer distinction (5 values instead of 3) and for a non-linear classification. Furthermore, we propose an index different according to the stage of production, allowing the data to determine if the same RoO represents a different cost for intermediate-goods-producing sectors or for final-goods-producing sectors.

Table 7.4 shows that the ranking of costs according to the estimates corresponds to Estevadeordal's selection of observation rule: costs of CC < costs of RVC < costs of TECH. However, the two indicators do not generate the same rank ordering. For instance, since the costs of an RVC is greater than the costs of a CC, a combination of CH + RVC is more costly than the cost generated by a CC.

Overall, however, for the sample of 3225 observations used in the estimations, the correlation between the two indices of costs of RoO is 0.66.

Comparisons based on RoO applied only for one preferential market access case cannot be expected to yield stylized facts, nor a robust assessment of the usefulness of a synthetic index. On the basis of the above, however, it is fair to say that the observation rule yields plausible results both in terms of relative rankings in terms of assumed costs of different types of RoO and in terms of restrictiveness when confronted with US tariff peaks (on the assumption that, for political-economy reasons, RoO should be expected to be more restrictive in sectors with tariff peaks compared with sectors with low rates of protection). However, if other comparisons point in the same direction, it might be worthwhile to distinguish changes in tariff classification in terms of the broad categories of sectors they apply to.

7.6 Value content restrictions

Import content requirements (either in the form of value or quantity) are frequently used (see Estevadeordal and Suominen 2005, Tables 1 and 3): Out of 87 PTAs, 68 require an import content for at least from products; 7 requiring some form of RVC, and another 67 use some restriction on the value of parts (VP). When applied, they usually require between 30% and 60% of the value (or quantity) under constraint to originate in the region. Among the types of RoO considered in this paper, import-content restrictions hold the greatest promise for direct quantification of their cost-raising effects. As a first step in this direction, one can check orders of magnitude suggested by some simple simulations imposing accepted functional forms and cost-minimizing behavior in a competitive environment. The simulations below compute the extent of preferential market access necessary that would leave a cost-minimizing firm indifferent under different import restrictions.

Suppose then that a Mexican firm, or some other Southern partner firm, produces under constant returns to scale and perfect competition a final good, X that it can sell either in the US (Northern) partner market, or on the ROW market. The final good is produced with value added, VA, and intermediates, Z, i.e. $X = F(VA, Z)$. Value added is produced by capital and labor, i.e. $VA = H(K, L)$ at exogenously determined prices, (w, r) while intermediates either come from the US partner, Z^A, or from the ROW, Z^C so that $Z = G(Z^A, Z^C)$, also with exogenously given prices $p^{Z,A}$ and $p^{Z,C}$. Let $F(.)$ be Leontief, and $H(.)$ and $G(.)$, be CES functions. Profit maximization will imply that the unit cost function can be written as:

$$c(.) = a_z P^z + a_v P^v, \qquad (7.9)$$

where a_z, a_v are the per-unit input coefficients for intermediates and value added, respectively, with P^z, P^v their corresponding per-unit prices. Under the CES aggregation functions, the expressions for unit prices are:

$$P^z = CES(P^{z,a}, P^{v,c}; \gamma_z, \alpha_z, \sigma_z), \qquad (7.10)$$

where γ_z is a calibration parameter, α_z is the share parameter and σ_Z is the elasticity of substitution between intermediates of different origin. Likewise, the unit value-added price is given by:

$$P^v = CES(w, r; \gamma_v, \alpha_v, \sigma_v), \tag{7.11}$$

where the parameters have the same meaning as in the previous expression. Perfect competition implies that the unit price for the good, P^x equals unit cost, i.e.:

$$P^x = C(.). \tag{7.12}$$

Finally, let there be some market segmentation (or product differentiation by destination) by assuming that it is costly to reallocate X across markets. Then unit prices obtained in each market are $P^{X,A}$ in the US and $P^{X,C}$ in the ROW. Let the ease of substitution across markets be captured by the constant elasticity of transformation (CET) function, with unit sales given by:

$$P^x = CET(p^{X,A}, p^{X,C}; \gamma_x, \alpha_x, \sigma_x), \tag{7.13}$$

where the parameters have the same meaning as in the CES case.

Let, t^A be the US *ad valorem* tariff, and let the RoO be a RVC in quantity terms. If subscript zero denotes the optimal per-unit use of the intermediate originating in the US, and subscript one, the corresponding choices by the firm when it faces a RoO and preferential access, on the cost side:

$$z^R = Z_1^A/Z^C > z^* = Z_0^A/Z^C; Z_1^A > Z_0^A,$$

leading to the restricted cost function, $c^R(.)$. Since $c^R(z^R) > c^0(z^0)$, one can ask what rate of preference in the US market is necessary to leave the Mexican firm indifferent between choosing to export under NAFTA or under MFN, i.e. compute $\tau = (P_1^{X,A})/(P_0^{X,A})$ so that:

$$P_1^x = CET(p_1^{X,A}, p^{X,C}) = c^R(.). \tag{7.14}$$

Table 7.5 reports the results of illustrative simulations that calculate the margin of preference that would leave indifferent a Mexican (Southern) exporter facing an RVC for intermediate purchases.

Columns (1) to (4) could be representative of a final-producing goods industry, with a relatively low value-added ratio, while columns (5) to (8) could be representative of an intermediate-goods industry with a higher value-added ratio (less roundaboutness in the methods of production).

All simulations start from an initial equilibrium situation in which all prices are unity and in which the share of exports to the US is 50%. For simplicity, we assume that the two elasticities in the simulations are

Table 7.5 RVC and compensating preference margins

	(1)	(2)	(3)	(4)	(5)	(6)	(7)	(8)
Value added	30%	30%	30%	30%	60%	60%	60%	60%
Intermediates	70%	70%	70%	70%	40%	40%	40%	40%
Initial Vus/(Vus + Vrow)	20%	30%	40%	50%	20%	30%	40%	50%
Final Vus/(Vus + Vrow) [RoO]	40%	40%	60%	60%	40%	40%	60%	60%
Initial share of exports to US	50%	50%	50%	50%	50%	50%	50%	50%
Final share of exports to US	55.9%	51.5%	55.3%	51.4%	53.6%	50.9%	53.2%	50.8%
Initial Pus*	1	1	1	1	1	1	1	1
New Pus*	1.13	1.03	1.11	1.03	1.07	1.02	1.07	1.02

unity: a Cobb–Douglas for the substitution for intermediates of different origin and an elasticity of transformation across export destinations of unity. In this partial equilibrium setup, we also assume that the industry is a price-taker in input markets and in the market for export sales. Finally, to ease the interpretation of results, we also limit the amount that is exported to the initial equilibrium quantities, so that all firms do is readjust the export mix in response to the change in incentives to sell in the US market.[14]

Interpreting the results, note first that the required preferential access is higher for each RVC constraint in the final (low value-added activity). This is of course inherent in the model setup. Next we turn to orders of magnitude, given that it is not clear what the extent of restrictiveness is. For example, Estevadeordal and Suominen report that, when they are used, RVC percentages are 50% or 60%. So suppose it is 60%. According to the simulations, if the initial RVC was 40% [50%], a preference margin of 11% [3%] would be needed to leave the Mexican exporter indifferent.

7.7 Conclusions

Exporters benefitting from preferential market access have to contend with a vast array of RoO whose cost-raising effects have, so far, escaped

---

[14] If one were interested in computing welfare effects, one would incorporate a price responsive demand curve for total exports, so that binding RoO would then have two effects: a change in volume and a change in export destination mix. The model would be closed by specifying an upward-sloping supply curve for primary factors on production in the industry.

quantification. Using the RoO map negotiated under NAFTA, this chapter has attempted to quantify these costs. Using non-parametric methods based on a widely used synthetic index, we have estimated total compliance costs and the administrative component of total costs. Comparisons between 2000 and 2001 reveal some learning effects as utilization rates increased in spite of insignificant changes in market access. Calculations also revealed that administrative costs fell in absolute terms, but also as a percentage of total compliance costs.

Turning to the econometric estimates carried out for broad categories of goods (final and intermediates), results are in accordance with *a priori* expectations with respect to the type of RoO and to the costs of a given set of RoO across broad categories of goods. Other things being equal, compliance costs are the least for a change of tariff classification (here captured by CC), followed by a regional value content (RVC) and by a technical requirement (TECH). Regarding stages of production, an RVC is more costly for final-goods producing sectors than for intermediate-goods producing sectors. Estimates also showed that the lower rate of utilization for final-goods producing sectors under NAFTA (presumably the sectors in which Mexico had a comparative advantage) could be attributed to the battery of RoO they faced (after controlling for differences in preferential access).

Synthetic indices, such as the one proposed by Estevadeordal, which will continue to be used notably when utilization rates are not available, can give a summary measure of overall restrictiveness of a given RoO map. We have therefore compared the lexicographic ordering used by Estevadeordal in his observation rule with the ordering emerging from our cost estimates. We find that his ordinal ranking is the same as ours when it comes to individual RoO. However, they differ when several RoO enter simultaneously, and especially when it come to the distinction between final-goods-producing activities and intermediate-goods-producing activities. This suggests that it might be useful to build different synthetic indexes for broad categories of activities.

Finally, we have estimated rates of preferential market access that would be needed to counteract the cost-raising effects for regional value-content requirements when they apply. Under cost-minimization assumptions, and under acceptable functional forms, it would appear that preference margins of about 10% would be needed to compensate for a 'typical' regional value content RoO. While much still remains to be done before we better understand the cost-raising effects of RoO, the evidence presented here suggests that RoO go a long way towards negating the benefits of preferential market access for the Southern partners that are the presumed beneficiaries of these preferences.

References

Anson, J., Cadot, O., Estevadeordal, A., de Melo, J., Suwa-Eisenmann, A., Bolorma T. 2005. Rules of Origin in North-South Preferential Trading Arrangements with an application to NAFTA. *Review of International Economics*, 13(3): 501–517.

Augier, P., Gasiorek, M., C. Lai-Tong. 2005. 'The Impact of Rules of Origin on Trade Flows'. In *The Origin of Goods: Rules of Origin in Regional Trade Agreements* edited by Cadot, O., Estevadeordal, A., Suwa, A., T. Verdier. *CEPR/ IADB / Oxford University Press*, this volume Chap. 14.

Brenton, P., M. Manchin. 2003. Making EU Trade Agreements Work: The Role of Rules of Origin. *World Economy*, Vol.26 (may): 755–769.

Brenton, P. 2005. 'Rules of Origin and Utilization of Trade Preferences in non-Reciprocal Agreements'. In *The Origin of Goods: Rules of Origin in Regional Trade Agreements* edited by Cadot, O., Estevadeordal, A., Suwa, A., T. Verdier. *CEPR/ IADB / Oxford University Press*, this volume Chap. 13.

Cadot, O., Estevadeordal, A., A. Suwa-Eisenmann. 2005. 'Rules of Origin as Export Subsidies'. In *The Origin of Goods: Rules of Origin in Regional Trade Agreements* edited by Cadot, O., Estevadeordal, A., Suwa, A., T. Verdier. *CEPR/ IADB / Oxford University Press*, this volume Chap. 6.

Estevadeordal, A. 2000. Negotiating Preferential Market Access: The case of the North American Free Trade Area. *Journal of World Trade* 34(1): 141–166.

Estevadeordal, A., K. Suominen. 2005. 'Rules of Origin A World Map and Trade Effects'. In *The Origin of Goods: Rules of Origin in Regional Trade Agreements* edited by Cadot, O., Estevadeordal, A., Suwa, A., T. Verdier. *CEPR/ IADB / Oxford University Press*, this volume Chap. 4.

Flatters, F., R. Kirk. 2005. 'Rules of Origin as Tools of Development: Lessons from SADC'. In *The Origin of Goods: Rules of Origin in Regional Trade Agreements* edited by Cadot, O., Estevadeordal, A., Suwa, A., T. Verdier. *CEPR/ IADB / Oxford University Press*, this volume Chap. 12.

Herin, J. 1986. Rules of Origin and Differences Between Tariff Levels in EFTA and in the EC. EFTA Occasional Paper no. 13.

Ju, J., K. Krishna. 2003. Firm Behavior and Market Access in a Free Trade Area with Rules of Origin. Mimeo, Penn State University.

Krishna, K. 2005. 'Understanding Rules of Origin'. In *The Origin of Goods: Rules of Origin in Regional Trade Agreements* edited by Cadot, O., Estevadeordal, A., Suwa, A., T. Verdier. *CEPR/ IADB / Oxford University Press*, this volume Chap. 2.

Maddala, G.S. 1983. *Limited-Dependent and Qualitative Variables in Econometrics*, Cambridge (GB).

Appendix: The model

This appendix develops the firm's decision to indicate the link between the variables determined at the firm level and the observed data at the HS-6 level, and justifies the econometric specification.

Firm' decision
Let index i refer to an HS-6 tariff line observation (this is the product line for which we have observations on utilization rates and preference rates). Let there be $j = 1, \ldots, n$ Mexican firms exporting to the US under product category i. Rank firms so that $j = 1, \ldots, k$ export to the US under NAFTA regime and $j = k + 1, \ldots, n$ export under the MFN regime. Let $u_j = 1[0]$ represent the firm's decision to export under NAFTA [MFN], and E_j firm's j exports to the US. Finally, total unit compliance costs, c_j, associated with RoO include an administrative component, δ_j, and a distortionary cost associated with implementing the RoO requirement itself, σ_j, i.e. $c_j = \delta_j + \sigma_j$. The above relations suggest that we can write the firm's costs as:

$$c_j = f(RoO_i, \delta_j). \tag{7.15}$$

Implicitly, in eqn (7.15) we have assumed that all firms differ in their costs when they sell product i only because of costs associated with implementing RoO, an assumption that will certainly be violated in practice. With this notation, the firm's decision will boil down to:

$$u_j = 0 \Leftrightarrow E_j = E_j^{MFN} \quad \text{if} \quad \tilde{\tau}_i < c_j$$
$$u_j = 1 \Leftrightarrow E_j = E_j^{NAFTA} \quad \text{if} \quad \tilde{\tau}_i \geq c_j. \tag{7.16}$$

Note that the rate of preference is observed at the HS-6 product level, while the utilization rate decision takes place at the firm level. However, the utilization rate in the data is also observed at the product level, and it is defined as:

$$u_i = \frac{\sum\limits_{j=1,\ldots,k} E_j^{NAFTA}}{\sum\limits_{j=1,\ldots,k} E_j^{NAFTA} + \sum\limits_{j=k+1\ldots,n} E_j^{MFN}} \quad \text{with} \quad \begin{cases} u_i = 0 & \text{if } k = 0 \\ u_i = 1 & \text{if } k = n \\ 0 < u_i < 1 & \text{if } 0 < k < n. \end{cases} \tag{7.17}$$

We assume linear specifications for the utilization rate of NAFTA at the product level:

$$u_i = \alpha(\tilde{\tau}_i - c_i) + \mu_i, \tag{7.18}$$

with c_i, the unit costs associated with RoO at the product level. c_i is a weighted average of the firms' costs c_j. Unfortunately, we have no information on the distribution of these c_j in each HS-6 level, i. However, we can reasonably assume that:

$$c_i = \delta + \beta' RoO_i + v_i, \tag{7.19}$$

where β is a $t \times 1$ vector of unknown parameters and RoO_i is a $t \times 1$ vector of explanatory variables.

Equations (7.18) and (7.19), lead to the reduced form for estimation:

$$u_i = \alpha(\tilde{\tau}_i - \delta - \beta' RoO_i) + (\mu_i - \alpha v_i). \tag{7.20}$$

Econometric specification

The dependent variable being truncated at both high and low values, the model becomes:

$$u_i^* = \lambda + \alpha\tilde{\tau}_i + \theta' RoO_i + \varepsilon_i. \tag{7.21}$$

where u_i^* is the latent variable, ε_i are residuals that are independently and normally distributed, with mean zero and a common variance σ^2 and:

$$\begin{cases} u_i = 0 & \text{if } u_i^* \leq 0 \\ u_i = u_i^* & \text{if } 0 < u_i^* < 1 \\ u_i = 1 & \text{if } u_i^* \geq 1. \end{cases}$$

Here, 0 and 1 are the lower and upper limits. The likelihood function for this model is given by:

$$L(\lambda, \alpha, \beta, \sigma | u_i, \tilde{\tau}_i, RoO_i, 0, 1)$$

$$= \prod_{u_i=0} \Phi\left(\frac{0 - \lambda - \alpha\tilde{\tau}_i - \theta' RoO_i}{\sigma}\right) \prod_{u_i=u_i^*} \frac{1}{\sigma} \phi\left(\frac{u_i - \lambda - \alpha\tilde{\tau}_i - \theta' RoO_i}{\sigma}\right)$$

$$\times \prod_{u_i=1} \left[1 - \Phi\left(\frac{1 - \lambda - \alpha\tilde{\tau}_i - \theta' RoO_i}{\sigma}\right)\right]. \tag{7.22}$$

In eqn (7.22), $\phi(.)$ and $\Phi(.)$ are, respectively, the density function and distribution function of the standard normal evaluated at $(\lambda + \alpha\tilde{\tau}_i + \theta' RoO_i)/\sigma$ (see Maddala 1983, Chap. 6 for algebraic details).

8

Implementing PTAs in the Southern Cone region of Latin America: Rules of Origin

Pablo Sanguinetti and Eduardo Bianchi

8.1 Introduction

The last 10 to 15 years have witnessed a significant rise in preferential trade agreements (PTAs) in the Americas. PTAs can take several forms, going from partial import tariff liberalizations to more ambitious schemes including total elimination of trade barriers, the setting up of a common external tariff, the allowance of free movements of factors of production, the co-ordination of other domestic policies and regulations affecting market transactions, monetary integration, etc.

Within this continuum, a Free Trade Agreement (FTA) is a PTA in which tariff rates among members are zero, although external tariffs may be set at different rates. A Customs Union (CU) is a PTA where, in addition to internal free trade, a common external tariff governs trade between members and third countries. In the Americas most of the PTAs have taken the form of FTAs, NAFTA being one of the leading examples, while few other initiatives have adopted the form of CU like Mercosur.

The fact that under FTAs external tariffs may differ across member countries has made the establishment of Rules of Origin (RoOs) a central ingredient of these schemes, since they are required to avoid trade deflection. It has been argued that this implementing feature of FTAs can alone reduce welfare compared to a CU (Krueger 1995). Now, if from a normative point of view a CU may be preferred to a FTA, from a political-economy perspective, the preference order may be inverted as the establishment of RoOs under FTAs adds a new instrument through which local producers can obtain 'enhanced protection' (Grossman and Helpman, 1995) and thus support the formation of a FTA.

The purpose of this chapter is to look at the role of Rules of Origin in the implementation of PTAs in the Southern Cone region of Latin America. In particular we are going to look at Mercosur and the FTAs signed between Mercosur and Chile and Mercosur and Bolivia. The case of Mercosur is interesting because as it is as an imperfect Custom Union it allows the establishment of RoOs under two quite different scenarios to be studied: for those products included and those excluded from the Common External Tariff (CET). For the first group trade deflection is not an issue, while it is quite relevant for the second one. Similarly, another piece of evidence to study the potential contrast in the design of RoOs under CU and FTA is to compare RoOs within Mercosur to those established in the FTA signed between Mercosur and Chile and Mercosur and Bolivia. In all these comparisons the key questions we want to address are the following: was there any significant difference in the design of RoOs under CU and FTAs? Were the latter more restrictive? To what extend did normative *vis-à-vis* political economy considerations play any role in the determination of RoOs?

The rest of the chapter is organized as follows. Section 8.2 presents an analytical framework in which we discuss the effect of RoOs in FTA and CU. We use this framework to derive our main working hypotheses. Section 8.3 describes the main criteria used in Mercosur and in the FTAs Mercosur-Chile and Mercosur-Bolivia to determine the origin of commodities. In Section 8.4 we calculate an index of RoOs restrictiveness by commodity and we use it to empirically investigate some of the hypotheses described in Section 8.2. We conclude in Section 8.5.

8.2 Rules of Origin in CU and FTAs: normative and political-economy considerations

8.2.1 *Normative issues*

Rules of Origin are established aiming at different objectives in Customs Unions and Free Trade Agreements. In CU RoOs are established to define when a good is produced within the region and so it can be granted preferential treatment. The existence of a common external tariff makes external protection uniform across member countries, so domestic prices of traded goods will tend to equalize (up to differences originated in transport cost). Clearly this is not the case with FTAs, where each country independently sets its tariff against non-members. Here the RoOs have the additional purpose of avoiding imports of any particular commodity to enter through the country with the lowest tariff rate and be re-exported to the other member with zero tariffs; this is called trade deflection. If intraregional transport costs are not negligible this could be welfare reducing. Thus the establishments of RoO are in this case justified to avoid socially costly trans-shipment of merchandises[1]. A simple prediction coming from this normative approach will imply that RoOs will be present whenever we find significant differences in external tariff across FTA partner countries.

Now, a RoO established to avoid trade deflection could serve as an 'export protection' mechanism depending on its degree of restrictiveness. That is, the more protectionist member of the FTA can indirectly impose its protectionist policies on the other members. Following Krishna and Krueger (1995), consider an FTA where country A is a high-cost producer (compared to world markets) of an intermediate input j that serves to produce a final good i, which it is also subject to high tariffs in country A, but it is an exportable good for country B, also an FTA member. Then, if country A imposes a very restrictive RoO on the assembly operations of good i in country B, it can force B firms to redirect purchases of intermediate goods j from worldwide low-cost producers to country A's manufactures in order to be able to enter into A's market for product i and realize the high internal prices. Thus, in this case we see that a given RoO forces country B to adopt (to pay) country A's protection-driven price of input j in exchange of high tariff preference for the final product. Of course this will happen whenever the tariff structure in country A gives a net positive effective protection to B producers once they meet the RoO requirement. If this net effective protection is negative then the RoO will simply imply that, at least in the short run, exports of good i by country B into A will not be further expanded by the formation of the FTA and the adoption of tariff preferences[2].

---

[1] Notice that if transport costs are negligible, a FTA without RoOs could eventually imply that the low-protection country of the FTA 'exports' its liberalizing policy to the remaining members and in this case the normative implication is to eliminate these regulations.

[2] In addition to affecting trade flows, a very restrictive RoO can induce a foreign producer to establish a plant to produce the intermediate input j (even though it could not be justifiable given country B costs and transport expenses from third countries) in order to allow producers

8.2.2 *Political economy*

But then, if we recognize that within the context of FTAs RoO could function as another protectionist device, how does a political-economy approach change the normative prescription about the emergence of FTAs and the role of these regulations? What are their determinants and how do they relate to other key trade-policy variables like tariff preferences?

Grossman and Helpman (1995) (GH95) provide a political-economy model of the emergence of FTAs. According to their approach, at the heart of whether to form a FTA there are political pressures for and against it coming from the potential losers and winners due to trade creation and trade diversion. GH95 use the term 'enhanced protection' to describe trade diversion and 'reduce protection' for trade creation (relative to the tariff-ridden pre-FTA situation). In a few words, this approach suggests that exporting interests that are expected to gain the most from trade diversion in the partner country are those that will be more in favor of the establishment of the trade agreement. At the same time, those import-competing sectors that are expected to suffer the most from trade creation originated in imports from the other members are the ones who most strongly will oppose the formation of a FTA. Thus from the point of view of producers' interest, a FTA will most probably emerge when the probability of generating trade diversion is maximized, while at the same time the occurrence of trade creation is minimized. As we know, this is the case when, from a normative point of view, a FTA is less justifiable. In practice, the final result will depend on how efficient these different groups are in influencing government policy through lobby activity, and also the weight in the government objective function of the consumer welfare *vis-à-vis* that of the producer groups.

The original Grossman and Helpman model does not address the issue of intermediate inputs and thus it cannot be easily applied to study the endogenous determination of RoO. This extension is provided in Cadot *et al.* (2003). They present a simple partial equilibrium model with two countries (North and South) engaging in a FTA and where both tariff preferences and the RoO are jointly determined. For tractability reasons they focus in the case where intermediate-good interests in the North country wish to use the FTA to create a captive market for their product. Thus they lobby their government (though GH-type political contribution) to establish strong RoOs to obligate southern producers of the final

of final good *i* in B to enjoy the tariff preference in A. Thus, again, we see how a RoO could also imply 'tariff jumping' FDI in B as a consequence of high protection in its FTA partner.

good to source in the northern country in order to qualify for preferential access. Of course this clearly reduces the effective protection the southern producers get for entering into the final good market in the north. They assume that the southern country is always on its 'participation constraint', that is, the effective protection is zero[3]. Now in this context, deeper tariff preference for the final goods can sustain stricter RoOs. This, in turn, favors the North producers because it raises the demand for their product and, more importantly, the intermediate-good price. In this sense the model delivers the interesting prediction that this price is not tariff ridden but depends on demand and supply (as if the market for this product were closed). This is not surprising as we can think of the RoO as a type of quantitative restriction. Within this framework then we can derive the testable implication that RoO's restrictiveness and tariff preferences are positively associated. We will empirically investigate this hypothesis in Section 8.4.

8.3 Rules of Origin in the Southern Cone: Mercosur, Mercosur-Chile and Mercosur-Bolivia

The RoO regulations that will be the main subject of this section were designed in the context of PTA negotiations that Southern Cone countries undertook since the beginning of the 1990s. In particular, we will concentrate our analysis in Mercosur, an imperfect CU signed by Argentina, Brazil, Paraguay and Uruguay established in 1995, and the FTAs between Mercosur and Chile and Mercosur and Bolivia, which came into effect in 1996 and 1997, respectively. The next subsection presents a background description of the tariff preference policies followed in each agreement, while RoOs regulations are described later.

8.3.1 *Preferential tariffs*

8.3.1.1 MERCOSUR

Mercosur was built on previous treaties that Argentina and Brazil had been negotiating since 1986. The treaty that created Mercosur, signed in

---

[3] Notice that in this case, exports of the final good will not rise as much due to the FTA initiative. Thus the lobby for stronger tariff preferences by the intermediate good industry in the North will not face strong opposition from the final-good industry in the same country. There will be very low trade creation in final goods and a strong trade diversion in intermediates.

March of 1991 also included Uruguay and Paraguay. The agreement was very broad in terms of integration goals. The first article of the Treaty of Asuncion states that the initiative aims at achieving 'the free circulation of goods, services and productive factors among the member countries, through the elimination of the tariff and non-tariff restrictions to the circulation of merchandises and of any other equivalent measure'. It also established the adoption of a Common External Tariff (CET) and of a common commercial policy with relationship to third countries or groupings of countries.[4] In addition to the Treaty of Asuncion, a key piece of legislation was the 'Protocol of Ouro Pretc', signed on December 17, 1994, which revised the institutional framework of Mercosur, set up dispute settlement mechanisms and established the Custom Union (Laird 1997).

The implementation of the Mercosur agreement in 1991 implied the complete elimination, among member countries, of import tariffs affecting most trade. The process of tariff elimination was intended, through progressive linear and automatic reductions in MFN applied import taxes, to reach a zero-tariff state by the end of 1994. After an initial drop taken in 1991 of 47% in the rates applied by each country to its imports from other members, successive reductions took place every six months so as to arrive at a zero tariff at the end of 1994. However, each state could maintain, transitorily and for a limited number of products, tariffs on imports from other Mercosur partners. Toward the end of 1994 these products were included in what was called the 'Adaptation Regime' that established another scheme of tariff reduction so that these items would be completely liberalized by January 1, 1999.[5]

In addition to the above exceptions, the sugar and automotive sectors were not included in the intra-Mercosur trade liberalization due to significant divergence across member countries (especially Argentina and

[4] The Treaty also stipulates far-reaching objectives in terms of co-ordination of policies in other areas. In particular, policies applied in the following sectors: agriculture, industry, public taxes and expenditures, monetary rules, exchange rates, capital market, services, transport and communications. The co-ordination of policies in these areas should aim at assuring appropriate conditions of competition in the broadened economic space created by the integration process.

[5] Argentina had 223 tariff line items on this list. 57% of the items were steel products, 19% were textiles, 11% were paper and 6% footwear. Brazil had only 29 such items, including wool products, peaches in can, rubber factories and wines. Paraguay had 272 such tariff items, with the majority in textiles, some agricultural products, wood and steel. Finally, Uruguay had an extensive list with 953 items, including textiles (22%), chemical products and pharmaceuticals (16%), and steel and electric machinery (8%) (see Bouzas (1997) and Terra (1998)). In the case of Argentina, the average tariff for these products was 21.9% in 1995 and 17.1% in 1996 (see Crespo Armengol and Perez Constanzó 1998).

Brazil) in their national policies toward these sectors. An *ad hoc* group for sugar and a technical committee for autos were created to ensure convergence in national policies. But in the interim, while the exchange of these products was subjected to a very complicated set of rules and restrictions. For example, Argentina maintained quotas and prohibitions on sugar imports from its Mercosur partners. The Argentine position was that this was necessary due to the generous subsidies enjoyed by Brazilian producers from their government. For autos, a managed trade arrangement was put in place. It featured local content, concessional entry of parts, and a bilateral trade-balance requirement.

A common external tariff (CET) was agreed by 1995, but it was going to be in full operation in year 2006. There were three types of temporal exceptions to the CET. First, there were general exceptions consisting of a list proposed by each country. Argentina, Brazil and Uruguay have selected 300 each while Paraguay has 399. It was established that the level of import taxes for these products would converge progressively toward the Common External Tariff by the year 2001 (except for Paraguay where the convergence culminates in the year 2006).[6] A second group of exceptions is constituted by some of the products included in the internal tariff adaptation list. These are the products for which the internal tariffs have been set at a level higher than the negotiated CET. Thus to avoid a negative preference margin, countries were allowed to set a higher external tariff for these items. The convergence of the external tariff to the CET was then linked to the reduction of internal tariff within the adaptation list.

Besides these country-specific exceptions to the CET, it was agreed that capital goods (machines and equipment) could also be subject transitorily to differential aliquots in each state. For capital goods a common external tariff of 14% was established, the level to which Argentina and Brazil must converge no later that year 2001 and Uruguay and Paraguay until the year 2006. These include approximately 1146 positions. For computers and telecommunication equipment there was also a process of convergence to the CET. The agreed Common External Tariff in this sector has a maximum level of 16% and a minimum of 0%. Each state must converge toward the common aliquot in a progressive way until the year 2006.

[6] Though a CET was also established for textiles, countries agreed not to put it into practice immediately. Thus, for example, Argentina maintained a specific tariff on large quantities of textile products as well as in footwear. A similar policy was followed by Uruguay for almost 100 textile items. More recently, and as a consequence that some of these policies have been denounced at the WTO (i.e specific tariffs levied by Argentina), external protection for these sectors has been granted using safeguards clauses (see Sanguinetti and Sallustro (2000)).

Table 8.1 Mercosur average tariffs

	External Tar.	Internal Tar.	Import weighted Ext. Tar.	Import weighted Int. Tar.	Av. Tariff CET exc. Items	Av. Tariff Exc. Int. Items
Argentina	11.78	0.36	13.37	0.86	14.33	11.69
Brazil	13.14	0.02	15.44	0.02	21.39	10.2
Paraguay	8.79	0.80	5.18	0.37	6.83	24.91
Uruguay	10.78	0.88	11.01	1.77	5.92	19.73
Mercosur	11.75	0.00	11.09	0.00	—	—

Source: Olarreaga and Soloaga (1998).

An overall assessment, as of 1996, of the result of the Mercosur internal and external liberalization process can be seen in Table 8.1, taken from Olarreaga and Soloaga (1998). The table contains data on average 8-digit HS tariff lines, external and internal, for the four Mercosur countries. We see that in spite of the commented exceptions, in 1996 on average countries were pretty close to the liberalization objectives. One interesting finding is that while the external tariff in Argentina and Brazil converge from above to the CET, those of Paraguay and Uruguay do it from below, reflecting the relative lower level of protection that those countries had compared to the big patterns in Mercosur.

Regarding the tariff levels observed for the exempted items, we see that the small countries set very high level of tariffs to the excluded items in the internal liberalization. On the other hand, the big countries, in particular, Brazil, have large tariffs on its external excluded items (21.39%). This fact could potentially play an important role in encouraging exports from Argentina and Uruguay into the Brazilian market benefitting from the high external protection. At the same time Brazilian import competing sectors may have tried to avoid this through stricter RoOs applied to this excepted sectors. We will analyse this in Section 8.3.2.

8.3.1.2 MERCOSUR FTA WITH CHILE AND BOLIVIA

The FTA signed by Mercosur with Chile and Bolivia were the first ones that Mercosur as an entity negotiated with third countries (actually as of March 2003 these were the only agreements completed by Mercosur). The agreements provided a comprehensive framework for implementing an integration initiative that not only incorporates trade in goods but also services, investment, and border infrastructure.

In the case of Mercosur-Chile, the adoption of tariff preferences was done automatically, on an annual basis, and the phase-out period varies

Table 8.2 Tariff concessions in Mercosur-Chile FTA

Product category	Preference margin	Phase-out period	No of 8-digit items			
			Chile	%	Mercosur	%
1. General list	40% or more	8	6367	92	6280	91
2. Low-sensitivity items	30%	10	312	5	291	4.2
3. Medium sensitivity	0%	10	208	3	194	2.8
4. High sensitivity	0%	15	139	2	153	2.2
5. Sugar	0%	15	4	0	4	0.1
6. Wheat	0%	18	3	0	3	0

Source: www.direcon.cl

according to the characteristic of the products. Table 8.2 presents the main features of the tariff-preference concessions negotiated by both parties. Products can be grouped into 6 categories depending on the adopted initial level of tariff preference and phase-out period. The first category includes those items where tariffs were initially reduced 40% or more and where the remaining taxes were going to be eliminated over an 8-year time period, ending in 2004. These products represented approximately 90% of the 8-digit tariff lines that were subject to negotiation. The second category corresponds to those products for which the phase-out period was extended to 10 years, while the initial cut in tariffs was set at a 30% level. These were around 300 items (312 for Chile and 291 for Mercosur). Next we have items that received zero initial tariff preference and a 10-year lapse to complete liberalization (around 200 products). The so-called high-sensitivity items are those for which a 15-year phase-out period is to be applied. Chile's list includes 139 positions among them bovine meat, rice, oils, wines and tubes, while in Mercosur's list we have 153 items including grapes, apples, wine and TV sets. Finally, we have two additional categories: one for sugar where the phase-out period is 15 years and one for wheat where complete elimination of MFN tariff will take 18 years. On the other hand, certain other trade barriers, like specific tariffs applied by Argentina and the system of price band applied by Chile to some agriculture prices (e.g. wheat) were not eliminated (though countries took the compromise of not extending their application). Finally, the automotive sector was left outside the initial agreement and subject to future negotiations.

In the Mercosur-Bolivia agreement we have a much simpler structure of tariff preference implementation. Most of the goods are liberalized during a 10-year time period and initial tariff preference varies between 30% and 80%, though for some sensitive items initial tariff preferences are only

10 or 15%. Very few high-sensitivity items receive a 15-year and 18-year adjustment period. Finally, we have a category of products for which a 100% preference was initially applied.[7]

8.3.2 Rules of Origin

Because of its discriminatory nature, a preferential agreement must distinguish 'non-member-originating' from 'member-originating' products in order for a product to be granted preferential access. The determination of origin does not constitute a problem when the product is 'wholly obtained or produced' in one country, although some rules are usually included in PTAs to define this concept. Nevertheless, when two or more countries have been involved in the manufacture of a product, the general principle widely accepted in international law is that the country where the 'last substantial transformation' took place should determine the origin of the product.

Since the term 'substantial transformation' is vague, leaving wide room for a discretionary enforcement, in practice there are three main methods to determine when such 'substantial transformation' has occurred. These are:

1. Change in Tariff Classification: confers origin if the process in the exporting country results in a product that is classified under a different tariff chapter, heading, subheading or item than that of its inputs.

2. Value Added (or Domestic Content): requires that the last substantial transformation has created a certain percentage of local value added in the originating country (or that imported inputs are not higher than a given proportion of the value of the final good).

3. Technical requirement: prescribes that the product must undergo a specified manufacturing or processing operation in the originating country.

These methods present different *ad hoc* levels of restrictiveness. As Estevadeordal (2000) points out, a change of tariff classification at the chapter level tends to be more stringent than at the heading level, a change at the heading level more than at the subheading level and a change at the subheading level more than at the item level. Domestic or

---

[7] It was impossible to quantify the number of 8-digit positions and to identify the products involved in each category given that the annexes to the Treaty were not available on the Internet.

regional content requirement follows up in the restrictiveness scale, while technical requirement can potentially be the most stringent rule. In what follows we briefly describe the Mercosur regime and those applied in the Mercosur-Chile and Mercosur-Bolivia FTAs. Table 8.3 summarizes the main features of all these regulations.

8.3.2.1 MERCOSUR RoO REGIME

Mercosur Rules of Origin are regulated by Decision No 06/94 of the Common Market Council (DEC/CMC 06/94), incorporated as Annex I of the 8th Additional Protocol to the Economic Complementation Agreement N° 18 (ECA 18) that created Mercosur. Complementary regulations regarding RoOs can be found in the 22nd and 39th Additional Protocols to ECA 18 and Decision 24/02 of the Mercosur's Council (DEC/CMC 24/02).[8]

The 8th Additional Protocol approved the regulations pertaining to the Mercosur Origin System and was applied from 1/1/1995 onwards.[9] It is interesting to note that DEC/CMC 06/94 argued that the existence of products exempted from the Mercosur Common External Tariff (CET), necessitated 'the implementation of clear, predictable Rules of Origin to facilitate the flow of intra-zone trade'. This last Decision also justified the adoption of RoOs 'so as not to extend the differential treatment to third countries'.

It is to be noted that according to these regulations, the scope of application of the Mercosur Origin System was: a) products in the process of convergence to the CET; b) products subject to the CET, but with inputs, parts, pieces and components in the process of convergence, except in cases wherein the total value of the extrazone inputs did not exceed 40% of the total FOB value of the end product; c) different trade-policy measures applied by one or more Mercosur countries, as anti-dumping duties, and d) in exceptional cases to be decided by the Mercosur Trade Commission.

In the case of products included in the list of exceptions to CET, RoOs would be applied to intra-Mercosur trade depending on the tariff being above or below the CET, i.e. if in a Mercosur country the tariff of a product

---

[8] This last Decision is dated on December 6th, 2002.

[9] These regulations define the Mercosur's RoOs, the provisions and the administrative decisions to be applied by Mercosur countries for purposes of classification and determination of the native product, the issuance of certificates of origin and the penalties for falsification of certificates of origin, or non-compliance with the verification and control processes. Prior to these regulations, Article III of the Treaty of Asunción established a transitional General Origin System, described in Annex 2 of the Agreement, that was in operation until 12/31/1994.

was above (below) the CET, RoOs would be applied to imports (exports) to (from) this Mercosur country. Notice that this requirement is clearly aimed at, on the one hand, discouraging trade-deflection import operations in cases of downward and/or upwards deviation from the CET. On the other hand, it also avoids Rules of Origin requirement (saving trade costs) when there is certainty that the divergence in external tariffs cannot induce the mentioned speculative operation with trade flows.

Thus Mercosur regime aimed, in theory, at taking full opportunity of the CU advantages regarding RoOs regulations. Nevertheless, in practice, and despite all these considerations, the lack of agreement among Mercosur countries on the distribution of customs collection implied that the Mercosur Origin System is applied to all intrazone trade independently of products being or not in the lists of exceptions.

The Mercosur Origin System considers that products are 'wholly obtained or produced' in Mercosur, when they are totally made in the territory of any of the Mercosur countries, using materials solely and exclusively native to these countries. The same category applies to products from the animal, mineral and plant kingdoms, including those obtained from hunting and fishing, extracted, harvested, or collected, born and raised in their territory.

In the case of products prepared with 'materials' not native to Mercosur countries, these rules consider them originated in Mercosur if they are the result of a transformation process carried out in Mercosur territory, defining this transformation process by a change in the Mercosur Common Tariff Classification (MCTC) at a heading (4-digit) level. When this method cannot be applied, because the transformation process carried out does not entail a change in the MCTC, it is required that the CIF value of the inputs from third countries does not exceed 40% of the FOB value of the goods involved. This last method is also applied for products resulting from assembly or mounting operations conducted in the territory of a Mercosur country, using materials coming from third countries. Finally, there are exceptions where the criterion of a change in tariff heading level plus 60% added value is deemed necessary. The expression 'materials' is interpreted as covering raw materials, inputs, intermediate products, and parts and pieces used in making the product.[10]

The Mercosur Origin System also contemplates the existence of specific origin requirements, many of them in the form of technical specifications,

---

[10] The Mercosur Origin System is based on LAIA tradition, where the general RoOs are conformed by a change in tariff classification at the heading level (4-digit) or, alternatively, a regional value content of at least 50% of the FOB value.

which take precedence over the general criteria explained above. These specific RoOs are applied mainly to products like dairy, chemical, steel, data processing and telecommunications.

Products from Paraguay could have 50% Mercosur value added until 1/1/2001 when the General Mercosur rule began to apply. This consideration was complemented by the possibility of applying safeguards measures in cases where exports of these products caused injury or threat of injury to the other Mercosur countries.

The 22nd Additional Protocol defines the products that are subject to General Mercosur rule (Annex 1) and substitutes the specific RoOs defined in the 8th Additional Protocol for new ones (Annex 2), while 39th Additional Protocol regulates the control of certificates of origin by Mercosur customs authorities. On the other hand, DEC/CMC 24/02 decision substitutes Annex 1 of the 22nd Additional Protocol, that contains the products wherein requirements different from the general rule apply.

8.3.2.2 MERCOSUR-CHILE AND MERCOSUR-BOLIVIA RoO REGIMES

The FTA between Mercosur and Chile entered into force in 1996 as Economic Complementation Agreement N° 35 (ECA 35), while the FTA between Mercosur and Bolivia entered into force in 1997 as Economic Complementation Agreement N° 36 (ECA 36). Both agreements have regulations on RoOs: Article 13 (with Annex 13 and Appendixes 1, 2, 3 and 4) in the case of ECA 35 and Article 12 (with Annex 9 and Appendixes 1, 2 and 3) in the case of ECA 36.

In both cases, the scope of application of RoOs is conformed by the products included in the liberalizing schemes. As in the Mercosur Origin System, in Mercosur-Chile and Mercosur-Bolivia FTAs the general rule is the change in the tariff classification at a heading (4-digit) level, although in the last cases the NALADISA classification is used instead of the MCTC.[11] If this change is not possible, then in both agreements it is required that the CIF value of the inputs from third countries does not exceed 40% of the FOB value of the goods involved; this last method is also applied for products resulting from assembly or mounting operations, even though the change in NALADISA classification is accomplished. The Mercosur-Chile FTA contemplates the possibility of exceptions where both a change in tariff heading and 60% added value are required, while Mercosur-Bolivia FTA does not include this provision.

---

[11] NALADISA is the tariff classification of LAIA (ALADI).

Table 8.3 Main characteristics of RoOs in the Southern Cone

Concept	Mercosur	Mercosur-Chile	Mercosur-Bolivia
1. Implementing regulation	8th, 22nd and 39th Additional Protocols to ECA 18	Art. 13 and Annex 13 of ECA 35	Art. 12 and Annex 9 of ECA 36
2. Scope of application	Exceptions to CET	Liberalizing scheme	Liberalizing scheme
3. General rule	Change in tariff classification and/or regional content	Change in tariff classification and/or regional content	Change in tariff classification or regional content
4. Classification & level of change in tariff	4-digit of MCTC	4-digit of NALADISA	4-digit of NALADISA
5. % Regional content & calculation basis	60% of FOB value	60% of FOB value	60% of FOB value
6. Rule for assembly & mounting operations	60% regional content	60% regional content	60% regional content
7. Presence of specific RoOs	Yes	Yes	Yes
8. Main sectors with specific RoOs	Milky, chemical steel, data processing and telecommunications	Milky, chemical, paper, apparel, steel, data processing and telecommunications	Milky, chemical, paper, apparel, steel, data processing and telecommunications

Source: Own elaboration based on ECA 18,35 and 36.

Both FTAs include provisions about the existence of specific technical-origin requirements that take precedence over the general criteria. For both agreements, and very similar to the case of Mercosur, these specific RoOs are applied mainly to dairy, chemical, paper, apparel, steel, data processing and telecommunications products.

Finally, for some items, mainly from the chemical, textiles, apparel and furniture sectors, Chile grants Paraguay RoOs with 50% of regional content until 12/31/2003. Mercosur countries granted the same rule to Bolivia up to 1/1/2002 for products pertaining mainly to processed food, chemical, leather, textiles and footwear sectors. Another group of products, pertaining mainly to chemical, textiles and apparel sectors could certificate origin from Bolivia with a 40% of regional content rule, while for the same products Bolivia granted to Paraguay the same treatment. We summarize the already described main characteristics of RoOs in Mercosur, Mercosur-Chile and Mercosur-Bolivia in Table 8.3.

8.4 The impact of RoOs in Southern Cone's PTAs

In this section we aim to quantify the coverage and restrictiveness of the RoO regimes described previously. We will also aim to assess the empirical relevance of some of the hypotheses discussed in Section 8.2.

Table 8.4 RoO restrictiveness index

RoO index	RoO family
1	Change in heading
2	Regional content 60%
3	Change in heading + regional content 60%
4	Technical requirement

8.4.1 *Quantifying the scope and restrictiveness of RoOs*

In order to quantify the coverage and the degree of restrictiveness of the RoO legislation we follow very closely the methodology presented in Garay and Estevadeordal (1996) and Estevadeordal (2000). First, we define four 'families' of origin rules and we assign to each of them an ordered categorical variable, which takes integer numbers from 1 to 4, 1 being the less restrictive and 4 the more restrictive. Thus, as indicated in Table 8.4, a change in heading is the less-restrictive RoO rule, followed by regional value content of 60%, then comes the case where both requisites are needed and finally, the more-restrictive RoO is that for which, in addition to the sum of the rules indicated before, a specific technical requirement is also required. The second step is to associate each six-digit position of the HS with one of the above categories as indicated by the RoO legislation corresponding to Mercosur and the FTAs Mercosur-Chile and Mercosur-Bolivia.

To perform this matching, we use the MCTCS (Mercosur Common Tariff Classification System) in the case of Mercosur, and NALADISA (ALADI Tariff Classification System) in the case of Mercosur-Chile and Mercosur-Bolivia FTAs. Both classifications coincide at the 6-digit level, although they differ at the item level (8 digits). In particular, NALADISA has a lower number of items than MCTCS, since it is used only to negotiate among LAIA countries, and the subheadings are broken down only when this is required in the negotiations.

Because RoOs are defined at the item level, to construct the RoO index it is necessary to assign the *ad hoc* value of restrictiveness at the subheading level. We assign to each tariff subheading, the number corresponding to the most stringent RoO defined at the item level. Notice that using this methodology it doesn't matter if the number of items differs between MCTC and NALADISA[12]. The index is defined at the subheading level and

[12] It might have mattered if instead we used an average of the restrictiveness indicator at the item level.

Table 8.5 Structure of Rules of Origin in Mercosur by manufacturing sector (ISIC R.2) (percentage of tariff subheadings in each category)

	Rules of Origin based on:				Total
	Change of heading	Regional content	Change of heading – regional content	Technical requirement	
Food, Beverages and Tobacco	84.7	0.0	14.3	1.0	100.0
Textiles, Apparel and Leather	60.0	2.3	37.7	0.0	100.0
Wood Products	98.6	1.4	0.0	0.0	100.0
Paper and Printing	90.8	2.6	6.5	0.0	100.0
Chemicals	48.5	0.4	1.9	49.1	100.0
Non-Metallic Products	97.4	0.0	1.9	0.6	100.0
Basic Metal Products	76.0	0.3	0.0	23.7	100.0
Metal Products, Machinery & Equipment	50.2	46.5	0.8	2.6	100.0
Other Manufactring Products	100.0	0.0	0.0	0.0	100.0
Total	62.5	14.3	9.4	13.7	100.0

Source: Own elaboration based on ECA 18.

again both classifications have the same number of positions at this level of aggregation.

Table 8.5 presents the structure of RoOs in Mercosur by manufacturing sectors, distinguishing among the above 4 different families of RoOs specifications. For all sectors, 62.5% of total tariff subheadings (4504 positions) corresponds to the change of heading rule, 14.3% to regional content, 9.4% to change of heading and regional content and 13.7% to technical requirements. Note that technical requirements, the most stringent rule, are particularly important in Chemicals (49.1%) and Basic Metal Products (23.7%). Change in heading plus regional content is applied especially in Textiles (37.7%) and Food (14.3%). Regional content specification is used predominantly in the case of capital and data-processing goods, i.e. Metal Products, Machinery and Equipment (46.5%). The general rule, change in heading, is the main rule in all sectors, except in Chemicals.

Table 8.6 illustrates the structure of RoOs in Mercosur-Chile FTA. The distribution of RoO rules across products already suggests that in this case these regulations are more stringent that in Mercosur, since the less strict rule (change in heading) is applied to 40.3% of the total 6-digit positions. The regional content rule is applied to 25.4%, while 11.5% of the products require a change of heading and regional content. Finally, specific technical requirements cover 22.8% of the total. When we analyse the distribution of RoO by industry sector, we see that the results are similar to

Table 8.6 Structure of Rules of Origin in Mercosur-Chile FTA by manufacturing sectors (ISIC R.2) (percentage of tariff subheadings in each category)

	Rules of Origin based on:				Total
	Change of heading	Regional content	Change of heading + regional content	Technical requirement	
Food, Beverages and Tobacco	78.2	10.1	4.7	7.0	100.0
Textiles, Apparel and Leather	19.7	2.0	51.4	27.0	100.0
Wood Products	65.7	27.1	5.7	1.4	100.0
Paper and Printing	82.4	5.2	10.5	2.0	100.0
Chemicals	40.8	6.7	0.9	51.6	100.0
Non-Metallic Products	89.0	11.0	0.0	0.0	100.0
Basic Metal Products	47.0	0.3	0.8	52.0	100.0
Metal Products, Machinery & Equipment	23.0	71.9	1.6	3.5	100.0
Other Manufactring Products	82.8	14.8	1.2	1.2	100.0
Total	40.3	25.4	11.5	22.8	100.0

Source: Own elaboration based on ECA 35.

the Mercosur case, with the specific technical requirements being more applied in Textiles, Chemicals, Basic Metal Products and Machinery and Equipment.

The structure of RoOs by industrial sectors for the case of the Mercosur-Bolivia FTA is presented in Table 8.7. The evidence suggests that the structure of RoO is more restrictive than that applied within Mercosur and also slightly more stringent than the one established for the Mercosur-Chile FTA. For the whole agreement 37.7% of total tariff subheadings corresponds to change of heading, 22.2% to regional content, 14.3% to change of heading and regional content and 25.8% to technical requirements. At the sectoral level the structure of RoOs is similar to that of Mercosur-Chile with the only visible difference that Food and Beverage products now have a relative high proportion of items where specific technical rules are required (21.6%).

Finally, in Table 8.8 we show the results for the calculation of the RoO restrictiveness index across PTAs and across sectors. As indicated above we constructed an index by weighting the different RoOs specifications by the *ad hoc* level of restrictiveness that is equal to 1 for changes of heading, 2 for regional content, 3 for change of heading plus regional content and 4 for technical requirements. In this way, each tariff subheading corresponds to one of these numbers, depending on the particular RoO that is being applied. Then, for each manufacturing sector we computed the average index, summing up through subheading and dividing by the

Table 8.7 Structure of Rules of Origin in Mercosur-Bolivia FTA by manufacturing sector (ISIC R.2) (percentage of tariff subheadings in each category)

	Rules of Origin based on:				Total
	Change of heading	Regional content	Change of heading + regional content	Technical requirement	
Food, Beverages and Tobacco	75.6	0.8	2.1	21.6	100.0
Textiles, Apparel and Leather	18.4	1.7	52.9	27.0	100.0
Wood Products	68.6	1.4	22.9	7.1	100.0
Paper and Printing	81.7	2.0	13.7	2.6	100.0
Chemicals	40.7	1.2	6.5	51.6	100.0
Non-Metallic Products	89.0	2.6	7.8	0.6	100.0
Basic Metal Products	46.5	0.3	0.5	52.8	100.0
Metal Products, Machinery & Equipment	16.1	71.8	3.5	8.6	100.0
Other Manufacturing Products	82.2	5.9	10.7	1.2	100.0
Total	37.7	22.2	14.3	25.8	100.0

Source: Own elaboration based on ECA 36.

Table 8.8 RoOs index by manufacturing sector

	Mercosur	Mercosur-Chile	Mercosur-Bolivia
Food, Beverages and Tobacco	1.3	1.4	1.7
Textiles, Apparel and Leather	1.8	2.9	2.9
Wood Products	1.0	1.4	1.7
Paper and Printing	1.2	1.3	1.4
Chemicals	2.5	2.6	2.7
Non-Metallic Products	1.1	1.1	1.2
Basic Metal Products	1.7	2.6	2.6
Metal Products, Machinery & Equipment	1.6	1.9	2.0
Other Manufacturing Products	1.0	1.2	1.3
Total	1.7	2.2	2.3

Source: Own elaboration based on ECA 18, 35 and 36.

number of subheading.[13] The index we obtain goes from 1 to 4, and a larger value means a higher level of RoO restrictiviness.

The results confirm the presumptions coming from the previous analysis. That is, RoOs are more restricted in Mercosur-Chile and Mercosur-Bolivia FTAs than in Mercosur. For the whole universe of 6-digit commodities, we computed an index of 1.7 for Mercosur, 2.2 for Mercosur-Chile and 2.3 for Mercosur-Bolivia. The estimation across sectors shows that the level

[13] In the cases where more than one RoO specification applied for one tariff subheading, the number corresponding to the most stringent was assigned.

of RoO's restrictiveness is particularly higher in Textiles, Chemicals and Basic Metal Products.

8.4.2 Regression analysis

In this section we want to present a preliminary assessment of the determinants of the structure of RoO across 6-digit tariff items, which main features were summarized in the previous section. In the theoretical analysis presented in Section 8.2 we highlighted some key correlations that we want to empirically explore below. In particular, from a purely normative point of view, RoOs are trade-policy instruments that help to avoid trade deflection that under certain circumstances could reduce welfare. Thus we should expect a positive correlation between the absolute differences in member countries' MFN tariffs and the level of restrictiveness of the RoO rule. On the other hand, from a political-economy perspective, we indicated that strong RoO regulations would be pushed by intermediate-goods export interest within FTA member countries as a way to create a captive market for their products. Now this trade-diversion-induced demand will be larger the more significant are the tariff preferences applied to the final-good product. Thus, this approach suggests a positive association between RoO and tariff preferences.

The information of tariffs we use in the following exercises corresponds to year 1996, which coincides with the first year in the convergence path toward the CU. Thus, the data will feature a large number of items that were excluded from the common external tariff and for which, at least from a normative point of view, the establishment of RoO was a key issue.

In Table 8.9 we present the test of the hypothesis derived from the normative analysis, which implies a positive correlation between RoO restrictiveness index and tariff differences. The partial correlations are calculated running ordered logit regressions.[14] In column 1 we show the partial correlation of MNF tariff (absolute) differences across all possible pairs of Mercosur countries to investigate which of those differences were relevant in the determination of RoO restrictiveness[15]. We find a positive and significant coefficient for the pairs Brazil-Paraguay and Brazil-Uruguay, while somewhat surprisingly we obtain a negative coefficient for

---

[14] We cannot apply OLS estimation methods in this case as the dependent variable takes only four alternative integer values between 1 and 4.

[15] Notice that, as we are using MNF tariff differences across members, in those cases that convergence to the common tariff was already achieved, the indicated difference will obviously be zero. So in this regression we are in practice estimating the marginal effect of tariff differences on RoO restrictions above that corresponding to the CU items.

Table 8.9 Normative determinants. RoO, MNF tariffs differences and CET tariff exceptions. Ordered logit estimation. Dependent variable: RoO restrictiveness index

Exp. variables	1	Exp. variables	2	Exp. variables	3
ln (1 + difargbra)	−0.379*	Devcetarg	−0.032*	Dposdevarg	−0.44*
	(−6.57)		(−4.30)		(−5.56)
ln (1 + difargpar)	−0.028	Devcetbra	0.009**	Dposdevbra	0.62*
	(0.42)		(2.40)		(9.64)
ln (1 + difarguru)	0.12	Devcetpar	0.001	Dposdevpar	0.43*
	(1.81)		(0.12)		(2.59)
ln (1 + difbrapar)	0.13*	Devceturu	−0.022**	Dposdevuru	0.2
	(2.00)		(−2.59)		(1.90)
ln (1 + difbrauru)	0.26*	—		—	
	(3.75)				
ln (1 + difparuru)	−0.088**	—		—	
	(−2.48)				
obs	4267		4267		4267
Wald chi2	214.4		125.5		171.8

All regressions include section dummies
robust standard errors in parentheses
*significative at 1% **significative at 5%
Definition of variables: (i) difargbra=abs(External Tariff Arg-External Tariff Brazil)
(ii Devcetarg=External tariff−CET; (iii) Dposdevarg= 1 if Devcetrarg > 0

Brazil-Argentina. Thus, this evidence suggests that, if RoO were established to avoid trade deflection, the Brazil external tariff was a key parameter[16]. This may not be surprising. We have already shown in Section 8.3 that Brazil had in 1996 the largest tariffs level for those products that were excluded from the CET. Thus trade deflection should have been a primary concern for Brazil. This conclusion is somewhat confirmed when instead of using MNF tariffs differences as our independent variable, we use the difference between each country external tariff and the CET. We have already indicated that trade deflection should be an issue of concern for the excluded CET items especially for those that have large positive values. Columns 2 and 3 of Table 8.9 show the results when we introduce two alternative ways of measuring this deviation. Devcet is just the difference between each country external tariff and the CET while Dposdev is a dummy that takes the value of 1 when this difference is positive. As we see, on average, RoO were more restricted for those six-digit items where Brazil excluded-CET products have the largest (positive) deviation. On the other hand, we find no partial correlation for Paraguay or even a negative one for the case of Argentina and Uruguay.

[16] The fact that the absolute difference between the MNF tariffs of Argentina and Brazil does not matter could imply that those differences, from the point of view of Brazil, were already taken care of by the other pairs included in the regression. In fact when we include difargbra alone the sign comes out positive and significant.

Table 8.10 Political-economy determinants. RoO and tariff preferences

A. Ordered logistic estimation. Dependent variable: RoO restrictiveness index

Exp. variables	1	Exp. variables	2	Exp. variables	3	Exp. variables	4 (IV)
lnprefarg	0.17	lnprefarg 1	0.16*	ln (1 + prefarg 1)	0.285*	lnprefarg 1	0.86*
	(1.82)		3.08		(4.71)		(3.58)
lnprefbra	0.36*	lnprefbra 1	0.31*	ln (1 + prefbra 1)	0.25*	lnprefbra 1	1.44*
	(4.23)		4.55		(3.7)		(9.88)
inprefpar	−0.052	lnprefpar 1	−0.1*	ln (1 + prefpar 1)	−0.11*	—	
	(1.21)		(−3.12)		(−2.72)		
lnprefuru	−0.15*	lnprefuru 1	−0.078*	ln (1 + prefuru 1)	−0.179*	—	
	(−3.9)		(−3.20)		(−4.70)		
obs	3920		4267		4267		4495
LR	151.8		165.1		184.4		250.3

B. First-stage IV estimation. OLS Dependent variable: tariff preferences

Exp. variables	prefarg 1	prefbra 1
concentration	0.00026*	0.00034
	(2.44)	(1.48)
labor share	−15.25**	14.8
	(−2.32)	(1.49)
labor/capital ratio	−0.034	−0.0033
	(8.63)	(−0.51)
unit wage	−339.8*	−553.2
	(−9.40)	(−5.32)
section dummies	yes	yes
AdjR2	0.33	0.28
Obs	4261	4261

All regressions include section dummies
robust standard errors in parentheses
*significative at 1%, **significative at 5%
Definition of variables: (i) lnprefarg = ln(External Tariff Arg-Internal Tariff Arg)
(ii) Prefarg 1 = (External tariff Arg−Internal tariff Arg)/(1 + internal tariff Arg)

In Table 8.10 we present the estimation of the hypothesis derived from the political-economy analysis, according to which we should find a positive association between RoO and tariff preferences.[17] Columns 1, 2 and 3 show the results for alternative definitions of the explanatory variable. We see that this political-economy explanation is consistent with the results we obtain for Argentina and Brazil. For these countries we find a positive and significant association between RoO restrictiveness and

[17] Cadot *et al.* (2003) also includes in the regression a input-output coefficient measuring the amount of upstream inputs *j* demanded by the final product *i*. This should be negatively associated with RoO's restrictiveness. We were not able to obtain this variable for the 4 Mercosur countries so we didn't include it in our regressions.

tariff preferences. In the cases of Paraguay and Uruguay the relationship is negative. Thus the above results suggest that export interests in Brazil and Argentina were more successful in pushing RoO regulations in their favor. Of course this is consistent with the fact that these two countries have a much larger industrial base capable of providing intermediate input to the final-good producers of the other members.

Now, if we were to assess between Argentina and Brazil which of the two countries have benefitted the most from this trade-diversion-induced demand in intermediates, Brazil would come out as the winner given the difference we find in the estimated coefficients. This is mostly shown in the estimation presented in column 4 where we have used IV to control for the presumed endogeneity bias affecting the tariff preference variable.[18] Panel B of Table 8.10 shows the first-stage regression we run for tariff preferences in the cases of Brazil and Argentina. We employ often-used industry control variables like concentration, labor share, labor/capital ratios and wages cost.[19] We see that the IV estimates for tariff preferences in Argentina and Brazil are positive and significant, but now the values of the coefficients are much larger, compared to the case where no correction is made, and also that the difference between Brazil and Argentina have become more significant in absolute terms.

Overall then, we conclude that there is evidence that both normative and political-economy considerations have played a role in the determination of RoO in Mercosur. In both cases Brazil has been a major player within the member countries. On the one hand, as it has the largest level of tariff for its CET-excluded items, it is intuitive that RoO were found to be on average more restrictive for these products. At the same time, being the largest economy within Mercosur, it has strong export interests that could benefit from trade-diversion-induced demand in intermediates. Thus it is not surprising that we find that for this country, and to a lesser extent for Argentina, there is a positive association between tariff preferences and RoO's restrictiveness.

8.5 Concluding remarks

In this chapter we have looked at the role of Rules of Origin in the implementation of PTAs in the Southern Cone region. In particular we

---

[18] Actually, this is what the Cadot *et al.* (2003) model suggests. Both RoO and tariff preferences are jointly determined.

[19] These variables were only available for the cases of Argentina and Brazil.

analysed with great detail the Mercosur legislation and that relating to the FTAs signed between Mercosur and Chile and Mercosur and Bolivia. We hypothesized that RoO within Mercosur should not be very restrictive as a large proportion of its tariff items are included within the CU. In this case trade-deflection arguments are not a concern. This is exactly what we obtain when we compute the RoO restrictiveness index. The value for Mercosur is well below that we find for the FTAs Mercosur-Chile and Mercosur-Bolivia. From the estimation of this RoO index we also learned that Textiles, Chemicals and Basic Metal Products are the sectors that are subject to the more restrictive origin rules.

The chapter also presents a first step in the analysis of the determinants of RoO restrictions. Following the existing literature we explore the empirical relevance of some simple hypotheses suggested by the normative and political-economy perspectives. We found that both considerations have been significant forces behind the determination of RoO in Mercosur. Brazil has been a major player within the member countries. On the one hand, as it has the largest level of tariff for its CET-excluded items, it is intuitive that RoO were found to be on average more restrictive for these products. At the same time, being the largest economy within Mercosur, it has strong export interests that could benefit from trade-diversion-induced demand in intermediates. Thus it is not surprising we find that for this country, and to a lesser extend for Argentina, there is a positive association between tariff preferences and RoO's restrictiveness.

References

Bouzas, R. (1997): El Mercosur: Una Evaluación sobre su Desarrollo y Desafíos Actuales.

Cadot, O., A. Estevadeordal, A. Suwa-Eisenmann (2003): Rules of Origin as Export Subsidies. Mimeo, IADB.

Crespo Armengol, E., G. Perez Constanzó (1998): 'El Regimen Arancelario Argentino.' Boletin Informativo Techint, 294.

Estevadeordal, A. (2000): 'Negotiating Preferential Market Access. The Case of the NAFTA', Journal of World Trade.

Garay, L., A. Estevadeordal (1996): 'Protection, Preferential Tariff Elimination and Rules of Origin in The Americas', Integration and Trade.

Grossman, G., E. Helpman (1995): 'The Politics of Free Trade Agreements', American Economic Review.

Krishna, K., A. Krueger (1995): 'Implementing Free Trade Areas: Rules of Origin and Hidden Proection', NBER Working Paper.

Krueger, A. (1995): 'Custom Unions vs FTAS: Rules of Origins', NBER Working Paper.

Laird, S. (1997): 'Mercosur: Objectives and Achievements', Economic Development Institute, Economic Note No 22.

Olarreaga, M., Soloaga (1998): 'Endogenous Tariff Formation: The Case of Mercosur', World Bank Economic Review 12, 297–320.

Sanguinetti, P., M. Sallustro (2000): 'El Mercosur y el Sesgo Regional de la Política Comercial: Aranceles y Barreras No Tarifarias'. Documento de Trabajo, Centro de Estudios de Desarrollo Institucional (CEDI).

Terra, I. (1998): Uruguay en el MERCOSUR: Perspectivas del Comercio Intrar-egional. Mimeo, Cepal.

9

Preferential trade arrangements production, and trade with differentiated intermediates[†]

Joseph Francois

9.1 Introduction

Rules of Origin are an important aspect of preferential trade agreements (PTAs). They affect both North-South free trade agreements (FTAs), like US-Mexico trade under the NAFTA, and North-North trade, like US-Canada trade and EU trade with other European economies under various FTAs. They have also been blamed for the failure of developing-country trade preference schemes. Baldwin (2001) warns of their potential use as technical barriers to trade.

The relevance of Rules of Origin in recent preferential trade schemes has spawned a new formal literature. This includes exploration of the importance of Rules of Origin for the political economy of regional agreements (Duttagupta and Panagariya 2001), as well as the impact of Rules of Origin on outside country access to internal markets (Ju and Krishna 1998). Other work of this type includes Falvey and Reed (1998) and Krishna and Krueger (1995).

The roots of Rules of Origin regimes can be found in the relative complexity of PTAs *vis-à-vis* customs unions. For example, because free trade agreements (FTAs) do not have a common external tariff, the risk exists that goods will be diverted through the lowest FTA-partner tariff and into the FTA block. For this reason, one stated reason for Rules of Origin is that

† Special thanks are due to Kala Krishna and Olivier Cadot for constructive comments on an earlier draft.

they are designed to ensure that only goods produced within a free trade block actually receive free-trade treatment. At least, that is the theory.[1] In practice, assigning the origin of a product is not simple, as value added is sometimes included and sometimes not, local-content thresholds vary, and products can and do lose their FTA origin as they cross borders. In addition, the assignment of origin is probably subject to political factors, much like contingent protection.

In Europe, a regime of 'Pan-European cumulation,' entered into force on 1 January 1997. It originally applied in all of the EEA countries (Norway, Iceland, Liechtenstein, Sweden, Finland, Denmark, the UK, Ireland, Germany, Luxembourg, the Netherlands, Belgium, France, Austria, Italy, Spain, Portugal and Greece), in Switzerland (EFTA member), and in Estonia, Latvia, Lithuania, Poland, the Czech Republic, Slovakia, Hungary, Bulgaria, Romania and Slovenia. Turkey joined in late 1999,[2] and is working to implement the regime. The European rules require that the inputs in fact originate within the free trade area. Otherwise, processing requirements in the Rules of Origin have to be complied with if the finished product is to have free trade status. A similar arrangement for the Mediterranean countries is due to take effect by 2010.

In the North American Free Trade Agreement (NAFTA), the Rules of Origin state that a product originates in the free trade area when it is wholly produced or substantially transformed in the free trade area. Substantial transformation occurs when processing causes a product to shift from one tariff classification to another. NAFTA Rules of Origin include a '*de minimis*' provision that permits a final NAFTA good to contain a small quantity of the same kind of good from a non-NAFTA source (up to 7 per cent of the value of each shipment, or 9 per cent in the case of cigarettes and cigars). The motor vehicle sector was heavily involved in the design of the NAFTA Rules of Origin, and from the beginning it was clear that their purpose was to provide additional protection to intermediate parts producers.

Much of the literature on Rules of Origin works from the premise of homogeneous goods. This is in keeping with a large part of the literature on trade creation and diversion under PTAs. In contrast, this chapter is concerned with Rules of Origin in the context of Ethier-type two-way trade in

---

[1] See Bhagwati and Panagariya (1996) and Panagariya (2000) for more on this point.

[2] Turkey originally signed protocols for accession to the system of European cumulation in late 1999, though by 2001 (relevant for the empirics in Sections 3 and 4) transitional arrangements were still being implemented. The most critical effect has been to strengthen the operational effectiveness of the customs union between the EU and Turkey.

differentiated intermediate goods (Ethier 1979, 1982). Such differentiation of intermediates is an important aspect of recent division of labor models of trade, geography, and growth (Francois and Nelson 2002). The analytical approach followed here is similar in spirit to that taken in *ex ante* studies of the impact of the NAFTA on the automobile industry.[3] Manufacturing involves use of intermediate inputs that are differentiated by intermediate firms, with two-way trade of intermediates and benefits from an increased division of labor through trade. Emphasis is placed on the pattern of production and trade in such a framework, and in particular on the relative importance of trade in intermediates *vis-à-vis* trade in final goods when Rules of Origin are imposed on a trade equilibrium.

While the literature stresses the discriminatory impact of PTAs with Rules of Origin, there is at the same time an inherent ambiguity regarding Rules of Origin, at least when we make comparisons to customs-union regimes. This is because regional agreements can reduce internal trading costs. In particular, while FTAs punish use of external intermediates, customs unions (CUs) and ancillary trade facilitation measures may reward the use of internal intermediates, reducing the costs of moving goods cross-border.[4] These carrot and stick mechanisms both work in the same direction, which means that the impact of use of Rules of Origin in FTAs on trade in intermediates *vis-à-vis* similar trade in a customs union without need of rules of original is actually ambiguous. We highlight this issue here, stressing the theoretical impact of Rules of Origin, while isolating these from border effects (impacted by cost reductions in customs unions) in the empirics.

The chapter is organized as follows. An analytical model is first developed in Section 9.2, from which basic expectations are developed regarding differences between Rules of Origin (i.e. FTAs instead of customs unions) and the pattern of trade and production in intermediate and final goods. (A technical innovation here involves the conceptual use of an actual set of global equilibrium prices for the examination of trade between different pairs of countries under various Rules of Origin.) The theory-based discussion is followed by a brief overview of recent experience in Turkey and Mexico in the auto sector, and then by a more formal econometric cross-sectional analysis of OECD bilateral trade in finished motor vehicles and parts. The econometric evidence suggests that FTA Rules of Origin can be an

---

[3] See Lopez-de-Silanes *et al.* (1994).

[4] In both the 200 + year-old North American customs union (i.e. the United States), and in the European Union since the single market was implemented in the early 1990s, goods move more or less freely across internal borders.

effective barrier against third-country suppliers of intermediate goods. In the context of Europe, trade-facilitation measures (the European carrot rather than the NAFTA stick) dominate, revealing the importance of border-effect mitigation within customs unions. In addition, while European accumulation rules are discriminatory against third countries, they appear to extend most of the benefits of customs union membership (apart from border effects) to the larger European Economic Area.

9.2 Analytical expectations

In this section the impact of PTAs on intermediates trade is explored in an analytical framework involving Ethier-type two-way trade in differentiated intermediates (Ethier 1979, 1982).[5] Domestic and imported intermediate goods are specialized compliments in production, and potential gains from the division of labor in intermediate goods, and with intermediate goods themselves being used to produce final, traded goods. In formal terms, we examine the properties of PTA partners within a global trading equilibrium. This allows us to take world prices as given at actual equilibrium values as we examine a given set of countries, and to then focus on differences across PTA country pairs within the equilibrium price set as implied by differences in Rules of Origin. We are able then to isolate expected intra-PTA differences related directly to rules-based costs for use of non-PTA intermediates.

We focus on Countries 1 and 2, on which we will impose a PTA that leaves out country 3. Country 3 represents the rest-of-world region *vis-à-vis* countries 1 and 2, and is represented in the system by world prices representing the trade equilibrium price set. For both countries, we assume a transformation technology $g(.)$ that maps production of the numeraire good wheat, represented by W, and intermediate factor bundles, represented by b, used in the production of manufactured goods, both as inputs to intermediate input production and as value added.

Formally, our transformation technology is represented by eqn (9.1). It has the usual properties of convexity.

$$b^i = g^i(W^i), \quad i = 1, 2 \quad g', g'' < 0. \tag{9.1}$$

Assuming W is homogeneous, we set the intra-PTA price of wheat at unity, and give it the job of serving as numeraire. We can then represent the

[5] The analytical model developed here is similar in spirit to Lopez-de-Silanes *et al.* (1994), Markusen *et al.* (1995) and Francois (1994).

supply price of bundles (assuming competitive factor markets) as an artifact of the transformation technology. These are formalized in eqns (9.2) and (9.3).[6]

$$p_b^i = - \left((g^i)' \right)^{-1} \tag{9.2}$$

$$P_W^i = 1 \quad i = 1, 2. \tag{9.3}$$

We next turn to intermediate goods. We are interested in two-way trade in intermediates. In reduced form, we will have a mapping from bundles prices to prices for composite intermediates. This is represented in eqn (9.4). The h function in eqn (9.4) is a consequence of increasing returns to specialization in intermediate goods, and from the primal functional mapping of bundles to intermediates (Francois and Nelson 2002). It builds on the following property of Ethier-type trade models with a CES-aggregator for traded intermediates. With some manipulation we can represent the reduced-form system as one involving a composite region-specific intermediate good m produced under external increasing returns to scale. In terms of the region-indexed intermediate good, the remainder of the intermediate demand system can then be modelled as one involving CES-type preferences with regional rather than firm indexing.[7]

$$P_m^i = h(m^i) \cdot P_b^i, \quad h > 0, \quad h' < 0, \quad i = 1, 2. \tag{9.4}$$

In working with eqn (9.4), we assume that we generally operate on the concave region of the product transformation surface, which simply means that the curvature of the $g(.)$ function in eqn (9.1), which reflects opportunity costs for bundles *vis-à-vis* wheat, dominates reduced-form scale effects as embodied in the h function over the range of relevant equilibria. When this is not the case we will be in unstable equilibria, with stability ultimately either involving equilibria like those assumed, or else corner solutions. Under constant returns, the h function would simply be a linear operator.

We are concerned with the impact of PTAs on trading costs as manifested as reduced-form trading costs. As such, we introduce them here as a markup on the cost of intermediates for final-goods producers.

$$P_{m,(i,j)}^k = P_m^k \cdot T_{m,(i,j)}^k \quad T \geq 1. \tag{9.5}$$

[6] Both superscripts and subscripts are used to denote countries. In general, superscripts denote values related to where an intermediate or final good originates, in terms of either quantities or prices. Subscripts denote the use of goods in production or consumption.

[7] A full derivation of this representation of monopolistic competition for traded intermediates can be found in Francois and Roland-Holst (1997).

In eqn (9.5), $P^k_{m,(i,j)}$ represents the trading-cost inclusive price of intermediates from region k when used in region i to produce a good for region j, given trading costs $T^k_{m,(i,j)}$. For final-goods production in the manufacturing sector, we assume a CES-based production function, defined over value added measured directly in units of bundles, and in terms of composite regional intermediate goods. In dual form, the cost function for a regional manufactured good is then as represented by:

$$P^{(i,j)}_Y = A^i \cdot \left(\sum_{k=1}^{3} \omega^k_{m,i} \left(P^k_{m,(i,j)} \right)^{\rho/(\rho-1)} + \omega_{i,VA} \left(P^i_b \right)^{\rho/\rho-1} \right)^{(\rho-1)/\rho}, \quad i = 1, 2$$

$$j = 1, 2, 3 \quad 0 < \rho < 1. \tag{9.6}$$

In eqn (9.6), the ω terms are exponential CES weights from the underlying CES production function. In the dual context shown here, they serve as inverse cost weights for mapping input prices into final-good prices.

Note that with constant returns under a CES production technology involving value added and assembly, we implicitly assume that production can be separated between production for home, partner, and ROW markets to reflect relative input-cost variations as detailed below. This means we can index cost of production of Y by destination market. Again, we are also interested in potential trading costs, and so again introduce a trading-cost wedge on final goods.

$$P^{(i,j)}_{Y,j} = P^{(i,j)}_Y T^i_{Y,j}, \quad T \geq 1, \quad i \neq j. \tag{9.7}$$

In eqn (9.7) $P^{(i,j)}_{(Y,i)}$ denotes the producer price of good Y produced in region i for consumption in region j, while $P^{(i,j)}_{(Y,i),j}$ denotes the consumer price of the same good given final-good trading cost $T^i_{Y,j}$.

From eqn (9.6), and the first-order conditions for cost-minimization in Y production, we can also map composite intermediate input demand to relative internal prices and the total quantity produced. This is represented below in eqn (9.8).

$$m^k_{(i,j)} = \omega^k_{m,i} \left(\frac{P^{(i,j)}_Y}{P^k_{m,(i,j)}} \right)^{\sigma} Y^{(i,j)}, \quad \sigma = \frac{1}{1-\rho}. \tag{9.8}$$

In eqn (9.8), $m^k_{(i,j)}$ denotes intermediates produced in region k and used in region i for final-goods production destined for region j. We can make a similar derivation for total value added VA, represented by eqn (9.9) below.

$$VA^{(i,j)} = \omega_{i,VA} \left(\frac{P^{(i,j)}_Y}{P^i_b} \right)^{\sigma} Y^{(i,j)}. \tag{9.9}$$

When we combine intermediates demand and value added we then have total demand for factor bundles in the manufacturing sector. This is shown in eqn (9.10), where the h function represents the primal mapping technology in eqn (9.4) from factor input bundles employed in m production to m itself.

$$b^i = h^i \left(\sum_{j=1}^{3} \sum_{k=1}^{3} m^i_{(j,k)} \right) + \sum_{j=1}^{3} VA^{(i,j)}. \tag{9.10}$$

Turning to final demand, we assume CES preferences defined over regional final manufactured goods. Since income itself can be mapped from the price of bundles, regional demand for regional varieties will be a function of the vector of goods prices within a national economy $\mathbf{P}$ and also of bundles prices. In total (and assuming third-country demand for regional goods is also a function of price in the observed equilibrium), total demand for regional varieties will be a function of the degree of substitution between varieties, as measured by the substitution elasticity ε, and of the price vectors for final goods and bundles.

$$Y^i = D(\mathbf{P}, \mathbf{T}, \varepsilon). \tag{9.11}$$

Together, eqns (9.1)–(9.11) give us 11 sets of functional relationships that determine a comparable set of unknowns:

$$P^i_b, P^i_W, P^i_m, P^j_{m,i}, b^i, P^i_Y, P^i_{Y,j}, VA^i, m^i_j, Y^i, W^i.$$

We now turn to the differential impact of FTAs and CUs. For a starting point, we assume a customs union within the framework spelt out above, meaning identical external tariffs and free movement of all goods internally. With this regional integrated equilibrium as the benchmark for the country pair, we then move to introduce trading costs to reflect the introduction of Rules of Origin, which characterizes an important difference in practice between FTAs and customs unions. Assuming that these rules are binding, then in reduced form we will see an increase in the effective cost of using intermediates from outside the CU/FTA (see eqn 9.5), which can in turn be mapped to an effective increase in the inverse cost weights (i.e. a drop in the weights) in eqn (9.8). How the increase is realized depends on how the rules are operationalized. They could range from a sliding scale involving tariffs on third-country inputs to tariffs on the whole product (including FTA inputs and value added). In practice these rules are constantly evolving. For our purposes here, we simply assume that third-country intermediates used for internally traded final goods effectively cost more to use once we introduce Rules of Origin. The implication of such a change is immediately clear from eqn (9.12), which is derived from eqn (9.8). Equation (9.12) defines the relative input mix of intermediates, by country of origin, as a function of relative input costs. With the consequent shift in the cost of using third-country inputs, as they imply a cost increase related to some financial penalty like loss of duty-free treatment for the final good, we will see a downward shift in the relative importance of third-country intermediates, and a shift toward FTA-originating inputs. Hence, there will be a shift toward intermediates that are internally produced, and away from third-country intermediates.

$$\frac{m^v_{(i,j)}}{m^k_{(i,j)}} = \frac{\omega^i_{m,v}}{\omega^i_{m,k}} \left(\frac{P^{(i,j)}_{m,k}}{P^{(i,j)}_{m,v}} \right)^\sigma \quad v \neq k. \tag{9.12}$$

Depending on the specific form of the Rules of Origin and related penalties, such a shift would be made to the point where the marginal value of product of imported third-country inputs exceeds penalty costs. For the present exercise (and the empirics that follow), the important point is just the end result. There will be a shift toward FTA inputs, if all other factors are held fixed.

At the same time, CUs themselves can involve lower cross-border trading costs than FTAs. For example, the European Union, with its single-market program, has led to the dismantling of border posts across Europe, and to cross-border co-operation to speed the clearing of goods. This has the effect of reducing the cost of using internal inputs. The obvious contrast is to the border crossing-points within NAFTA, where FTA inputs still have to clear border checks. This effect will work in the opposite direction from Rules of Origin. In our controlled experiment, where we only introduce Rules of Origin on an otherwise clean slate, the impact will be a relative shift toward internal intermediates. However, when we move from our hypothetical to actual data, we will also expect to see a rising border cost as we shift from a CU to an FTA. This would imply a rising cost for use of internal intermediates, so that the shift may be in the opposite direction. The net effect is an empirical question.

A second impact of this increase in the effective cost of external inputs (relative to our integrated customs union benchmark equilibrium) will be to increase the cost of producing final manufactured goods for export to the relevant CU/FTA partner. This is shown in eqn (9.13) for exports from Country 1 to Country 2, which follows from manipulation of eqn (9.6).

$$\frac{\partial P_Y^{(i,j)}}{dP_{m,(i,j)}^k} = A^i \cdot \left(\sum_{k=1}^{3} \omega_{m,i}^k \left(P_{m,(i,j)}^k \right)^{\rho/(\rho-1)} + \omega_{i,VA} \left(P_b^i \right)^{\rho/(\rho-1)} \right)^{-1/\rho}$$

$$\omega_{m,i}^k \left(P_{m,(i,j)}^k \right)^{1/\rho-1} > 0. \tag{9.13}$$

Assuming CES demand for the final manufactured good, we will then also have a version of eqn (9.12) that involves final goods.

$$\frac{Y^{(k,i)}}{Y^{(v,i)}} = k \left(\frac{P_{Y,i}^{(v,i)}}{P_{Y,i}^{(j,i)}} \right)^{\varepsilon}. \tag{9.14}$$

Since we translate Rules of Origin into increases in the cost of using non-FTA intermediates when producing goods for sale to an FTA partner,[8] from eqn (9.13) we can derive directly the elasticity of the price of supplying a final good to an FTA partner with respect to this increase in the price of non-FTA intermediate inputs.

$$\eta_{P_Y^{(i,j)} P_{m,(i,j)}^k} = 1 > \frac{\omega_{m,i}^k P_{m,(i,j)}^k}{\sum\limits_{k=1}^{3} \omega_{m,i}^k \left(P_{m,(i,j)}^k \right)^{\rho/(\rho-1)} + \omega_{i,VA} \left(P_b^i \right)^{\rho/(\rho-1)}} > 0. \tag{9.15}$$

In eqn (9.15), the term $\eta_{P_Y^{(i,j)} P_{m,(i,j)}^k}$ is the elasticity of the cost of producing good Y in country i for market j, with respect to rules-induced increases in the price of intermediates from country k when used for good destined for market j. What happens to the demand for inputs? Starting from eqn (9.8), we can derive the change in demand for non-FTA intermediates as follows.

$$dm_{(i,j)}^k = -\sigma \omega_{m,i}^k \left(\frac{P_Y^{(i,j)}}{P_{m,(i,j)}^k} \right)^{\sigma} Y^{(i,j)} \frac{dP_{m,(i,j)}^k}{P_{m,(i,j)}^k}$$

$$+ \sigma \omega_{m,i}^k \left(\frac{P_Y^{(i,j)}}{P_{m,(i,j)}^k} \right)^{\sigma} Y^{(i,j)} \frac{\partial P_Y^{(i,j)}}{\partial P_{m,(i,j)}^k} \frac{dP_{m,(i,j)}^k}{P_Y^{(i,j)}}. \tag{9.16}$$

This in turn can be manipulated, by dividing through our definition of $m_{(i,j)}^k$, to yield the percentage change in intermediate demand.

$$\frac{dm_{(i,j)}^k}{m_{(i,j)}^k} = -\sigma \frac{dP_{m,(i,j)}^k}{P_{m,(i,j)}^k} + \sigma \frac{\partial P_Y^{(i,j)}}{\partial P_{m,(i,j)}^k} \frac{dP_{m,(i,j)}^k}{P_Y^{(i,j)}} \frac{P_{m,(i,j)}^k}{P_{m,(i,j)}^k}. \tag{9.17}$$

[8] Obviously, such rules do not apply directly to the choice of inputs used to serve third (non-FTA) markets. Neither are they immediately relevant for production for the home market. Where they bite is in the production of goods for export to the FTA partner.

Finally, dividing through by relative price changes, and making a substitution from eqn (9.15), we arrive at an elasticity representation of the impact of rules-induced non-FTA intermediate-goods price increases on the use of intermediates for FTA partner-destined final goods.

$$\eta_{m_{(i,j)}^k, P_{m,(i,j)}^k} = -\sigma(1 - \eta_{P_Y^{(i,j)} P_{m,(i,j)}^k}) < 0. \tag{9.18}$$

In the context of a given set of world equilibrium prices, deviations in internal prices from world benchmark prices are directly defined by deviations in the effective trading cost imposed by Rules of Origin.

$$\hat{P}_{m,(i,j)}^k = \hat{T}_{m,(i,j)}^k. \tag{9.19}$$

This in turn means that eqn (9.18), following a substitution from eqn (9.19), yields the impact of such trading costs on intermediate input demand.

$$\eta_{m_{(i,j)}^k, T_{m,(i,j)}^k} = -\sigma(1 - \eta_{P_Y^{(i,j)} T_{m,(i,j)}^k}) < 0. \tag{9.20}$$

Note that in eqn (9.20), we have also taken advantage of eqn (9.19), which implies that $\eta_{P_Y^{(i,j)} T_{m,(i,j)}^k} = \eta_{P_Y^{(i,j)} P_{m,(i,j)}^k}$ and where the second term is defined in eqn (9.15). The shift in relative intermediate import demand in the production process for each final product line follows directly from the definition of substitution elasticities as used in the cost and input demand equations above.

$$\hat{m}_{(i,j)}^v - \hat{m}_{(i,j)}^k = \sigma\left(\hat{P}_{m,k}^{(i,j)} - \hat{P}_{m,v}^{(i,j)}\right) \quad v \neq k$$
$$\eta_{\frac{m_{(i,j)}^v}{m_{(i,j)}^k}, \frac{P_{(i,j)}^k}{P_{(i,j)}^v}} = \sigma > 0. \tag{9.21}$$

Consider next the impact on relative final-product demands, and hence on relative trade shares for final products. Again, assuming CES final demands, the shift in relative final goods demand follows directly from the definition of the substitution elasticity, this time from eqn (9.14).

$$\left(\hat{Y}^{(k,i)} - \hat{Y}^{(v,i)}\right) = \varepsilon\left(\hat{P}_{Y,i}^{(v,i)} - \hat{P}_{Y,i}^{(j,i)}\right)$$
$$\eta_{\frac{Y^{(3,1)}}{Y^{(2,1)}}, T_{m,(2,1)}^3} = \varepsilon\eta_{P_Y^{(2,1)} T_{m,(2,1)}^3} > 0. \tag{9.22}$$

In eqn (9.22), $\eta_{\frac{Y^{(i,1)}}{Y^{(2,1)}}, T_{m,(2,1)}^3}$ represents the elasticity of relative final-product demand for goods consumed in region 1, with respect to a rules-induced change in the cost of using intermediates from country 2 (an FTA partner) to produce goods for consumption in region 1. Again, we have taken advantage of the relationship of rules-induced costs to prices, given that we are working in the context of a given set of world equilibrium prices. Consider next the impact on actual rather than relative trade flows. This follows from final-product demand elasticities, and the impact of rules-based trading costs for intermediates on the price of final goods (from eqn 9.15).

$$\eta_{Y^{(2,1)}, T^3_{m(2,1)}} = \eta_{Y^{(2,1)}, P^{(2,1)}_{Y,1}} \eta_{P^{(2,1)}_{Y}, T^3_{m(2,1)}} < 0. \tag{9.23}$$

Taken together, eqns (9.20) and (9.23) say that we expect a drop in intra-FTA trade in final goods under increasingly restrictive Rules of Origin.

Next, we turn to the cross-price effects of rules-induced trade costs on intra-FTA demand for intermediate inputs. We again start from eqns (9.5) and (9.8). Differentiating eqn (9.8) for cross-price effects yields eqn (9.24).

$$\eth m^k_{(i,j)} = \sigma \omega^k_{m,i} \left(\frac{P^{(i,j)}_Y}{P^k_{m,(i,j)}} \right)^\sigma Y^{(i,j)} P^{(i,j)-1}_Y \frac{\partial P^{(i,j)}_Y}{\partial P^v_{m,(i,j)}} dP^v_{m,(i,j)}$$

$$+ \omega^k_{m,i} \left(\frac{P^{(i,j)}_Y}{P^k_{m,(i,j)}} \right)^\sigma \frac{\partial Y^{(i,j)}}{\partial P^v_{m,(i,j)}} dP^v_{m,(i,j)} \quad v \neq k. \tag{9.24}$$

Some further manipulation yields eqn (9.25), which can then be summarized in elasticity form as in eqn (9.26).

$$\frac{\eth m^k_{(i,j)}}{m^k_{(i,j)}} \frac{P^v_{m,(i,j)}}{dP^v_{m,(i,j)}} = \sigma \omega^k_{m,i} P^{(i,j)-1}_Y \frac{\partial P^{(i,j)}_Y}{\partial P^v_{m,(i,j)}} P^v_{m,(i,j)}$$

$$+ (Y^{(i,j)})^{-1} \frac{\partial Y^{(i,j)}}{\partial P^v_{m,(i,j)}} P^v_{m,(i,j)} \tag{9.25}$$

$$\eta_{m^k_{(i,j)}, P^v_{m,(i,j)}} = \sigma \omega^k_{m,i} \eta_{P^{(i,j)}_Y, P^v_{m,(i,j)}} + \eta_{Y^{(i,j)} P^v_{m,(i,j)}} . \tag{9.26}$$
$$ (+) (-)$$

In eqn (9.26), the term $\eta_{m^k_{(i,j)}, P^v_{m,(i,j)}}$ measures the marginal shift toward region k inputs as Rules of Origin discriminate against region v inputs. The equation says that at the margin, Rules of Origin may yield more or less trade in intermediate inputs. On the one hand, they force a substitution toward FTA-origin parts and away from outside supplies of intermediates in the production of goods destined for the FTA partner. This has a positive effect on intra-FTA demand for intermediates (and hence on internal trade). On the other hand, these rules also drive up prices, which forces overall demand toward non-FTA supplies of final goods. This depresses overall demand for intermediate goods.

Finally, we turn to the relative composition of intermediate and final goods in bilateral trade flows. We define the change in imported FTA intermediates used for intra-FTA exports of the final good Y relative to the change in intra-FTA imports of the final good from that same partner in the form of the elasticity $\eta_{m^2_{\frac{(1,2)}{Y^{(2,1)}}}}$, where we are indexing trade of goods produced in region 1 and sold in region 2. Working from eqns (9.23) and (9.26), we then have the following result:

$$\eta_{m^2_{\frac{(1,2)}{Y^{(2,1)}}}} = \eta_{m^2_{(1,2)}, P^3_{m,(1,2)}} - \eta_{Y^{(2,1)}, P^3_{m(2,1)}}$$

$$= \sigma\omega^2_{m,1}\eta_{P_Y^{(1,2)}, P^3_{m,(1,2)}} + \eta_{Y^{(1,2)}P^3_{m,(1,2)}} - \eta_{Y^{(2,1)}, P_{Y,1}^{(2,1)}}\eta_{P_Y^{(2,1)}, P^3_{m(2,1)}}. \qquad (9.27)$$
$$(+)(-)(+)$$

Starting with a customs union as a benchmark, these results imply a set of stylized shifts in the pattern of production and trade that can be expected if we observe different Rules of Origin across pairs of countries within a given global trading equilibrium. These can be summarized as follows:

Observation 1: With the introduction of binding Rules of Origin against third-country intermediate goods, the volume of trade in finished goods will fall between FTA partners, all other things being equal. This follows from eqn (9.23).

Observation 2: Import demand for finished goods in the manufacturing sector will shift away from FTA partners and toward third-country suppliers as a result of imposing Rules of Origin for intermediate goods onto an FTA. This follows from eqn (9.22).

Observation 3: In contrast to final goods, demand for intermediate goods will shift away from third-country suppliers, and toward FTA-partner suppliers as a result of imposing binding Rules of Origin. This follows from eqn (9.21).

Observation 4: The volume of internal trade in intermediates may rise or fall, depending on substitution effects at given levels of production, weighed against the drop in final-good production for the internal market. This follows from eqn (9.25).

What happens to the relative composition of intra-FTA trade, in terms of intermediates and final goods? We expect a drop in intra-FTA trade in finished goods from Observation 1. The effect on intermediates is murkier. Two opposing forces drive the trade in intermediates. It may go up due to substitution or down if the impact on the cost of production is strong enough to drive down total production of final goods sufficiently. This second effect is probably second order though, so that the intermediate-goods volume should also go up. If we focus on the FTA imports of final goods by Country 1 from Country 2 and exports of intermediates from Country 1 to Country 2, this ratio will fall, since even if exports of intermediates fall, they will fall at less than any drop in total targeted production of final goods for Country 1 in the Country 2 industry (because of offsetting substitution effects). We can say the same thing for comparable FTA imports of final goods and exports of intermediates between Country 2 and Country 1. However, when we look strictly at bilateral exports of Country 1 to Country 2, or Country 2 to Country 1, we have an ambiguity following from Observations 1 and 4. We summarize these results as follows:

Observation 5: The expected relative allocation of total trade between Countries 1 and 2 will shift from final goods to intermediates as we introduce binding Rules of Origin.

Observation 6: For Country 1, the expected relative allocation between total exports of intermediates to Country 2 and imports of final goods from Country 2 will shift to intermediates as we introduce binding Rules of Origin.

Observation 7: For Country 1, the expected relative allocation between total imports of intermediates from Country 2 and imports of final goods from Country 2 will be ambiguous.

One way to read Observation 6 is that binding Rules of Origin will drive down the size of offshore assembly activities as measured in terms of final goods within the FTA, even as the FTA content of those activities goes up, measured in terms of the mix of intermediate goods consumption. Of course, in all the discussion of final goods here we are holding discrimination against finished vehicles constant. If FTA implementation also introduces discrimination against third-country finished goods, such direct effects will likely outweigh the indirect ones stressed here.

In all fairness, when moving from theory to empirics, these results must be approached with caution. By construction, CUs and FTAs involve a great deal more than just Rules of Origin. They are packages that can include harmonization and mutual recognition of standards, acceleration of customs-clearance procedures, and deregulation of foreign direct investment. Such regime shifts and policy differences, which have been effectively sterilized in this section, can be quite dramatic, and may outweigh the direct effects of Rules of Origin in the data.

9.3 Anecdotal evidence: autos, EU-Turkey, and NAFTA

We can build anecdotal evidence that Rules of Origin have an important effect on the pattern of production and trade in intermediate and final goods.

This is based on recent experience with the NAFTA and the EU-Turkey Customs Union.

Turkey had free trade with the EU in industrial products by the early 1990s. This followed a long process that culminated in the EU-Turkey Customs Union. First, in 1963 the Treaty of Ankara envisaged Turkey becoming a full member of the EU with preparation being phased over a series of stages. An additional Protocol to this Ankara Agreement outlined a framework of the Customs Union between the EU and Turkey in 1970. Turkey's application for full membership of the EU in 1987 was rejected. However, Turkey continued to pursue unilateral trade liberalization with the EU. As a result, when the Customs Union was finally established for industrial products on January 1st 1996, after a transition period of 22 years, much of the required tariff changes for industrial products had already been implemented. Tariffs were generally harmonized, as was the regulatory regime. It has been estimated that the average reduction in tariffs required by the CU for Turkey was only 7% (Harrison *et al.* 1997). It has also been estimated that the combination of adopting the Common Customs Tariff (CCT) structure and Uruguay Round commitments should have produced a trade-weighted average tariff on industrial goods of 3.5% by 2001 (WTO 1998). There has also been further harmonization across the regulatory spectrum.[9]

At first glance then, the EU-Turkey customs union appears to offer a natural experimental shift from FTA to customs union, with the ease of entry (and escape from Rules of Origin control) that goes along with it. Figure 9.1 presents the pattern of Turkey's trade in automobiles with Germany over this period. The left axis maps the value of trade in US dollars, while the right maps the ratio of intermediate goods (motor vehicle parts) to total trade in motor vehicles and parts. The pattern is rather striking, with a dramatic shift from being a parts supplier to being a supplier of finished motor vehicles.

We should not, however, rush to conclusions from this picture. Figure 9.2 presents the same type of data, involving trade with the US and Mexico, over the same period. Both pictures offer the same pattern, though for opposite thought experiments. In both cases we see a significant shift

---

[9] In theory, the objective of the customs-union agreement is to prepare Turkey for full membership of the EU and the agreement is, therefore, not only deeper than the EU's free trade agreements, but goes well beyond the basic requirements of a customs-union agreement. In particular, it requires Turkey to introduce a wide range of legislation covering all aspects of trade, competition law, industrial commercial and intellectual property rights and the harmonization of EU technical standards. In this sense, the Customs Union agreement carries with it many of the consequences that would follow from full EU membership.

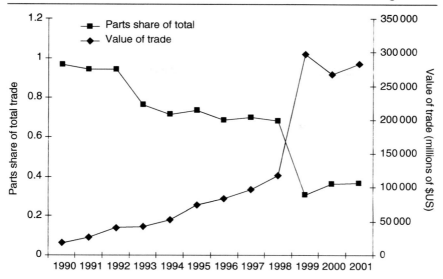

Fig. 9.1 Turkey's motor vehicle exports to Germany.

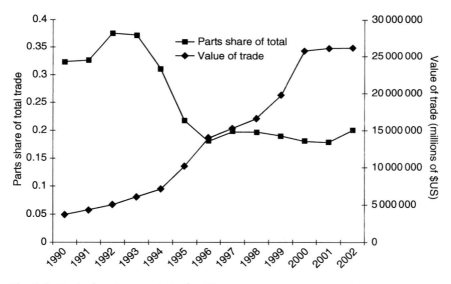

Fig. 9.2 Mexico's auto exports to the US.

from intermediates to finished motor vehicles, combined with a dramatic rise in the value of trade. This may point to first-order effects, such as FDI liberalization and harmonization of product-recognition standards in the context of both the NAFTA and EU-Turkey customs union that simply dominate the differential effect of Rules of Origin. The next section therefore turns to a more formal cross-country econometric assessment.

9.4 Evidence from regression analysis

9.4.1 *The data*

We next turn to a more formal empirical assessment. This involves data on the value of motor vehicles trade from UNCTAD's COMTRADE dataset for 2001, supplemented with estimates of bilateral tariff rates taken from the World Bank's WITS dataset. The data are for trade in motor vehicles, represented by SIC (rev1) 732, which is all motor vehicles and parts, and SIC 7328 (rev 1), which is motor vehicle parts only. We have relatively complete data for bilateral trade between 27 OECD Member and associate countries: Australia, Austria, Belgium, Canada, Switzerland, the Czech Republic, Germany, Denmark, Spain, France, Great Britain, Greece, Hungary, Ireland, Italy, Japan, Korea, Mexico, the Netherlands, Norway, Poland, Portugal, Sweden, Turkey, and the United States. These countries cover a range of preferential arrangements. In addition to the NAFTA (US, Canada, Mexico), and the European Union, we also have FTAs within Europe through EFTA (Norway and Switzerland), the European Economic Area (EFTA and the EU, but without Switzerland), and an EU-Turkey customs union. In addition, the EU has extended FTA status to the East-European economies in this period (Poland, Hungary and the Czech Republic), as has EFTA. Japan, Korea, and Australia are left out of these arrangements entirely (though Australia and New Zealand have an FTA). Critically, since roughly 1997, the EU has also negotiated a set of European accumulation rules on most though not all of its FTA partners. As a result, many countries that were in a hub-and-spoke arrangement with the EU now benefit from Europe-wide Rules of Origin, with the net effect being a relatively large Europe-wide FTA, with the EU15 at the center. The implementation of the arrangement, however, excluded Turkey at the time, though it did include candidate countries (the new 10 EU Members). In short, the cross-section provides a nice sample of Rules of Origin arrangements.

9.4.2 *Regression model and results*

We are interested in the apparent relationship between FTA vs. customs union membership, on the one hand and hence the assumed or explicit application or non-application of Rules of Origin, and on the other hand the pattern of trade and the relative importance of intermediate- and final-product trade as outlined in Section 9.2 above. Our focus will be on the relative importance of individual partners for trade in motor vehicles and parts. By implication, and as summarized above in Section 9.2, a shift toward traded intermediates also implies a shift in production toward intra-FTA intermediates.

We define an index for intermediates trade, $\zeta 1$. This measures the relative importance of a trading partner in total imports of intermediates.

$$\zeta 1^{i,j} = \log\left(\frac{z1^{i,j}}{1 - z1^{i,j}}\right) \tag{9.28}$$

$$z1^{i,j} = \frac{V_{SIC7328}^{i,j}}{\sum_k V_{SIC7328}^{i,k}}. \tag{9.29}$$

From Observation 3 above, we expect $\zeta 1$ to rise for an FTA imposing binding Rules of Origin, relative to an otherwise comparable customs union.

An econometric model is estimated for our index as defined above. Since the $z1$ index is a share, a logistic transformation is first performed. Two samples are covered in the estimates in Table 9.1. One is a subsample, restricted to European countries with free trade either as part of the European Union, or as part of various European FTAs, all subject to pan-European accumulation rules. The second set of regressions involves a full sample of OECD countries as both importers and/or exporters. The right-hand side variables are explained in the tables.

Turning to our regressions on the share of total intermediates trade (Table 9.1) several results stand out. First, there is a border effect, both in Europe, and globally. This means that national shares of intermediates trade increase when countries share a border. This implies that multiple border crossings add economic distance. However, a second effect relates to borders within a customs union. Borders do not matter (i.e. the border effect goes away) when we focus on intermediates trade within the European Union (our customs union in the sample) though they matter otherwise, both within Europe, and globally. Another point to note is that, apart from borders, there is no discernible difference between the EU and EEA pattern of trade within Europe. The rules governing pan-European accumulation do seem to work, in that they confer most of the benefits that follow from trade between EU Members. Again, this is apart from the border effects. Finally, both European and NAFTA preferential

Table 9.1 OLS estimates with robust standard errors: $\zeta 1$ partner share of total imports of parts

Variable	Description	Sample 1: European customs union or European accumulation rules	Sample 2: All countries
BORDER	1: country pair shares a border 0: otherwise	0.628 (2.06, .040)	0.716 (2.32, .021)
CU_BORDER	1: country shares a border and both are EU Members 0: otherwise	−0.712 −(1.59, .066)	−0.661 −(1.75, .081)
LNDISTW	The natural log of distance	−1.435 −(6.64, .000)	−1.002 −(5.98, .051)
lnT	Log $(1 + t)$	N/A	−2.141 −(1.11, .267)
not-EU	1: importer is and EU Member, but partner is not 0: otherwise	−0.334 −(0.69, .493)	N/A
not_NAFTA	1: importer is a NAFTA member, but partner is not	N/A	−3.215 −(6.68, .000)
not_EEA	1: importer is an EEA member (EU, EFTA, CEFTA) and partner is not 0: otherwise	N/A	−1.084 −(2.36, .019)
		R-sq: .8800 obs: 297 d.f.: 257	R-sq: .8310 obs: 621 df: 563

Estimates are based on OLS regressions with robust standard errors. Since left-hand side variables are measured as shares, dependent variables in the regressions are logistic transformations of the original share terms. t ratios are given in parentheses '( )' with significance levels in italics. For the first regression, sample is restricted to EU Members and countries that have otherwise implemented pan-European accumulation rules.

trade arrangements lead to discrimination against third countries. However, the NAFTA regime is much stronger, leading to a greater shift away from third-country suppliers, even after we control for differences in tariffs.

9.5 Summary

This chapter is concerned with preferential trade agreements with two-way trade in intermediates, emphasizing patterns of production and trade and the relative importance of trade in intermediates with third countries. This includes a discussion of the analytical implications of Rules of Origin in a world with Ethier-type two-way trade in differentiated intermediate goods. The analytical approach introduces an innovation involving construction of a theoretical framework around an actual trade equilibrium. Individual pairs of countries are examined within the equilibrium defined by this set of world prices, to isolate and identify the impact that Rules of Origin will have on preferential free trade. Results point to systematic differences in the composition of trade between final and intermediate goods, and the relative importance of preferential trade partners as suppliers of final and intermediate goods.

The analytical discussion is followed by an empirical examination of the implied impact of PTAs, Rules of Origin (a critical divide between FTAs and customs unions), and border effects on the pattern of intra-OECD trade in motor vehicle parts. There is evidence that such rules do cause a systematic shift in the composition of trade in intermediate goods away from third countries, after we control for actual tariff preferences. There appears to be a particularly strong shift toward inputs sourced from FTA partners with the NAFTA, relative to expected trade under a customs union or European pan-accumulation rules. At the same time, there is no apparent evidence that North American rules are different from European ones in the pattern of final-goods trade relative to intermediates.

References

Baldwin, R.E. (2001), 'Regulatory Protectionism, Developing Nations and a Two-Tier World Trading System,' *Brookings Trade Forum*, 3: 237–280, The Brookings Institution, 2001.

Bhagwati, J., A. Panagariya (1996), 'The Theory of Preferential Trade Agreements: Historical Evolution and Current Trends,' American Economic Review, 86(2) pp. 82–8.

Duttagupta, R., A. Panagariya (2001), 'Free Trade Areas and Rules of Origin: Economics and Politics,' University of Maryland mimeo.

Ethier, W. (1979), 'Internationally Decreasing Costs and World Trade,' *Journal of International Economics*, 9: 1–24.

Ethier, W. (1982), 'National and International Returns to Scale in the Modern Theory of International Trade,' *American Economic Review*, 72 (June), 950–959.

Falvey, R., G. Reed (1998), 'Economic Effects of Rules of Origin,' *Weltwirtschaftliches Archiv* 134:2.

Francois, J., D. Nelson (2002), 'A Geometry of Specialization,' *Economic Journal*, 112 (481): 649–667.

Francois, J.F., D.W. Roland-Holst (1997), 'Scale Economies and Imperfect Competition,' in J.F. Francois, K.A. Reinert (ed.), *Applied Methods for Trade Policy Analysis: A Handbook*, Cambridge University Press, 1997.

Harrison, G.W., T.F. Rutherford, D. Tarr (1997), 'Economic Implications for Turkey of a Customs Union with the European Union,' *European Economic Review*, 41(3–5): 861–870, April.

Ju, J., K. Krishna (1998), 'Firm Behavior and Market Access in a Free Trade Area with Rules of Origin,' NBER Working Paper No 6857.

Krishna, K., A.O. Krueger (1995), 'Implementing Free Trade Areas: Rules of Origin and Hidden Protection,' in *New Directions in Trade Theory*, A. Deardorff, J. Levinsohn, R. Stern (ed.), University of Michigan Press.

Lopez-de-Silanes, F., J.R. Markusen, T.F. Rutherford (1994), 'Complementarity and increasing returns in intermediate inputs', *Journal of Development Economics*, 45: 133–151.

Markusen, J.R., T.F. Rutherford, L. Hunter (1995), 'Trade liberalization in a multinational-dominated industry', *Journal of International Economics*, 38: 95–118.

Panagariya, A. (2000), 'Preferential Trade Liberalization: The Traditional Theory and New Developments,' *Journal of Economic Literature* XXXVIII: 287–331.

Part V

Rules of Origin and development

10

Rules of Origin as tools of development? Some lessons from SADC

Hennie Erasmus, Frank Flatters, and Robert Kirk[†]

10.1 Introduction

There are two quite different and competing economic visions of the Southern African Development Community (SADC). The alternate policy directions they imply are well illustrated in the negotiation of Rules of Origin under the SADC Trade Protocol.[1]

- The first vision is of SADC as a fortress within which member states can develop themselves through privileged access to an enlarged market area that remains protected and relatively isolated from external markets.
- The second vision sees SADC as a platform for directly improving the competitiveness of individual members in international markets

† This chapter is based in part on earlier USAID-supported work for the SADC Secretariat. We are grateful to IADB, Fédération Paris-Jourdan, ADRES, INRA and CEPR for facilitating the updating and completion of the work in its present form. The chapter has also benefited from presentations and discussions at an authors' meeting at INRA, Paris in May 2003. Numerous officials in SADC member states, representatives of private firms in many industries, and researchers in the SADC region provided valuable information and many useful insights through interviews, workshops, seminars and informal discussions. They would not all agree with all the analysis and conclusions presented here. For that reason their inputs are even more greatly appreciated. The views expressed in the chapter are those of the authors and should not be attributed to the IADB, USAID, SADC Secretariat, any of its member states or any of the staff or officials of these organizations.

1 See Flatters (2001).

and/or for improving consumption opportunities of their citizens. Regional integration is seen as part of a more general strategy for full and meaningful participation in global markets.

The vision that has driven the development of the SADC Trade Protocol has been distinctly inward-looking. Development of policies on Rules of Origin has responded defensively to fears of external (international and regional) competition and proactively to desires to develop linkages through administrative requirements. A central issue has been the extent to which Rules of Origin can or should be used to promote economic development in the region. In this sense, Rules of Origin are similar to local content regulations, a more familiar tool that is a common feature of failed import substitution regimes. Little attention has been paid to the Trade Protocol as an instrument to capitalize on opportunities for improving international competitiveness and for participating in global markets.

Rules of Origin have been among the more contentious issues in SADC Trade Protocol negotiations. Indeed, even four years after implementation of the Protocol, rules have not yet been agreed in some sectors. In many sectors in which rules have been agreed, resolution of outstanding differences has been put off for consideration in a mid-term review of the Trade Protocol that is currently underway.

Rules of Origin are an essential element of regional trading arrangements. But their use as protectionist devices, whether in North-South or South-South agreements, can also undermine and subvert the benefits of the trade liberalization they are meant to support. This is one of the great dangers of regionalism as a strategy for global integration.

The chapter is structured as follows. Sections 10.2 and 10.3 present the general context, focusing on the roles of international fragmentation of production and trade in middle products in economic development (Section 10.2) and on the purposes, types and effects of Rules of Origin, and their evolution in SADC (Section 10.3). Sections 10.4 and 10.5 provide a detailed and critical analysis of selected SADC Rules of Origin in agriculture (Section 10.4) and manufacturing (Section 10.5). Section 10.6 discusses links and lessons from this work on SADC for other studies included in this project. Section 10.7 briefly summarizes the principal conclusions about Rules of Origin in SADC and in preferential trading arrangements (PTAs) more generally.

10.2 Background

To put the discussion of Rules of Origin into a broader context, we begin with a brief review of lessons from several strands of recent literature on trade and development.

10.2.1 *Trade in middle products*

Following on the earlier theory of effective protection that recognized the key role of intermediate inputs in shaping the protective effects of tariffs, Sanyal and Jones (1982) and later Jones and Kierszkowski (1990, 2001a, 2001b and 2001c) set out a framework for analysing international 'fragmentation' of production and the corresponding necessity for trade in 'middle products'. Improvements in the infrastructure of trade and investment create enormous possibilities for the international division of labor and for the global spread of production according to differences in relative costs at different stages in the production process and in different markets. This is really a formalization and extension of Adam Smith's insight into the economic gains from specialization.

This framework also focuses attention on the role of international transport costs and of the costs and efficiency of a variety of non-tradable services from telecommunications to ports and customs administration in shaping possibilities for international production sharing.

The twin phenomena of fragmentation of international production and the large share of international trade in middle products are central features of globalization. In products from autos and electronics to garments, manufacture of subcomponents and assembly of components and of final products can and do take place in many different locations. The geographic distribution of these activities can be sensitive to small changes in local cost conditions and in the cost of international transport and communications. Systematic changes in these conditions in the process of a country's development produce corresponding changes in the local mix of production and assembly activities.

The study of fragmentation of production sheds new light on the link between exports and imports. To participate as a successful exporter in the global manufacturing system a country must be a successful importer; flexibility and low costs in sourcing imported materials are critical ingredients in exporting. Slow and/or costly Customs and port procedures raise the cost of importing; administrative requirements on the sourcing of inputs raise costs and reduce flexibility. They raise the cost of undertaking any stage of the production process and so reduce investment and exports.

10.2.2 *Lessons from Southeast Asia and elsewhere*

10.2.2.1 SOUTHEAST ASIA

Southeast Asia integrated highly successfully into the global manufacturing system in the final decades of the twentieth century. While the lessons of this experience remain the focus of considerable analysis and debate, certain things are clear. One is that the success of Southeast Asian exporters depended heavily on access to imported inputs. There are few examples of successful manufactured export activities that involved full manufacture of components and final products in a single country. Production of components and subcomponents of almost all products was scattered across many locations according to local cost conditions. The standard pattern, of course, was for skill and capital-intensive parts of production operations to take place in higher-income countries and for labor-intensive activities to be undertaken in low-income countries.

The pattern was far from static, however. As skill levels and wages rose countries specializing in labor-intensive production moved 'up the ladder' to more skill- and capital-intensive activities. But regardless of what took place in any location, production remained heavily dependent on imports.

Another lesson was that there are limits to the degree of production fragmentation that is possible or desirable. Benefits of close communication and the costs of transporting goods over long distances and across international borders mean that assemblers or producers of components always prefer, all other things being equal, to have subcomponents suppliers close at hand. The degree of local sourcing (or the limits of international fragmentation of production) depends on a trade-off between the centrifugal force of differences in relative production costs and the centripetal force of proximity advantages.

As Japanese and Korean television or VCR producers responded to labor-cost differences by moving assembly operations from Malaysia to Indonesia, for instance, they worked closely with components and subcomponents suppliers in the region and in their home countries to persuade them to invest near their new factories in Indonesia. According to one investor, moving an assembly operation from Malaysia to Indonesia with no change in existing local supply networks would increase production costs by 20 per cent. However, when capacities of local sourcing industries reached Malaysian levels, Indonesian costs would be 20 per cent lower than in Malaysia. Investors in electronic assembly industries had a strong incentive to encourage the development of local supply networks.[2]

The key to the development of local supply networks, however, was not to force them through local-content rules, but rather to clear the way for development of downstream production in order to create a demand for the products of upstream suppliers. This meant facilitating trade and investment through regulatory and tariff reform, improving port and customs services and removing administrative barriers. Having chosen to invest in a particular location, internationally experienced and competitive downstream producers then play an important mentoring role for local suppliers with respect to product design, sourcing of materials, production methods and logistics, thus ensuring to the greatest possible extent that they become internationally competitive suppliers.[3]

Some policy-makers have taken exactly the wrong lesson from the observed correlation between the development of competitive downstream producers and upstream sourcing industries, and have tried to force the development of upstream suppliers. High tariffs designed to encourage local production of consumer goods for local markets encouraged the development of small-scale and high-cost local assembly industries. Disappointed by the low levels of local content policy-makers devised complex tariff-rate structures, often combined with specific local-content rules intended to encourage the development of domestic supporting industries. The almost inevitable result was not the development of internationally competitive industrial 'clusters' but rather high-cost import-substitution enclaves for which consumers paid a double price through protection of the original product and the further increase in costs incurred in meeting local-content requirements.

10.2.2.2 MAURITIUS

Mauritius is a member of SADC and is one of the few African successes in global integration. At independence, Mauritius' economic prospects were bleak.[4] It was among the poorest countries in the world. The population was too high to be supported by the island's limited land and natural resources. Any wage sufficient for landowners to hire the available labor

---

[2] Source: author's (Flatters) interviews in Malaysia, Indonesia and Singapore.

[3] This key role of export-oriented international investors in attracting and mentoring upstream suppliers is a major theme of Moran (2001).

[4] For an elegant and highly readable overview of the findings of British government-commissioned studies at the time, see Meade (1964).

force would be too low to support a subsistence standard of living. It appeared that the only hope was large increases in sugar yields or significant increases in world sugar prices. Neither of these was very likely. Mauritius appeared to be stuck in a Malthusian trap, condemned to grinding poverty, inevitable ethnic strife and political and economic instability.

Thirty years later Mauritius would be unrecognizable to those who participated in British-commissioned studies at independence. Per capita income (PPP adjusted) is more than 5 times higher than the average for sub-Saharan Africa and more than two and a half times that of all developing countries. Rates of growth and other human development indicators outperform these other countries by a wide margin.

Central to this achievement have been:

- recognition of special opportunities available in world markets, and
- trade-promoting policy reforms—facilitation of the import of raw materials and the export of processed products, with minimal regulation or other interference.

Outward-oriented investors in Mauritius were permitted to import what they wanted from any source they wished, to engage in any processing of these materials that they could do economically in Mauritius, and to export to any market in the world.

At the same time, an interesting feature of trade policy over the same period has been the continuation of relatively high rates of protection to a wide range of import substitution industries. Until very recently, the tariff structure has been characterized by high and variable rates, with an escalating pattern that encouraged inefficient local assembly industries. A long-entrenched myth about the importance and fragility of such import-substitution industries perpetuated a high-cost policy regime for an unusually long time.

It is only relatively recently, after recognizing the small amounts of employment in these industries and the high costs they impose on consumers, and after introducing a VAT that reduces budgetary reliance on import duties that Mauritius has begun to rationalize its import-duty regime.[5]

It is a testimony to the effectiveness of the EPZ system and to the market-friendliness of the rest of the investment and industrial policy regime that the export-oriented economy in textiles and other sectors developed so successfully in spite of these persistent import substitution

---

[5] See Box 7 of Flatters (2002b).

measures. Mauritius now exports a wide range of manufactured products, including of course garments and textiles, but also sunglasses, watches and their parts, medical equipment and many other goods. In addition, she continues to earn considerable income from tourism, and has begun to export banking and information-processing services.

One of the achievements of this 'miracle' was huge job creation in outward-oriented manufacturing. Mauritius is now facing labor shortages rather than surpluses; wages and skill levels have risen to the point that Mauritius is rapidly losing its comparative advantage in labor-intensive manufacturing. Mauritius is graduating from producing low-skill manufactures to exporting more skill-intensive products. It has become a regional growth engine—a hub for co-ordination and logistical support of production and exports of a wide range of services and manufactures, including textiles and garments.

Mauritius is an African example of the gains from participation in global markets. Central to its success has been a policy environment that has made trade as easy as possible and has permitted investors, domestic and foreign, to engage in activities that could be done best in Mauritius.

10.2.2.3 SUMMARY OF GENERAL LESSONS

The broad lessons from international experience are clear. Participation in global markets is a necessary condition for sustainable economic development and poverty reduction. The extent and type of participation of any country is largely the result of its own policy choices. Countries that have pursued relatively open trade-policy regimes have performed better than those that have not. No country that has closed itself from world markets has achieved rapid economic growth.

The key to openness in trade is the minimization of distortions and restrictions to imports and exports. Successes in Asia and elsewhere have often been characterized as 'export-led growth.' An equally accurate and more informative description would be 'import-led growth.' Freedom of access to imports—at the lowest possible cost and with a minimum of logistical and bureaucratic barriers—is a *sine qua non* of efficient growth of exports of manufactured goods.

The comparative advantage of poorer countries in labor-intensive exports is the guarantee that outward-oriented development is job and equity enhancing and that it is a powerful instrument of poverty reduction. International experience has shown time and again that trade is one of the most effective tools available for achieving sustainable growth and poverty reduction.

Within SADC, Mauritius provides an excellent case study of the economic achievements that are possible through outward-oriented trade policies.

10.3 The functions of Rules of Origin[6]

10.3.1 *General uses of Rules of Origin*

Rules of Origin are required in any preferential trading arrangement (PTA) in order to *authenticate* that goods claiming tariff preferences result from significant economic activity in an eligible country. The rules prevent 'trade deflection'—importing products from outside the PTA into a member country with a relatively low external tariff and re-exporting them under PTA tariff preferences into another member with a higher external tariff. Their importance depends on the height and intra-PTA variance of external tariffs. The greater the height and variance of external tariffs of PTA members, the greater will be the dangers of trade deflection.

The basis for Rules of Origin in most PTAs is the definition of a minimum level of processing or manufacturing within the region as a requirement for preferential tariff treatment.

A second purpose for which Rules of Origin are sometimes used is to encourage certain regional activities or to protect them from potential competition arising from the formation of the PTA. This is the *protective* effect (intended or unintended) of Rules of Origin. This protection can be of two forms—preventing the emergence of regional competition as a result of regional trade liberalization, and encouraging regional production of intermediate or primary products.

- Restrictive Rules of Origin deprive producers of access to raw materials or intermediate products from low-cost international sources and hence raise the cost of producing for sale in the PTA.[7] If they have any effect at all, they force producers to source inputs locally when they would not otherwise have done so, forcing them into cost-raising production patterns. This reduces the ability of producers to take

---

[6] This section draws on Flatters (2002b).

[7] Producers are free, of course, to source raw materials wherever they wish, subject to import regulations and taxes in their own countries. But if they do not meet the requirements of the PTA's Rules of Origin, they will not qualify for preferential access to other markets in the PTA.

advantage of regional preferences. In this way restrictive Rules of Origin shield existing producers from new regional competition, and deprive consumers from potential benefits of regional tariff reductions.

This is sometimes rationalized as a defensive measure to protect producers from cost-raising effects of their own countries' MFN import tariffs on raw materials and intermediate inputs. Forcing potential regional competitors to operate under similar policy-induced handicaps has no economic rationale. At best it makes the PTA irrelevant for globally competitive producers who source materials from the best international sources. At worst it induces producers to adopt high-cost production methods, simply to satisfy a rule of origin.

- Strict Rules of Origin can induce producers to use regional raw materials, thus giving protection and encouragement to the producers of such goods. Such an incentive is necessary only to the extent that their local/regional costs of these materials are higher than international prices of the same goods. Therefore, the burden of Rules of Origin designed for this purpose are borne in the form of higher costs by downstream user industries, making them less competitive internationally and forcing them to charge higher prices domestically. Such a strategy reduces rather than increases the global competitiveness of regional producers and deprives consumers of the benefits of trade liberalization.

Rules of Origin can have substantial protective effects. To reduce tariffs on regional trade only to replace them with less transparent and often more restrictive Rules of Origin is a questionable way to achieve the benefits of trade liberalization.

10.3.2 *Proposed uses of Rules of Origin in SADC*

Under some interpretations the SADC Trade Protocol Rules of Origin are intended to be used not only for authentication, but also to serve a broader developmental role. The 'developmental' function is justified by Article 2 of the Trade Protocol that identifies the enhancement of economic development, diversification and industrialization of the region as major goals. This has been seen as counsel for protection as a development tool, getting to the heart of much more general debates about the role of trade polices in development.

Proposed uses of Rules of Origin in SADC have not been confined to authentication and protection. Other justifications have included consumer and industrial safety, environmental protection, and preventing the dumping of foreign goods in regional markets.

Liberalization of regional trade, it has been claimed, might impose new threats in these areas. There is very little evidence about the likelihood of these threats, and in most instances it appears that the risks are low. In each case there also exist a wide range of instruments that should be more suitable, more effective and have less costly side effects than Rules of Origin.

Fears have been expressed that the 'normal' instruments for dealing with these problems might not work. This is not an argument for using Rules of Origin; rather, it points out the need to improve the design or implementation of the normal tools. The use of restrictive Rules of Origin would be a much less effective (often completely ineffective) and more costly alternative.[8]

Another frequently expressed belief is that regional Customs administrations are incapable of enforcing Rules of Origin. As a result, it is feared that low-cost goods from Asia will enter SADC through porous borders of weak member states, be granted SADC tariff preferences, and destroy regional industries. More restrictive Rules of Origin are the suggested solution. This begs the question of why a weak administration should be more capable of enforcing complex and restrictive rules than simpler and less restrictive ones.

Solving problems of weak administration by making it difficult, if not impossible, for any trade to qualify for SADC preferences subverts the trade-liberalization process. Improving administrative systems and capabilities would be a more direct, appropriate and less costly alternative.

10.3.3 Evolution of SADC Rules of Origin

The Rules of Origin in the original SADC Trade Protocol were simple, general and consistent with those in other developing country PTAs, including most importantly neighboring and overlapping COMESA.[9] They included both general conditions stipulating that simple packaging, assembly and labelling, for instance, are insufficient to confer originating status (Rule 3 of Annex I to the Protocol), and specific rules setting out

---

[8] See Box 2 of Flatters (2002b) for a discussion of a proposal to use Rules of Origin for the enforcement of safety standards for electrical cable.

[9] In fact the COMESA rules was relaxed slightly to bring them into greater conformity with those originally agreed in SADC. This is ironic in light of the fact that the original SADC rules were never implemented and were replaced instead with much more complex and restrictive

minimum levels of economic activity. Under the specific rules goods would have to undergo a single change of tariff heading, contain a minimum of 35 per cent regional value added, or include non-SADC imported materials worth no more than 60 per cent of the value of total inputs used. Agricultural and primary products needed to be wholly produced or obtained in the region.

Certain member states, led by South Africa, pressed for exceptions to these rules. South Africa accounts for over 75 per cent of SADC GDP and is the only member state with a significant manufacturing base. After signalling his government's intent to promote regional free trade, South Africa's Minister of Trade then clarified that this was subject to the important constraint that it not endanger existing domestic industries. In particular, for goods to benefit from SADC preferences, they must be 'genuinely produced in SADC'. This was interpreted to mean that if an intermediate product was produced within SADC it should be used instead of one from outside the region.

This led to the development of a regime of more restrictive sector-specific rules. Most of the arguments for such rules boiled down to attempts to increase or preserve protection in domestic markets. The rule of origin regime in the amended Trade Protocol is very different from what was originally agreed, characterized by made-to-measure product-specific rules that are far more restrictive. The change of tariff heading requirement has been replaced by multiple transformation rules and/or detailed descriptions of required production processes. Value-added requirements have been raised, and permissible levels of import content have been decreased.[10]

The rules are now much more like those in the EU and in PTAs with rich, highly industrialized countries.[11] They are most similar to the rules in the EU-South Africa and EU-ACP trade agreements. This is no coincidence. The EU-South Africa rules were often invoked by special interests in South Africa as models for SADC. Such claims were too often accepted at face value and not recognized as self-interested pleading for protection by already heavily protected domestic producers. There was little or no discussion about the appropriateness of the underlying economic model (whatever it might be) for SADC.

rules. The irony is compounded by the current pressure from some parties in COMESA to follow SADC once again and 'tighten' the COMESA rules.

[10] The amended Trade Protocol had replaced the original one before the Protocol was actually implemented. Therefore the relatively simple and liberal rules in the original Protocol never were applied in regulating intra-SADC trade.

[11] Estevadeordal and Suominen (2003) refer to this as the PANEURO model.

The complex and asymmetric pattern of tariff phase-down schedules agreed under the Trade Protocol was another factor in shaping the Rules of Origin. Undue attention was paid to transitional rules rather than the end product. During the transition it was agreed to permit the relatively less-developed member states to phase down their tariff rates at a slower rate than South Africa/SACU.[12] In order to take account of the divergent levels of development between the SACU members the non-SACU countries were permitted to phase down preferential tariffs more slowly towards South Africa than towards the rest of SADC.[13]

The complexity of the compromises involved in the tariff phase downs made it virtually impossible to reopen discussions later to deal with unforeseen problems.[14] This placed the burden of dealing with any *ex post* complaints of excessively rapid liberalization on other instruments, most importantly Rules of Origin. Stakeholders wishing to forestall increases in competition arising from preferential tariff reductions found Rules of Origin to be a wonderful tool. The ability to appeal to the 'EU model' added further credibility to the process of tightening the rules.

The following sections discuss and summarize the findings of numerous case studies of the effects of alternative Rules of Origin discussed in the development of the SADC regime.

10.4 SADC Rules of Origin: agriculture and processed agricultural products

The SADC economies are still heavily dependent on agriculture and on other primary products. For those who see Rules of Origin as a development tool, these sectors are important targets. The 'EU model' has provided considerable guidance.

As already observed, primary agricultural products must be wholly produced in a member state in order to qualify for SADC preferential tariffs. This ensures that products produced elsewhere do not gain access to preferences by being imported initially into a low-tariff member-state market.

[12] SACU is the Southern Africa Customs Union and comprises Botswana, Lesotho, Namibia, South Africa and Swaziland. With a common external tariff SACU presented one tariff phase-down offer to the rest of SADC.

[13] This transitional asymmetry was even carried over into Rules of Origin in the textile sector.

[14] South Africa's entry into other trade agreements, especially with the EU, together with its commitment in SADC never to offer better preferential access to its markets than to SADC producers added to the difficulty of slowing down or reversing agreed SADC tariff reductions.

In addition, however, there has been strong pressure to use Rules of Origin to encourage the use of local raw materials in downstream processing industries. There are two variations on this argument.

- Requiring the use of regional raw materials will protect and/or encourage development of local agricultural production. Without such protection processors, especially those in member states with low agricultural tariffs, will harm regional producers by substituting international for regional raw materials. Restrictive Rules of Origin on processed products will do the opposite and increase demand for regional agricultural products.

- Insisting on the use of regionally produced raw materials will encourage greater regional value added in agriculture. Rather than exporting unprocessed raw materials, restrictive Rules of Origin will encourage further downstream processing.

These arguments have been heard in many forms in many agricultural sectors. They often have been used together, with no apparent recognition of the inherent contradiction between them. Underlying the discussions in some key sectors as we shall see has been a third, often unstated presumption—that requiring the use of local raw materials will reduce the amount of competition in markets for processed goods as a result of SADC tariff reductions.

In any event, following the 'EU model' and what were perceived to be the interests of agricultural producers and processors, the Rules of Origin for many processed agricultural products require that many of the raw materials used be wholly originating in the region in order for the regionally processed products to qualify for SADC preferences.

The most interesting and informative cases during the negotiations were sectors in which the absurdity of such a rule was too great to be ignored. We briefly discuss a few such cases here.

10.4.1 *Wheat flour*[15]

The rule of origin for wheat flour and its products have not been agreed. The main differences among the proposed rules for flour hinge on the amount of local/regional wheat that is required. At one extreme is a proposal requiring that 70 per cent of the wheat used (by weight) be sourced in the region. At the other is a rule that requires simply that the

[15] The argument in this and the following section is developed in more detail in Erasmus and Flatters (2003).

flour be milled in the region—i.e. that wheat undergoes a change of tariff heading. The main differences in the proposed rules for downstream flour products also relate to whether there are any requirements on the local wheat content of flour used.

There are large variations in production capacities and in the regulatory environments for these products in SADC member states. Several members produce significant amounts of wheat, although none are self-sufficient. Others produce almost no wheat at all. South Africa is by far the dominant producer, in terms of both total production and the proportion of domestic demand that can be met from local production.

Some member states have a history of providing considerable protection to local wheat growers and others provide none. Similarly, there are large variations in the amount of protection given to downstream producers of flour and its products. There has been significant and rapid deregulation in these industries in some member states recently, especially South Africa.

Member states with large and protected wheat and wheat flour industries have resisted liberalization of intra-SADC trade. In particular, they have advocated restrictive Rules of Origin as a means of insulating their producers against competition from other member states.

Even in member states that have resisted liberalization, however, there are significant and growing interests whose focus extends beyond national markets. This is especially true in certain downstream industries. These producers compete in regional and world markets and have a strong interest in a more liberal trading environment. The conditions that permit them to compete in international markets—especially unrestricted access to key raw material inputs—would not apply if SADC markets were governed by high tariffs, stringent Rules of Origin and other restrictions.

SADC is not self-sufficient in wheat. Outside of South Africa and Zimbabwe (until recently), only modest volumes of wheat are produced within SADC. Indeed even South Africa and Zimbabwe have always needed to import wheat in order to meet the requirements of the flour millers. South Africa is the dominant producer in SADC accounting for about 80 per cent of total regional production.

The discussions have raised questions about downstream milling industries. What are the implications of wheat policies on the competitiveness of flour milling in different member states and how might this change as a result of SADC free trade under different Rules of Origin? Less attention has been paid to the implications of these policies for consumers of flour and flour products in member states.

Less openly discussed, but of equal or maybe even greater importance has been the type and extent of protection of SADC milling industries. How much protection is currently enjoyed by different SADC milling industries? How will this protection be affected by intra-SADC free trade under different Rules of Origin?

Tanzania and South Africa are the only members to place significant import duties on wheat. Tanzania's MFN duty is 25 per cent, while South Africa has a specific duty that is triggered by a world price less than its 'long-term average.' Whenever this happens the specific duty is set at the difference between the actual and long-term average wheat price.[16] The actual duty has been zero or very close to zero for the past two years.

The wheat duty, arguably intended to protect local wheat growers provides South Africa's main justification for a restrictive Rule of Origin for flour. Without such a rule, it is argued, millers in other member states would be able to import 'cheap' wheat on world markets, undermine South African millers in their domestic market and ultimately deprive wheat growers of their only source of demand.

However, any Rule of Origin requiring significant amounts of regionally sourced wheat could never be met by non-SACU millers. Therefore a Rule of Origin allegedly designed to protect South African millers and grain growers would also prevent all preferential SADC trade among non-SACU members. Only SACU millers would ever be able to satisfy the South Africa-proposed rule of 70% local content by weight.

A closer study of the South African/SACU grain markets reveals another problem with the South African justification for a restrictive rule of origin. In recent years at least, the SACU wheat tariff provides very little if any assistance to local grain growers. For the past two years the duty has been set at zero or close to zero. Previously, under the competitive structure of the grain market (few buyers, many sellers), domestic wheat prices in South Africa were equal to or less than the import parity price before import duty.[17] In some regional markets they were closer to export parity than to import parity. Simple evidence is provided by the preference of non-South African SACU millers to purchase local South African wheat even when they could use the rebate facility to buy imported wheat on a duty-free basis. In other words, the South African wheat tariff has not helped grain growers and has not imposed a significant cost penalty on millers. The only negative impact on millers is the effect it has on the

---

[16] While the SACU wheat duty applies to all SACU members, all except South Africa provide a full rebate. The stated purpose of the rebate is to reduce the cost of flour, an important ingredient of many basic foodstuffs. [17] See Box 2 of Erasmus and Flatters (2003).

price of imported wheat, which comprises only 20 to 30 per cent of their needs.

What protection is given to the SADC milling industries? All member states except Malawi tax imports of wheat flour. Outside of SACU these duties range from 15 to 40 per cent. The SACU duty is more complex. Until the beginning of 2003 it comprised two elements, a specific duty equal to 150 per cent of that on wheat, and an additional *ad valorem* duty that started at 40 per cent several years ago, had been phased down to 10 per cent in 2002 and to zero in 2003.

MFN tariff structures in the early stages of the SADC negotiations gave substantial protection to millers in most SADC member states. Effective protection to milling most member states ranged from 25 to 127 per cent. Only Malawi and Mauritius gave no protection to local milling industries. In more recent years, with the disappearance of the duties on wheat and flour, SACU millers received no effective tariff protection.

Within each domestic market, most SADC milling industries have tended to be oligopolistic and face little threat from external competition. It is understandable that they would wish to use Rules of Origin to protect them from new regional competition from SADC.

The SACU millers have been quite successful at delaying preferential trade in wheat flour. Tariff phase downs on wheat flour are among the slowest in all sectors. A number of member states have erected non-tariff barriers against imports of wheat flour, the most notable of which is a recently enacted ban on all wheat flour imports in Namibia (a member of SACU). And the milling industries, especially those in SACU, have captured almost complete control of negotiations in this sector and have ensured complete deadlock so that no rule can be agreed.[18] Claiming to represent the interests of South African wheat farmers against those of non-South African millers, the major South African flour producers have convinced negotiators that any non-restrictive Rule of Origin will provide a back door through which SADC free trade in flour will destroy the South African grain industry, despite the fact that current protection, at most, helps only millers and provides no benefit to grain growers.

Rent-seeking behavior by key stakeholders has stalled regional trade liberalization in this sector and has even created new trade barriers. Incorrect but nevertheless plausible-sounding claims about support for agriculture have been manipulated to justify policies that benefit

---

[18] Senior management from the major milling interests are principal actors at all trade negotiating meetings and have played major roles in writing the position papers for several of the member states.

particular parties but deliver none of the promised benefits to the supposed beneficiaries.

Similar but even less plausible arguments are being used to argue for the use of flour milled from local wheat in downstream flour products such as bread, pasta and biscuits. As with wheat flour, no rule has been agreed.

10.4.2 Coffee, tea, spices and other processed agricultural products

Member states in which there is significant primary production of coffee, tea, spices or other agricultural products, and especially those that impose significant external tariffs on these products have often advocated restrictive Rules of Origin (high regional content requirements) for their downstream products, and those that are not major producers of the raw materials generally prefer less-restrictive rules. The raw-material producers have tended to have a louder voice and greater influence.

The principal argument for restrictive Rules of Origin in these sectors is to encourage regional economic activity by:

- increasing demand for a regional agricultural product and hence the incomes of its producers; and/or
- encouraging downstream processing.

The original chapter rule for coffee, tea and spices required that locally produced materials account for at least 80 per cent by weight of the final product in order for them to qualify for SADC tariff preferences. The only exception was for mixtures of spices where the requirement was that at least 80 per cent of the *value* of the final product (ex-works price) be attributable to regional inputs. Following pressure from non-producing member states it was eventually agreed that:

- for tea, coffee and spices at least 60 per cent by weight of the raw materials must originate in the region, and
- for curry and mixtures of spices, there must be a change of tariff heading and all cloves used in such mixtures must be wholly originating in the region.

For many other products, the rules require that certain primary products produced in the region be fully sourced in the region in order for the downstream products to receive SADC tariff preferences.

Insistence on highly restrictive Rules of Origin reflects a fundamental misunderstanding of their likely effects. In the case of spice mixes, many of the relevant spices are not even available in the region, at any cost.

Therefore the proposed rules would not accomplish any of their intended goals, for primary producers or for processors, and they would have the unintended consequence of preventing any intra-SADC preferential trade. They would impede rather than encourage the development of downstream processing activities, at least for the SADC market.

Two of the keys to successful downstream coffee, tea and spice blending are a) sourcing a variety of appropriate raw materials—in terms of quality, price and other characteristics—for blending purposes and b) efficient processing, creative packaging and marketing of the final products. See Box 1 for the case of instant coffee.

High-quality coffee, tea and spices are grown in a number of SADC Member States. A wide variety of lower-quality products are also grown. Many of these products are exported internationally. Those of higher quality command correspondingly high prices in world markets. Growers' participation in international markets means that restrictive Rules of Origin in SADC will have no effect on them. Any sales that might be diverted to regional markets as a result of restrictive Rules of Origin would simply replace one customer by another, with no impact on the sellers or the producers of the raw materials. A restrictive rule of origin for coffee, tea or spices will be of no benefit to local growers.

Consider the case of Tanzania, a competitive world producer and net exporter of coffee and cloves. Any diversion of its coffee or cloves to local or regional use would simply detract from international exports, with no net gain. The world price would obtain in either case.

Furthermore, a restrictive rule of origin for these products will not assist in the development of downstream processing industries. In fact, it would most likely have the opposite effect; it would decrease the overall competitiveness of coffee, tea, and spice processors. However, it would prevent any new competition for existing producers arising from SADC tariff reductions.

Processed coffee, tea and spices are heterogeneous and highly differentiated products. The raw materials used are similarly heterogeneous and their characteristics are generally very location specific—a product of climate, soil conditions and many other factors.[19] Relative to the variety of raw materials available in the world, SADC Member States produce only a very narrow range and a similarly limited set of varieties of the few products that are grown in the region.

---

[19] The time, effort and resources devoted to exploration and colonial wars over several centuries in China and the East Indies is testimony the location-specific nature of growing conditions for a wide variety of spices, teas and coffees.

---

1. INTERNATIONAL SOURCING FOR INSTANT COFFEE

As is well known to any aficionado, 'coffee' is not a homogeneous product. With few exceptions, most coffees available in the market are blends of beans from different sources, each with its distinct taste characteristics.

Instant coffee is no different. Coffee producers source beans from around the globe in light of differences in price, quality and flavor. For example, one major manufacturer in SADC sources beans from at least seven different countries in order to achieve a product at the right cost and with the appropriate flavor. The basic mix is roughly 60% robusta and 40% Arabica. Suitable robusta is not available anywhere in the SADC region, and so it is sourced in other parts of Africa (mainly Ivory Coast) and Asia (primarily Indonesia and Vietnam at the moment). Arabica is sourced in a number of countries, including South Africa, Tanzania, Uganda and Zimbabwe. Overall, however, only five to ten per cent of their coffee inputs are sourced in SADC.

The low degree of local sourcing is of no consequence to regional growers. Arabica coffee grown in the region is sold internationally—indeed some high-quality Arabica products command very high premiums in Europe and other international markets. Increased local sourcing by regional processors would not affect the world prices of these products and hence would be of no benefit to local growers.

Instant coffee production is a substantial manufacturing process, with value added in the range of 40 to 50 per cent of the ex-works price. The rule of origin for chapter 21 that includes instant coffee puts an upper limit of 60 per cent of the ex-works price on the amount of imported materials that can be used. A 70 or 80 per cent regional-content requirement as was originally set for processed coffee and tea would make regionally manufactured instant coffee ineligible for SADC trade preferences.

Source: Case study interviews. See Flatters (2002b).

Producers would prefer to source locally whenever possible—for reasons of transport costs, speedy and reliable communication with suppliers, etc. They work closely with regional suppliers and growers to develop local sources of raw materials where this can be done competitively.

For some products such as rooibos tea,[20] the raw materials can be obtained only in the SADC region. For others, such as Ceylon tea, green tea and many of the raw materials that are essential in curries and other mixed spices, there are no local sources of supply in SADC. Branding, licensing, local health regulations and many other factors often determine where inputs must be sourced, and Rules of Origin cannot be used to overcome these requirements. Skillful sourcing and selection of raw materials in the global market is a key to the international competitiveness of these producers. Therefore, restrictive Rules of Origin simply

---

[20] This is a popular herbal tea in South Africa and the region, made from the leaves of the 'red bush.'

---

2. GHERKINS: THE NEED FOR FLEXIBLE SOURCING OF RAW MATERIALS

An example from a different tariff heading illustrates the importance of flexibility in sourcing raw materials and the absurdity of rules such as those governing coffee, tea and spices. A company investigated in the course of this work produces a wide variety of food products, including pickled gherkins.

Gherkins are grown competitively in SADC and the company routinely buys locally. However, a recent crop failure created an emergency and required the company to source gherkins from Turkey, at considerable extra cost. Under a restrictive rule such as those proposed for coffee and tea, the use of imported gherkins would disqualify these pickles from SADC trade preferences. This would provide no benefit to local gherkin growers and would be harmful to regional producers and consumers.

In any other year, the rule would be easily satisfied. But it would be redundant; producers would source locally regardless of the Rules of Origin. In normal years, the restrictive rule would be unnecessary, and in unusual years, such as that described here, it could not be fulfilled and would only cause harm to local producers and consumers.

Source: Case study interviews. See Flatters (2002b).

---

hinder the development of downstream processing industries. See Box 2 for an example from another sector.

There are a number of internationally successful SADC producers of processed agricultural products. They already export within the immediate region, to the rest of Africa and many other places, including Asia, Europe and North America. Arbitrary and restrictive rules that limit flexibility in raw-material sourcing will reduce their competitiveness and harm regional consumers.

Restrictive Rules of Origin would exclude from SADC preferences most of the products currently produced in the region, including many in which non-preferential trade is already taking place. Even member states that might have some comparative advantage in tea, coffee or spice blending by virtue of local availability of some of the necessary ingredients would be deprived of preferential access to SADC markets under current rules.

10.5 Manufacturing industries

10.5.1 *Light manufacturing*

Some of the most contentious issues on manufacturing Rules of Origin rules arose in the light manufacturing industries in HS Chapters 84, 85 and 90. These include machinery, electrical and electronic goods and components, and various kinds of technical and medical equipment.

The initially proposed general rule for products in Chapters 84, 85 and 90 was that non-originating raw materials used could not exceed 65 per cent of their ex-factory cost. In other words, a minimum local/regional content of 35 per cent of ex-factory cost was required.

The basis for value calculations was then changed from ex-factory cost to ex-works price and the domestic content threshold was raised to 40 per cent (i.e. the maximum import content became 60 per cent of the ex-works price).

The more interesting story concerns the exceptions to the chapter rule. Several member states, most importantly South Africa, identified certain chapter subheadings in which they had a special interest and for which they advocated more restrictive rules. As might be expected, these were subheadings in which South Africa had existing (or potential) producers selling behind high import tariff barriers.

After tortuous negotiations that went on until mid-2002 it was finally agreed that eight four-digit HS chapter subheadings would 'benefit from' a more restrictive 45 per cent maximum import content. This is subject to reconsideration under the mid-term review of the Trade Protocol.

Several justifications were provided for such strict rules. Most were based simply on the desire to protect existing or potential industries against the possibility of increased competition arising from the freer trade in the region. This insurance was often unnecessary and misguided, not only because it violated the intention of using the Trade Protocol to promote freer trade in SADC, but also because the members in question had no significant local industry to protect anyway.[21]

A variation on the same argument is the fear that trade liberalization will lead to a flood of imports from new 'screwdriver' industries set up in neighboring countries to take advantage of the Trade Protocol. These concerns ignore specific prohibitions set out in the Protocol against the granting of preferential tariff treatment for screwdriver-assembly activities.

---

[21] In one instance in which a Member State pressed for restrictive Rules of Origin it turned out that the industry in question comprised only two firms. One was an internationally competitive exporter and had no need for or interest in a restrictive Rule of Origin. The other firm, a high-cost import substitution producer, had already gone out of business—apparently unbeknownst to the country's negotiators. In another such sector the firm that allegedly needed protection through a restrictive Rule of Origin had already received an offer of a government-funded investment grant covering almost 100 per cent of its capital costs and had not yet even located a piece of land on which to build.

A variety of other arguments based on safety, environmental protection and the possibility of dumping have been presented in particular cases as well. Without questioning the importance of achieving these social and economic goals, it is clear that Rules of Origin are not an appropriate instrument. In fact, the use of SADC Rules of Origin for these purposes would be very costly and almost certainly ineffective.[22]

There are many types of industries and firms represented in these sectors. These include a significant and growing number of successful exporters. There is intraindustry trade—trade in middle products—within the region as well as exports in a variety of niche markets to various parts of the world, including Europe and North America. Extraregional exports account for a growing share of production. Many of these are 'new exports' that have become more competitive due to MFN-based trade liberalization in the region over the past decade. What were once inward-looking import substitution industries have become global players. This has generated many new regional jobs—far more than can be created in uncompetitive import substitution activities.

Boxes 3 and 4 give examples of the sourcing practices in two sectors, water valves and small electric appliances, which have become competitive exporters as a result of liberalization of the South African economy over the past decade. Although their experience with international sourcing has been quite different, both provide important lessons for the design of Rules of Origin.

The actual degree of local content achieved in existing regional industries varies considerably. Some have levels of local content that are less than those specified by the relevant chapter rules, and many achieve considerably higher levels. In general, it is unlikely that the chapter rules would be a serious impediment to competitive trade for most existing industries. However, for some highly competitive global export industries in these sectors, a less restrictive Rule of Origin would undoubtedly enhance trading opportunities in the region.

The more restrictive special rules for particular subheadings would be much more of a problem.

In almost all cases in which a more restrictive rule has been agreed or proposed, the amendments are in respect of goods that already are produced in the region, most usually in South Africa and/or Zimbabwe (until the recent troubles). In most cases it is SACU that has proposed the alternative, more restrictive rule.

---

[22] See Box 2 of Flatters (2002b) for a discussion of these dumping and safety issues with respect to the case of electric cable.

---

3. RoO AND INTERNATIONALLY COMPETITIVE EXPORTERS: VALVES

The term 'valves' covers a wide range of industrial and consumer products. The two main local markets are water systems and the mining industry. South Africa imports valves of some types and exports others. Because of the relatively small size of the domestic market, it tends to import standardized products that benefit from economies of scale in production. On the other hand, South African producers are competitive in a number of products with smaller niche markets and shorter production runs.

As a result of their long experience supplying the South African mining sector, local producers have built up expertise in production of valves used in the mining industry, especially for the transport of slurry. This has generated a steady demand from the mining industry around the world. Exports account for over one-third of total production.

By the nature of the materials and production processes, valves rely heavily on domestic materials. The bulk and weight of iron castings make them costly to import. Therefore, a relatively restrictive Rule of Origin would not be a major hindrance. On the other hand, the natural protection provided by production and transport costs also means that producers have nothing to fear from a liberal Rule of Origin. Competitors planning to rely on imported components would have much higher costs than local producers. Furthermore, a more liberal rule would provide flexibility for these internationally competitive local producers to take advantage of any cost-saving import possibilities that might arise.

Source: Case study interviews. See Flatters (2002b).

A principal justification for the more restrictive rules can be paraphrased as follows.

'Our domestic industry already achieves a high level of domestic content; achieving high levels of local content is costly, and allowing competitors to "get away with" lower levels of local content would give them an unfair advantage under SADC free trade.'

Producers would not voluntarily engage in cost-raising methods of production unless government policies required it and/or unless they were given some financial incentives for doing so. Assembly of products from CKD kits for sale in a protected domestic market is an example of a cost-raising activity encouraged by high tariffs on final products and lower tariffs on kits and components.[23]

Of course, not all increases in local content raise costs. To be able to compete, whether in the local or international market, producers actually would prefer to be able to source raw materials and inputs locally (recall

---

[23] See Box 7 in Flatters (2002b) on refrigerator production in Mauritius for a good example of this.

**4. RoO AND INTERNATIONALLY COMPETITIVE EXPORTERS:
ELECTRIC APPLIANCES**

The South African electrical appliance industry has evolved in response to the opening up of the domestic economy. Production has been rationalized considerably. There is still some production aimed specifically at the protected domestic market. Some is of a relatively simple assembly nature and accounts for correspondingly low levels of employment. At the other extreme are examples of internationally competitive export production, which account for much more employment than domestically oriented sales. One domestic company now accounts for about 4 per cent of the entire global market for electric kettles.

Exporting is a tough business. Exporters of electric appliances prefer to source components locally, but only if price, quality and terms of delivery meet international standards. The degree of local sourcing varies considerably across products. To remain competitive producers must have the flexibility to source anywhere in the world. Internationally branded vacuum cleaners exported to the Middle East use motors from Italy. Simple cord sets for kettles and other exports are sometimes sourced domestically and sometimes from as far away as China. *It is the flexibility to source from anywhere that permits exporters to remain competitive.*

A SADC Rule of Origin requiring 60 per cent local content could be met for some products. A 45 or 50 per cent rule would broaden the range of possibilities. But a 35 per cent rule would be much preferred. This would provide the kind of flexibility currently used to compete in the much larger and much more interesting global market.

Restrictive Rules of Origin are a hindrance, not a benefit, to internationally competitive exporters.

Source: Case study interviews. See Flatters (2002b).

---

the lessons from Southeast Asia discussed earlier). But to remain competitive, they also must have the flexibility to obtain such materials from the best sources.[24]

When high levels of local content are motivated by cost savings and by efficient production, existing producers have nothing to fear from competitors that might set up operations with lower levels of local content in other member states. Even if changing technology or new marketing possibilities make lower local content production methods more competitive, existing producers are better placed to adjust than new competitors.

---

[24] The agreed rules now also include a requirement for the local assembly ('population') of printed circuit boards (PCBs) in television receivers and video monitors. There is no obvious justification for such a requirement in order to prevent trade deflection. If local population of PCBs makes economic sense (i.e. is less costly than importing already assembled boards), then self-interested actions of profit-seeking producers will ensure that this happens. But if it is less costly to import than to assemble PCBs, there is no economic argument for using SADC Rules of Origin to encourage such assembly.

The chapter rule requiring 40 per cent local content is sufficient to authenticate origin of manufactured goods in these chapters. Additions to these requirements are at best unnecessary, and at worst will inhibit intra-SADC competition and make SADC irrelevant for producers that are or wish to be internationally competitive.

Two member states have recently proposed that the chapter rule be relaxed in favor of one that is *less* restrictive for a number of industries in which they hope to attract export-oriented investors. This recognizes that international competitiveness rests on flexibility in sourcing of raw materials, not on the imposition of arbitrary barriers such as restrictive Rules of Origin.

10.5.3 *Textiles and garments*[25]

Textiles and garments are of particular interest in SADC. This is one of the few manufacturing sectors in which there is significant production in a number of member states. Differences in labor intensity and other determinants of comparative costs at various stages in the textile and garment 'value chain' also mean that there are potentially significant complementarities among member states that could enhance the region's competitiveness in world markets. It is a sector in which some member states, most importantly Mauritius, have already demonstrated the potential of the region. The opportunities opened up through the Africa Growth and Opportunities Act (AGOA) together with the looming uncertainties arising from the end of the Agreement on Textiles and Clothing (ATC) make this a crucial time for remedying domestic and regional policy weaknesses.

The successes of Lesotho and other countries that benefit from a non-restrictive Rule of Origin under AGOA are an important lesson for SADC. Lesotho, a small, least-developed and landlocked country has experienced strong growth in this sector in recent years. Foreign direct investment (FDI) into export-oriented manufacturing accounted for the bulk of new investments.

Most inputs to foreign-owned firms established in Lesotho come from East Asia, the cheapest and most efficient source. This has been possible because Lesotho has benefitted from a single-transformation Rule of Origin under AGOA. Due to the growing scale of garment production, however, there have been recent investments in upstream textile production as

---

[25] This section draws heavily on Flatters (2002a).

well. This is similar to what happened in Mauritius earlier. Garment production for exports to the US market has increased almost threefold between 2000 and 2003. Over 30 000 jobs have been created. This contrasts with Lesotho's export performance to the EU where a double-transformation rule is required to qualify for preferential market access.

As currently agreed, the movement to SADC free trade in textiles and garments will be slow and there are relatively complex transitional arrangements. Most non-SACU Member States have postponed significant tariff reductions until very late in the transition process. Even SACU has postponed full tariff liberalization in this sector until 2005 (and even later in the case of clothing).[26]

With a few exceptions and except for yarn, the Rules of Origin require double transformation in order to qualify for SADC tariff preferences—garments must be made from regionally produced textiles; fabric must be made from regionally produced yarns; yarn must be made from uncarded, uncombed fiber or from chemical products. The double-transformation rules for garments and fabric are waived for the four poorest member states, Malawi, Mozambique, Tanzania and Zambia (known as the MMTZ countries), on exports to SACU, but only until July 2006, and subject to small quotas. It was agreed early on that this derogation and its phase out would be reassessed as part of the mid-term review of the Trade Protocol.

The current SADC Rules of Origin will be very difficult to satisfy for most regional garment producers.

The stated rationale for the double-transformation rule was that it would encourage regional sourcing and deeper integration of the regional textile and garment industries. An examination of the regional industry, however, reveals very little such integration at the moment, especially for import-substitution-oriented producers. The scale of the local and regional markets alone is simply too small to make such integration economic.

Even in South Africa the vast majority of garment producers use imported fabric. When asked how it would respond to a requirement that its garments be made from domestic or regional fabric (i.e. to meet the SADC Rules of Origin), the owner of one of South Africa's most successful garment producers replied: 'We could not compete; we would shut our doors tomorrow.'[27] This is despite import duties of 40 per cent on its products. Another manufacturer of brand name apparel uses Italian cotton fabric for

---

[26] South Africa has recently proposed an acceleration of the tariff phase down in these sectors, conditional on similar actions by other member states. However, it must be noted that the sector will remain constrained by SADC's very restrictive two-stage transformation Rule of Origin requirement.   [27] Source: case study interviews.

its high-end products. Such fabric cannot be obtained from a South African producer at any cost.[28] The same is true, and in fact even more so, of SADC garment makers outside of South Africa. This is not surprising in light of the much lower stage of development of upstream textile industries and the small scale of the domestic markets in most of SADC.

Enshrining in the Trade Protocol Rules of Origin that cannot be met even by South African garment producers arose in part from the structure of MFN tariff protection of this industry in SACU.[29] South African garment makers that sell in the domestic market and hence do not benefit from duty rebates or additional export incentives suffer from the cost-raising impact of high fabric import duties, generally in excess of 20 per cent. At the same time, they are more than adequately compensated for this by much higher import duties on garments, generally in excess of 40 per cent. The net effect is very high rates of effective protection when selling domestically.

As long as they are penalized by high duties and other restrictions on yarn and fiber imports, South African textile makers do not want duty-free competition from regional weaving and knitting industries that have access to duty-free yarn. Similarly, South African garment makers do not wish to compete with those in other Member States that do not suffer the cost-raising effects of high tariffs on fabric. A double-transformation rule of origin 'solves' this problem by ensuring that such competition will never occur. The rule is designed, not to encourage use of regional textile inputs (not even South African garment makers do so at the moment), but rather, to ensure that SADC preferential trade does not take place when South African garment makers labor under the handicap of high domestic textile duties. The same explanation applies one stage further back in the production chain.

Since most South African producers cannot satisfy this Rule of Origin, it is highly unlikely that it could be met by non-SACU producers. The double-transformation rule will prevent preferential intra-SADC garment trade, thus permitting South Africa to preserve its high protection policies on garments and fabric. It certainly will not promote intra-SADC trade in this sector—not even among non-SACU Member States. And it will do nothing to promote the global competitiveness SADC textile and garment producers.

The real challenge facing the SADC textile and garment industries is the expiry of the Agreement on Textiles and Clothing (ATC) at the end of

---

[28] See Box 3 of Flatters (2002a).   [29] See Box 4 of Flatters (2002a).

2004. The post ATC world will be one of ruthless competition, with competitive producers sourcing fabrics and other raw materials from the most economical sources. Market shares will no longer be determined by quota arrangements in rich-country markets. They will depend solely on suppliers' abilities to compete on the basis of cost, quality and timeliness of delivery. Producers that are burdened by cumbersome Customs procedures and administrative requirements of dealing with restrictive Rules of Origin in regional markets will find it difficult to compete.

For export-oriented garment and textile production, any SADC Rules of Origin are redundant in the face of any restrictive rules imposed by AGOA and the EU and/or unnecessary and cost raising where exports are not constrained by such rules in export markets.

The stringent Rules of Origin and back-loaded tariff reduction schedules that are currently agreed will be especially unhelpful to SADC as a means of taking advantage of US or EU preferences or adjusting to the challenges that will soon arise with the end of the ATC. They impede rather than promote the increased competitiveness that will be necessary to survive in the post-ATC world in 2005 and beyond.

10.6 General observations

This chapter has taken a 'bottom up' approach to Rules of Origin, looking at the details of a particular agreement and critically examining its likely effects against the claims put forth by stakeholders and decision-makers in the course of and subsequent to the negotiations. Arguments have been supported by qualitative and quantitative information obtained not only from verifiable market data but also from a variety of individual agents.

The methodology is quite different from most of the other chapters. Before summarizing our main conclusions, we pause here to ask what light this work might shed on some of the other exercises conducted under this project, especially the construction and use of various summary indices of Rules of Origin regimes as exemplified by the pioneering work of Estevadeordal (2000) and Estevadeordal and Suominen (2003) and built upon by a number of other papers.

10.6.1 *Constructing and interpreting an index*

To construct an overall index of restrictiveness of the SADC Rules of Origin regime would not have revealed almost all of the useful insights and information that have come from our own work on SADC. Furthermore, it would not be very helpful in guiding or persuading decision-makers in developing, evaluating or contemplating changes in the regime.

Nevertheless, it is useful to identify simple summary measures of complex phenomena. The concept and measurement of national income has been one of the greatest and most useful simplifications in economics. Trade-policy analysis is replete with indices of the average levels (and variances) of nominal and effective protection provided by tariffs. While there are issues about whether to use trade, production or other weights, the concept of a tariff rate is at least quite well founded. A 10 per cent tariff can generally be interpreted in terms of the magnitude of an important economic variable, the distortion between domestic and international prices.

The quantification of non-tariff barriers such as import quotas and other quantitative restrictions is more difficult, but has had real usefulness when the restrictions are conceptualized in terms of their tariff or subsidy equivalents.

Rules of Origin are more difficult still. The approach taken by Estevadeordal is to classify Rules of Origin according to their administrative types, make prior assumptions about the restrictiveness of each type and assign an index of between 1 and 7, in order of increasing restrictiveness to each type.

A change of tariff-heading rule is assumed to be more restrictive than a change of subheading. This is certainly a plausible assumption. However, as Estevadeordal and Suominen observe, the HS coding system was not designed as a policy-implementation tool for Rules of Origin. As experience in SADC and other PTAs has shown, a change of chapter requirement in most agricultural or primary commodities might be much easier to meet than even a change of subheading in some chemical, electrical or mechanical goods sectors where inputs and outputs are often included in the same subheading.

While tariff chapters versus subheadings might seem to be relatively simple, what about technical and value requirements? Is a technical requirement more or less restrictive than a restriction on import content? And if there are both a technical and value-content requirement in a sector, is that more restrictive than having just a technical requirement or just a value requirement? Clearly, the answer depends at least in part on the nature of the technical requirement and on the amount of import content allowed under the value requirement. And when there are two requirements, the answer depends on which one is binding for producers or potential regional exporters in the sector.

And once again the restrictiveness of any given requirement will vary according to the sector in which it is applied (compare instant coffee, valves and electrical goods described in Boxes 1, 3 and 4 above). The Estevadeordal index makes no allowance for such differences and in fact does not distinguish among different levels of permissible import content at all. All other things being equal, a 60 per cent local-content requirement gets the same restrictiveness index as a 35 per cent requirement. Some of the most heated discussions in SADC have been precisely over issues such as this. Yet according to this index, they do not matter.

What then do we make of measures of intersectoral variances of the restrictiveness index? Once again it surely depends on the details. One thing that is certain is that the imposition of uniform Rule-of-Origin requirements across sectors will ensure differences in their restrictiveness across these sectors. The question becomes whether variations in Rule-of-Origin requirements across sectors increase or decrease the degree of restrictiveness of the regime, by sector or overall.

The SADC negotiations offer a number of interesting examples. In HS 84, for instance, South Africa started by proposing a uniform and highly restrictive value-content requirement as a chapter rule, to which in some subheadings was added a technical requirement that printed circuit boards (PCBs) be populated in the region. Faced with an attack on the chapter rule, the response was to slowly agree to less-stringent value requirements and removal of the technical requirement in sectors 'of no importance' to South Africa (i.e. in which there was no local production). This has eventually led to a less-restrictive chapter rule with exceptions for all the sectors of interest to South Africa. In these sectors the required value content remains high (but subject to reconsideration under the Mid Term Review of the Trade Protocol). The result has been a reduction in the restrictiveness of the chapter rule, an increase in its variance, and no change in its real restrictiveness.

The variance in type and level of Rule-of-Origin requirements across many sectors in SADC can be described in a similar way. In sectors of interest to a major player (usually South Africa) rules were adjusted to ensure maximum protection against new preferential imports arising from SADC tariff liberalization. In sectors of no interest to South African producers, less-stringent rules were often agreed. The result is high variance and a highly restrictive regime.

A quick and admittedly superficial examination of the rules in the new US FTAs with Chile and Singapore, on the other hand, suggests that, except for textiles and garments, variance in the rules (change of chapter versus change of subheading, etc.) reflects an attempt to remove some of the unnecessary restrictiveness that would result from application of a uniform rule. This appears to be the case at least in sectors that have been particularly contentious in the SADC negotiations. Despite their high variance, a substitution of US-Chile or US-Singapore rules for those in SADC would almost surely reduce the restrictiveness of the SADC regime.

Estevadeordal and Suominen (2003) place the US-Chile and US-Singapore rules in the same category as NAFTA's. This is consistent with US public pronouncements on the new regimes. However, based again on a less than complete examination of all the details, these new FTA's would appear to have less-restrictive rules than NAFTA. The value-content requirements certainly tend to be less in the bilaterals than in NAFTA. However, this is not regarded as important in the Estevadeordal index.

None of this is meant to cast undue aspersion on the Estevadeordal index or its use by Estevadeordal and Suominen. Indeed the information provided in this exercise is of enormous value. But any attempt to summarize a complex reality by a few numbers is bound to lose a great deal of the information that went into its construction. An important lesson from SADC is that a great deal of the most interesting information is in the details of the rules and their effects in different sectors. This points to the importance of undertaking work on specific sectors—the case-study approach—and would caution against relying solely on aggregate or average measures of protection.[30]

10.6.2 Political economy and other elements of trade policy

The SADC Rules of Origin are the result primarily of the influence of special interests and a lack of understanding of the economic consequences. We concentrate here on self-interest.

Implementation of the SADC Trade Protocol will lead to the eventual removal of most import tariffs on intra-SADC trade. This has the potential to erode protection of producers in members' domestic markets. It also opens up opportunities for preferential access to regional markets. Rules of Origin can protect against domestic preference erosion by making it impossible, or at least very costly to take advantage of PTA preferences.

---

[30] This finding mirrors the argument of economists that argue for firm-level analysis of effective protection rather than relying on Social Accounting Matrices. Analyses based on average rates of protection will underestimate the level of protection since they smooth out the effects of the tariff peaks. Almost invariably import-substituting activities will produce items with higher than average rates of duty rather than lower than average ones.

They can also be used to keep out unwanted competition in regional markets. As the examples in earlier sections have shown, this is clearly a large part of the story in the negotiation of SADC Rules of Origin.

Rules of Origin work in conjunction with members' MFN tariff structures and possibly with other elements of the trade-policy regime as well. They are more important the greater the levels of tariffs in the PTA and the greater their differences among members, especially on inputs. A Rule of Origin that might otherwise be very restrictive will have little impact in the absence of significant MFN import tariffs.

This has some interesting implications.

It suggests an alternative way of quantifying the restrictiveness of a Rule of Origin—i.e. to estimate the effective protection that producers would face in PTA markets with and without that rule, with the rule's restrictiveness indicated by the increase in effective protection due its imposition. Such estimates are mentioned in a number of the SADC cases discussed earlier.[31] This is analogous to the quantification of the tariff or subsidy equivalents of other non-tariff trade barriers. This would dispense with the need for arbitrary assumptions about the restrictiveness of different types of administrative requirements and would provide a way of examining different effects of similar rules in different sectors.

It also suggests that any attempts to measure the effects of Rules of Origin without reference to the tariff structure and other elements of the trade-policy regime are likely to be very seriously misspecified. This is true in looking at behavior both within and across different PTAs. Estevadeordal and Suominen (2003), for instance, report on an examination of the effects of Rules of Origin on trade in intermediate goods in the motor industry. The model includes no trade or industrial-policy variables other than Rules of Origin. This is an industry that is known in many places to be riddled not only with complex tax and tariff structures but also long legacies of local-content requirements and other incentives. South Africa's Motor Industry Development Program (MIDP), for instance, has recently replaced a set of cumbersome and costly local-content rules with export-subsidy programs based on the granting of import privileges on vehicles and components in an otherwise heavily protected market.[32] An attempt to explain trade in vehicles and components in South Africa without consideration of these complex incentives would certainly be misspecified.

---

[31] A firm-level survey of effective protection throughout SADC supported this finding. See SADC Economic Impact Assessment Study, TSG, September 30, 2003.

[32] See Flatters (2002c) and Flatters (2003).

Returning to the more general link between Rules of Origin and MFN tariff structures and the case of SADC, there can be little doubt that a major effect of this regime's restrictive Rules of Origin will be to maintain protection and trade patterns that might otherwise be eroded by intra-SADC free trade. While there has been some talk about development of interregional linkages between upstream and downstream industries and especially about using SADC Rules of Origin to promote the development of upstream trade linkages, this is mostly rhetoric hiding some combination of self-interest in and ignorance of the true effects of the rules.

10.6.3 *Harmonization of Rules of Origin*

Estevadeordal and Suominen (2003) use their indices to characterize different Rule-of-Origin regimes around the world. Among their interesting findings is a convergence of many of them towards two main types—the PANEURO and the NAFTA models. There is then a suggestion that this *de facto* convergence might and arguably should be encouraged to be translated into some kind of *de jure* convergence at the global level.

There can be little economic argument against some disciplines on the application of restrictive Rules of Origin in PTAs. However, caution should be exercised in advocating either the PANEURO or the NAFTA type of regime as the model. Use of these models in preferential agreements involving developing countries would be a serious setback to global trade liberalization.

Just as the restrictiveness of similar rules varies across sectors in any country, similar Rule-of-Origin regimes among countries and regions at different economic levels will not have a symmetric impact. This is especially true in key manufacturing sectors in which poorer countries might expect to begin to participate in the global division of labor. As the experiences of Southeast Asia and Mauritius have shown, international fragmentation of production enables poorer countries to participate in particular stages of the process. But requiring them to engage at the same time in stages in which they do not yet have technological capabilities or relative cost advantages would cripple their ability to participate.

On the basis of our investigations, it is apparent that adoption of the PANEURO model as the basis for the Rules of Origin in SADC will doom this PTA to failure. There is circumstantial evidence that imposition of some NAFTA-type rules in AGOA and of PANEURO rules in economic partnership agreements (EPAs) that are now under negotiation between the EU and ACP countries are having or will have similar effects.[33]

If Estevadeordal and Suominen (2003) are correct about the current convergence towards the PANEURO and NAFTA models, the correct focus of attention should be radical reform of Rules-of-Origin regimes, and not on harmonization. It is necessary to get back to basics, to consider the effects of alternative Rules of Origin in light of their only necessary function and to discard their use for protection and other distorting and counterproductive uses. Failure to do so will doom regionalism to the fate of its greatest critics.

Policy researchers could help by building on the information assembled by Estevadeordal and Suominen and others, not just by running global or regional regressions on questionable data and crude indices, but also by examining and documenting how Rules of Origin actually work. Discussions are now underway in various policy fora; investments in research of this type might have a high rate of return.

10.7 Conclusion

Rules of Origin are necessary in preferential trading arrangements. However, they are needed for only one reason, to authenticate that the goods claiming preferences are the product of significant economic activity in a participating member state. The originally agreed rules in the SADC Trade Protocol would have achieved this purpose without imposing any significant unintended distortions on private production or investment decisions.

Before the Trade Protocol was implemented, however, the rules were tightened. The stated goal was to use Rules of Origin to encourage the development of linkages between upstream and downstream industries. This strategy, however, is based, at least implicitly, on a development model that is contrary to evidence from recent experience in Asia and Africa and that has failed in many places.

Global commerce is characterized by large volumes of trade in middle products. This facilitates 'fragmented' production to take advantage of differences in economic circumstances across locations. To interfere in this process through local-content regulations or restrictive Rules of Origin is a dangerous form of protectionism. It raises the costs of participating

---

[33] See Brenton (2003) and Mattoo *et al.* (2002).

in the global production and trading system. It is an invitation for investors to go elsewhere.

The idea of developing clusters of linked industries and activities through Rules of Origin has a superficially appealing plausibility. Accepting these arguments without question is encouraged by vocal stakeholders with a vested interest in the protection the rules provide. And it is further reinforced by the appeal to existing models, especially those provided by the EU in a variety of trade arrangements with developing countries.

To impose restrictive Rules of Origin in a large and technologically sophisticated market such as the EU is one thing. However, the entire SADC market is smaller than Turkey and its industrial structure is still thin and undiversified. To burden SADC producers with the constraints of such rules in this market is not a sensible development strategy. The best it can do is to make SADC irrelevant as a tool for increasing the participation of its members in world markets.[34]

The tendency to expand the scope of Rules of Origin beyond their simple task of authentication is one of the major flaws of regionalism and other types of preferential trading arrangements as approaches to global trade and investment liberalization.

References

Brenton, P. (2003) 'The Value of Trade Preferences: The Economic Impact of Everything But Arms' Washington DC: The World Bank *mimeo*.

Erasmus, H., F. Flatters (2003) 'Rent-Seeking in Regional Trade Liberalization: Rules of Origin and Other Barriers to Trade in Wheat and Wheat Products' http://qed.econ.queensu.ca/faculty/flatters/main/writings.html.

Estevadeordal, A. (2000) 'Negotiating Preferential Market Access: The Case of the North American Free Trade Agreement' *Journal of World Trade* 34, 1 February.

Estevadeordal, A., K. Suominen (2003) 'Rules of Origin: A World Map and Trade Effects' paper prepared for the workshop 'The Origin of Goods: A Conceptual and Empirical Assessment of Rules of Origin in PTAs' INRA-DELTA, Paris, May.

Flatters, F. (2001) 'The SADC Trade Protocol: Impacts, Issues and the Way Ahead' http://qed.econ.queensu.ca/faculty/flatters/main/writings.html.

Flatters, F. (2002a) 'Rules of Origin and AGOA: Hard Choices for Textiles and Clothing in SADC' http://qed.econ.queensu.ca/faculty/flatters/main/writings.html.

Flatters, F. (2002b) 'SADC Rules of Origin: Undermining Regional Free Trade' http://qed.econ.queensu.ca/faculty/flatters/main/writings.html.

---

[34] See Flatters (2001) for further discussion.

Flatters, F. (2002c) 'From Import Substitution to Export Promotion: Driving the South African Motor Industry' http://qed.econ.queensu.ca/faculty/flatters/main/writings.html.

Flatters, F. (2003) 'Is the MIDP a Model for Selective Industrial Policies?' http://qed.econ.queensu.ca/faculty/flatters/main/writings.html.

Jones, R. W., H. Kierzkowski (1990) 'The Role of Services in Production and International Trade: A Theoretical Framework' in R.W. Jones and A. Krueger (ed.) 1990 *The Political Economy of International Trade* Oxford: Basil Blackwell.

Jones, R. W., H. Kierzkowski (2001a) 'Globalization and the Consequences of International Fragmentation' in R. Dornbusch, G. Calvo, and M. Obstfeld (ed.) *Money, Factor Mobility and Trade: The Festschrift in Honor of Robert A. Mundell* Cambridge MA: MIT Press.

Jones, R. W., H. Kierzkowski (2001b) 'A Framework for Fragmentation' in S. Arndt and H. Kierzkowski *Fragmentation: New Production Patterns in the World Economy* Oxford: Oxford University Press.

Jones, R. W., H. Kierzkowski (2001c) 'Horizontal Effects of Vertical Fragmentation' chap.3 in L. K. Cheng and H. Kierzkowski (2001) *Global Production and Trade in East Asia* Norwell MA: Kluwer Academic Publishers.

Mattoo, A., D. Roy, A. Subramanian (2002) 'The Africa Growth and Opportunities Act and its Rules of Origin: Generosity Undermined?' IMF Working Paper WP/02/158.

Meade, J. E. (1964) *Efficiency, Equality and the Ownership of Property* London: G. Allen and Unwin.

Moran, T. H. (2001) *Parental Supervision: The New Paradigm for Foreign Direct Investment and Development* Policy Analyses in International Economics 64, Washington DC: Institute for International Economics.

Sanyal, K. K., R. W. Jones (1982) 'The Theory of Trade in Middle Products' *American Economic Review* 72, 16–31.

TSG, SADC Economic Impact Assessment Study, September 30, 2003, prepared under USAID project PCE—I–98–00017–00 TO823.

11

Trade preferences for Africa and the impact of Rules of Origin

Paul Brenton and Takako Ikezuki[1]

11.1 Introduction

Industrial countries offer developing countries preferential access to their markets through lower duties. The rationale for granting these preferences is that improving the ability of developing countries to participate fully in world markets can accelerate development and poverty reduction. In practice, however, many developing countries, particularly least-developed countries (LDCs), have remained marginalized in world trade. For example, the share of sub-Saharan African countries in US imports of agricultural products fell from 4.3 per cent in 1982 to 2.5 per cent in 2002. Similarly, the share of the African, Caribbean, and Pacific countries in total EU agricultural imports fell from 11.7 per cent in 1982 to 7.8 per cent in 2002. And the share of low-income countries in Japanese imports fell from 1.2 per cent to 0.5 per cent over the same period.

The inability of many developing countries to effectively participate in world markets primarily reflects severe constraints on domestic supply, macroeconomic instability and often very hostile business environments. In addition, trade preferences appear to have had little impact for most developing countries. The direct impact on countries whose exports are dominated by primary products has been limited since these products are subject to zero duties in industrial countries, and therefore no trade preference can be given. The key issue for these countries is export diversification and, in most cases, preferences seem to have done little to

[1] The views expressed here are those of the authors and should not in any way be attributed to the World Bank.

facilitate such structural change. However, the design of trade-preference schemes has limited the role they can play in fostering the export of a wider range of products based upon inherent comparative advantages in labor-intensive products and processes. First, agricultural and manufactured products with high duties are typically excluded from preferences or the preference margin is very small.[2] Secondly, when sensitive high-duty products are covered they are typically subject to restrictive Rules of Origin. These factors have severely limited the role of trade preferences in encouraging export diversification in developing countries. Many countries remain dependent on the export of staple products, for which world prices have fluctuated wildly.

In practice, only a proportion of the exports from developing countries that are eligible for preferential access to the EU, US and Japan actually request zero or reduced duties. But why would exports at the overseas border not request the preferences that are available? The main reason why financial incentives such as trade preferences are not fully utilized, that is, why traders forego a transfer of money that is available to them, is that there must be some accompanying costs that outweigh the benefits. The main cost factor relating to trade preferences are the Rules of Origin. It is important to recognize that the recorded utilization rates do not capture situations where the Rules of Origin are prohibitive, in that they prevent any preferential exports and there are no exports at the full duty. In other words, there may be cases where the beneficiaries can only export with preferences but the Rules of Origin constrain any take up of those preferences. In this sense the utilization rates understate the constraining impact of the Rules of Origin.

This chapter briefly describes the trade preference schemes provided by the EU, US and Japan and then concentrates on their impact on sub-Saharan African developing countries, which, as a group, are the countries most marginalized in world trade. We then present information on the utilization of these preferences and discuss why Rules of Origin may constrain their take-up. Unlike previous studies, which have concentrated on the overall level of utilization of available preferences[3], we highlight the variation in the rate of utilization of preferences across beneficiaries and across the three developed-country preferential schemes.

---

[2] As we shall discuss below, for a small number of products, however, preference margins are substantial, though usually within strict quantitative limits and only for certain countries. Countries that have been granted preferential access for sugar and tobacco, for example, have received large transfers due to preferences.

[3] For example, Inama (2002).

11.2 The preference schemes of the US, EU and Japan

US preferences under the GSP and AGOA: The US has offered preferences under the GSP since the mid-1970s with a significant increase in coverage for LDCs taking place in 1997. The current GSP program expires at the end of 2006. In 2003, 143 developing countries were eligible for preferences under the GSP. The preferential rate on all included products is zero. There are no partial preferences. However, these preferences can be withdrawn at any time. In addition, the GSP contains certain safeguards in the form of ceilings of GSP benefits for each product and country, known as competitive need limitations, although these do not apply to LDCs. A country's GSP eligibility for a product is automatically removed if that country provides more than 50 per cent of US imports of that product or a certain dollar value is exceeded.[4]

Table 11.1 shows that the GSP provides preferences on 3635 products (defined at the level of the tariff line), which amounts to 35 per cent of the total number of products in the US tariff schedule and 51 per cent of the total number of dutiable products. Sensitive products, such as dairy products, meats, sugar, many processed foods, textiles and clothing are excluded from the GSP. LDCs receive preferences on an additional 1626 products under the GSP so that 73 per cent of dutiable products are eligible for preferential access to the US.

AGOA, introduced in 2000 and recently extended until 2015, offers potential improved market access to 48 sub-Saharan African countries subject to certain criteria regarding basic human rights and the rule of law. At present 38 of these countries have been granted eligibility for AGOA preferences. The competitive needs limitations of the GSP do not apply to AGOA preferences. However, most of the products covered by AGOA had already been liberalized for the LDCs under the GSP. AGOA makes available preferences on 225 additional products for the LDCs but on an additional 1790 products for non-LDCs.

The key further feature of AGOA is the inclusion of clothing products. Access to preferences on clothing products is not automatic, countries must apply for these benefits that are conditional on the satisfaction of certain criteria regarding measures to prevent illegal trans-shipment including an effective visa system for clothing products. In 2004, 25 countries had requested and been granted eligibility for clothing preferences. AGOA grants duty-free preferences to clothing products.

---

[4] For a more comprehensive description of US preferences for agricultural products see Wainio and Gibson (2003).

Table 11.1 US preferences under the GSP and AGOA—the number of tariff lines liberalized

	Non-LDCs	LDCs
Total tariff lines	10 383	10 383
Total GSP	3635	5261
GSP LDC but not AGOA	. . .	61
AGOA	1 790	225
AGOA clothing	557	557
Duty-free lines	3 213	3 213
Lines excluded from GSP	3 535	1 909
Lines excluded from AGOA (with clothing)	1188	1127

We treat tariff lines for out of quota quantities of products subject to tariff quotas as excluded from preferences–see Brenton and Ikezuki (2004a) for a more detailed discussion.

Although as we shall discuss below there are specific rules governing the granting of preferences for clothing that determine the ability of countries to exploit these preferences.

EU preferences under the GSP and Cotonou Agreement: Under the recent GSP scheme of the EU, which ran until the end of December 2004, there are two categories of products covered by the scheme: non-sensitive, for which duties are suspended, and sensitive. A number of products, including meats, dairy products, certain vegetables, cereals, some prepared foodstuffs and wine are excluded from the scheme. For the sensitive products there is a flat-rate reduction of 3.5 percentage points from the MFN rate. This entails high proportionate reductions for most industrial products, for which the average EU MFN tariff is around 4 per cent, but relatively low proportionate reductions for many agricultural products where the average MFN duty is much higher, being at least 20 per cent. However, the EU tariff structure for agricultural products is incredibly complicated with more than 45 per cent of agricultural product lines subject to non-*ad valorem* duties. This in turn is reflected in the convoluted nature of preferences granted.

Specific duties, those in which the duty is related to physical rather than monetary values, are reduced by 30 per cent. However, when duties comprise both *ad valorem* and specific components, as is the case for a range of processed agricultural products of interest to developing countries, such as, sugar confectionary, the specific duties are not reduced. Typically, the greatest part of the protection of these products is provided by the specific duties. For a number of products, primarily fruit and vegetables, the EU applies a system of minimum reference prices that vary according to the season, despite the dubious compatibility of such an approach with WTO rules. This can lead to a very complex structure of preferences. When minimum duties are specified in the EU's Common Customs Code, for example, the EU duty on beans is 13.6 per cent subject to a minimum duty of 1.6 euro per 100 kg being paid, these no longer apply for products covered under the GSP.

Within the GSP, the EU discriminated in favor of the least-developed countries. All imports of industrial products and a range of agricultural products from these countries entered the EU duty free. However, a significant number of agricultural products still faced some market-access barriers. These were removed under the EBA initiative, introduced in 2001, which grants duty-free access to imports of all products from the least-developed countries, with the exception of arms and munitions, and without any quantitative restrictions. Liberalization was immediate except for three products, fresh bananas, rice and sugar where tariffs will be gradually reduced to zero (in 2006 for bananas and 2009 for rice and sugar). The effect of the EBA in the short run will be limited since the LDCs were not exporting the products subject to immediate liberalization (see Brenton (2003)).

A key difference between the EBA and other unilateral preferences granted by the EU is that preferences for the least-developed countries are granted for an unlimited period and are not subject to periodic review. As such, it is argued that the EBA should provide exporters and investors with greater certainty of market access to the EU and therefore stimulate greater capacity in the production of existing products and an environment conducive to the export of a wider range of products. However, this may be undermined to an extent by the inclusion of a new reason for the temporary suspension of preferences: 'massive increases in imports of products originating in the LDCs in relation to their usual levels of production and export capacity'. This could act as a constraint upon large-scale investment that transforms production capacities in a particular country and may limit diversification into new products.[5]

The EU offers enhanced preferences beyond those of the GSP to all sub-Saharan African countries and countries in the Caribbean and Pacific (ACP countries) under the Cotonou Agreement. There are individual protocols for bananas, beef, veal and sugar. McQueen (1999) reports that these products accounted for three-quarters of the total value of ACP preferences,

---

[5] This clause was initially discussed in the context of combating fraud, however, this is not made clear in the legislation and it would appear that it could be invoked in more general circumstances.

Table 11.2 EU preferences under the GSP and Cotonou Agreement—the number of tariff lines liberalized

	Non-LDCs	LDCs
Total tariff lines	10 486	10 486
Total GSP	7200	10 461 (EBA)
Cotonou	8 134	8134
Duty-free lines	2 226	2226
Lines excluded from GSP	1060	25 (arms)
Lines excluded from Cotonou	126	126

Note: that under the GSP individual countries are excluded from preferences for particular sectors.

including industrial products all of which are eligible for duty-free access to the EU.

The EU GSP scheme is quite comprehensive in coverage with 69 per cent of the total number of tariff lines, or 87 per cent of the dutiable lines (those for which the MFN tariff is greater than 0), being eligible for preferences (see Table 11.2). However, many of these products are only eligible for partial preferences and a range of sectors are excluded for many countries. The Cotonou Agreement covers close to an additional 1000 tariff lines and enhances preferences on industrial products relative to the GSP. Only 126 products (mainly wine) are entirely excluded from the scheme, but around 800 agricultural products have (often very) limited preferences subject to tariff quotas.

The Japanese GSP scheme: Trade preferences under the GSP of Japan are offered to 164 developing countries. The current scheme expires in 2011. There are enhanced preferences for LDCs, with partial preferences deepened to 100 per cent cuts and, from April 2003, greater product coverage. Data for this exercise are only available for 2002 and so we are not able to capture this extension of the Japanese scheme. There are no explicit quantitative ceilings on preferences for particular products although there are safeguard mechanisms and a product exported by a country is excluded if imports from that country exceed 25 per cent of total imports and exceed one billion yen in value.

Under the Japanese scheme there are preferences for 36 per cent of the total number of tariff lines or 56 per cent of the number of dutiable lines (Table 11.3). More than 2600 lines are excluded. The enhanced preferences available to LDCs leads to the inclusion of a further 1110 lines, but LDCs still have to pay duties on more than a quarter of the total number of dutiable lines.

Table 11.3 Japanese preferences under the GSP—the number of tariff lines liberalized

	Non-LDCs	LDCs
Total tariff lines	9311	9311
Total GSP	3391	4501
Duty-free lines	3268	3268
Lines excluded from GSP	2652	1542

11.3 The value of preferences offered by the United States, the European Union, and Japan

Table 11.4 presents the calculated value of EU, US and Japanese preferences for African countries. This is derived from the value of exports that actually request preferences multiplied by the preference margin and is the implicit transfer of tariff revenue due to the preference scheme.[6] This is presented in the table as a share of the total value of exports to each market. The economic impact of the preferences offered by the United States, the European Union, and Japan vary enormously across beneficiary countries. For some countries exports are dominated by non-preference-receiving products and there has been little success in diversification. This is especially the case for countries dependent on products that are currently subject to zero import duties in developed countries, such as coffee and cocoa. For other countries, however, all exports are eligible for preferences to a particular market and the potential impact of preferences much greater.

In the EU market there are substantial preferences for Swaziland, Mauritius, Seychelles and Malawi, for whom the value of preferences exceeds 10 per cent of the value of exports. For Swaziland, Mauritius and Malawi these preferences are derived mainly from sugar (see Brenton and Ikezuki (2004b)). For Seychelles the main product receiving preferences is prepared fish. There are then 11 countries for whom the value of preferences lies between 5 and 10 per cent of the value of exports to the EU. For 14 countries the value of preferences is between 1 and 5 per cent of the

---

[6] The extent to which the available rents are actually obtained by suppliers in developing countries depends upon a number of factors including the nature of competition in the industry and the rules and regulations governing the granting of preferential access. If there is little effective competition among buyers/importers of the product then the suppliers/exporters may be unable to acquire much of the price premium. Ozden and Olareaga (2003) find evidence that only one third of the available rents for African exports of clothing to the US under AGOA actually accrue to the exporters. Satisfying the rules governing preferences and proving conformity with those rules raises costs, which reduces the extent to which the preferences raise actual returns.

Table 11.4 The value of preferences and preference utilization for African countries exports to EU, US and Japan

	Value of preferences requested (% of total exports)			Utilization of available preferences		
	EU	US	Japan	EU	US	Japan
Angola	0.19	0.37	0.06	77.07	93.20	100.00
Benin	1.39	0.00	0.00	64.75	*	*
Botswana	2.09	2.98	0.00	95.99	63.10	*
Burkina Faso	5.6	0.07	0.02	93.65	96.20	44.90
Burundi	0.12	0.00	0.00	36.22	*	0.00
Cameroon	4.31	0.24	0.10	84.31	73.10	83.30
Cape Verde	2.79	0.01	0.00	94.45	0.10	0.00
Central Africa Rep.	0	0.53	0.00	35.18	93.40	*
Chad	0.01	0.00	0.00	2.97	0.00	*
Cote d'Ivore	5.97	0.06	0.10	88.70	57.90	71.70
Comoros	3.08	0.01	0.00	57.94	55.50	*
Rep. Congo	1.43	0.19	0.00	87.23	78.90	0.00
Dem. Congo	0.02	0.28	0.10	24.94	96.00	88.60
Djibouti	0.31	0.39	0.00	15.50	69.00	0.00
Eq. Guinea	0.24	0.97	0.00	68.42	95.00	*
Eritrea	2.14	0.18	0.00	45.35	9.40	0.00
Ethiopia	3.13	1.39	0.13	87.18	98.60	76.10
Gabon	0.95	0.31	0.00	92.31	92.70	*
Gambia	5.26	0.16	2.98	87.38	2.00	97.90
Ghana	3.01	0.66	0.00	76.86	93.80	87.30
Guinea	0.62	0.00	0.00	73.40	14.60	0.00
Guinea-Bissau	5.24	0.00	**	98.55	*	**
Kenya	5.16	12.77	0.40	70.13	95.80	82.70
Lesotho	3.68	19.01	1.42	87.24	98.80	12.80
Liberia	0.02	0.00	0.00	77.25	0.00	0.00
Madagascar	8.26	5.97	0.00	90.94	86.30	1.10
Malawi	14.24	9.89	0.64	94.00	83.90	100.00
Mali	0.42	0.70	0.40	66.80	87.50	49.80
Mauritania	3.37	0.09	6.36	97.70	1.80	97.60
Mauritius	21.35	6.59	0.01	96.90	41.60	38.80
Mozambique	6.87	1.76	0.00	92.71	97.50	0.00
Namibia	6.98	0.55	0.30	93.48	25.00	80.00
Niger	0.03	0.13	0.02	35.28	22.00	0.50
Nigeria	0.22	0.38	0.00	71.89	97.40	0.00
Rwanda	0.33	0.01	0.00	66.14	18.00	*
Sao Tome and Principe	1.03	0.00	**	53.13	0.00	**
Senegal	8.47	0.25	4.36	94.97	38.80	78.10
Seychelles	16.84	0.00	0.00	89.84	5.00	0.00
Sierra Leone	1.13	0.23	0.00	71.51	20.40	100.00
Somalia	0.31	0.00	**	17.72	0.00	**
South Africa	FTA	1.27	0.08	FTA	74.00	34.30
Sudan	2.35	No GSP	0.00	88.18	No GSP	96.80
Swaziland	39.67	12.72	0.00	88.51	84.30	0.00
Tanzania	5.34	0.38	0.11	84.46	42.70	99.90
Togo	2.59	0.08	0.02	85.54	97.70	1.70
Uganda	3.53	0.01	0.00	79.53	7.60	0.00
Zambia	5.33	0.06	1.02	37.06	50.30	60.60
Zimbabwe	7.12	2.12	0.60	84.36	98.75	42.40

* signifies that no exports are eligible for preferences
** signifies no export

value of exports whilst for 16 countries preferences account for less than 1 per cent of the value of exports to the EU.

In the US preferences under AGOA and the GSP lead to substantial transfers, equivalent to more than 10 per cent of exports to the US, for three countries: Lesotho, Kenya and Swaziland. These preferences are almost entirely due to exports of clothing (see Brenton and Ikezuki (2004a)). There are 3 countries for whom the value of preferences amounts to between 5 and 10 per cent of the value of exports, for a further 3 countries preferences account for between 1 and 5 per cent of exports. For 37 countries the value of preferences amounts to less than 1 per cent of the value of exports to the US.

Japanese preferences lead to a transfer in excess of 5 per cent of the value of exports, for only one country, Mauritania. There are 7 countries for whom the transfer amounts to between 1 and 5 per cent of the value of exports to Japan. For the remaining 40 countries the value of preferences is less than 1 per cent of the value of exports. The key product generating preferences in Japan is fish.

Hence, for the majority of countries in Africa, the value of preferences requested in the EU, US and Japan are very small fractions of the value of exports. This entails that for these countries the impact of trade preferences will be very limited. Nevertheless, for a small number of countries the preferences requested are substantial in relation to the value of exports. These are driven mainly by sugar in the EU, clothing in the US and fish in Japan.

11.4 Utilization rates vary across beneficiaries and across preference-giving markets

We can observe from Table 11.4 that there is a high degree of variation in the utilization of available preferences across the beneficiaries of a given trade-preference scheme. It is important to stress that the rate of utilization of preferences that we discuss measures the proportion of exports from developing countries to the EU, US and Japan that are recorded *at the border* as requesting preferences. In previous studies it is the value of exports requesting preferences divided by the value of exports eligible for preferences that is presented. However, this does not take into account that the value of preferences (determined by the difference between the applied MFN duty and the preferential tariff) varies by product and that it is important to take into account that utilization rates may be lowest exactly where preferences are greatest if Rules of Origin are stricter for sensitive products. Hence, here we calculate the utilization rate as the value of preferences requested divided by the total available transfer.[7]

We also do not capture situations where the Rules of Origin are prohibitive, in that they prevent any preferential exports, and there are no exports at the full duty. In other words, they may be cases where the beneficiaries can only export with preferences but the Rules of Origin constrain any take up of those preferences. Also, it is important that the under-utilization of preferences that we measure, the fact that some exports do not request and therefore are not granted the preferential access to which they are in principle eligible, cannot reflect the inability of the recipients to meet other requirements to access the relevant market, such as health and safety or sanitary requirements or deficiencies in their infrastructure, as is sometimes suggested. These factors cannot explain why at the border some products that are eligible for preferences do not request those preferences.

The second set of columns in Table 11.4 show the utilization rates for African beneficiaries of the preference schemes of the US, EU and Japan. The figures clearly show that some countries are utilizing a much higher proportion of the preferences available to them in each of these markets. For example, Madagascar and Ivory Coast export similar amounts of products that are eligible for preferences in the US market (about $95 million in 2002) yet whilst 86 per cent of the value of preferences available to Madagascan exporters are taken up only 58 per cent of the amount available to exports from the Ivory Coast are requested. Lesotho, on the other hand is utilizing 99 per cent of the preferences that are available on products exported to the US. Similarly, 96 per cent of the value of preferences available to Botswana in the EU are requested, whilst Zambia utilizes only 53 per cent of the available preferences in this market. In Japan, utilization rates vary across countries from 0 to 100 per cent.

It is also interesting to note that *utilization rates for a given beneficiary vary across the preference giving markets*. For example, Ethiopian exporters request 92 per cent of the preferences to which they are eligible in the US, 74 per cent of the available preferences in Japan but only 46 per cent of the available preferences in the EU are requested. Mauritius utilizes 91 per cent of the available preferences in the EU, 58 per cent of those available in Japan and 43 per cent of those in the US. Overall there is a very low

---

[7] Hence, we calculate at the tariff-line level the value of exports requesting preferences multiplied by the preference margin and the value of exports eligible for preferences multiplied by this margin.

degree of correlation between the series of utilization rates for these three markets.[8]

11.5 Rules of Origin and trade preferences

Rules of Origin are essential to ensure that preferences are granted only to exporters from countries that are eligible beneficiaries. However, the nature of the Rules of Origin are a key element determining the extent to which countries are able to utilize the preferences that are available to them. When a product is produced in a single stage or is wholly obtained in one country the origin of the product is relatively easy to establish. This applies mainly to 'natural products' and goods made entirely from them and hence products that do not contain imported parts or materials. Primary agricultural products typically fall into this category. Proof that the product was produced or obtained in the preferential trade partner is normally sufficient. If, however, obtaining the certificate of conformity with the Rules of Origin incurs significant costs, then the value of the preferences granted will be reduced.

For processed manufactured products the Rules of Origin stipulate the amount of processing or the nature of the domestic processing that must take place to ensure a substantial transformation has taken place and to confer origin. Under the US GSP scheme there is a value-added requirement of 35 per cent that is common across all products. The US scheme also allows for cumulation between selected countries, whereby value added in those countries can be counted towards the overall value-added requirement for the product exported to the US. Under AGOA the basic rule of origin is the same as under the GSP although cumulation can take place amongst all the sub-Saharan beneficiaries. However, there are specific Rules of Origin for clothing.

Three categories of products are defined in terms of the Rules of Origin:

- Products assembled from fabrics and yarns formed and cut in the United States.
- Products assembled from fabrics formed in one or more of the AGOA beneficiaries from US or regional yarns, subject to quantitative limits.
- Products assembled in LDCs from any fabric or yarn. This provision, recently extended, expires at the end of September 2007.

---

[8] The simple correlation coefficients are Japan-EU: –0.16, EU-US: 0.03, Japan-US: –0.01.

The first rule is extremely restrictive. Clothing assembled from non-US fabrics (categories 2 and 3 above) is subject to quantitative restrictions that are related to the overall level of US imports of clothing. Within this there is a sublimit on imports under the special rule of origin that allows for global sourcing of fabrics (category 3 above). For the year October 2002 to end of September 2003 the overall quota was 36 per cent filled. Within this the limit on products subject to liberal Rules of Origin was 62 per cent utilized. Whilst the quota on products assembled from regional fabric was less than 10 per cent filled. This reflects in large part the differences in the restrictiveness of the Rules of Origin.

It is important to note that access to preferences on clothing products is not automatic for AGOA beneficiaries. Countries must apply for these benefits and there are requirements regarding measures to prevent illegal trans-shipment including an effective visa system for clothing products. These requirements are unlikely to be a barrier to the granting of clothing preferences in many countries and technical assistance in meeting the requirements is available. What is important is that the US sought to deal with the issue of illegal trans-shipment through the visa system and co-operation between customs authorities, including regular monitoring of customs data. This contrasts to arguments that have been made elsewhere that strict Rules of Origin are necessary to deal with such illegal activities. This is a misinterpretation of the role of the Rules of Origin. Illegal activity may take place whatever the nature of the Rules of Origin and procedures need to be put in place to identify and prevent such activity. The Rules of Origin should be set only with regard to legal activity and define the amount of processing that is required to assign country of origin to a product.

EU Rules of Origin are product specific and sometimes complex. Some products require change of tariff heading, others a value-added requirement, whilst others are subject to a specific manufacturing-process requirement. In some cases these methods are combined. For certain industrial products alternative methods of conferring origin are specified, for example, change of tariff heading or satisfaction of a value-added requirement. This is clearly more flexible but such an approach is not available for any agricultural products.

For many products, the EU rules require change of chapter, which is more restrictive than change of heading. In certain cases the EU rules provide for a negative application of the change of tariff classification by proscribing the use of certain imported inputs. For example, the rule of origin for bread, pastry, cakes, biscuits, etc., requires change of tariff heading except any heading in Chapter 11 (products of the milling industry). Hence, the production of bakery products cannot use imported flour, which is very restrictive for countries that do not have a competitive milling industry. All products that include sugar have to demonstrate that the value of any imported sugar does not exceed a certain proportion of the price of the product. EU Rules of Origin for clothing are restrictive since they require production from yarn. This entails that a double-transformation process must take place in the beneficiary with the yarn being woven into fabric and then the fabric cut and made-up into clothing. Countries cannot import fabrics and make them up into clothing and receive preferential access, which constrains the value of the scheme for countries that do not have an efficient textile industry.

Whilst the EU has sought to harmonize the specific processing requirements for each product a number of the general rules vary substantially across different schemes particularly with regard to the nature and extent of cumulation and the tolerance rule. In this regard there are important differences between the Rules of Origin for the EBA and the GSP and those of the Cotonou Agreement. For example, under the Cotonou Agreement there is full cumulation. Under the GSP there is more limited partial or diagonal cumulation that can only take place within four regional groupings: ASEAN, CACM, the Andean Community and SAARC but not amongst ACP countries. Hence LDC members of the ACP who are eligible to export to the EU under the EBA may, and often do,[9] prefer to continue exporting under Cotonou, in part, due to the more liberal Rules of Origin under the latter.

The Rules of Origin for the Japanese GSP specify a basic requirement of change of tariff heading to demonstrate that a substantial transformation has taken place, although there is a list of products for which specific criteria are defined. Thus, for example, flour or similar products cannot be produced from imported cereals. The rule for clothing is particularly restrictive, requiring manufacture from fibers and hence a triple-transformation process of spinning, weaving and then making up into final clothing must all take place within the beneficiary. The Japanese scheme allows cumulation amongst a limited group of South-East Asian countries (Indonesia, Malaysia, Philippines, Thailand and Vietnam).

Strict Rules of Origin, such as those for clothing requiring a double or triple transformation, are viewed by some as a mechanism for encouraging the development of integrated production structures within

---

[9] See Brenton (2003) for more details.

developing countries to maximize the impact on employment and to ensure that it is not just low value-added activities that are undertaken in the developing countries. There are problems with this view. First, such rules discriminate against small countries where the possibilities for local sourcing are limited or non-existent. Since most developing countries are small countries they are particularly disadvantaged by restrictive Rules of Origin relative to larger countries. Secondly, there is no evidence that strict Rules of Origin over the past 30 years have done anything to stimulate the development of integrated production structures in developing countries. In fact, such arguments have become redundant in the light of technological changes and global trade liberalization that have led to the fragmentation of production processes and the development of global networks of sourcing. Globalization and the splitting up of the production chain does not allow the luxury of being able to establish integrated production structures within countries. Strict Rules of Origin act to constrain the ability of firms to integrate into these global and regional production networks and in effect act to dampen the location of any value-added activities. In the modern world economy flexibility in the sourcing of inputs is a key element in international competitiveness.[10]

11.6 Utilization rates and the costs of satisfying Rules of Origin

The nature of the Rules of Origin are a key determinant of the ability of firms in beneficiary countries to take advantage of trade preferences. Recent experience of the clothing sector under AGOA provides an example of the impact of Rules of Origin. AGOA has had a profound impact on the exports of a small group of sub-Saharan African countries, almost entirely as a result of the provisions regarding clothing. All of the countries that have been able to substantially increase exports of clothing to the US have been eligible for the liberal rule of origin and to source fabrics globally. All exports of clothing products from countries eligible for the liberal rule of origin have received preferential access to the US. Mauritius and South Africa are the only two countries that are eligible for clothing preferences but that have not been granted liberal Rules of Origin. In 2002, 90 per cent of exports from Mauritius to the US were clothing

---

[10] Flatters (2002) and Flatters and Kirk (2003) highlight these points in the case of SADC. They show that the adoption of restrictive Rules of Origin is more likely to constrain than to stimulate regional economic development.

products, yet only 41 per cent of the available preferences for these products were taken up. Clothing only accounts for about 4 per cent of South African exports to the US, although the absolute amount is similar to that exported by Mauritius. In 2002, only 47 per cent of the available preferences for South African clothing products were actually utilized. In other words, for more than half of the clothing exports of Mauritius and South Africa to the US the traders preferred to pay the full MFN duty than to satisfy the requirements of the rule of origin. Presumably the costs of satisfying these requirements exceeded the value of the tariff preferences. The issue with the more restrictive Rules of Origin is not just the constraints that these rules impose on the sourcing of inputs, forcing producers to use higher-cost fabrics and materials, but also the costs and difficulties in proving conformity with these rules compared to the more liberal rules where fabrics can be globally sourced.

Anson *et al.* (2003) and Carrere and de Melo (2004) develop the idea that utilization rates reveal information concerning the upper and lower bounds of the cost of obtaining preferential access. The margin of preference for products with a utilization rate of 100 per cent provides an upper bound for these costs. On the other hand, the margin of preference for products with zero utilization of preferences provides a lower bound on the costs associated with obtaining those preferences. These authors then proceed to argue that for products with utilization rates between 0 and 100 per cent, if compliance costs are homogeneous across exporters then exporters would be revealed indifferent between exporting under preferences and paying the full MFN tariff. In this case, the rate of tariff preferences is revealed as being equal to the costs of compliance. Carrere and de Melo (2004) find that this approximation of compliance costs in the case of Mexican exports under NAFTA is around 6.1 per cent.

A feature of the NAFTA agreement is the high degree of variation in the Rules of Origin across product categories. This is reflected in the specification of the rules comprising more than 200 pages! Different rules are specified for different products: sometimes the rule may be a change of tariff heading, sometimes a change of tariff chapter, for other products there will be a value-added requirement, elsewhere the Rules of Origin may specify a particular technical process. The amount of value added required can vary across products. The change of tariff classification can be used to provide a positive test of origin, by stating the tariff classification of imported inputs that can be used in the production of the exported good but also can be defined to provide a (more restrictive) negative test by stating cases where change of tariff classification will not confer origin.

For example, in NAFTA, the rule of origin for Tomato Ketchup, which is defined at the subheading or 6-digit level of the HS, states that a change to Ketchup (HS 210320) from imported inputs of any chapter will confer origin except subheading 200290 (Tomato Paste). In other words any Ketchup made from imported fresh tomatoes will confer origin but Ketchup made from tomato paste imported from outside of the area will not qualify for preferential treatment even though the basic change of tariff classification requirement has been satisfied.[11] The outcome of highly detailed product-specific Rules of Origin is a complex set of rules the restrictiveness of which varies across products. Box 1 provides an example of the sort of complexity that can arise.

Anson *et al.* (2004) and Carrere and de Melo (2004) exploit this variation in the Rules of Origin across products under the NAFTA to separate out the administrative costs of complying with Rules of Origin from the pure distortionary element. They exploit an index of the restrictiveness of the Rules of Origin developed by Estevadeordal (2000) that takes change of tariff heading to be the least restrictive. They then compute the margin of preferences for products with high rates of utilization and a change of tariff-heading requirement and conclude that administrative costs of satisfying Rules of Origin are in the region of 1.8 per cent. This in turn implies that the distortionary element is substantially higher at around 4.3 per cent. Carrere and de Melo (2004) conclude that for the NAFTA, other things being equal, compliance costs are lower for a change of tariff-heading rule, followed by a value-added rule with a specific technical process requirement having the highest compliance costs. They also find that a value-added requirement is more costly to satisfy in final-goods sectors than in intermediate-goods sectors.

As noted above, the Rules of Origin of the EU preference schemes are product specific and, like the NAFTA, different rules are often set for different products, value-added requirements for certain products, change of tariff classification for other and sometimes specific technical requirements are defined. However, the US GSP and AGOA schemes and the Japanese GSP scheme define rules of origin that are common across products. The Japanese scheme defines the basic rule as change of tariff heading, although a large number of product-specific exceptions to

---

[11] The apparent reason for this rule in the NAFTA is to protect producers of tomato paste in Mexico from competition from producers in Chile. See Palmeter D., (1997), 'Rules of Origin in Regional Trade Agreements,' in Demaret, P., J. F. Bellis and G. Garcia Jimenez (ed.), 'Regionalism and Multilateralism after the Uruguay Round: Convergence, Divergence, and Interaction', European Interuniversity Press, Brussels.

1. RESTRICTIVE RULES OF ORIGIN UNDER NAFTA: THE CASE OF CLOTHING

The following example is for men's or boys' overcoats made of wool (HS620111)

A change to subheading 620111 from any other chapter, except from heading 5106 through 5113, 5204 through 5212, 5307 through 5308 or 5310 through 5311, Chapter 54 or heading 5508 through 5516, 5801 through 5802 or 6001 through 6006, provided that:

The good is both cut and sewn or otherwise assembled in the territory of one or more of the Parties.

The basic rule of origin stipulates change of chapter but then provides a list of headings and chapters from which inputs cannot be used. Thus in effect the over-coat must be manufactured from the stage of wool fibers forward since imported woollen yarn (HS5106–5110) or imported woollen fabric (HS5111–5113) can be used. However, the rule also states that imported cotton thread (HS5204) or imported thread of manmade fibers (HS54) can be used to sew the coat together. This rule in itself is very restrictive, however, the rule for this product is further complicated by requirements relating to the visible lining:

Except for fabrics classified in 54082210, 54082311, 54082321, and 54082410, the fabrics identified in the following sub-headings and headings, when used as visible lining material in certain men's and women's suits, suit-type jackets, skirts, overcoats, car coats, anoraks, windbreakers, and similar articles, must be formed from yarn and fin-ished in the territory of a party: 5111 through 5112, 520831 through 520859, 520931 through 520959, 521031 through 521059, 521131 through 521159, 521213 through 521215, 521223 through 521225, 540742 through 540744, 540752 through 540754, 540761, 540772 through 540774, 540782 through 540784, 540792 through 540794, 540822 through 540824 (excluding tariff item 540822aa, 540823aa or 540824aa), 540832 through 540834, 551219, 551229, 551299, 551321 through 551349, 551421 through 551599, 551612 through 551614, 551622 through 551624, 551632 through 551634, 551642 through 551644, 551692 through 551694, 600110, 600192, 600531 through 600544 or 600610 through 600644,

This stipulates that the visible lining used must be produced from yarn and finished in either party. This rule may well have been introduced to constrain the impact of the tolerance rule that would normally allow 7 per cent of the weight of the article to be of non-originating materials. In overcoats and suits the lining is probably less than 7 per cent of the total weight. Finally, it is interesting to note that the Rules of Origin also provide a number of very specific exemptions to the Rules of Origin for materials that are in short supply or not produced in the US and reflects firm-specific lobbying to overcome the restrictiveness of these Rules of Origin when the original NAFTA Rules of Origin were defined. The most specific example is where apparel is deemed to be originating if assembled from imported inputs of

Fabrics of subheading 511111 or 511119, if hand-woven, with a loom width of less than 76 cm, woven in the United Kingdom in accordance with the rules and regulations of the Harris Tweed Association, Ltd., and so certified by the Association.

Table 11.5 The average costs of complying with requirements to obtain preferential access (2002)

	Ad valorem equivalent of compliance costs (%)
US	6.7
EU	8.4
Japan	5.6

this rule are also defined, whilst the US schemes are based on a common value-added rule.

Table 11.5 shows the computed average *ad valorem* equivalent compliance costs for the preference schemes of the 3 countries across the limited but common sample of beneficiaries used in this exercise. This is the average margin of preference for those products for which the utilization rate lies between zero and 100 per cent. Interestingly, the average compliance cost of 5.6 per cent is lowest for the Japanese scheme that appears to have the least restrictive general requirements—change of tariff heading. The US scheme that has a common rule across products but that specifies a more demanding value-added requirement has average compliance costs that are a little higher at 6.7 per cent.[12] Finally, the EU scheme, which has product-specific Rules of Origin reveals an average compliance cost of over 8 per cent.

However, these values also reflect that the EU scheme covers a much wider range of products. The Japanese scheme excludes many sensitive high-duty products. What the table suggests is that when countries include sensitive products that have higher MFN duties they are typically accompanied by more restrictive Rules of Origin. This is consistent with Estevadeordal (2000) who finds a strong and statistically significant correlation between the MFN tariff differential under NAFTA and a measure of the stringency of the Rules of Origin. However, the recent experience under AGOA shows that when developing countries are offered preferences on labour-intensive sensitive products with simple Rules of Origin there can be a significant supply response. The challenge for these countries is to capitalize on these short-run benefits to ensure that the

---

[12] The value-added rule is generally more demanding, particularly for developing countries, since countries experiencing exchange-rate fluctuations will find that the value of non-qualifying materials will change. Land-locked countries may incur greater costs due to the requirement of direct transportation in all preference schemes. The costs of compliance will also vary according to the availability of competitive local inputs, and if the country is part of a region of cumulation, the availability of competitive inputs from regional partners.

local industry develops quickly to be able to effectively compete on world markets as preferences are eroded.

11.7 Conclusions

The impact of trade preferences on the majority of sub-Saharan African countries is very weak. Many of these countries are exporting products for which no preferences can be given since MFN duties have already been reduced to zero. Where preferences are available they are not always fully utilized. The rates of utilization vary across beneficiaries of a particular scheme and across schemes for a particular beneficiary. This implies that the impact of preference erosion following multilateral negotiations to reduce MFN tariffs will fall more heavily on some countries (those with higher utilization rates) than on others. Thus, it is important to take into account differences in utilization rates in modelling exercises of the impact of global tariff reductions. Preference-receiving countries with low utilization rates stand to gain from multilateral tariff reductions.

Obtaining preferences requires that costs are incurred in complying with the stipulated Rules of Origin. These costs imply that the impact of preference erosion is not continuous. Once the margin of preference falls below the cost of compliance, preferences will no longer be utilized. Hence, models of the impact of multilateral tariff reductions in the presence of trade preferences should seek to capture the endogeneity of the rate of utilization of preferences. Such models could also usefully show how policy initiatives aimed at reducing the costs of complying with Rules of Origin as MFN tariffs decline would mitigate some of the adverse impacts from preference erosion, if they occur.

Finally, compliance costs for a given rule of origin may vary across beneficiaries. Hence the ability of different beneficiary countries to exploit a given preference will differ. This clearly argues for developing countries to be provided with greater flexibility in satisfying the requirements to demonstrate that sufficient processing has been undertaken to justify preferential access. Thus, Rules of Origin that provide for alternative methods for satisfying sufficient processing are more likely to lead to higher rates of utilization of available preferences. For example, a scheme that stipulates general rules, common across products, of a value-added requirement *or* a change of tariff heading, is more likely to promote trade with the beneficiaries. Preferences schemes would be enhanced if all countries were to adopt the same simple and easy-to-apply rules. This would then entail that a producer in a least-developed country could make production and investment decisions on the basis of equal and predictable access to all industrial markets.

References

Anson, J., O. Cadot, A. Estevadeordal, J. de Melo, A. Suwa-Eisenmann, B. Tumurchudur (2003) 'Assessing the Costs of RoO in North-South PTAs with an Application to NAFTA', Discusión Paper2476, CEPR, London.

Brenton, P. (2003) 'Integrating the Least Developed Economies into the World Trading System: The Current Impact of EU Preferences under Everything but Arms', *Journal of World Trade*, 37, 623–46.

Brenton, P., T. Ikezuki (2004a) 'The Initial and Potential Impact of Preferential Access to the U.S. Market under the African Growth and Opportunity Act' Policy Research Working Paper 3262, World Bank.

Brenton, P., T. Ikezuki (2004b) 'The Impact of Agricultural Trade Preferences, with Particular Attention to the Least Developed Countries', A. Aksoy J. Beghin (ed.) *Global Agricultural Trade and Developing Countries*, Oxford University Press and the World Bank, Washington D.C. (forthcoming).

Carrere, C., J. de Melo (2004) 'Are Rules of Origin Equally Costly? Estimates from NAFTA', paper presented at IDB conference, Washington, Feb. 2004.

Estevadeordal, A. (2000) 'Negotiating Preferential Market Access: The Case of the North American Free Trade Area', *Journal of World Trade*, 34, 141–66.

Flatters, F. (2002) 'SADC Rules of Origin: Undermining Regional Free Trade,' paper presented at the TIPS Forum, Johannesburg, September 2002.

Flatters, F., R. Kirk, (2003) 'Rules of Origin as Tools of Development? Some Lessons from SADC,' presented at INRA conference on Rules of Origin, Paris, May 2003.

McQueen, M. (1999) 'After Lome IV: ACP-EU Trade Preferences in the 21st Century', *Intereconomics*, 34, 223–232.

Ozden, C., M. Olarreaga (2003) 'AGOA and Apparel: Who Captures the Tariff Rent in the Presence of Preferential Market Access?', Mimeo, World Bank, forthcoming in The World Economy.

Wainio, J., P. Gibson (2003) 'The Significance of Nonreciprocal Trade Preferences for Developing Countries', mimeo.

Index

Note: Authors of cited works appear under the name of the first cited author only. As the entire book relates to 'Rules of Origin', there are only a few broad references under this heading; the reader is advised to search under a more specific heading. Page numbers in **bold** refer to tables, and those in *italics* to figures. Page numbers followed by 'n.' (e.g. 259 n.) refer to footnotes.

absorption principle *see* roll-up principle
accounting services 121
Adaptation Regime, Mercosur 218
administration of RoO 90–2
administrative component, compliance
    costs 197
administrative costs, RoO 76, 310
ADRES (Association for the Development
    of Economics and Statistics) 259 n.
Africa Growth and Opportunity Act
    (AGOA) 2, 3, 8, 182, 191, 283, 291,
    297–**8**
    RoO 305–6, 312
    effects 32, 308–9
African PTAs 79–80
    see also Common Market for Eastern
        and Southern Africa (COMESA);
        Economic Community of West
        African States (ECOWA); South
        African Development Community
        (SADC)
after-sales service, value-added 119
Agreement on Textiles and Clothing
    (ATC) 283, 285–6
agricultural products
    EU tariffs 298–9
    restrictiveness of RoO 95, **96**
    SADC RoO 270–8
    trade preferences 296
ALADI (Asociación Latinoamericana de
    Integración), facilitation index *97*
Americas, RoO regimes 78–9, **84**, **86**, 90
    see also Andean Community (CAN);
        Central American Common Market
        (CACM); Central American Free

Trade Agreement (CAFTA); Latin
    American Integration Agreement
    (LAIA); Mercosur; North American
    Free Trade Agreement (NAFTA)
analytical coding methodology 92–3
    restrictiveness of RoO 93–5
Andean Community (CAN) 78
    certification **91**, 92
    facilitation index *97*
    reductions in RVC level 99
    restrictiveness of RoO **94**
Andean Community Decision 439 134
Angola, value of trade preferences **302**
Ansolobehere, S. *et al.* 156 n.
Anson, J. *et al.* 150, 192, 196, 197, 309,
    310
anti-dumping legislation 116 n.,
    184, 185
apparel *see* garments; textiles and apparel
approved exporters, EU 91
architectural services 121
Argentina 235
    Adaptation Regime items 218 n.
    sugar quotas 219
    trade-diversion-induced demand in
        intermediates 234
Argentina–Netherlands BIT
    corporate nationality 131
    nationality of natural persons 129
Armengol, C. and Constanzó, P. 218 n.
arms and ammunition
    NAFTA RoO **194**
    restrictiveness of sectoral RoO **96**
Articles of Confederation period, external
    tariffs 21

315

art works, restrictiveness of sectoral
RoO **96**
ASEAN Agreement for Promotion and
Protection of Investments,
corporate nationality criteria 137
ASEAN Framework Agreement on Services
(1995) 136
ASEAN Free Trade Area (AFTA) 79, 81, *82*,
84, **87**, **89**, 90, **91**, 92, **108**, **110**
facilitation index *97*
restrictiveness *94*
ASEAN investor, definition 139
Asian PTAs 79–80
see also Japan-Singapore Economic
Partnership Agreement (JSEPA)
Asia–Pacific Cooperation (APEC) 70 n.
audiovisual sector, GATT rules 127–8
auditing services 121
Augier, P. *et al.* 192
Auguste, B. G. *et al.* 120 n.
Australia, cigarette industry RoO 24
Australia–New Zealand Closer Economic
Relations Trade Agreement
(ANZCERTA) 79, 81, *82*, 83, **84**, **87**,
89, 90, **108**, **110**
certification **91**, 92
facilitation index *97*
restrictiveness of RoO *94*
automobile industry
exclusion from Mercosur 218–19
exclusion from Mercosur-Chile
FTA 221
intermediate goods trade 250–1, 290
regression analysis of COMTRADE
dataset 252–5
Mexico's exports to US 250–*1*
NAFTA RoO 12, 176–7, 179–80, 187,
238, 239
Turkey's exports to Germany 250, *251*

bakery products, EU RoO 306–7
Baldwin, R. E. 237
Baltic Free Trade Agreement
(BAFTA) **108**, **110**
bananas, EU tariffs 299
Bangkok Agreement 81, *82*, **84**, **87**, **89**,
91, 92, **108**
facilitation index *97*
restrictiveness of RoO *94*
banking services 121
Barcelona Traction Case 122 n.

base metals
NAFTA RoO **194**
restrictiveness of sectoral RoO **96**
Benin, value of trade preferences **302**
best-response functions, outsourcing 44–5
beverages
Mercosur restrictiveness indices **230**
NAFTA RoO **194**
restrictiveness of sectoral RoO **96**
structure of Mercosur–Bolivia RoO **230**
structure of Mercosur–Chile RoO **229**
structure of Mercosur RoO **228**
Bhagwati, J. 126 n.
Bhagwati, J. and Panagariya, A. 238 n.
Bianchi, E. 13
bilateral cumulation 75
bilateral investment treaties (BITs) 115,
128–33
bilateral trade agreements 128
binary variables vector, RoO 163
biscuits, EU Single List RoO 8
Bolivia, FTA with Mercosur 13
Bond, E. and Syropoulos, C. 32
border effects, intermediates trade 255
Botswana, trade preferences **302**, 304
Brazil 235
Adaptation Regime items 218 n.
tariff levels 220, 232
trade-diversion-induced demand in
intermediates 234
Brenton, P. 191, 198, 292 n., 299
Brenton, P. and Ikezuki, T. 14, 301, 303
Brenton, P. and Imagawa, H. 7 n., 8 n.
Brenton, P. and Manchin, M. 22, 192 n.
build-down method 111
build-up method 111
Burkina Faso, value of trade
preferences **302**
Burundi, value of trade preferences **302**
Bush, G. H. W. 180, 182

CACM *see* Central American Common
Market
Cadot, O. 11, 184 n., 191 n., 200, 237 n.
Cadot, O. *et al.* 7 n., 22, 76 n., 153 n., 192,
216–17, 233 n.
Caflisch, L. 122 n.
CAFTA *see* Central American Free Trade
Agreement
Cameroon, value of trade preferences **302**
CAN *see* Andean Community

Canada–Chile FTA 81, *82*, **86**, **88**, **91**
  facilitation index *97*
  nationality of service providers 135
Canada–Israel FTA **89**, 90
  facilitation index 95, *97*
Canada–Singapore FTA 80
Canada–US Free Trade Agreement
    (CUSFTA) 73, 176
capacity constraints 28
Cape Verdi, value of trade pre-
    ferences **302**
capital goods, Mercosur CET 219–20
Caribbean Basin Initiative 117
Caribbean Community (CARICOM) 78,
    89, **110**, 113
  certification **91**, 92
  corporate nationality criteria 137
  facilitation index *97*
Carrère, C. 149 n.
Carrère, C. and de Melo, J. 12–13, 151,
    158, 309, 310
Cartagena Agreement, corporate
    nationality criterion 139
Central African Customs and Economic
    Union, Multinational Companies
    Code 139
Central Africa Republic, value of trade
    preferences **302**
Central American Common Market
    (CACM) 78–9, 90, **91**
  CACM–Chile FTA 81, *82*, **86**, **88**, **109**
  certification **91**, 92 n.
  restrictiveness of RoO *94*
  facilitation index *97*
Central American Free Trade Agreement
    (CAFTA) 78–9, 83, *83*, **84**, **88**, 90,
    109, **110**
  certification **91**, 92
  facilitation index *97*
  resistance in US 174, 179
  restrictiveness of RoO *94*, **96**
  tariff preference levels (TPLs) 101
Central European Free Trade Agreement
    (CEFTA) **108**, **110**
Centre for Economic Policy Research
    (CEPR) 259 n.
Centre National de la Cinématographie
    (CNC) 128 n.
certification methods 76, **91**–2
CES (constant elasticity of substitution)
    production function 241,
    242, 243

CET (constant elasticity of
    transformation) 154, 163 n., 207
Chad, value of trade preferences **302**
change of chapter criterion 93, 287
  NAFTA RoO 196
  costs 203, **205**, 209
  SADC light manufacturing 278–9, 283,
    288
change-of-heading criterion 74, 93
  global distribution 81, *82*
  NAFTA RoO 196
  restrictiveness index **227**
change in tariff classification (CTC)
    criterion 73–4, 222–3, 287
  in EU trade preferences 306–7
  global distribution 81, *82*
  Mercosur 224
  in NAFTA 309–10
  and observation rule 107
  SADC RoO 269
  wheat/flour 272
  and services trade 119
cheese, Canada–US FTA 8, 23
chemicals
  Mercosur restrictiveness indices **230**
  NAFTA RoO **194**
  restrictiveness of sectoral RoO **96**
  structure of Mercosur–Bolivia RoO **230**
  structure of Mercosur–Chile RoO **229**
  structure of Mercosur RoO **228**
Chile
  FTA with EU 77
  FTA with Mercosur 13
Chile–CACM FTA 83, **84**
  restrictiveness **96**
Chile–Canada FTA 78
Chile–Panama FTA, nationality of service
    providers 135
Chile–South Korea FTA 79, 80, 81, *82*, **87**,
    89, **91**–2, **91**
  origin of services 133 n., 135
  restrictiveness of RoO *94*, **96**
China–Hong Kong Closer Economic
    Partnership Arrangement
    (2003) 139
CIF (cost, insurance, and freight) value,
    inclusion in RoO 112
cigarette industry RoO, Australia 24 n.
citizenship, in definition of
    nationality 134
cleaning 75
Cline, W. R. 182

Clinton, W., NAFTA negotiations 179
Closer Economic Relationship (CER),
    Australia and New Zealand 23 n.
clothing see garments; textiles and
    apparel
cloves, SADC RoO 275
CMT (cut, make and trim) operations 2
coffee, SADC RoO 275, 276–7, 278
Colin, D. 149 n.
Colonia Protocol (1994), corporate
    nationality criteria 137
combinations of RoO 83, **86–7**
Committee on Regional Trade
    Agreements (CRTA), WTO 103
Committee on Rules of Origin (CRO),
    WTO 80–1
Common Customs Tariff (CCT) 250
common external tariffs (CETs) 70,
    214
    in Mercosur 218, 219–20, 223–4, 232
Common Market for Eastern and
    Southern Africa (COMESA) 8, 79,
    81, *82*, **84**, **87**, **89**, **91**, **108**, **110**
    definition of COMESA investor 124 n.
    facilitation index *97*
    reductions in RVC level 99
    RoO 268–9 n.
    restrictiveness *94*
Community juridical person, EU
    criteria 137 n.
Comoros, value of trade preferences **302**
companies, nationality determination see
    corporate nationality
'company', definition within BITs 130
competitive liberalization 174
competitive need limitations, GSP 297
complexity of RoO 8–11
    NAFTA 177
compliance-cost heterogeneity,
    North-South PTA model 158
compliance-cost homogeneity,
    North-South PTA model 158
compliance costs, NAFTA RoO 197, 198–9
computers, Mercosur CET 219
COMTRADE dataset 252
    regression analysis 252–5
Congo, value of trade preferences **302**
constant elasticity of transformation
    (CET) 154, 163 n., 207
constraints on RoO 185–7
consumer's welfare, effects of RoO 49,
    50–1

contracts, incomplete see incomplete
    contractual problems
contribution effect in North-south
    PTA 160
control of companies 123, 143
Cooper, R. 183
corporate nationality criteria 121–3,
    143–4, 145
    GATS 141
    service providers 134–40
    within BITs 130–3
Costa Rica–Netherlands BIT, corporate
    nationality 132–3
costs
    of outsourcing 38–9, 42, 52–3
    of RoO 12–13, 15, 22, 24–5, 76, 191–2,
        208–10, 310
    comparison with Estevadeordal's
        index **205**
    effect of value content restric-
        tions 206–8
    estimates by RoO type and category of
        activity 200–3
    non-parametric estimates,
        NAFTA 196–8
    of utilizing trade preferences **312**, 313
cost versus price in RoO
    definitions 29–30
Cote d'Ivore, trade preferences **302**, 304
Cotonou Agreement 77, 117, 299–**300**
    incorporation criterion 136–7
    RoO 307
Council for Trade and Economic
    Development (COTED) 113
country of ownership or control
    criterion 132, 139
country-specific export restraints 175
Croatia, Stabilization and Association
    Agreements 77
cross-border trade 121
cross-regime differences in RoO 101–2
cumulation 8, 9–10, 75, 85, 90, 95
curry, SADC RoO 275
CUSFTA (Canada–US Free Trade
    Agreement) 73, 176
customs administration, enforcement of
    RoO 268
customs unions 20, 70, 175, 213, 214
    border effects 254
    EU–Turkey 250–1
    impact on intermediates trade 243–9
    objectives of RoO 214–15

use of intermediates 239
see also European Union; Mercosur

Daimler Company Ltd. 123 n.
DEC/CMCs, Mercosur 223, 225
definition of RoO 23–4, 71
  significance 29–30
Demaret, P. *et al* 310 n.
de Melo, J. 149 n., 184 n.
de Melo, J. and Panagariya, A. 19
de minimis rule 74, 85, 95, 98, 238
denial of benefits clause, GATS 142
design services 121
Destler, I. M. 12, 14, 173n., 179 n., 181 n.,
  184 n., 185 n.
Destler, I. M., Fukui, H. and Sato, H. 181 n.
details of RoO, significance 23, 29–30
developing countries, trade preferences 295–6, 313–14
  EU schemes 298–300
  Japanese GSP scheme 300–**1**
  RoO 305–8
  US schemes 297–**8**
  utilization rates **302**, 303–5
    impact of RoO 308–13
  value 301–3, **302**
developmental function, SADC RoO 267
diagonal cumulation 75, 95
distortionary component, compliance
  costs 197, 199
distribution, value added 119
Dixit, A. and Grossman, G. 38, 151
Djibouti, value of trade preferences **302**
documentation costs 22
Doha Trade Round 70–1, 103–4, 173
domicile, as condition of nationality 130
double-transformation rules, garments
  trade 28, 284, 307–8
drawback *see* duty drawback
Driessen, B. and Graafsma, F 77 n.
dual nationality 134
Duttagupta, R. 150
Duttagupta, R. and Panagaryia, A. 11, 19,
  150, 183–4, 237
duty drawback 75–6, 90, 95, 113
dyeing provision, textiles 182–3

e-commerce 120–1, 122
Economic Community of West African
  States (ECOWAS) 79, 81, *82*, **84**,
    87, **89**
  certification **91**, 92

facilitation index *97*
restrictiveness of RoO *94*
Economic Complementation Agreements
  (ECAs), Mercosur 225
economic growth, requirement for global
  market participation 264–5
Economic Integration clause, GATS 142
economic justification of RoO 70
Economic Partnership Agreements
  (EPAs) 1, 291
ECTC (exception attached to a CTC) 74
EEA *see* European Economic Association
effective nationality 129
effects of RoO on outsourcing 36–8
EFTA *see* European Free Trade Association
Eisenhower, D. D., textile quotas 180
electrical equipment
  NAFTA RoO **194**
  restrictiveness of sectoral RoO **96**
electric appliance industry, South
  Africa 282
electronic industry, Southeast Asia 262–3
Elliott, K. A. 184 n.
empirical analysis of RoO 150
endogenous RoO determination 150–1
Energy Charter Treaty (1994) 136
energy services 118, 125
enforcement of RoO 268
engineering services 121
enhanced protection 216
environmental services 118
Equatorial Guinea, value of trade
  preferences **302**
equilibrium, effect of RoO 40–1, 45–8, 56,
  60–*2*, *61*
Erasmus, H. 259 n.
Erasmus, H. and Flatters, F. 271 n.
Eritrea, value of trade preferences **302**
establishment-related transactions 121
Estevadeordal, A. 11, 21, 22, 70 n., 72, 93,
  150, 152, 162, 163, 182, 200, 222,
  227, 312
  synthetic index 163, 165, 192, **194**,
    195, 196, 203, 209, 286, 287,
    288, 310
  evaluation 204–6, **205**
Estevadeordal, A. and Robertson, R. 70 n.
Estevadeordal, A. and Suominen, K. 8, 9,
  71 n., 99 n., 192, 204, 206, 269 n.,
  286, 289, 290, 291.292
Ethier-type trade models 240, 241
Ethier, W. 239, 240

Ethiopia, trade preferences **302**, 304
Euro–Mediterranean Association
    Agreements 77
Europe, Pan-European cumulation
    regime 238
European Community Treaty,
    incorporation criterion 136
European Economic Association (EEA) 85,
    108, 110
    EEA Agreement (1992), incorporation
        criterion 136
    facilitation index *97*
    intermediates trade **254**
European Free Trade Association
    (EFTA) 77, **108, 110**
    EFTA–Chile FTA, corporate nationality
        criteria 138 n.
    EFTA–Israel FTA, facilitation index *97*
    EFTA–Mexico FTA 81, *82*
        corporate nationality, service
            providers 137
    EFTA–Singapore FTA, corporate
        nationality criteria 138
    incorporation criterion 136
European Union (EU)
    certification methods 91
    dismantling of border posts 244
    EU–ACP FTA 269
    EU FTAs 8–9, **84, 86, 88,** 90, **91,**
        108, 252
        EU–Slovenia FTA 77
        EU–South Africa FTA 85, 90, 95,
            97, 269
        facilitation index *97*
        phase-in periods 99
        reductions in RVC level 99
        restrictiveness of RoO 93, *94*, **96**
    EU–Mexico Joint Council (2001),
        corporate nationality criteria 137 n.
    EU model, RoO 270
    intermediates trade **254**
    negotiations with Mercosur 70
    semiconductor imports 20
    trade preferences 298–300
        compliance costs **312**
        RoO 306–7
        utilization rates **302**, 303–5
        value 301, **302**, 303
    use of RoO 83
    see also PANEURO system
EU–Turkey Customs Union 250–1

Everything But Arms (EBA) initiative 2,
    191, 192 n., 198, 299, 307
exception attached to a CTC (ECTC) 74
export diversification, LDCs 295–6, 299
export-led growth 265
export processing zones (EPZ) system 264
export protection function, RoO 215
exports, link with imports 261
ex post bargaining, effect of RoO 57–8
ex post hold up 51, 52
external tariffs 20–1
ex-works price 110

facilitation index 9–10, 95, *97*, 98
Falvey, R. and Reed, G. 21 n., 30, 36, 71
    n., 150, 237
fats and oils
    NAFTA RoO **194**
    restrictiveness of sectoral RoO **96**
Fédération Paris–Jourdan 259 n.
Feenstra, R. 36 n.
Feenstra, R. and Hanson, G. 2 n.
film industry, GATT rules 127–8
films, determination of nationality 128 n.
final assembly process 175–6
final-good producers
    costs of RoO **201**, 203, 204, 209
    relationships with intermediates
        producers 37
final goods
    effect of RoO 170, 248
    price changes 30–1
finance services 121, 125
firm's decision problem, cost estimation
    model 198 n., 211–12
firm-suppliers relationships 37
first-mover advantages, services
    trade 126, 145
fish, EU RoO 9
flags of convenience 122
Flatters, F. 259 n., 263 n., 264 n., 266 n.,
    268 n., 277, 278, 280 n., 281, 283
    n., 285 n., 290 n., 293 n., 308 n.
Flatters, F. and Kirk, R. 13–14, 191, 308 n.
flexibility of RoO 98
flexible sourcing, SADC 277–8, 282
flour, SADC RoO 271–5
food
    Mercosur restrictiveness indices **230**
    NAFTA RoO **194**
    restrictiveness of sectoral RoO **96**

structure of Mercosur–Bolivia RoO **230**
structure of Mercosur–Chile RoO **229**
structure of Mercosur RoO **228**
footwear
    NAFTA RoO **194**
    restrictiveness of sectoral RoO **96**
Foreign Investment Protection Agreement
    (FIPA), Canada and Panama 131
four quadrant diagrams, garment
    trade 4–7
fragmentation of production 261, 291,
    292, 308
    effect of RoO 36
    limits 262
Francois, J. F. 13, 240 n.
Francois, J. F. and Nelson, D. 239, 241
Francois, J. F. and Roland-Holst, D.
    W. 241 n.
free riding 144
free trade agreements (FTAs) 19–22, 70,
    117, 175, 213–14
    constraints 186
    effects of RoO 22–3, 26–31, 149–50,
    183–4, 239–40
    effect of tariff preferences and RoO 3–8
    impact on intermediates trade 243–9
    models of outsourcing 41–51
    objectives of RoO 215, 237–8
    political-economy issues 216–17
Free Trade Area of the Americas
    (FTAA) 70, 78
French nationality, films 128 n.
Friedman, T. 115 n.
full cumulation 75, 95

G-3 *see* Mexico–Colombia-Venezuela
    (G-3) FTA
Gabon, value of trade preferences **302**
Gambia, value of trade preferences **302**
game-theoretic analysis 7–8
Garay, L. and Cornejo, R. 78
Garay, L. and Estevadeordal, A. 227
garments
    cost of RoO 12–13
    EU RoO 307
    four quadrant diagrams 4–7
    inclusion in AGOA 297–8
      RoO 305–6, 308–9
    Japanese RoO 307
    Multi-Fiber Arrangement (MFA) 175, 180
    NAFTA RoO 7, **194**, 195, 311

restrictiveness of RoO 95, **96**
SADC RoO 283–6
triple transformation test 12, 24, 181–2
    see also textiles and apparel
gatekeeper role of RoO 71
GATT (General Agreement on Tariffs and
    Trade) 170
    Article XXIV 1, 149
    rules for films 127–8
GCC *see* Gulf Cooperation Council
General Agreement on Trade in Services
    (GATS) 114, 115, 126–7, 133, 134
    determination of origin of
    services 140–2
general equilibrium, effects of RoO 31–2
Generalized System of Preferences (GSP)
    schemes 69 n., 117, 191
    EU 77, 192 n., 298–**300**, 307
    Japanese 300–**1**, 307
    US 152, 297, **298**, 305
General Mercosur Rule 225
Germany–Swaziland BIT, corporate
    nationality 132
Ghana, value of trade preferences **302**
gherkins, flexible sourcing in SADC 278
Ghosh, S. and Yamarik, S. 70 n.
glass
    NAFTA RoO **194**
    restrictiveness of sectoral RoO **96**
globalization 175–6, 261, 292, 308
    US business 178
global market participation, requirement
    for economic development 264–5
governmental certification 76
governments, use of RoO 71
Grossman, G. 3
Grossman, G. and Dixit, A. 38
Grossman, G. and Helpman, E. 11, 19,
    150, 151, 152, 214, 216
Grossman–Helpman model 156, 170
Grossman, S. and Hart, O. 37, 51
GSP *see* Generalized System of Preferences
    (GSP) schemes
Guinea, value of trade preferences **302**
Gulf Cooperation Council (GCC) 79, 81,
    82, **87**, **89**, **108**, **110**
    facilitation index *97*
    restrictiveness of RoO *94*

Hamilton, A. 173
Hanson, G. 150

harmonization of RoO 102–4, 186, 291–2
  non-preferential RoO 80–1
Harrison, G. W. *et al.* 250
Haveman, J. 149 n.
Herin, J. 22, 26 n., 192
heterogeneous regime 1
hidden protection 183
Hirsch, M. 71 n.
Hoekman, B. 119 n., 120 n.
homogeneous goods 238
homogeneous regime 30
Honduras–US BIT, corporate
  nationality 131–2
Hotelling's lemma 160
Hummels, D. *et al.* 2–3

illegal activities 306
impact of RoO 12–14, 15
import content (MC) criterion 74, 83,
  84, 112, 287
import-led growth 265
imports, link with exports 261
Inama, S. 296 n.
incomplete contractual problems,
  outsourcing 37, 51–63
incorporation criterion 122, 143
  BITs 130–2
  service providers 136–7
  use in GATS 141
indices of intermediates trade 253
indices of restrictiveness 286–8
  see also synthetic index, Estevadeordal
Indonesia, electronic assembly
  operations 262–3
industrial-organization (IO) perspective,
  impact of RoO on
  outsourcing 36–65
industries, benefits from RoO 179
infant-industry protection 126
information technology (IT), impact on
  services trade 120 n., 144
in-house production costs 52–3
innovations in RoO 98–101
input price change allowances 30–1
INRA (Institut National de la Recherche
  Agronomique) 259 n.
instant coffee, international sourcing 277
insurance services 121
integrated sourcing initiative (ISI) 100
Inter-American Development Bank
  (IADB) 69 n., 259 n.

interest groups, lobbying for RoO 19, 23,
  29, 33, 35
intermediates
  differentiation 239
  effect of RoO 170
  internal price, marginal effect of
    RoO 158, 159
  price change allowances 30–1
  trade-diversion-induced demand,
    Mercosur 231, 234
intermediates producers 11–12
  benefits from RoO 21
  costs of RoO **201**, **203**, 209
  relationships with final-good
    producers 37
  see also outsourcing
intermediates trade 261–2
  impact of PTAs 240–9, 255
    automobile trade 249–52, 290
    regression analysis 252–5
  impact of RoO 239, 240
intermediates trade indices 253
internal intermediates, movement within
  customs unions 239
internal intermediates trade, effect of
  RoO 248
internal tariffs, Mercosur 218–19
international sourcing, instant coffee 277
Internet, impact on services trade 120–1,
  122
intrabloc tariffs, phasing-out 152,
  155, 156
intra-PTA industry linkages, benefits of
  RoO 71 n.
investment
  definitions in BIT practice 129
  RoO 124
  see also bilateral investment treaties
    (BITs)
investment flows, effect of RoO 26
'investor'
  definition within ASEAN Investor
    Area 139
  definition within BITs 129, 130
  definition within Energy Charter Treaty
    (1994) 136
invoice declaration 91
Irwin, 115 n.
Ishii, J. and Yi, K. 2 n.
Israel *see* US–Israel FTA
Ivory Coast, trade preferences **302**, 304

Japan
    electronics industry 262–3
    trade preferences 300–**1**
        compliance costs **312**
        RoO 307, 310
        utilization rates **302**, 303–5
        value **302**, 303
Japan–Korea BIT 132
Japan–Singapore Economic Partnership
    Agreement (JSEPA) 79–80, 81, *82*,
    87, **89**, **91**, 92, **109**, **110**
    corporate nationality criteria 138
    facilitation index *97*
    restrictiveness of RoO **96**
Jensen-Moran, J. 71 n.
jewellery
    NAFTA RoO **194**
    restrictiveness of sectoral RoO **96**
Jones, R. W. and Keirszkowsi, H. 261
Jordan *see* US–Jordan FTA
Ju, J. and Krishna, K. 7, 30, 31, 32, 159,
    198, 237
juridical persons 130–3, 134–40, 137 n.,
    141–2

Katz, J. 180, 187
Kennedy, J. F., textile quotas 180
Kenya
    cut flower exports 2
    trade preferences **302**, 303
ketchup, NAFTA RoO 8, 24, 310
Kingston, E. I. 118 n.
Kirk, R. 259 n.
Korea, electronics industry 262–3
Kowalczyk, C. and Davis, D. 70 n.
Krishna, K. 7, 8 n., 31–2, 198, 237 n.
Krishna, K. and Krueger, A. O. 23, 24,
    26, 29, 43, 71 n., 117, 149, 183,
    184 n., 215
Krishna, K. and Panagariya, A. 29 n.
Krueger, A. O. 7 n., 21 n., 71 n., 149
Krugman, P. 32
Kuhn-Ticker conditions 160
Kyoto Convention 73

labeling 75
labor costs, Southeast Asia 262–3
Laird, S. 218
LaNasa, J. A. 184 n.
Lasswell, H. D. 177 n.
Latin American Integration Agreement
    (LAIA) 8, 78, 81, *82*, **84**, **91**, **108**

NALADISA classification 225, 227
reductions in RVC level 99
restrictiveness of RoO 94
Lawrence, R. Z. 126 n., 183, 186 n.
Lawrence-Snape remedy 185
laws of RoO 22–3
least-developed countries (LDCs), trade
    preferences 14, 295–6, 313–14
    EU schemes 298–300
    Japanese GSP scheme 300–**1**
        RoO 305–8
    US schemes 297–**8**
    utilization rates **302**, 303–5
        impact of RoO 308–13
    value 301–3, **302**
leather goods
    Mercosur restrictiveness indices **230**
    NAFTA RoO **194**
    restrictiveness of sectoral RoO **96**
    structure of Mercosur–Bolivia RoO **230**
    structure of Mercosur–Chile RoO **229**
    structure of Mercosur RoO **228**
legal criteria for RoO 23–4
legal persons 137 n., 141–2
    nationality determination within
        BITS 130–3
    nationality of service providers 134–40
legal services 121
Lesotho
    garment industry 2
    textiles and garments trade 283–4
    trade preferences 04, **302**, 303
liberalizing effects, RoO 183
Liberia, value of trade preferences **302**
light manufacturing, SADC RoO 278–83
live animal trade
    NAFTA RoO **194**
    restrictiveness of RoO **96**
Lloyd, P. 21, 151
lobbying
    NAFTA 176–7
    North-South PTA 156
local-content requirement,
    restrictiveness 288
local raw materials, SADC RoO 271
local suppliers
    effect of RoO 51–62, 63
        on investment 58, *59*
local supply networks, Southeast Asia 263
location of seat criterion 122–3, 130–2,
    136–7, 143
location-specific sunk costs 125

locus classicus 122n.
Lopez-de-Silanes, F. *et al.* 239 n., 240 n.
Luce, E. and Merchant, K. 115 n.

Macedonia, Former Yugoslav Republic of,
    Stabilization and Association
    Agreements 77
McGillivray, F. and Green, M. 21
machinery
    Mercosur restrictiveness indices **230**
    NAFTA RoO **194**
    restrictiveness of sectoral RoO **96**
    structure of Mercosur–Bolivia RoO **230**
    structure of Mercosur–Chile RoO **229**
    structure of Mercosur RoO **228**
McQueen, M. 299
Madagascar, trade preferences **302**, 304
Maddala, G. S. 199, 212
'mailbox' companies 129
Malawi
    textiles and garments, trade RoO 284
    value of trade preferences 301, **302**
    wheat imports 274
Malaysia, electronic assembly
    operations 262–3
Mali, value of trade preferences **302**
Mann, C. L. 120 n.
manufactured products, trade
    preferences 296
manufacturing industries, SADC
    RoO 278–86
mappings of PTAs 69–70
marginalization, least-developed
    countries 295
market-access equations 163
    regression results **167**, **168**–9
market access and RoO
    determination 162–71
market clearing condition, intermediate
    goods 157, 158
marketing, value added 119
marking 75
Markusen, *et al.* 240 n.
Mattoo, A. 123 n.
Mattoo, A, and Fink, C. 125 n., 126 n.
Mattoo, A, Rathindran, R. and
    Subramanian, A. 125 n.
Mattoo, A, Roy, D. and Subramanian,
    A. 32, 182 n., 292 n.
Mattoo, A. and Wunsch-Vincent, S. 121 n.
Mauritania, trade preferences **302**, 303

Mauritius
    economic growth 263–5
    flour milling industry 274
    garment industry 2, 3
    refrigerator production 281 n.
    textiles and garments trade 283, 284,
        308–9
    trade preferences 301, **302**, 304, 308–9
maximization problems
    outsourcing 43–5
    incomplete contractual
        problems 54–60
Mayda, A. M. 191 n.
Mayer, F. W. 176, 177, 180
MC *see* import content criterion
Meade, J. E. 263 n.
measurement of RoO 163
    see also restrictiveness indices
medical instruments, NAFTA RoO **194**
Mercosur 13, 70, 78, 90, **91**, 92, **110**, 213,
    214, 217
    association between RoO and tariff
        preferences **233**–4
    average tariffs **220**
    Colonia Protocol (1994), corporate
        nationality criteria 137
    correlation between restrictiveness
        index and tariff differences 231–**2**
    facilitation index *97*
    preferential tariffs 218–20
    RoO 111, 223–5, **226**, 235
        restrictiveness 93–4
        restrictiveness indices 229–31, **230**
        structure **228**
Mercosur–Bolivia FTA 81, *82*, **84**, **89**, 220,
    221–2
    certification **91**, 92 n.
    facilitation index *97*
    RoO 225–**6**
        restrictiveness *94*
        restrictiveness indices 229–31, **230**
        structure 229, **230**
Mercosur–Chile FTA 81, *82*, **84**, **86**, **89**,
    108, 220–1
    certification **91**, 92 n.
    facilitation index *97*
    phase-in period 98
    RoO 225–**6**
        restrictiveness *94*
        restrictiveness indices 229–31, **230**
        structure 228–**9**

Mercosur Common Tariff Classification
System (MCTCS) 224, 227
Mercosur Origin System 223–5, **226**
Mercosur Protocol of Montevideo
(1997) 133
metals
    Mercosur restrictiveness indices **230**
    NAFTA RoO **194**
    structure of Mercosur–Bolivia RoO **230**
    structure of Mercosur–Chile RoO **229**
    structure of Mercosur RoO **228**
Mexico
    automobile exports to US 250–*1*
    criteria for juridical person 137 n.
    FTA with EU 77, 81, *82*
    market access, effect of NAFTA's
        RoO 150–1, 162–71
Mexico–Bolivia FTA 78, 81, *82*, **86**, **88**,
    91, 108
    facilitation index *97*
    nationality of service providers 135
    phase-in period 98
    restrictiveness of RoO *94*
Mexico–Chile FTA 78
Mexico–Colombia-Venezuela (G-3)
        FTA 78, 81, *82*, **86**, **88**, **108**, **110**
    certification **91**, 92 n.
    facilitation index *97*
    nationality of service providers 135
    restrictiveness of RoO *94*, **96**
Mexico–Costa Rica FTA 78, 81, *82*, **86**,
    88, 91, 108
    facilitation index *97*
    nationality of service providers 135
    restrictiveness of RoO *94*, **96**
Mexico–Israel FTA **89**, *97*, **109**
Mexico–Japan FTA 80
Mexico–Korea FTA 80
Mexico–Nicaragua FTA 78, *97*
Mexico–Northern Triangle FTA 78
Mexico–Singapore FTA 80
MFN (Most Favored-Nation) principle 1,
    174
    exceptions 140
    liberalization 124, 125, 126, 145
    MFN tariffs 102, 104, 191, 199, 200
        correlation with restrictiveness
            index 231–**2**
        links with RoO 290, 291
        pre-determination 154
        reduction 187
        within SADC 274

Middle Eastern PTAs 79–80
MIGA (Multilateral Investment Guarantee
    Agency) Convention, dual
    nationality 134
milling industries, SADC 272–5
Milner, H. V. 70 n.
mineral products
    NAFTA RoO **194**
    restrictiveness of sectoral RoO **96**
Mkandawire, W. 124 n.
MMTZ countries, textiles and garments,
    trade RoO 284
Mode3 trade 121
modeling
    costs of RoO 198–200
    econometric specification 212
    North–South FTAs 3–8
    strategic outsourcing 38–51
    with incomplete contracts 52–62
monopoly's output and profit, effect of
    RoO 59–*60*, 62–3
Moran, T. H. 263 n.
Motor Industry Development Program
    (MIDP), South Africa 290
movement certificates 91
Mozambique
    textiles and garments trade RoO 284
    value of trade preferences **302**
Multi-Fiber Arrangement (MFA,
    1973) 175, 180
Multinational Companies Code, Central
    African Customs and Economic
    Union 139
multinational companies, nationality
    determination *see* corporate
    nationality
multinationalization 36, 116, 175–6
multistage production models 151
multimodal transport services 118

NALADISA classification 225, 227
Namibia
    ban on wheat flour imports 274
    value of trade preferences **302**
Namibia–Zimbabwe FTA 79, 81, *82*, **87**
Nash equilibria, outsourcing 40–1,
    45–8, 56
nationality determination 115
    of films 128 n.
    of natural persons129–30, 141
        service providers 134, 140
        within BITs 129–33

see also corporate nationality criteria
negotiations game 200
network-based services 117, 118
Niger, value of trade preferences **302**
Nigeria, value of trade preferences **302**
Nixon, R. M., Multi-Fiber Arrangement
    (MFA, 1973) 180
non-parametric cost estimates, NAFTA
    RoO 196–8, 209
non-preferential RoO 72–3, 80–1
    harmonization 102–3, 104
normative issues, RoO 214–15, 231, 234
North American Free Trade Agreement
    (NAFTA) 8–9, 73, 78, 79, **84**, 85, **86**,
    88, 90, **108**, **110**, 213, 291–2
  border checks 244
  certification 91, **91**, 92 n.
  cost estimates
    by RoO type and category of
      activity 200–3
    non-parametric 196–8
    simple model 198–200
  enactment 174
  facilitation index 95, *97*
  intermediates trade **254**–5
  legal persons, nationality
    determination 135
  negotiations 200
  origin of services 133
  political–economy model 151–62
  RoO 8, 12, 81, *82*, 238
    automobile industry 12, 176–7,
      179–80, 187
    complexity 177
    costs 12–13
    effect on Mexican market
      access 150–1, 162–71
    for garments 7, 24, 181–2, 311
    for ketchup 24
    preferences and utilization
      rates 193–6, **194**
    restrictiveness *94*, **96**, 289
    variation across product
      categories 309–10
  tariff preference levels (TPFs) 101
  triple transformation test 181–2
North–South FTAs
  effect of tariff preferences and
    RoO 149–50
  modeling 3–8
  NAFTA as example 152

North–South PTA, political-economy
    model 216–17
  economy 153–4
  equilibrium 157–62
  politics 155–7
  preferential regime 154–5
Nottebohm Case 129 n.

O'Brien, R. 126 n.
observation rule, Estevadeordal's
    index 93, 107, 192–3, 203
Odell, J. S. 184 n.
Offshore Assembly Provision (OAP) 3 n.
off-shoring, service trade 120
Olarreaga, M. 149 n., 184 n., 191 n.
Olarreaga, M. and Soloaga, I. 70 n.
oligopolists, effect of RoO 7–8
OLS regressions, intermediates trade
    data **254**
open trade, broadening US domestic
    support 186
operations insufficient to confer origin 75
optics, restrictiveness of sectoral RoO **96**
Organization of the Islamic Conference,
    Agreement on the Promotion,
    Protection and Guarantee of
    Investment (1981) 134–5
out of equilibrium outcomes 37
outsourcing
  analysis 38–42
    incomplete contractual
      problems 51–63
    outside an FTA 49–51
    within an FTA 42–9
    effects of RoO 36–8
  service trade 120
outsourcing best response function 39
outward processing (OP) 22, 100, **101**
over-outsourcing 40, 41
overseas processing trading (OPT)
    arrangements 192 n.
ownership of companies 143
Oye, K. A. 183

packaging 75
painting 75
Palmeter, D. 8 n., 23 n., 310 n.
Panagariya, A. 23 n.
Pan-European cumulation regime 238
PANEURO system 76–8, 81, *82*, 83, **84**,
    85, **86**, **88**, **91**, **108**, 291–2

facilitation index 95, *97*
restrictiveness *94*, **96**
paper
Mercosur restrictiveness indices **230**
NAFTA RoO **194**
restrictiveness of sectoral RoO **96**
structure of Mercosur–Bolivia RoO **230**
structure of Mercosur–Chile RoO **229**
structure of Mercosur RoO **228**
Paraguay
Adaptation Regime items 218 n.
Mercosur RoO 225, 226
partial equilibrium, effects of RoO 26–31
participation constraint 5, 6, 7, 56, 58,
151 n.
in model of North–South PTA 155, 157,
159, 161, 170, 217
Pastor, R. A. and de Castro, R. F.
179–80 n.
phase-in periods 98–9
length 21–2
phasing-out, intrabloc tariffs 152,
155, 156
physical content requirements 24
relationship to costs 25
physical presence, requirement in service
trade 117, 120
plastics
NAFTA RoO **194**
restrictiveness of sectoral RoO **96**
policy, role of RoO 123
political-economy issues
RoO 48–9, 50–1, 216–17, 234
association between RoO and tariff
preferences **233**–4
political-economy model, North–South
PTA 152–3
economy 153–4
equilibrium 157–62
politics 155–7
preferential regime 154–5
political-economy use of RoO 71
political equation 164
political role of RoO 177
politics, in model of North–South
PTA 155–7
Portugal-Pérez, A. 191 n.
potential outcomes 37
Powell, A. A. and Gruen, F. H. G. 163 n.
preferences, NAFTA RoO 193–6, **194**
preferential access to markets, developing
countries 295

preferential bilateral agreements 118
preferential regime in North–South
political-economy model 154–5
preferential RoO 73, 116
harmonization 103, 104
preferential tariffs, Mercosur 218–20
Preferential Trade Agreements (PTAs) 1–3,
8–11, 69–70, **108–10**, 117, 213–14
disaggregation 72
impact on intermediates trade 240–9,
255
automobile trade 249–52
regression analysis 252–5
inclusion of RoO 70
see also customs unions; free trade
agreements
preservation 75
price change allowances 30–1
price determination in North–South
PTA 157–60
price versus cost in RoO
definitions 29–30
principal place of management 122–3,
130–2, 136–7
printed circuit boards, (PCBs), SADC
RoO 282 n., 288
processing activities 119
producers
determination of origin 118
restrictiveness of RoO 119
see also services trade
product-specific RoO (PSRO) 8–10, 73–4
global mapping 81–4
profit functions 39, 43, 44
profits, effects of RoO 48–9
protectionism 21–2, 215, 260, 266–7,
292–3
decline in US 173, 178
and quantification of RoO 290
in SADC 269, 288
wheat/flour 272, 273
Protocol of Ouro Preto 218
PTAs *see* Preferential Trade Agreements
public companies
country of ownership or control 132
see also corporate nationality
pulp and paper
NAFTA RoO **194**
restrictiveness of sectoral RoO **96**

quota agreements 175
US, textiles 180–1

ranking of RoO, services trade 142–4
raw materials 195
  SADC RoO 271
real seat 122–3, 130–2, 136–7
recognition arrangements 127
reduced protection 216
refrigerator production, Mauritius 281 n.
regime-wide RoO 8, 74–6, 84–5, **88–9**, 90
regional integration agreements 118
regional liberalization 126–7
regional production networks 2, 150
Regional Trading Agreements (RTAs), RoO
  for services 123–7, 128
Regional Value Content (RVC) 6–7, 74,
  83, **84**, 111, 112, 159, 193, 206, 238
  and compensating preference
    margins **208**
  flexibility in calculation 100
  NAFTA RoO 196, 201
    cost estimates **201**, **205**, 209
  reductions in level 99
  restrictiveness index **227**
  SADC RoO 269
regression results, RoO equation 165–9
rent-seeking behavior, SADC wheat/flour
  trade 274–5
residence, as condition of nationality 130
restricted cost function 207
restrictiveness indices 93, **227**, 286–8
  correlation with MFN tariff differ-
    ences 231–**2**
  Mercosur and Mercosur FTAs 229–31,
    230, 235
  synthetic index, Estevadeordal 20, 150,
    192, **194**, 195, 196, 287, 288–9
    evaluation 204–6, **205**
restrictiveness of RoO 191–2, 266–7
  comparative analysis 93–5, *94*
  quantification 290
  reduction 101–4
  in services trade 119, 120, 124–5, 126–7
  see also stringency of RoO
revealed preference, use in estimation of
  costs of RoO 192, 202
Reyna, J. V. 73
rice, EU tariffs 299
Richardson, M 21 n.
Roach, S. 120 n.
Rodriguez, P. 21 n., 151
roll-up principle 75, 85
rooibos tea 277
Rosellon, J. 21 n.

rubber, NAFTA RoO **194**
rules of origin (RoO) 222–3
  definition of 23–4, 71
  significance 29–30
  estimation of costs 191–210
  lack of public attention 184
  preferences and utilization rates in
    NAFTA 193–6, **194**
  purpose 115–17, 149, 174–6, 214–15,
    237–40, 266–7
Rules of Origin Agreement, WTO 185–6
Rwanda, value of trade preferences **302**

SACU *see* South Africa Customs Union
SADC *see* South African Development
  Community
SAFTA *see* Singapore–Australia Free Trade
  Agreement
Sanguinetti, P. 13, 149 n., 151, 191 n.
Sanguinetti, P. and Salustro, M. 219 n.
Sanyal, K. K. and Jones, R. W. 261
Sao Tome and Principe, value of trade
  preferences **302**
Sauvé, P. 124 n.
Schiff, M. 149 n., 160 n.
Schott, J. J. 183 n.
Schumer, C. and Roberts, P. C. 115n.
screen-time quotas 128
'screwdriver' industries, SADC 279
'seat' of a company, location 122–3,
  130–2, 136–7
sectoral RoO 183
  comparison of restrictiveness 94–5, **96**
self-certification 76, 91–2, 95
semiconductor imports, EU 20
Senegal, value of trade preferences **302**
sequential entry 125
services, tradability 120
services trade 114–15
  determination of origin of services 117
  impact of Internet 120–1
  learning by doing 126
  RoO 11, 117–23, 144–5
    current practice 127–42
    economic considerations 123–7
    ranking of rules 142–4
    restrictiveness 119, 120, 124–5,
      126–7
Seychelles, value of trade preferences 301,
  302
shared borders 253
shareholders, nationality 122, 130

'shell' companies 129
Shibata, H. 20
shipping, flags of convenience 122
Shy, O. and Stenbarcka, R. 36, 38
siège social 130, 131
Sierra Leone, value of trade
    preferences **302**
Silveira, M. 184 n.
Singapore, FTAs 90
Singapore–Australia Free Trade Agreement
    (SAFTA) 79, 81, *82*, **84**, **87**, **89**
    certification **91**, 92
    corporate nationality criteria 138
    restrictiveness of RoO *94*
Singapore FTAs
    with EFTA 77
    flexibility in value content
        calculation 100, **101**
    see also Canada–Singapore FTA;
        Japan–Singapore Economic
        Partnership Agreement; Mexico–
        Singapore FTA; US–Singapore FTA
Smith, A. 261
Smoot–Hawley Act (1930) 187
Snape, R. H. 183
soft RoO 83
Somalia, value of trade preferences **302**
sorting 75
South Africa
    electric appliance industry 282
    FTA with EU 77
    light manufacturing, RoO 279
    Motor Industry Development Program
        (MIDP) 290
    SADC RoO 269, 288
    sourcing practices, valves 281
    textiles and garments trade 284 n., 285,
        309
    trade preferences **302**, 309
    wheat duty 273–4
    wheat production 272
South Africa Customs Union (SACU) 270
    wheat duty 273, 274
South African Development Community
    (SADC) 13–14, 79, 81, *82*, 83, **84**,
        87, **89**, **91**, **109**, **110**, 259–60
    adoption of PANEURO model 291
    facilitation index *97*
    flexibility in value content
        calculation 99
    lessons from international
        experience 265–6
    from Mauritius 263–5
    from Southeast Asia 262–3
    RoO 191, 269, 288, 292–3
        agricultural products 270–8
        evolution 268–70
        manufacturing industries 278–86
        proposed uses 267–8
        restrictiveness *94*, **96**, 288–9
        trade policy issues 289–91
        tariff preference levels (TPLs) 101
Southeast Asia, export trade
    success 262–3
Southern Cone
    impact of RoO 226–34
    see also Mercosur
South Pacific Regional Trade and
    Economic Cooperation
        (SPARTECA) 79, 81, *82*, **84**, **87**,
        89, 90, **91**, **108**, **110**
    facilitation index *97*
South–South PTAs 13, 15, 126
special interests 11–12
specific origin requirements
    Mercosur 224–5
    Mercosur FTAs 226
spices, SADC RoO 275–6
Spilimbergo, A. 12
steel safeguards, US (2002–2003) 174–5
Stein, A. 191 n.
Stenbarcka, R. and Shy, O. 36, 38
Stern, B. 122 n.
stone
    NAFTA RoO **194**
    restrictiveness of sectoral RoO **96**
strategic outsourcing, analysis 38–51
    incomplete contracts 52–62
stringency of RoO 9, 10–11, 21–2, 23, 28,
        191–2, 222–3
    effects on costs 25
    effects on outsourcing 43–8, 50
    effects on profits 48–9
    qualitative index of 150
    see also restrictiveness indices;
        restrictiveness of RoO
structure of RoO
    Mercosur **228**
    Mercosur–Bolivia FTA 229, **230**
    Mercosur–Chile FTA 228–**9**
studies of PTAs 69–70
subject-matter coverage 118
substantial business operation test,
        corporate nationality 122, 143, 145

substantial transformation criterion 24,
73–4, 222
NAFTA 238
and services trade 119
substitution elasticities 246
Sudan, value of trade preferences **302**
sugar
EU tariffs 299
trade preferences 296 n.
sugar trade
exclusion from Mercosur 218–19
tariff preferences, Mercosur–Chile
FTA **221**
sunk costs, in service industries 125
Suominen, K. 69 n., 71 n., 72, 95 n., 149
n., 182
surrogate local presence requirement 121
Suwa, A. 11
Swaziland, trade preferences 301, **302**,
303
synthetic index, Estevadeordal 20, 150,
192, **194**, 195, 196, 287, 288–9
evaluation 204–6, **205**

tailoring of RoO 71
Tanzania
coffee and cloves trade 276
textiles and garments trade RoO 284
value of trade preferences **302**
wheat duty 273
tariff-free status 2
tariff liberalization 71
tariff peaks 204
tariff phase downs, SADC 270
tariff preference levels (TPLs) 100–1
tariff preference margins 195
tariff preferences 215
effect 5–6
influences 167
Mercosur 217–**20**
Mercosur–Bolivia FTA 221–2
Mercosur–Chile FTA 220–**1**
positive association with RoO 231,
233–4
tariffs 20–1
purpose of RoO 116
tea, SADC RoO 275, 276, 277
Technical Committee on Rules of Origin
(TCRO), WCO 80
technical requirement (TECH) 74, 222,
223, 287

NAFTA 196
costs 201, 203, **205**, 209
restrictiveness index **227**
telecommunications equipment,
Mercosur CET 219
telecommunications services 118, 125
temporal exceptions, Mercosur CET 219
temporary entry privileges 127
textiles and apparel
AGOA 297–8, 305–6, 308–9
costs of RoO 203
dyeing provision 182–3
EU RoO 307
Japanese RoO 307
Mercosur RoO structure **228**
Mercosur–Bolivia FTA, RoO
structure **230**
Mercosur–Chile, RoO structure **229**
Mercosur CET 219 n.
Mercosur restrictiveness indices **230**
NAFTA RoO **194**, 195, 311
RoO 180–3
Multi-Fiber Arrangement 175, 180
restrictiveness 95, **96**
within SADC 283–6
triple transformation test 12, 24,
181–2, 191
tariff preference levels (TPFs) 101
Thoenig, M. and Verdier, T. 7–8, 38, 42,
49, 51, 58 n.
Thorstensen, V. 103
tightening of RoO, effect 7
time period of RoO 23
tobacco
Mercosur restrictiveness indices **230**
NAFTA RoO **194**
restrictiveness of sectoral RoO **96**
structure of Mercosur–Bolivia RoO **230**
structure of Mercosur–Chile RoO **229**
structure of Mercosur RoO **228**
trade preferences 296 n.
Tobit model 199 n.
Togo, value of trade preferences **302**
tomato ketchup, NAFTA RoO 8, 24, 310
tradability of services 120
tradable services, RoO 11
trade creation 216
trade deflection 70, 213, 215, 231, 266
within Mercosur 214, 224
trade diversion 150, 216, 237
trade-diversion-induced demand in
intermediates, Mercosur 231, 234

trade policy issues, SADC 289–91
trade preferences 14, 295–6, 313–14
  EU schemes 298–**300**
  Japanese scheme 300–**1**
  and RoO 305–8
  US schemes 297–**8**
  utilization rates **302**, 303–5
    impact of RoO 308–13
    value 301–3, **302**
Trade Promotion Authority (TPA),
    approval 179, 182–3
Trade Protocol, SADC 260, 269, 270, 279,
    289, 292
trade-related investment measures
    (TRIMS) 103, 104
trade remedy laws 174–5, 184
transformation technology 240
transition phase, North–South PTA 155–6
transportation equipment
  NAFTA RoO **194**
  restrictiveness of sectoral RoO **96**
transport costs 261
transport services 118, 125
trans-shipment 20, 71, 149, 175, 215
Treaties of Commerce and Naviga-
    tion 127
Treaty of Ankara 250
Treaty of Asuncion 218, 223 n.
Treaty of Rome 175
triple transformation test, garment
    trade 12, 24, 181–2, 191, 307–8
Tunisia–Turkey BIT, definition of
    'company' 130
Turkey
  accession to pan-European cumulation
    regime 238
  automobile exports to Germany 250,
    251
  EU–Turkey Customs Union 250–1
types of RoO 72–6, 222–3
  and cost estimates 200–3, 204, 209

Uganda, value of trade preferences **302**
'unfair trade' statutes 184
unit cost function 206
United States, Africa Growth and
    Opportunity Act (AGOA) 2, 3
unit value-added price 207
upstream coefficient 165, 166
Uruguay, Adaptation Regime items 218 n.
Uruguay Round 120, 127, 173, 175, 179,
    181, 250

US
  bipartisan trade consensus,
    erosion 178–9
  negotiation of FTAs 174
  RoO
    automobile industry 179–80
    textile industry 180–3
    trade preferences 297–**8**
    compliance costs **312**
    RoO 305–6
    utilization rates **302**, 303–5
    value **302**, 303
  treaty with Arab Republic of
    Egypt 133 n.
USAID (United States Agency for
    International Development) 259 n.
US–Australia FTA 80
US business, globalization 178
US–Central America FTA 78, 81, *82*
US–Chile FTA 78, 79, 81, *82*, 83, **84**,
    88, 91
  certification **91**, 92 n.
  facilitation index *97*
  origin of services 14
  restrictiveness of RoO *94*, **96**, 288–9
US–El Salvador BIT
  definition of 'company' 130 n.
  nationality of natural persons 129
US–Israel FTA 79, 81, *82*, **87, 89**,
    90, **108**
  facilitation index *97*
  restrictiveness of RoO *94*
US–Jordan FTA 79, 81, *82*, **87, 89, 91**,
    109, 176
  restrictiveness of RoO *94*
US–Singapore FTA 79, 80, **89**, 90, **91**, 100
  origin of services 133, 135
  restrictiveness of RoO 288–9
US Trade Representative 174
US–Vietnam Bilateral Trade Agreement
    (2000) 133
utilization rates
  NAFTA RoO 193–6, **194**
  trade preferences 296, **302**, 303–5
    impact of RoO 308–13
  use in estimation of costs of RoO 192,
    198–200

value added 4, 117, 119, 206
  inclusion in RoO 238
  in political-economy model 153–4
  unit value-added price 207

Value Added (Domestic Content)
  criterion 222
value content (VC) criterion 74, 83, **84**,
  111, 287, 312
  effect on costs of RoO 206–8
  flexibility in calculation 99–100
  US GSP scheme 305
value of parts (VP) restrictions 74, 206
valves, sourcing practices in South
  Africa 281
VanGrasstek, C. 181 n.
vector of binary variables, RoO 163
vegetable products trade
  NAFTA RoO **194**
  restrictiveness of RoO **96**
vehicles, RVC calculation 100 n.
Vermulst, E. 19 n., 116 n.
Vermulst, E., Waer, P. and Bougeois,
  J. 118 n.
vertical integration 37, 52
vertical trade 2–3
'vessel', definition under EBA 191
Viner, J. 21
Voluntary Export Restraint agreements
  (VERs) 175

Wainio, J. and Gibson, P. 297 n.
water distribution services 118, 125
weighted RoO 95
welfare effects 26, 27, 28, 184
  North–South PTA 160–2
wheat, tariff preferences, Mercosur–Chile
  FTA **221**
wheat flour, SADC RoO 271–5
wholly obtained or produced
  category 73, 83
  Mercosur 224

SADC RoO 269, 270
wood products
  Mercosur restrictiveness indices **230**
  NAFTA RoO **194**
  restrictiveness of sectoral RoO **96**
  structure of Mercosur–Chile RoO **229**
  structure of Mercosur RoO **228**
World Bank 125 n.
  WITS dataset 252
World Customs Organization (WCO) 73 n.
World Trade Organization (WTO) 69 n.,
  71 n., 72 n., 76
  Committee on Regional Trade
    Agreements 103
  Committee on Rules of Origin
    (CRO) 80–1
  constraining RoO 185–6
  General Agreement on Trade in Services
    (GATS) 114
  harmonization of RoO 102–3
  preparation for Doha Trade
    Round 70–1
  Technical Committee on Rules of
    Origin (TCRO) 80
Wunsch-Vincent, S. 120 n.

yarn forward rule *see* triple
  transformation test

Zambia
  textiles and garments trade RoO 284
  trade preferences **302**, 304
Zampetti, A. and Sauvé, P. 11
Zimbabwe
  value of trade preferences **302**
  wheat production 272
Zoellick, R. 174